# Shugo Chara!

## 12

### PEACH-PIT

Translated by
**Satsuki Yamashita**

Lettered by
**North Market Street Graphics**

KC
KODANSHA
COMICS

A Kodansha Comics Trade Paperback Original.

*Shugo Chara!* volume 12 copyright © 2010 PEACH-PIT
English translation copyright © 2011 PEACH-PIT

Published in the United States by Kodansha Comics, an imprint of Kodansha USA Publishing, LLC, New York.

Publication rights for this English edition arranged through Kodansha Ltd., Tokyo.

First published in Japan in 2010 by Kodansha Ltd., Tokyo.

ISBN 978-1-935429-84-5

Original cover design by Akiko Omo.

Printed in the United States of America.

www.kodanshacomics.com

9 8 7 6 5 4 3 2

Translator: Satsuki Yamashita
Lettering: North Market Street Graphics

# Contents

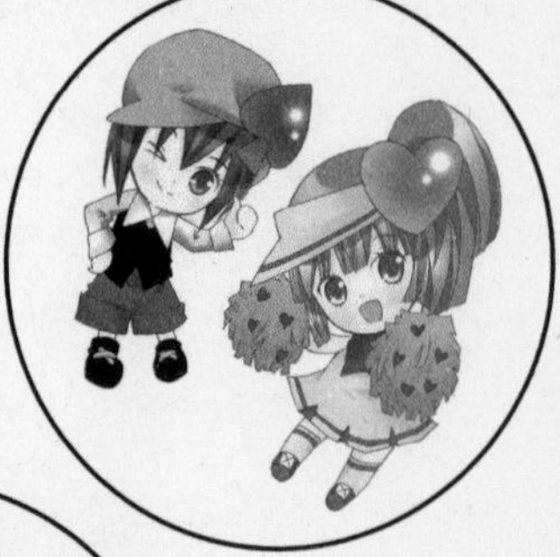
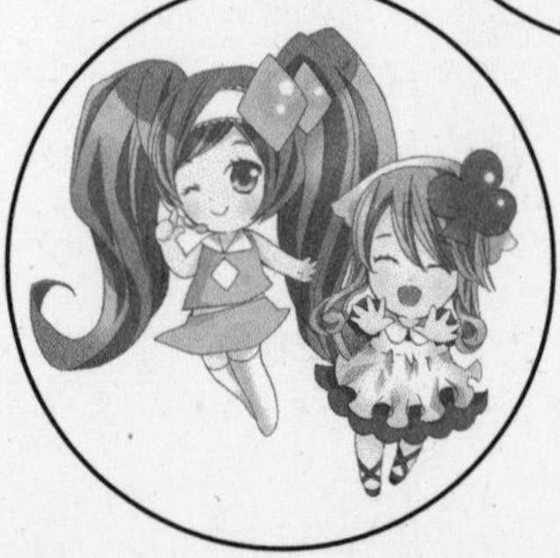

# Honorifics Explained

Throughout the Kodansha Comics books, you will find Japanese honorifics left intact in the translations. For those not familiar with how the Japanese use honorifics and, more important, how they differ from American honorifics, we present this brief overview.

Politeness has always been a critical facet of Japanese culture. Ever since the feudal era, when Japan was a highly stratified society, use of honorifics—which can be defined as polite speech that indicates relationship or status—has played an essential role in the Japanese language. When addressing someone in Japanese, an honorific usually takes the form of a suffix attached to one's name (example: "Asuna-san"), is used as a title at the end of one's name, or appears in place of the name itself (example: "Negi-sensei," or simply "Sensei!").

Honorifics can be expressions of respect or endearment. In the context of manga and anime, honorifics give insight into the nature of the relationship between characters. Many English translations leave out these important honorifics and therefore distort the feel of the original Japanese. Because Japanese honorifics contain nuances that English honorifics lack, it is our policy at Kodansha Comics not to translate them. Here, instead, is a guide to some of the honorifics you may encounter in Kodansha Comics books.

-san:   This is the most common honorific and is equivalent to Mr., Miss, Ms., or Mrs. It is the all-purpose honorific and can be used in any situation where politeness is required.

-sama:  This is one level higher than "-san" and is used to confer great respect.

-dono:  This comes from the word "tono," which means "lord." It is an even higher level than "-sama" and confers utmost respect.

-kun:   This suffix is used at the end of boys' names to express familiarity or endearment. It is also sometimes used by men among friends, or when addressing someone younger or of a lower station.

| | |
|---|---|
| -chan: | This is used to express endearment, mostly toward girls. It is also used for little boys, pets, and even among lovers. It gives a sense of childish cuteness. |
| Bozu: | This is an informal way to refer to a boy, similar to the English terms "kid" and "squirt." |
| Sempai/ Senpai: | This title suggests that the addressee is one's senior in a group or organization. It is most often used in a school setting, where underclassmen refer to their upperclassmen as "sempai." It can also be used in the workplace, such as when a newer employee addresses an employee who has seniority in the company. |
| Kohai: | This is the opposite of "sempai" and is used toward underclassmen in school or newcomers in the workplace. It connotes that the addressee is of a lower station. |
| Sensei: | Literally meaning "one who has come before," this title is used for teachers, doctors, or masters of any profession or art. |
| -[blank]: | This is usually forgotten in these lists, but it is perhaps the most significant difference between Japanese and English. The lack of honorific means that the speaker has permission to address the person in a very intimate way. Usually, only family, spouses, or very close friends have this kind of permission. Known as *yobisute,* it can be gratifying when someone who has earned the intimacy starts to call one by one's name without an honorific. But when that intimacy hasn't been earned, it can be very insulting. |

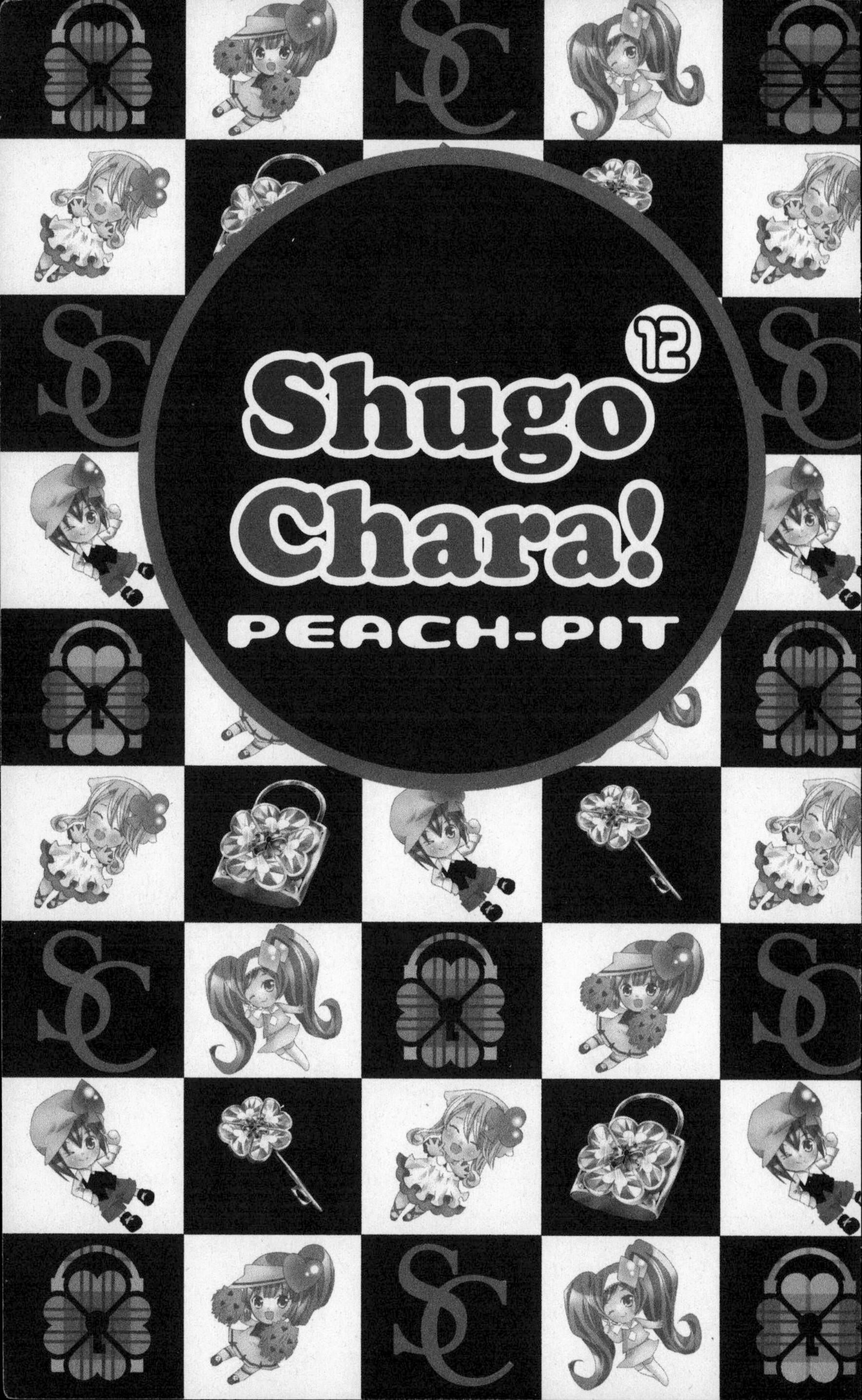
12
Shugo Chara!
PEACH-PIT

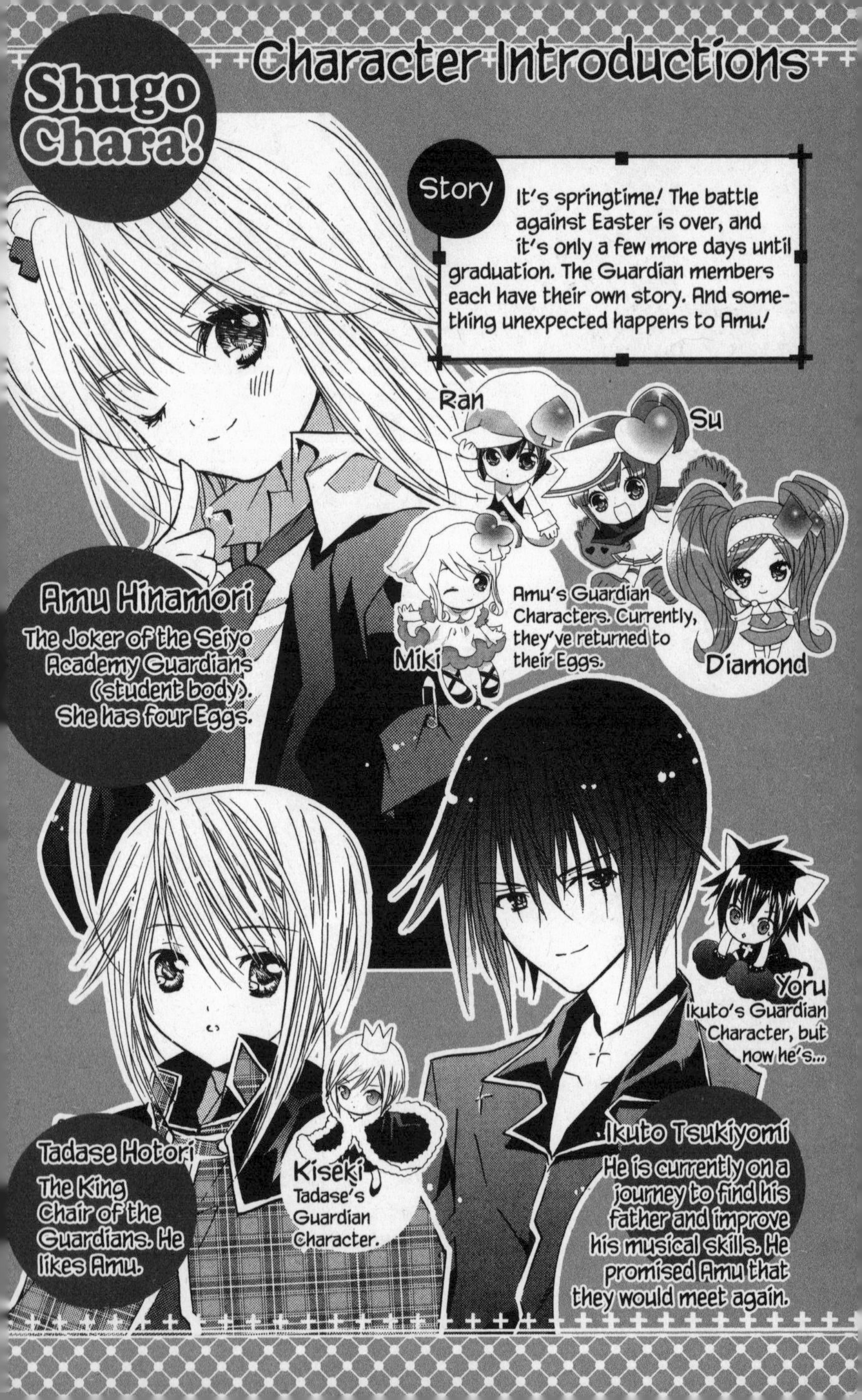
Character Introductions
Shugo Chara!
Story
It's springtime! The battle against Easter is over, and it's only a few more days until graduation. The Guardian members each have their own story. And something unexpected happens to Amu!
Ran
Su
Miki
Diamond
Amu's Guardian Characters. Currently, they've returned to their Eggs.
Amu Hinamori
The Joker of the Seiyo Academy Guardians (student body). She has four Eggs.
Yoru
Ikuto's Guardian Character, but now he's...
Ikuto Tsukiyomi
He is currently on a journey to find his father and improve his musical skills. He promised Amu that they would meet again.
Kiseki
Tadase's Guardian Character.
Tadase Hotori
The King Chair of the Guardians. He likes Amu.

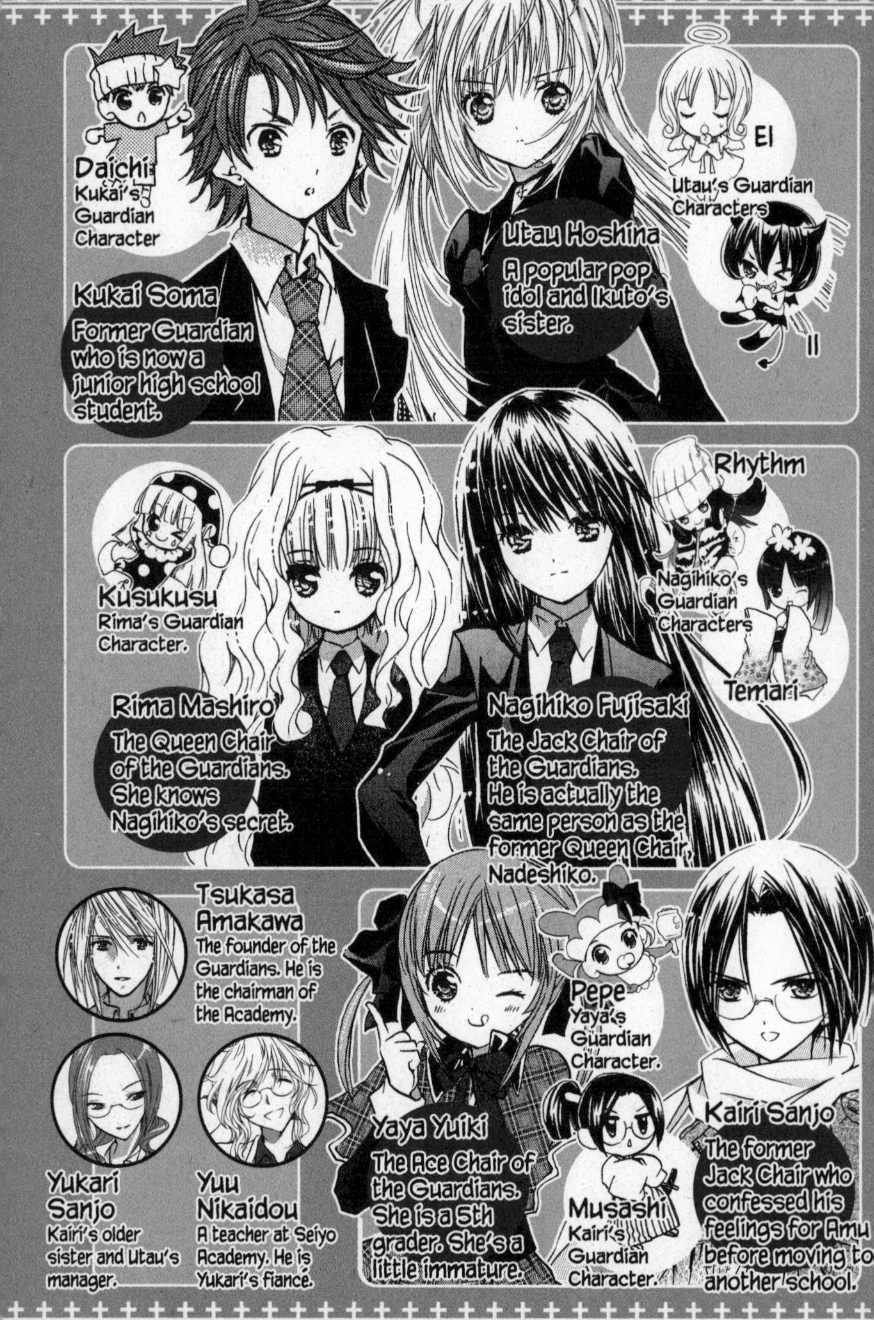
El
Utau's Guardian Characters
Il
Utau Hoshina
A popular pop idol and Ikuto's sister.
Kukai Soma
Former Guardian who is now a junior high school student.
Daichi
Kukai's Guardian Character
Rhythm
Nagihiko's Guardian Characters
Temari
Nagihiko Fujisaki
The Jack Chair of the Guardians. He is actually the same person as the former Queen Chair, Nadeshiko.
Rima Mashiro
The Queen Chair of the Guardians. She knows Nagihiko's secret.
Kusukusu
Rima's Guardian Character.
Kairi Sanjo
The former Jack Chair who confessed his feelings for Amu before moving to another school.
Musashi
Kairi's Guardian Character.
Pepe
Yaya's Guardian Character.
Yaya Yuiki
The Ace Chair of the Guardians. She is a 5th grader. She's a little immature.
Tsukasa Amakawa
The founder of the Guardians. He is the chairman of the Academy.
Yuu Nikaidou
A teacher at Seiyo Academy. He is Yukari's fiancé.
Yukari Sanjo
Kairi's older sister and Utau's manager.

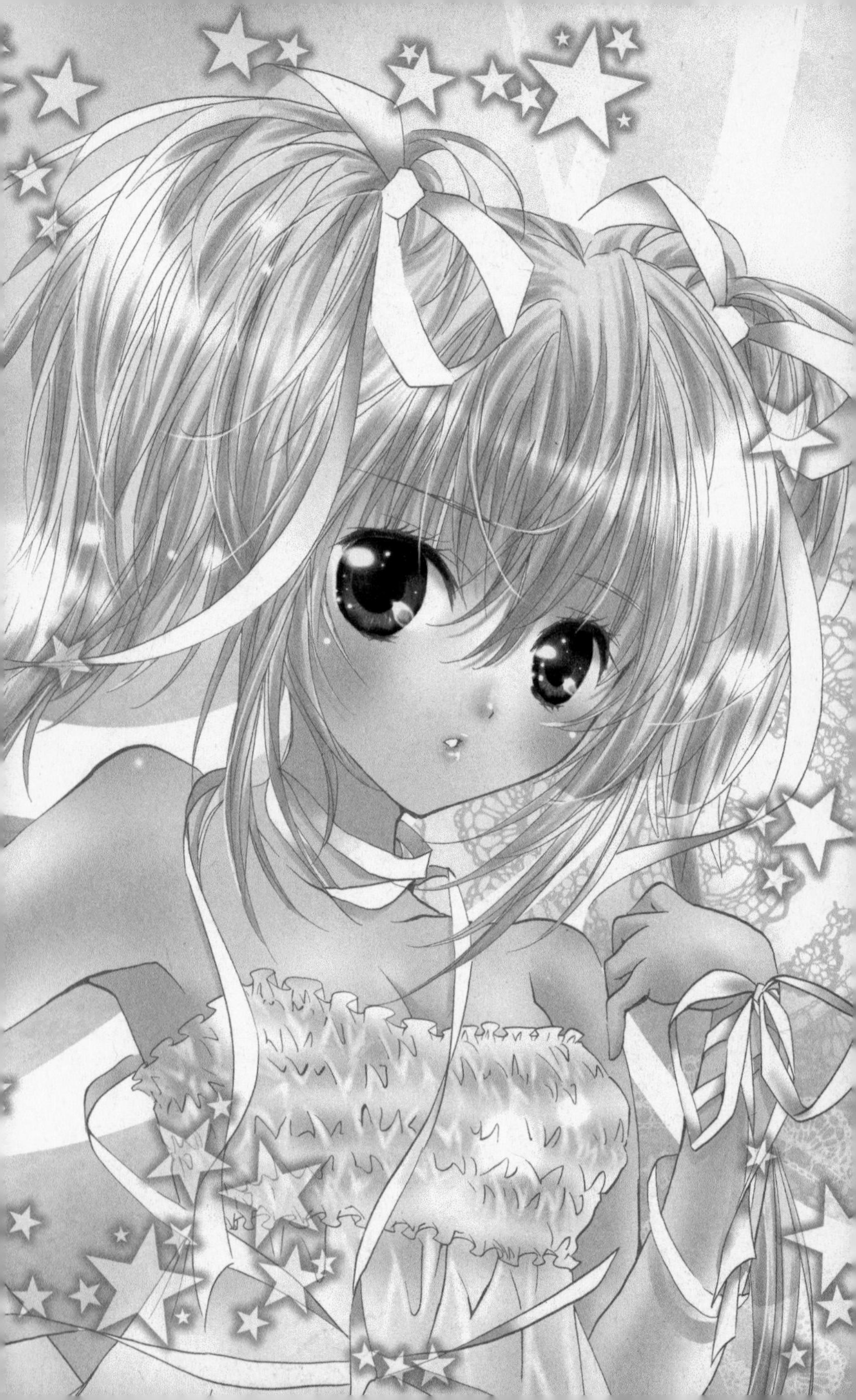

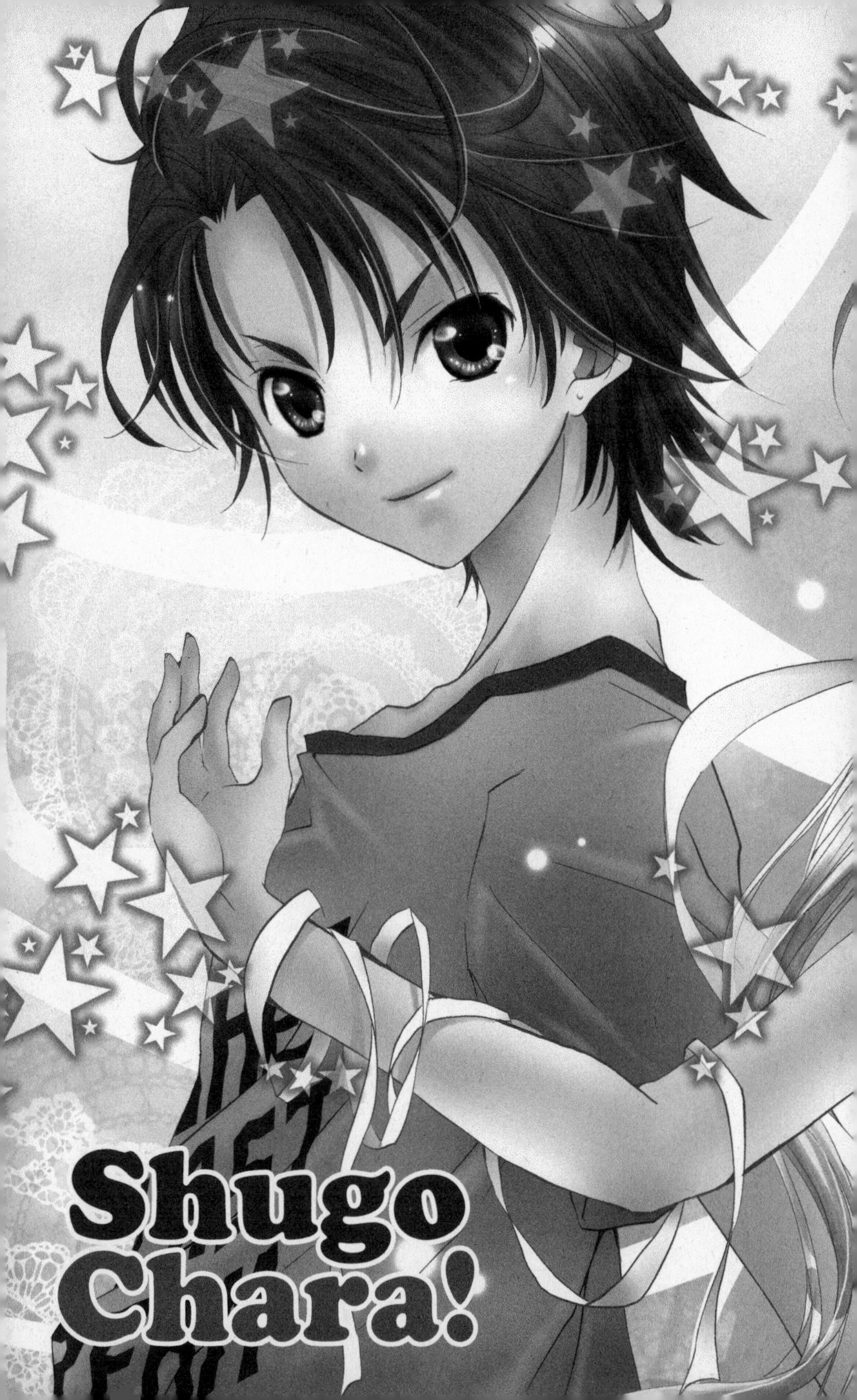
Shugo
Chara!

Shugo Chara!

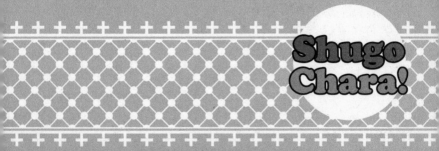

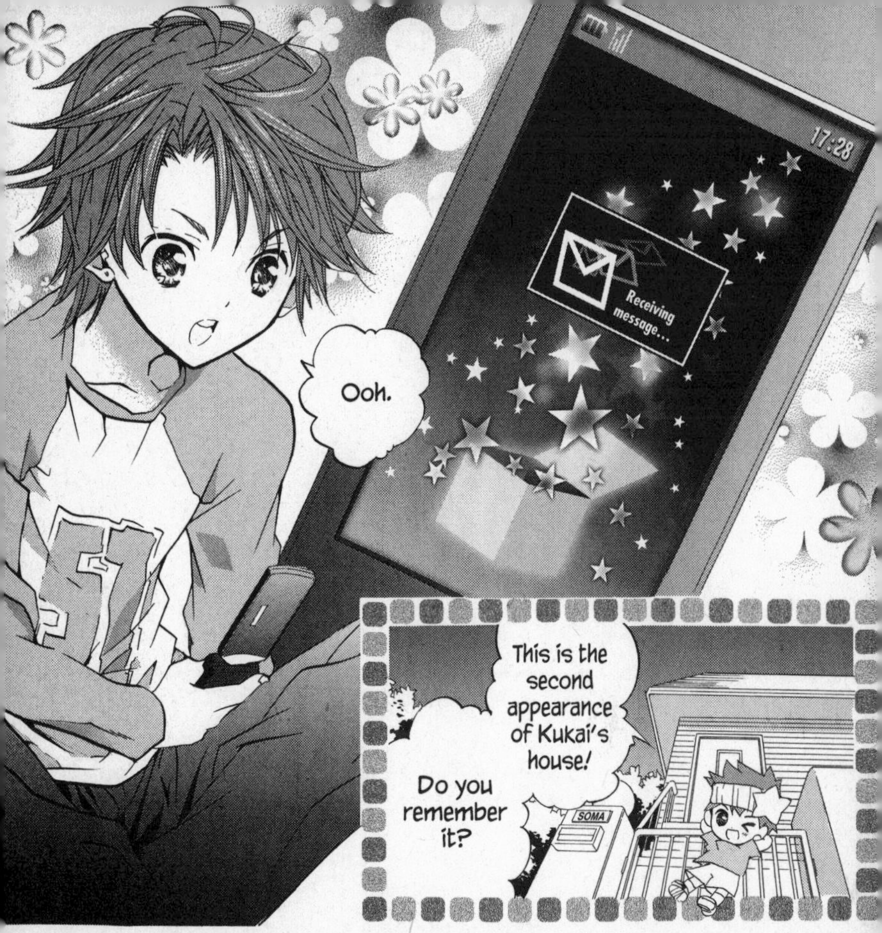
17:28
Receiving message...
Ooh.
This is the second appearance of Kukai's house!
Do you remember it?
SOMA

SOB

Hello-peach! Can you believe it? It's the final volume of "Shugo Chara!" This is PEACH-PIT ♥ I know I wrote in this segment last volume too, but once again, it's Shibuko Ebara! Banri-san will appear in the afterword, so please read that at the end ★ I've always looked forward to this Q&A segment, but this will be the last. We're such lucky people that we were able to work on this series for so long. Wait, we're lucky peaches! We were very happy to receive so many letters from the readers too. Now, on with the questions! ♥

Seriously!

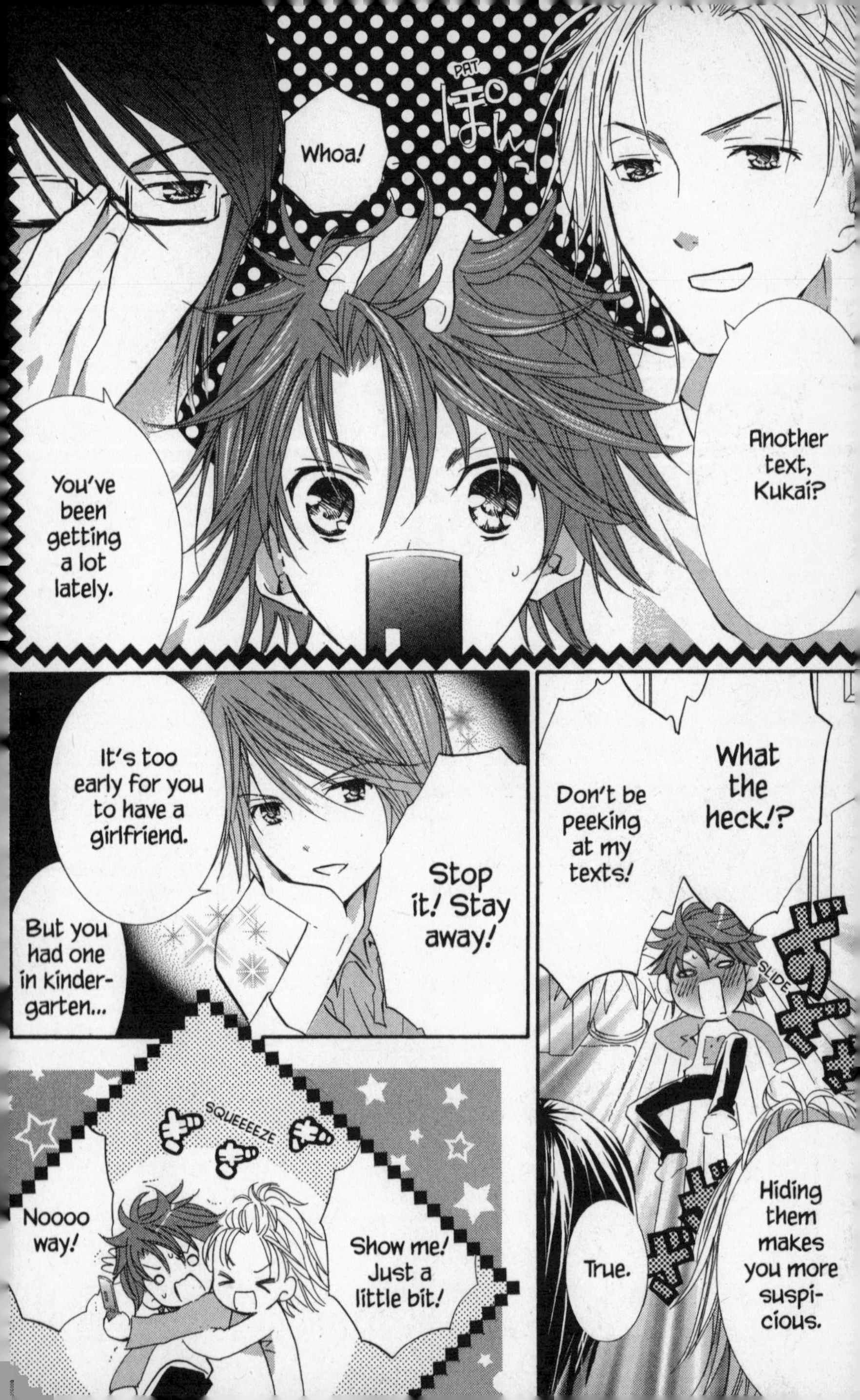
Another text, Kukai?
PAT
Whoa!
You've been getting a lot lately.
What the heck!?
Don't be peeking at my texts!
SLIDE
Hiding them makes you more suspicious.
True.
Stop it! Stay away!
It's too early for you to have a girlfriend.
But you had one in kinder-garten...
Show me! Just a little bit!
SQUEEEEZE
Noooo way!

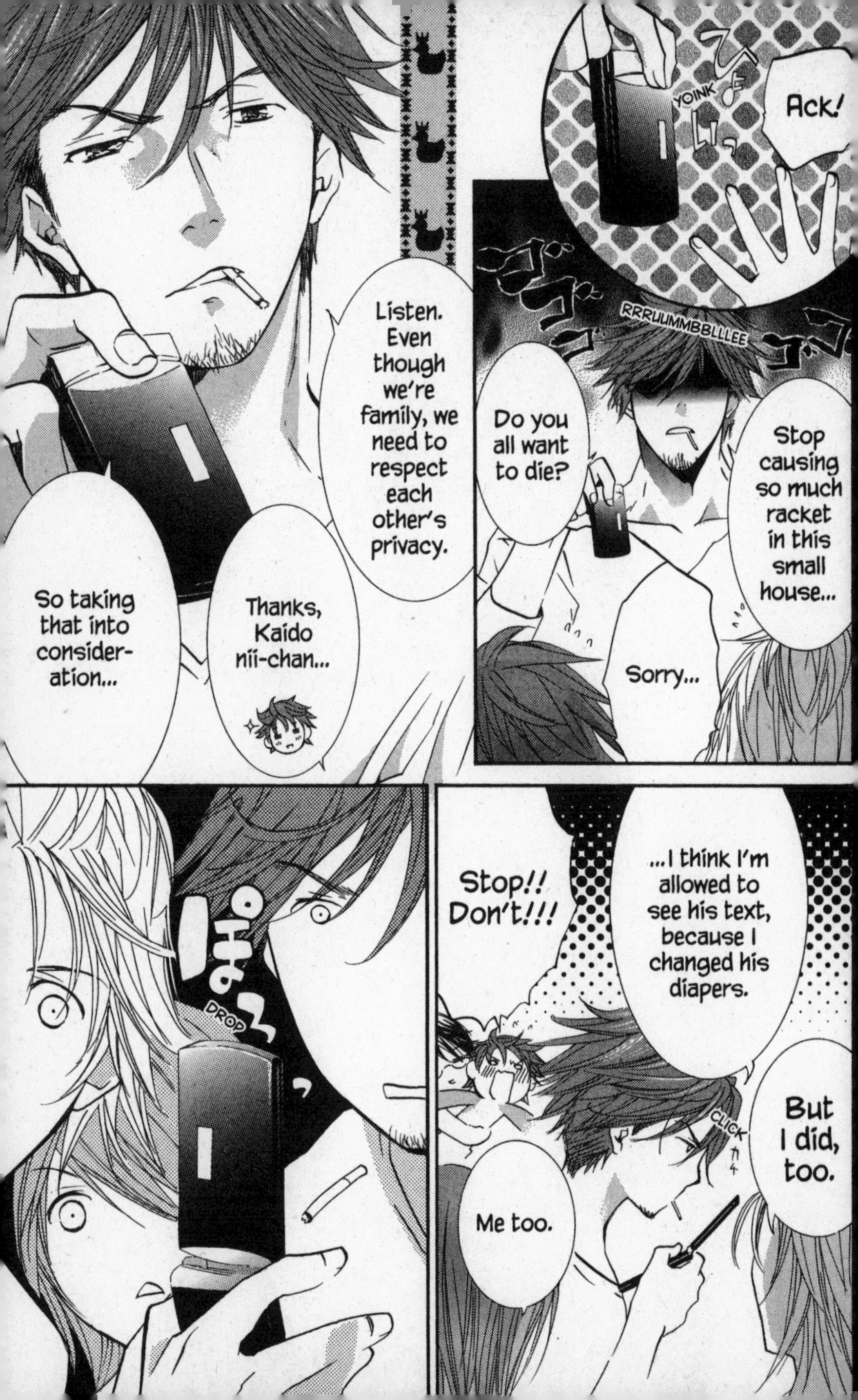
YOINK
Ack!
RRRUUMMBBLLLEE
Stop causing so much racket in this small house...
Do you all want to die?
Sorry...
Listen. Even though we're family, we need to respect each other's privacy.
Thanks, Kaido nii-chan...
So taking that into consideration...
...I think I'm allowed to see his text, because I changed his diapers.
Stop!! Don't!!!
But I did, too.
CLICK
Me too.
DROP

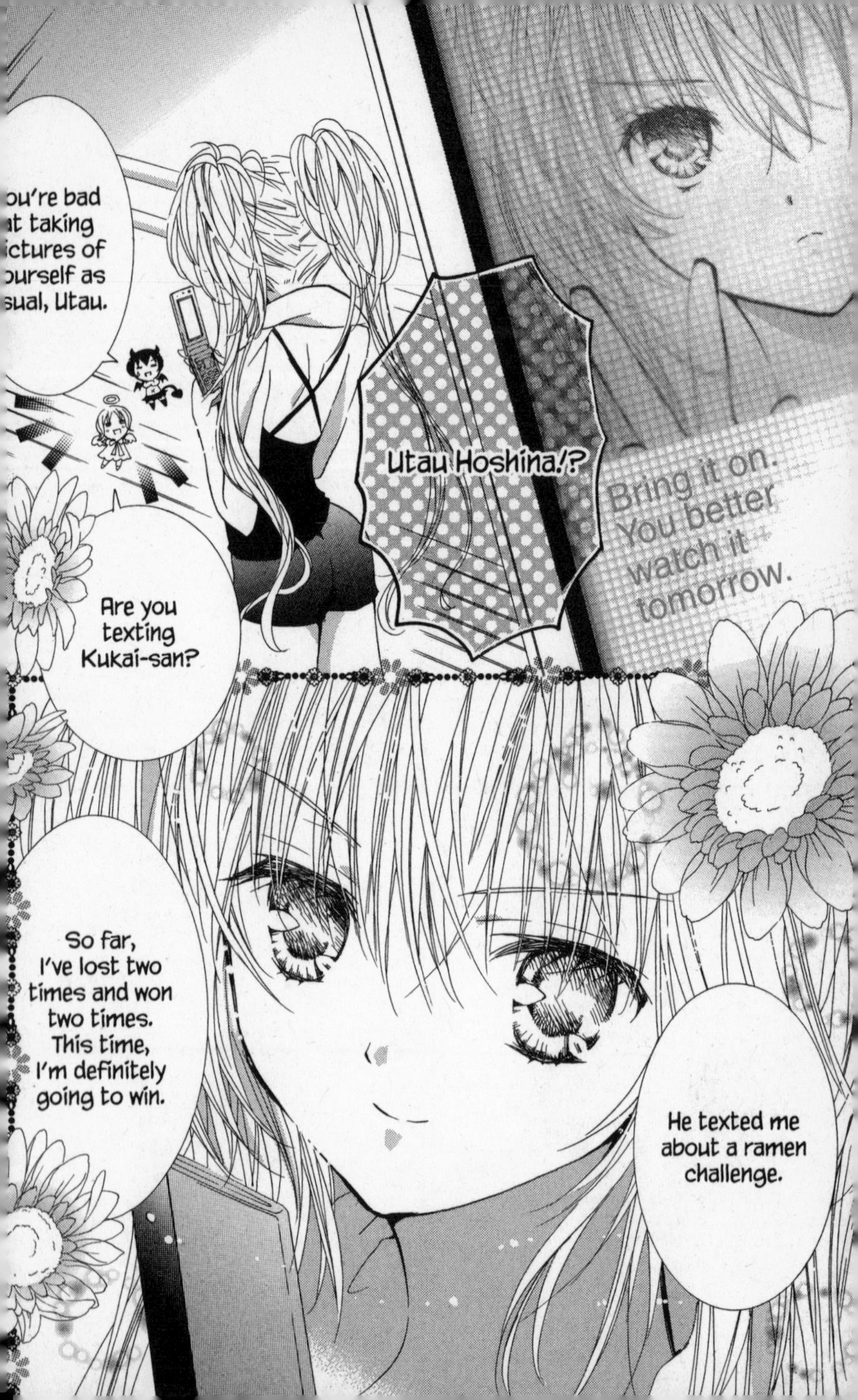

Bring it on. You better watch it tomorrow.
Utau Hoshina!?
ou're bad at taking ictures of ourself as sual, Utau.
Are you texting Kukai-san?
He texted me about a ramen challenge.
So far, I've lost two times and won two times. This time, I'm definitely going to win.

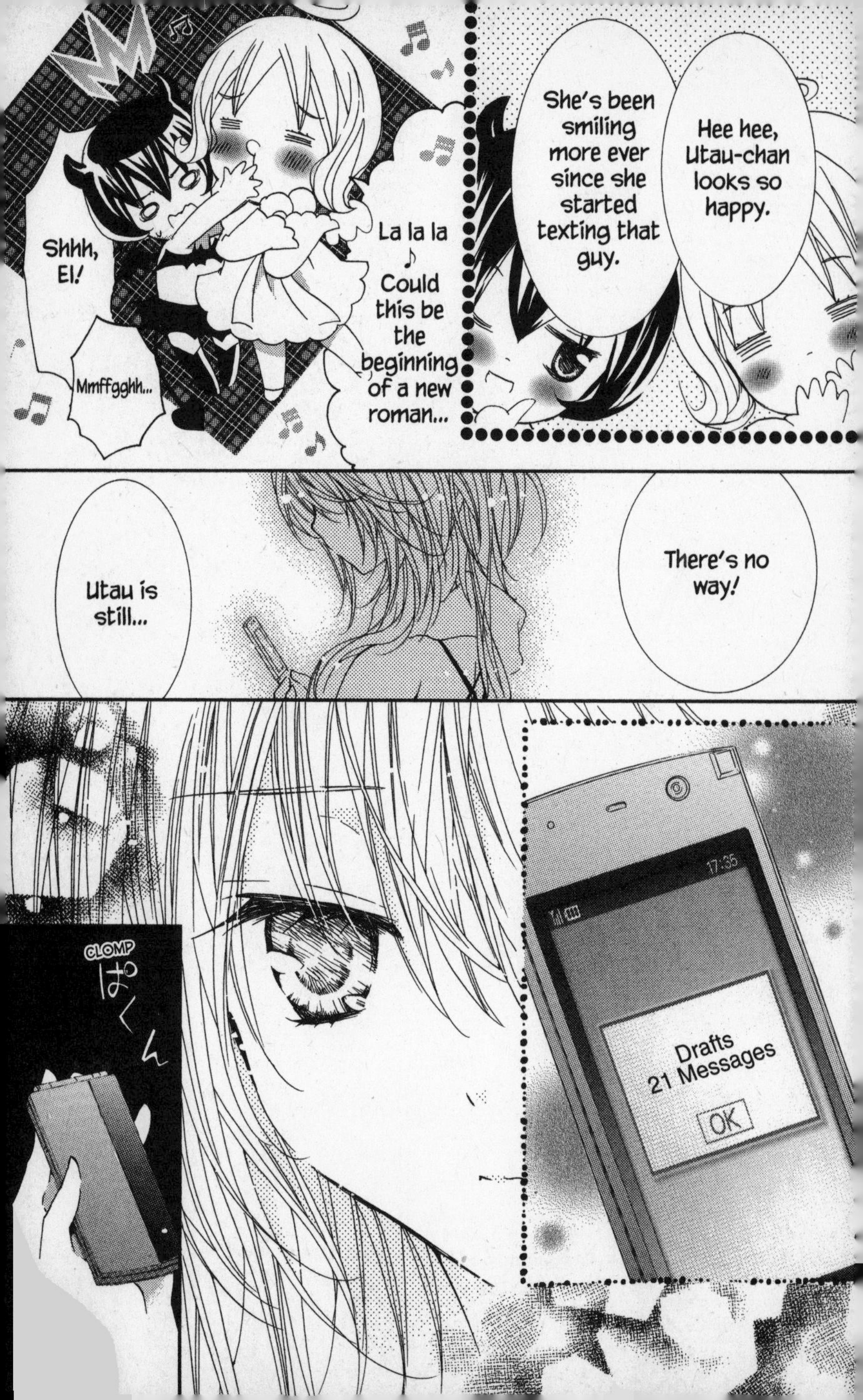
Hee hee, Utau-chan looks so happy.
She's been smiling more ever since she started texting that guy.
La la la ♪ Could this be the beginning of a new roman...
Shhh, El!
Mmffgghh...
There's no way!
Utau is still...
17:35
Drafts
21 Messages
OK
CLOMP
ぱくん

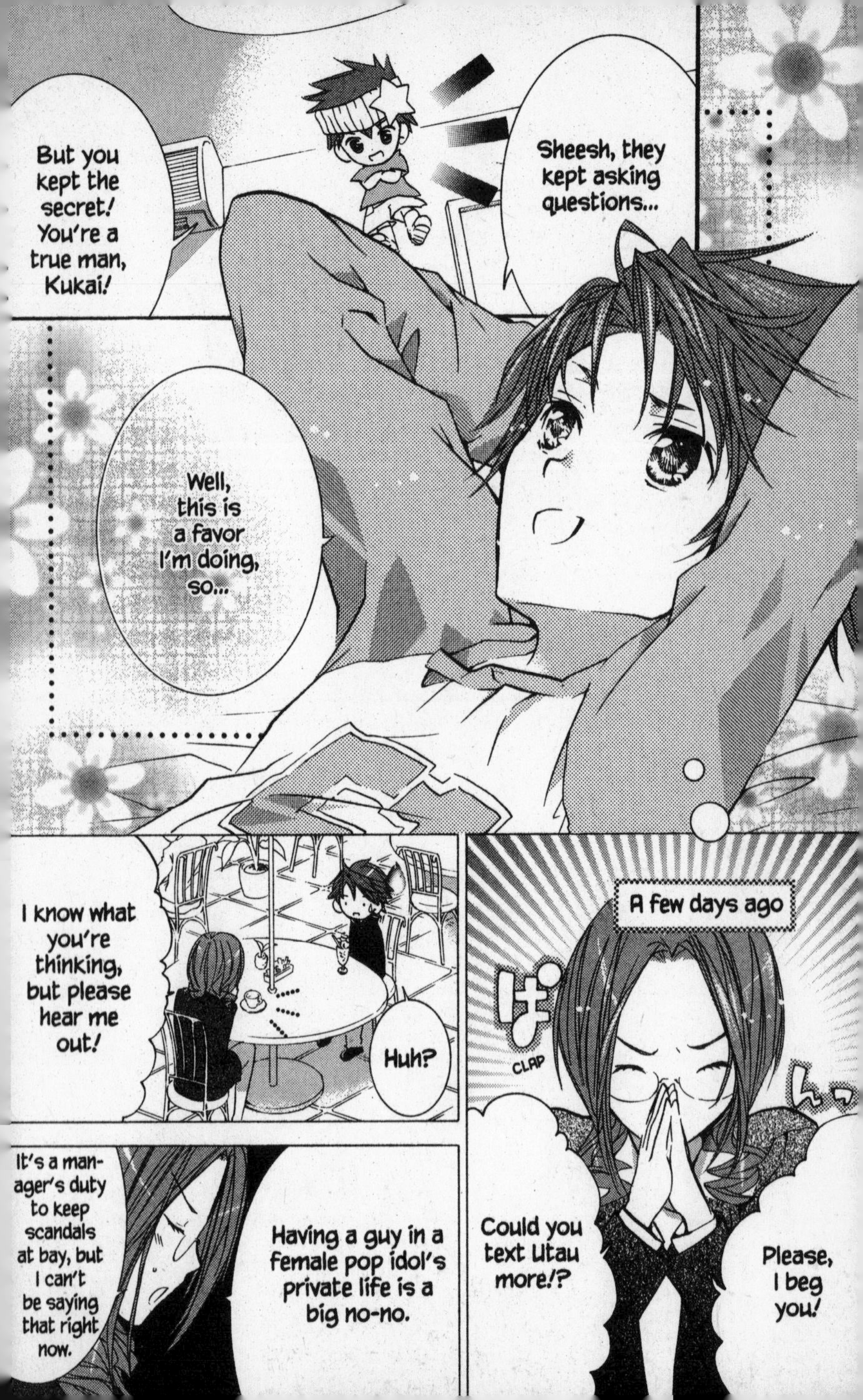
Sheesh, they kept asking questions...
But you kept the secret! You're a true man, Kukai!
Well, this is a favor I'm doing, so...
A few days ago
CLAP
Please, I beg you!
Could you text Utau more!?
Huh?
I know what you're thinking, but please hear me out!
Having a guy in a female pop idol's private life is a big no-no.
It's a manager's duty to keep scandals at bay, but I can't be saying that right now.

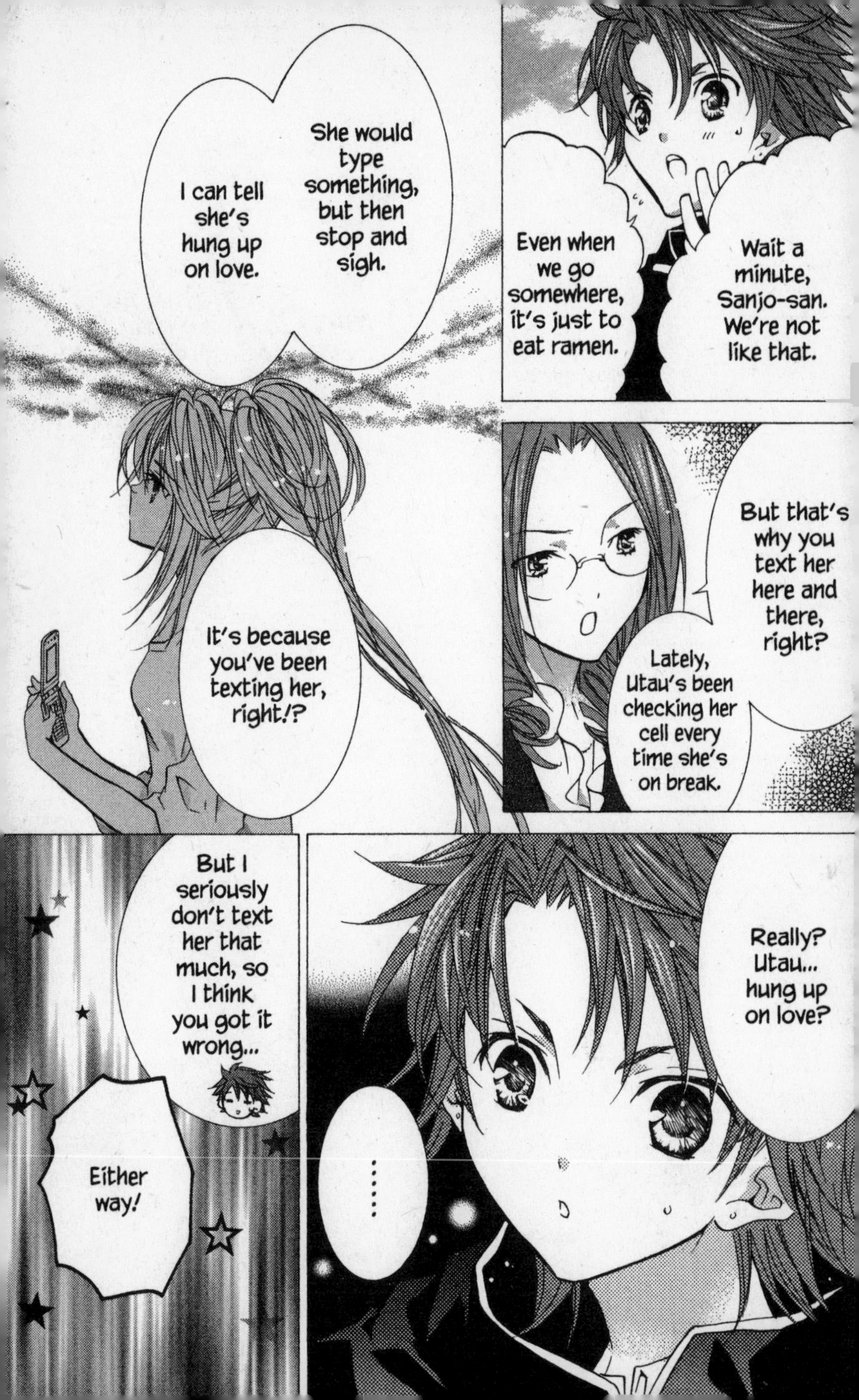
Wait a minute, Sanjo-san. We're not like that.
Even when we go somewhere, it's just to eat ramen.
But that's why you text her here and there, right?
Lately, Utau's been checking her cell every time she's on break.
She would type something, but then stop and sigh.
I can tell she's hung up on love.
It's because you've been texting her, right!?
Really? Utau... hung up on love?
......
But I seriously don't text her that much, so I think you got it wrong...
Either way!

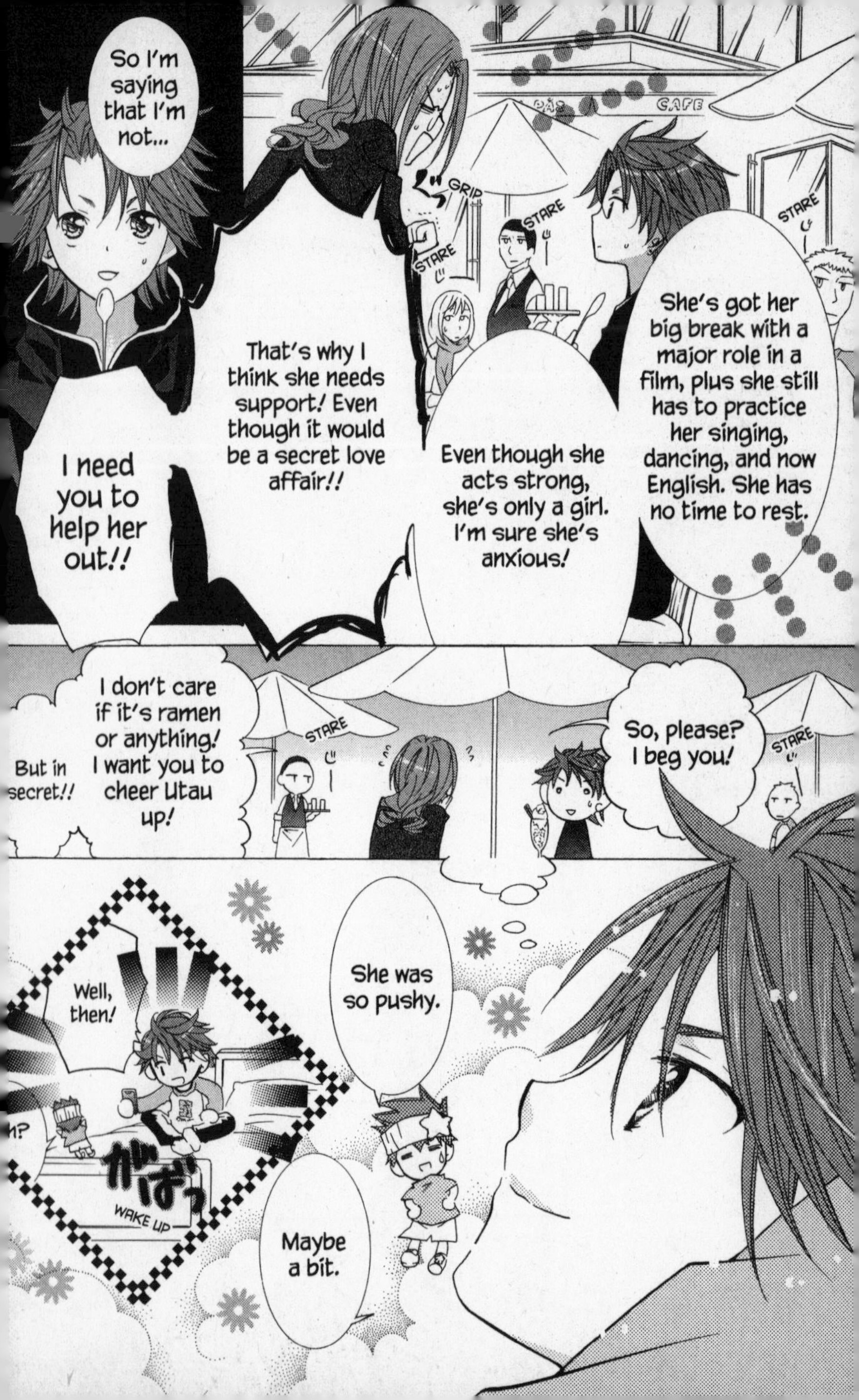
GRIP
STARE
STARE
STARE
She's got her big break with a major role in a film, plus she still has to practice her singing, dancing, and now English. She has no time to rest.
Even though she acts strong, she's only a girl. I'm sure she's anxious!
That's why I think she needs support! Even though it would be a secret love affair!!
So I'm saying that I'm not...
I need you to help her out!!
STARE
So, please? I beg you!
STARE
I don't care if it's ramen or anything! I want you to cheer Utau up!
But in secret!!
She was so pushy.
Maybe a bit.
Well, then!
がばっ
WAKE UP

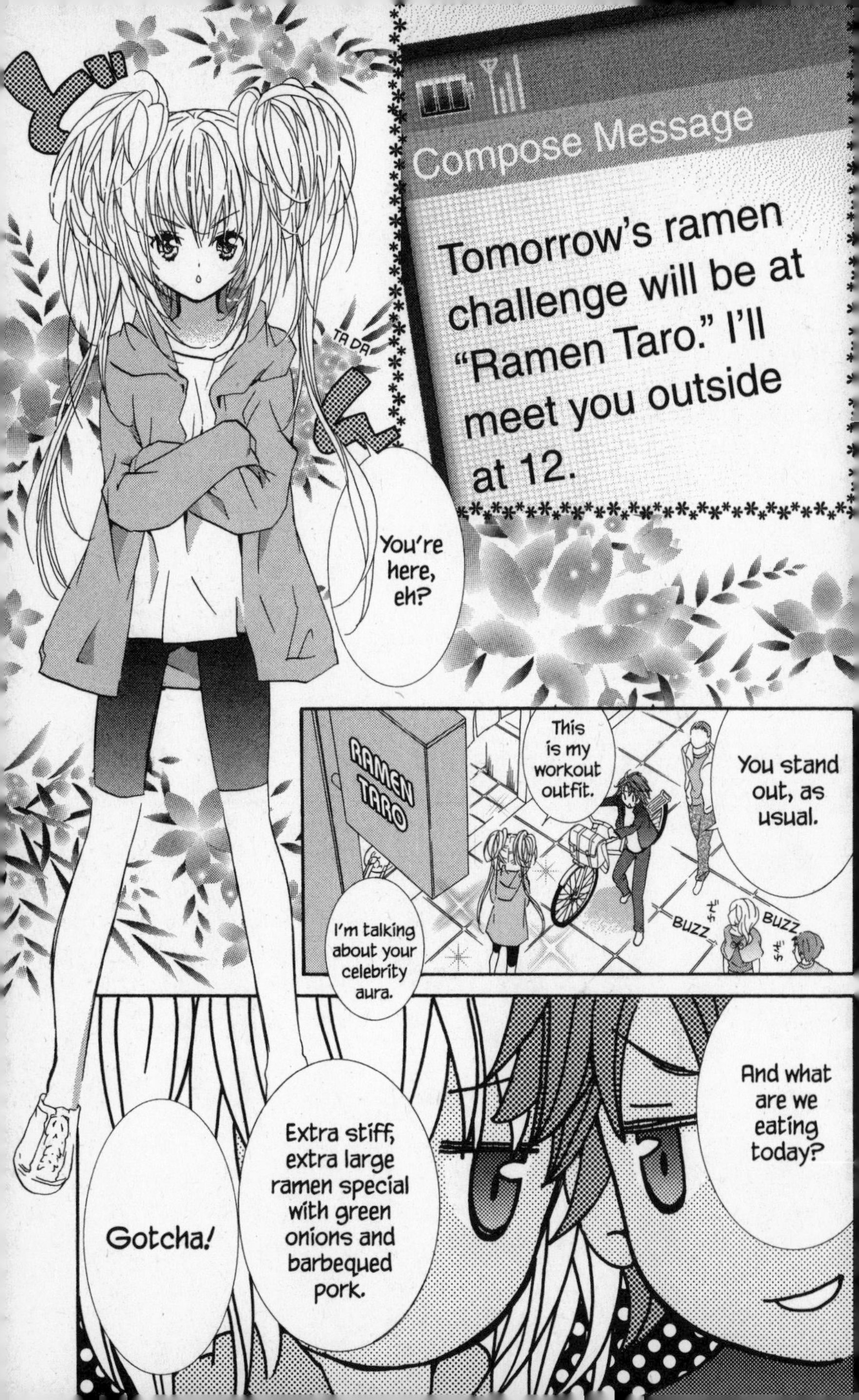
Compose Message
Tomorrow's ramen challenge will be at "Ramen Taro." I'll meet you outside at 12.
TA DA
You're here, eh?
RAMEN TARO
You stand out, as usual.
This is my workout outfit.
BUZZ
BUZZ
I'm talking about your celebrity aura.
And what are we eating today?
Extra stiff, extra large ramen special with green onions and barbequed pork.
Gotcha!

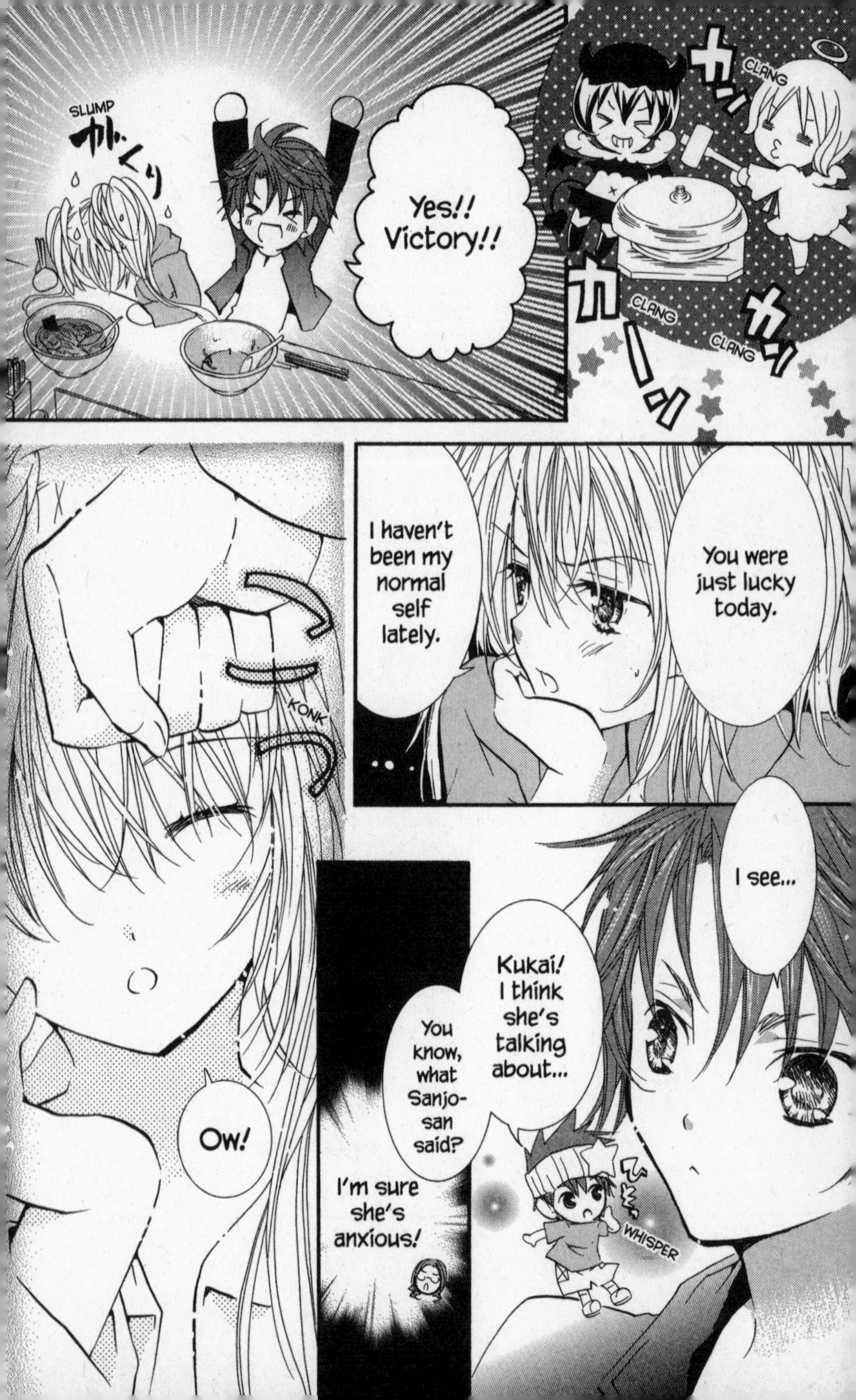
CLANG
CLANG
CLANG
Yes!! Victory!!
SLUMP
You were just lucky today.
I haven't been my normal self lately.
...
I see...
Kukai! I think she's talking about...
You know, what Sanjo-san said?
I'm sure she's anxious!
WHISPER
KONK
Ow!

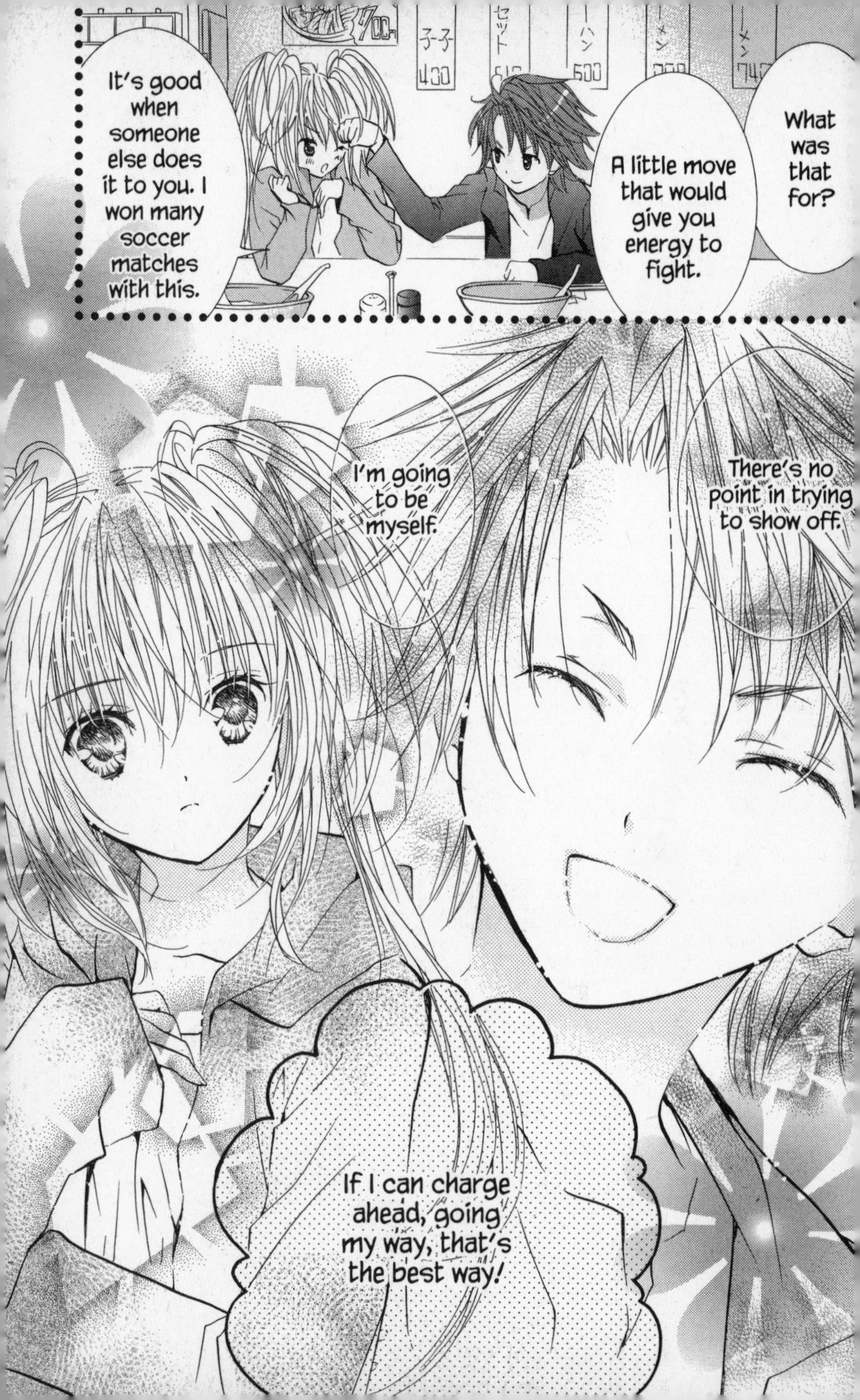
What was that for?
A little move that would give you energy to fight.
It's good when someone else does it to you. I won many soccer matches with this.
There's no point in trying to show off.
I'm going to be myself.
If I can charge ahead, going my way, that's the best way!

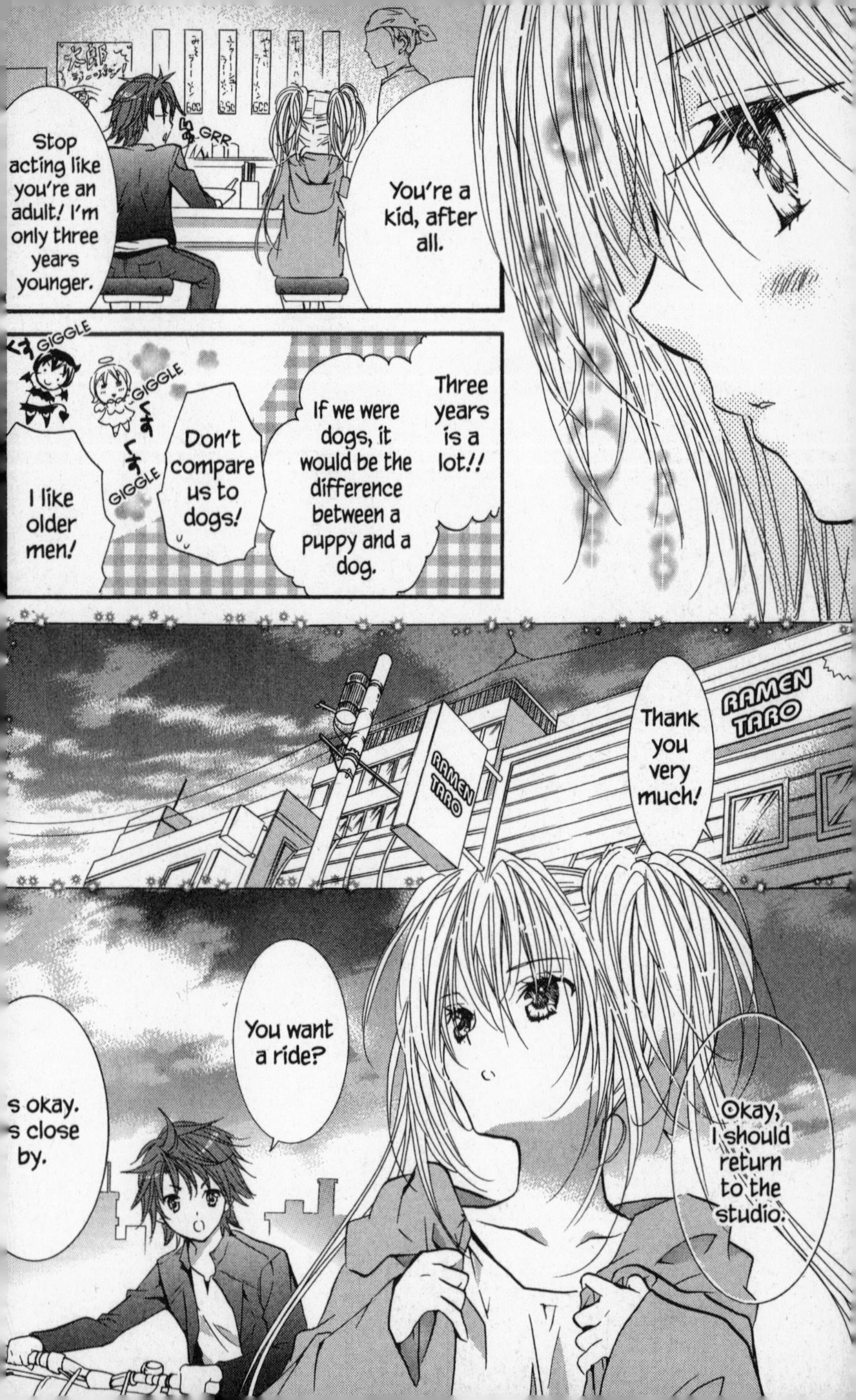
You're a kid, after all.
GRR
Stop acting like you're an adult! I'm only three years younger.
Three years is a lot!!
If we were dogs, it would be the difference between a puppy and a dog.
Don't compare us to dogs!
GIGGLE
GIGGLE
GIGGLE
I like older men!
RAMEN TARO
Thank you very much!
RAMEN TARO
Okay, I should return to the studio.
You want a ride?
s okay. s close by.

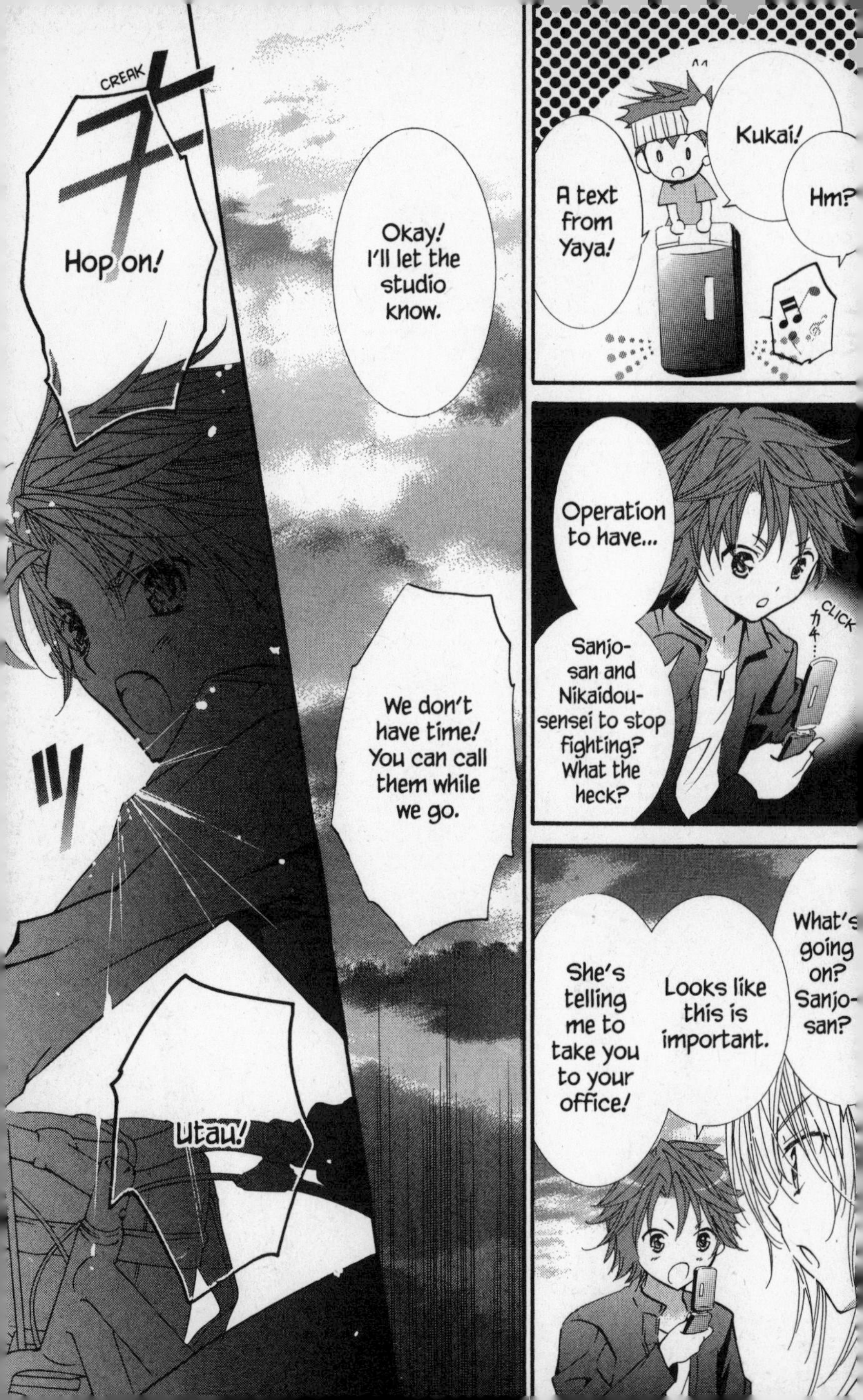
Hm?
Kukai!
A text from Yaya!
Operation to have...
CLICK
Sanjo-san and Nikaidou-sensei to stop fighting? What the heck?
What's going on? Sanjo-san?
Looks like this is important.
She's telling me to take you to your office!
Okay! I'll let the studio know.
CREAK
Hop on!
We don't have time! You can call them while we go.
Utau!

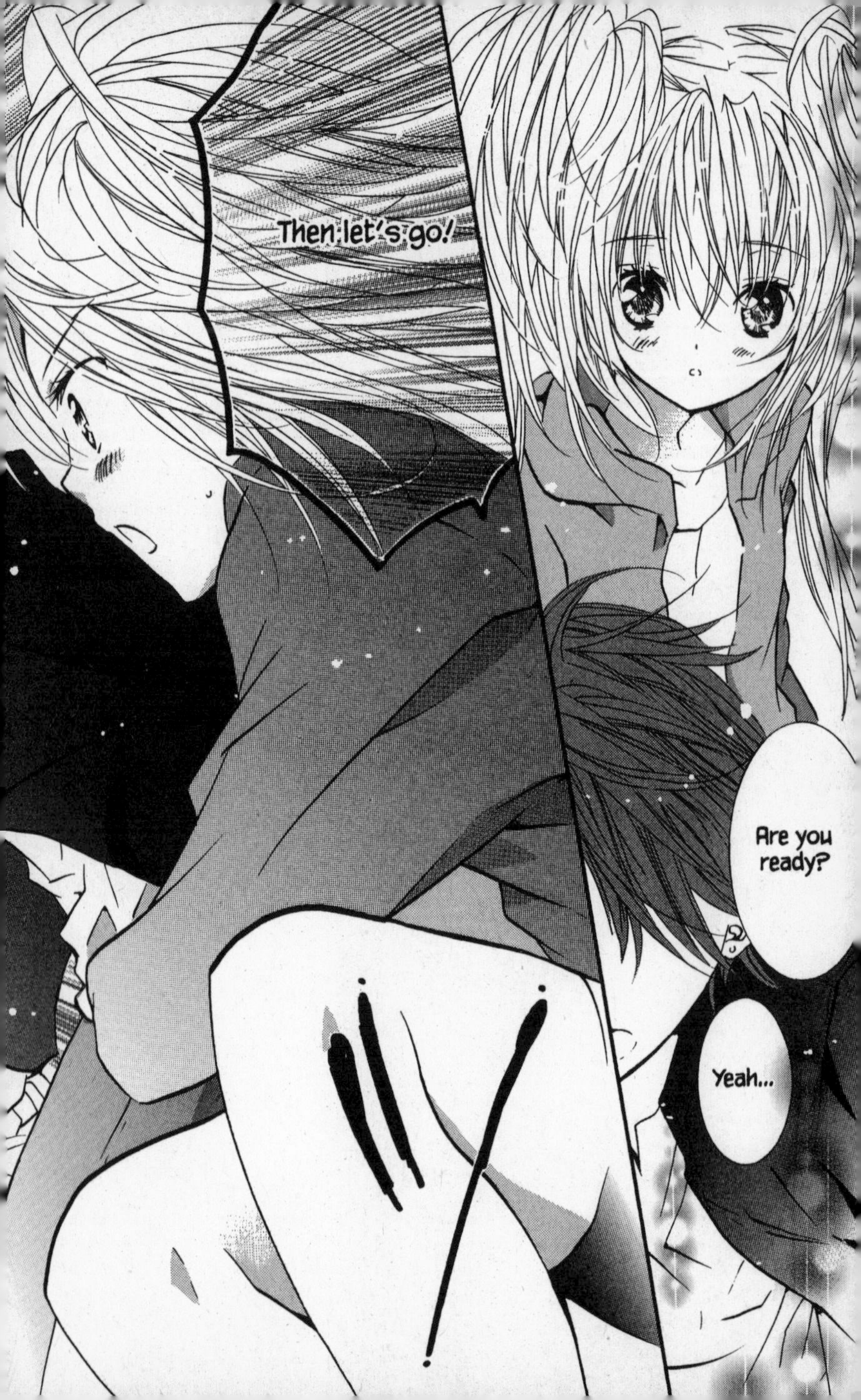
Are you ready?
Yeah...
Then let's go!

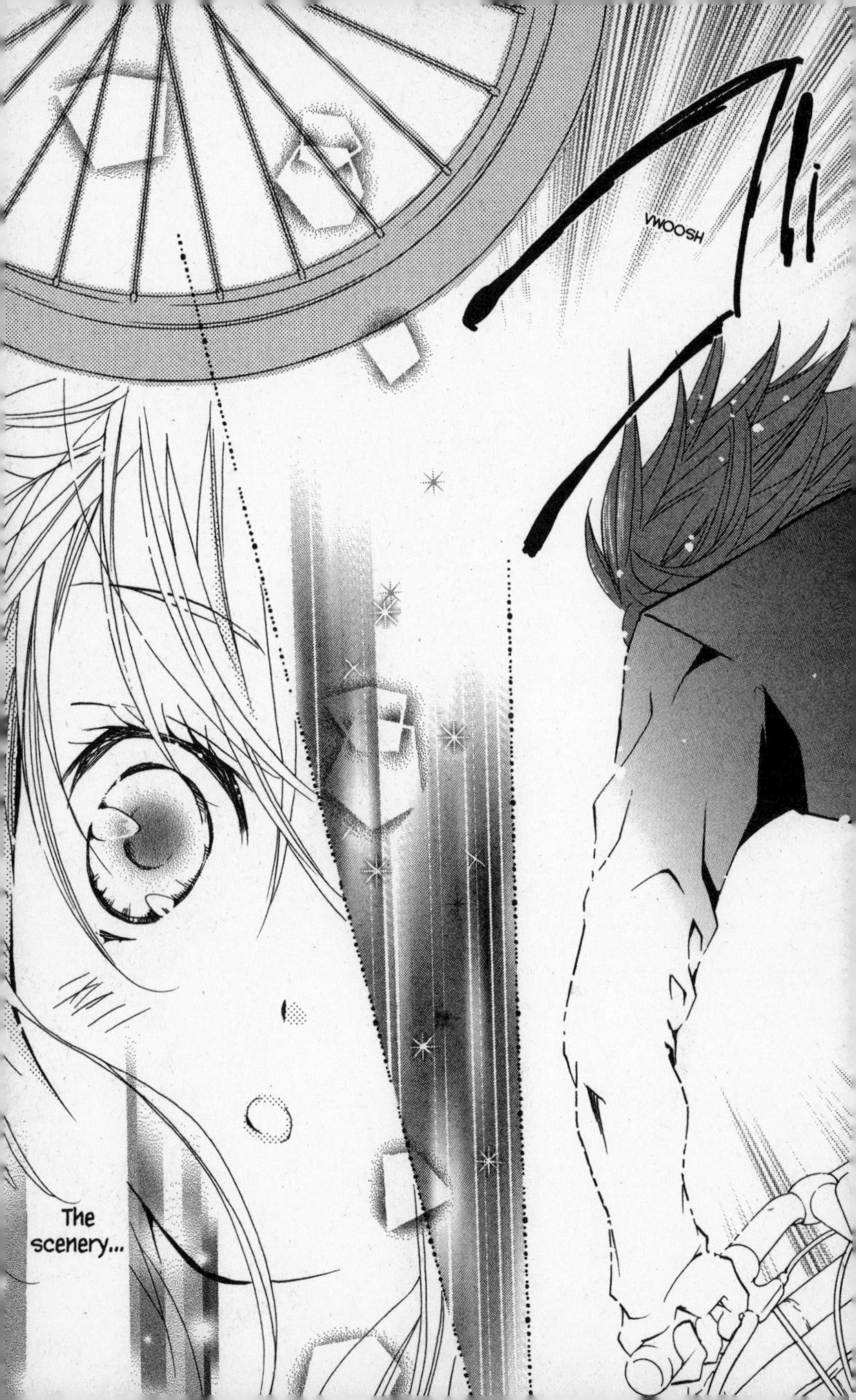
VWOOSH
The scenery...

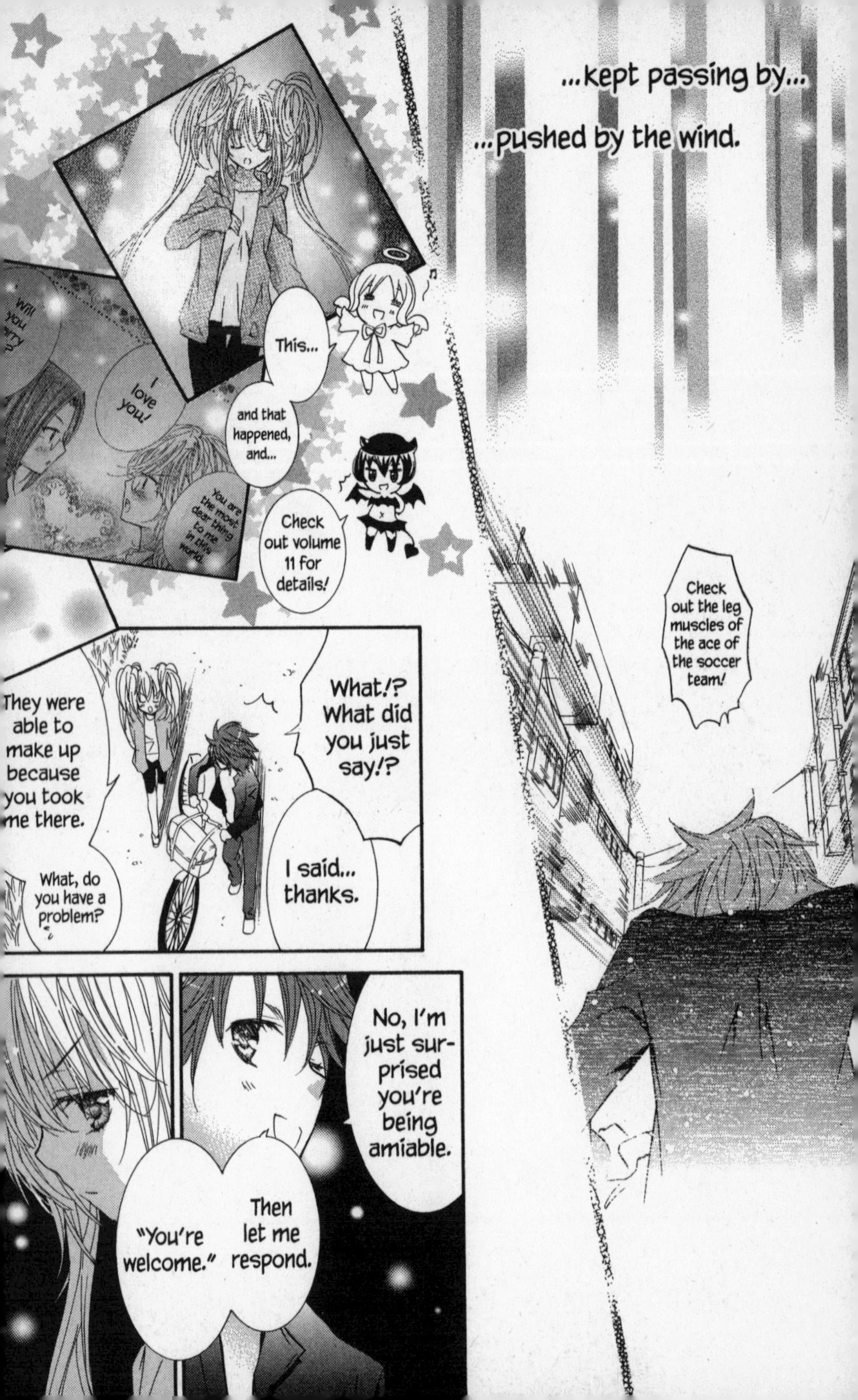

...kept passing by...
...pushed by the wind.
Check out the leg muscles of the ace of the soccer team!
Will you
I love you!
You are the most dear thing to me in this world.
This...
and that happened, and...
Check out volume 11 for details!
What!? What did you just say!?
They were able to make up because you took me there.
I said... thanks.
What, do you have a problem?
No, I'm just surprised you're being amiable.
Then let me respond.
"You're welcome."

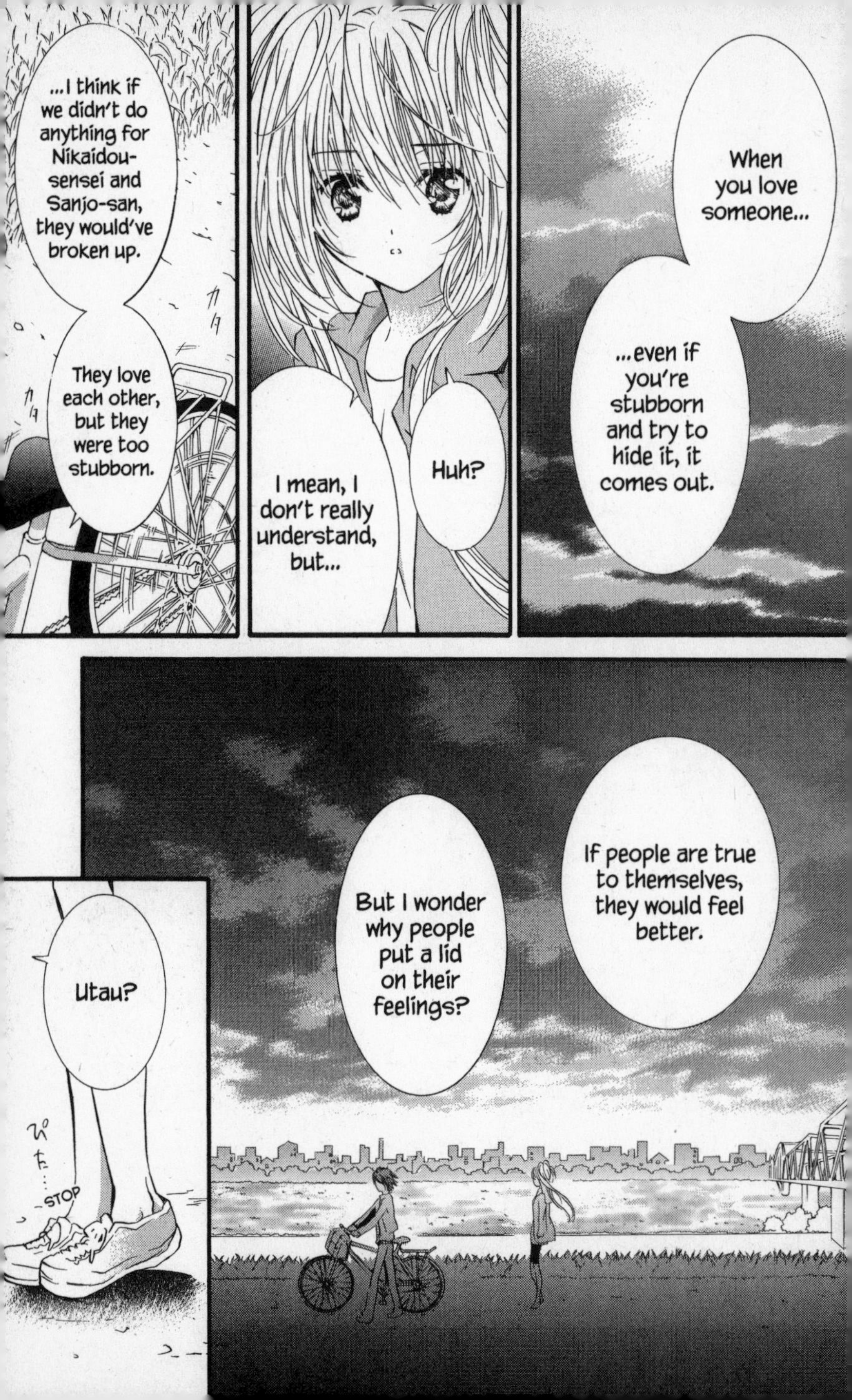
When you love someone...
...even if you're stubborn and try to hide it, it comes out.
Huh?
I mean, I don't really understand, but...
...I think if we didn't do anything for Nikaidou-sensei and Sanjo-san, they would've broken up.
They love each other, but they were too stubborn.
If people are true to themselves, they would feel better.
But I wonder why people put a lid on their feelings?
Utau?
STOP

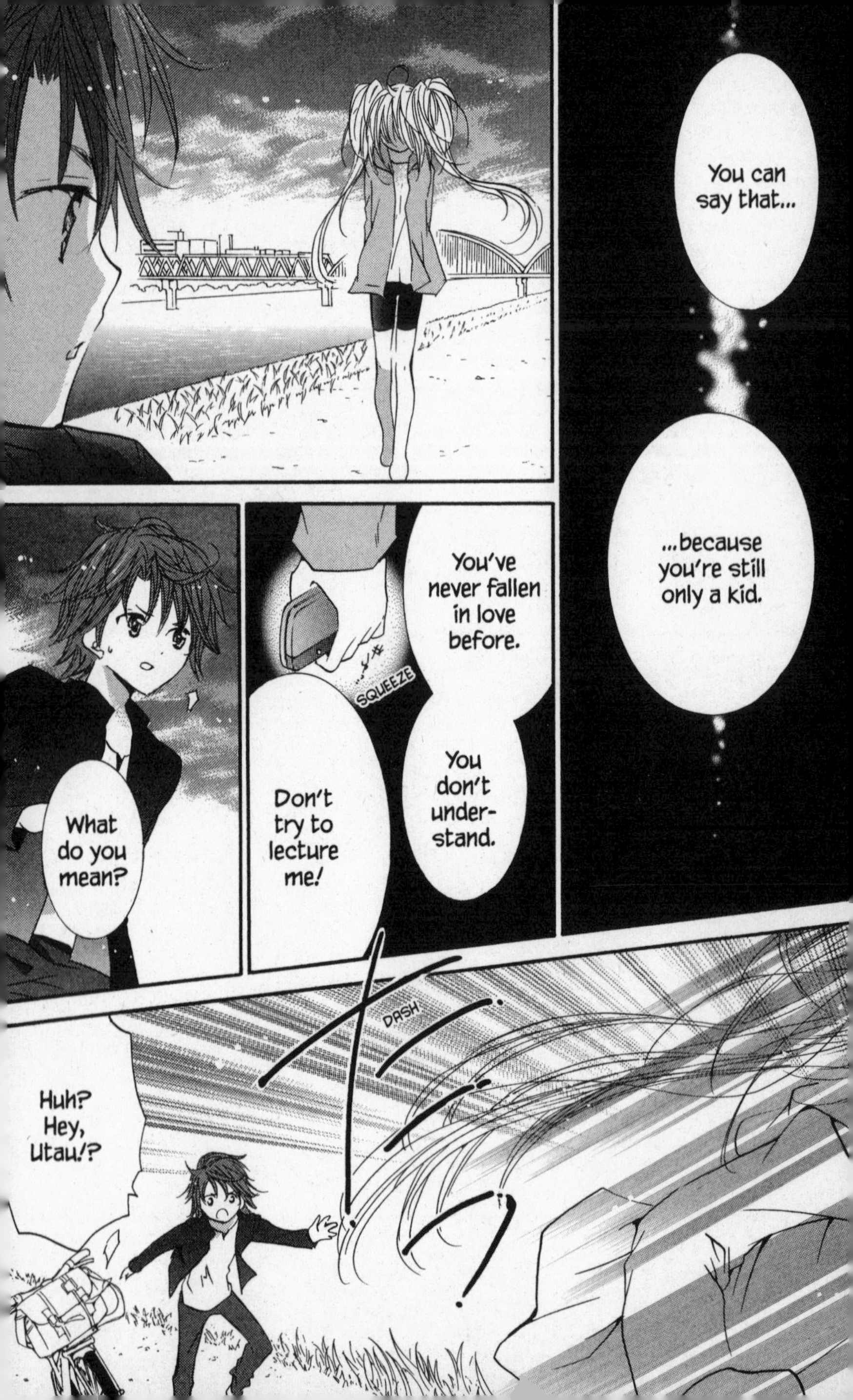

You can say that...
...because you're still only a kid.
You've never fallen in love before.
SQUEEZE
You don't under-stand.
Don't try to lecture me!
What do you mean?
DASH
Huh? Hey, Utau!?

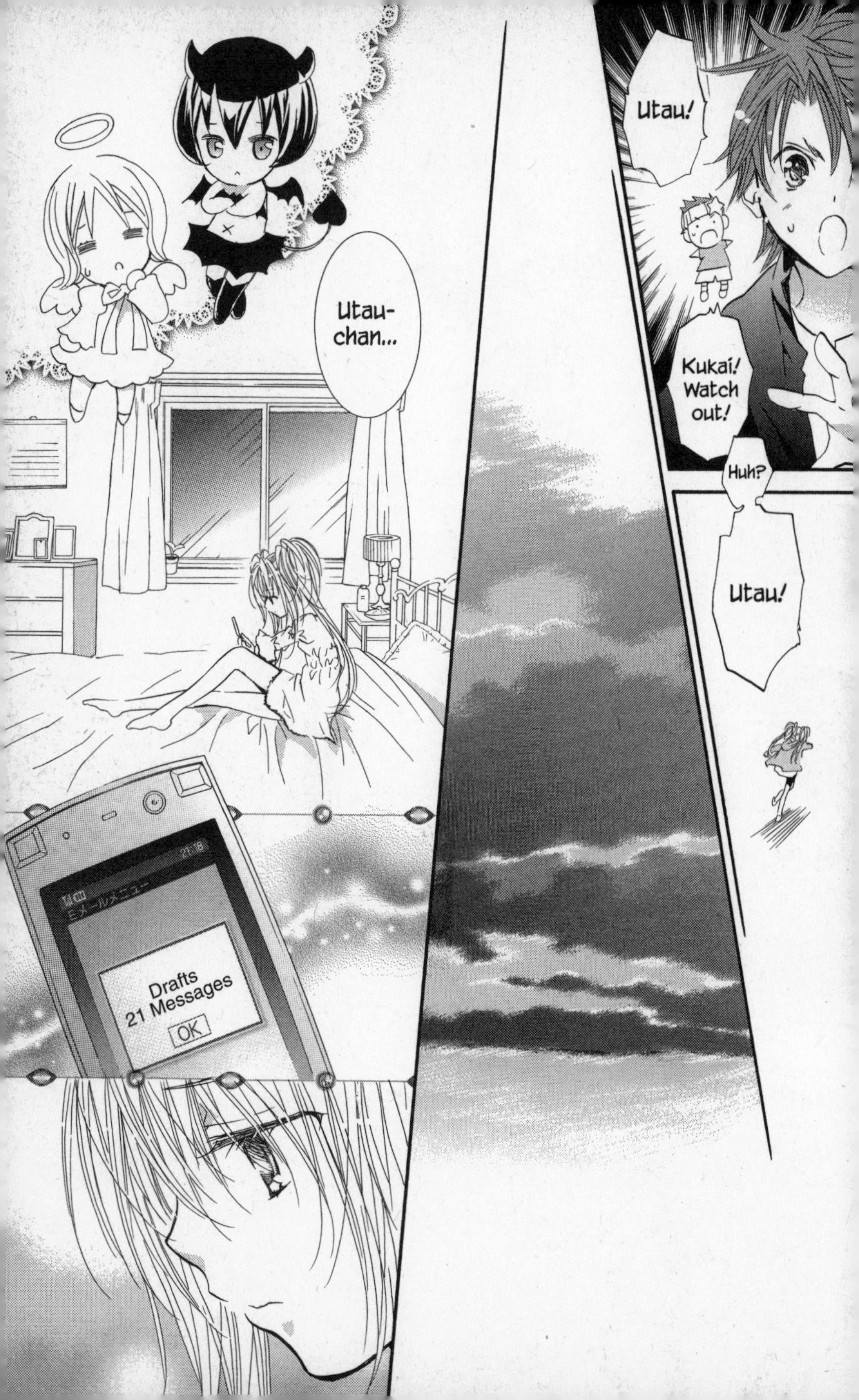
Utau!
Kukai! Watch out!
Huh?
Utau!
Utau-chan...
Drafts
21 Messages
OK

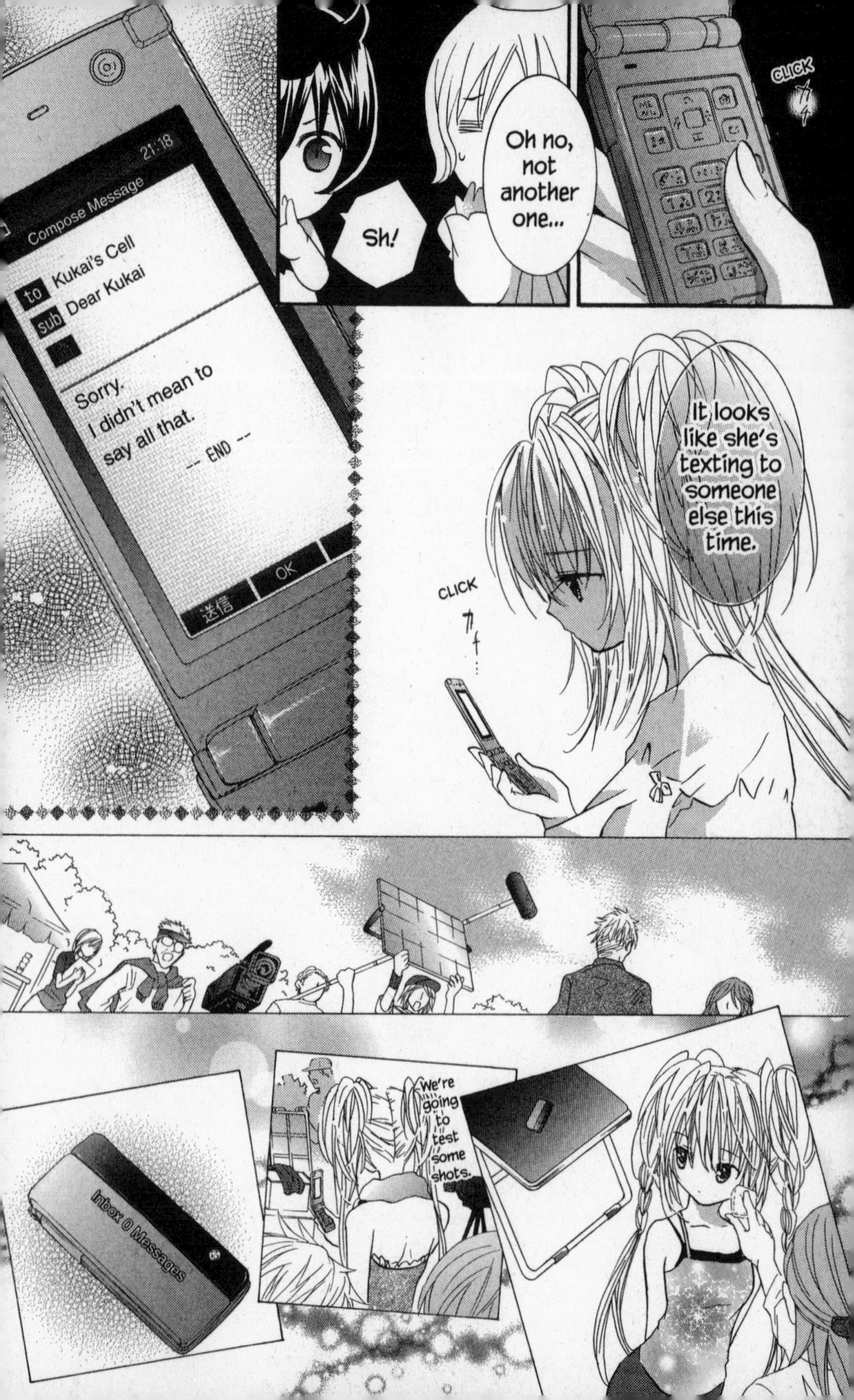
CLICK
Oh no, not another one...
Sh!
It looks like she's texting to someone else this time.
CLICK
カチ…
21:18
Compose Message
to Kukai's Cell
sub Dear Kukai
Sorry.
I didn't mean to
say all that.
-- END --
送信
OK
We're going to test some shots.
Inbox 0 Messages

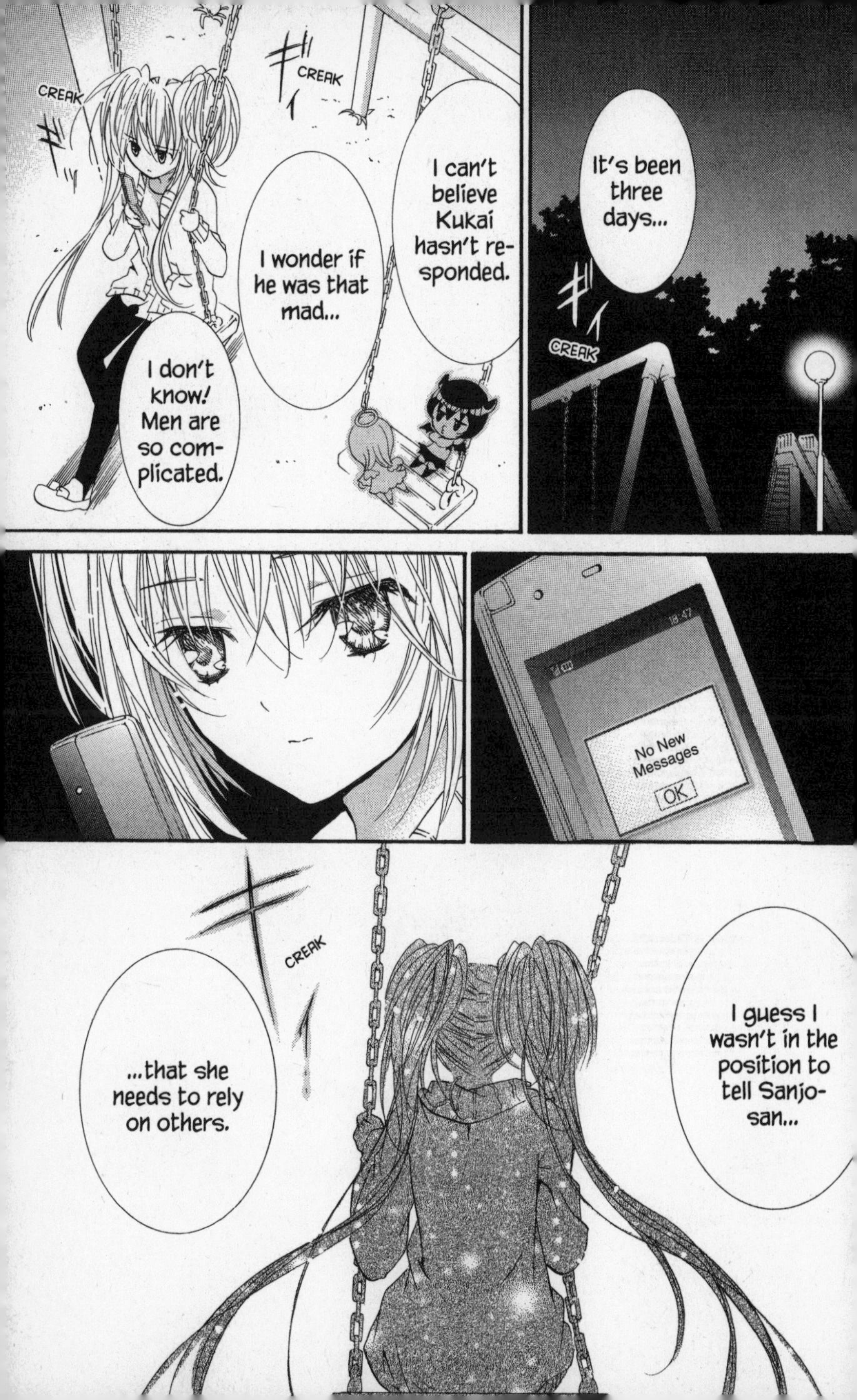
It's been three days...
CREAK
CREAK
I can't believe Kukai hasn't responded.
I wonder if he was that mad...
CREAK
I don't know! Men are so complicated.
No New Messages
OK
I guess I wasn't in the position to tell Sanjo-san...
CREAK
...that she needs to rely on others.

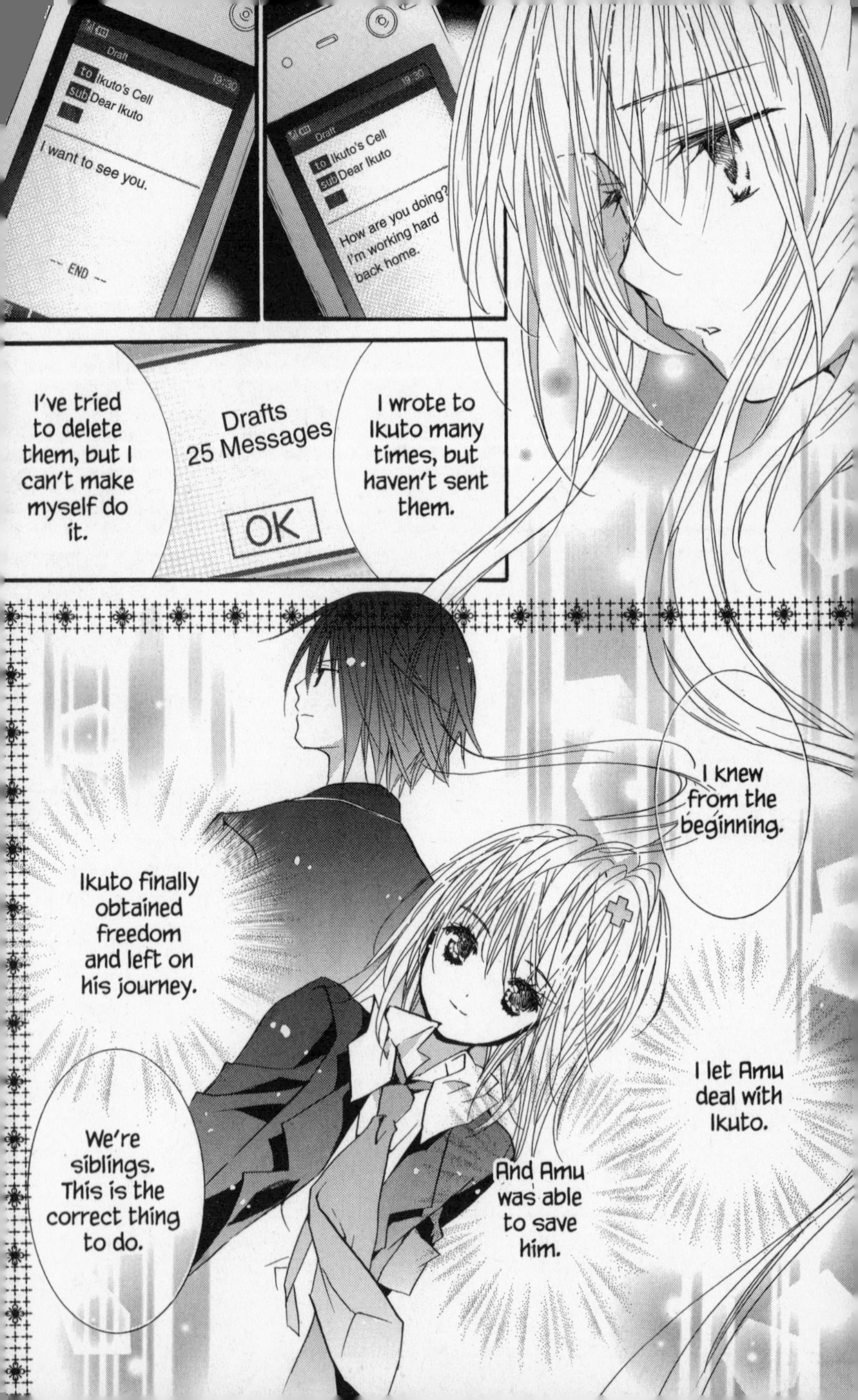

Draft
19:30
to Ikuto's Cell
sub Dear Ikuto
How are you doing? I'm working hard back home.
Draft
19:30
to Ikuto's Cell
sub Dear Ikuto
I want to see you.
-- END --
I wrote to Ikuto many times, but haven't sent them.
Drafts 25 Messages
OK
I've tried to delete them, but I can't make myself do it.
I knew from the beginning.
I let Amu deal with Ikuto.
And Amu was able to save him.
Ikuto finally obtained freedom and left on his journey.
We're siblings. This is the correct thing to do.

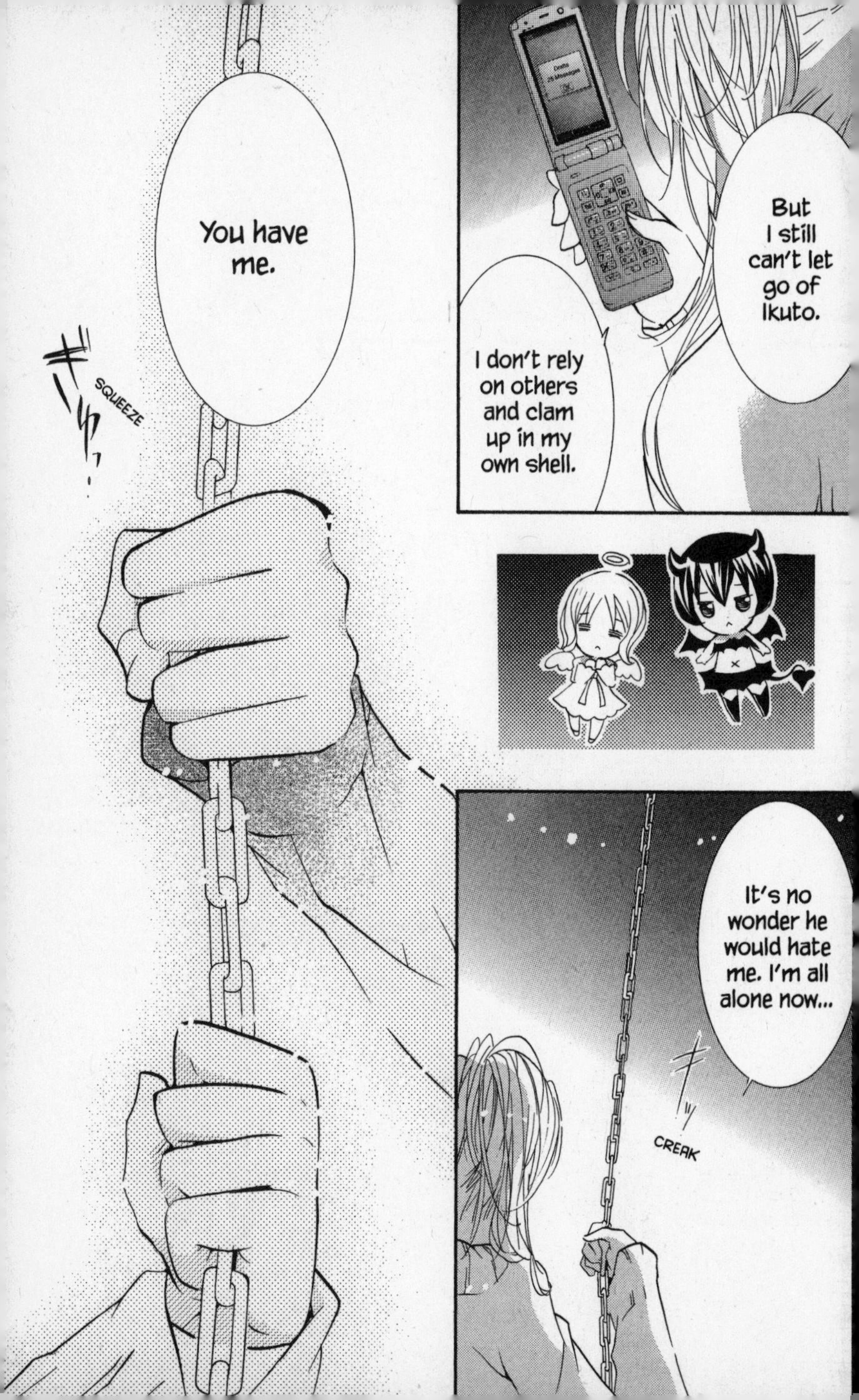

But I still can't let go of Ikuto.
I don't rely on others and clam up in my own shell.
It's no wonder he would hate me. I'm all alone now...
CREAK
You have me.
SQUEEZE

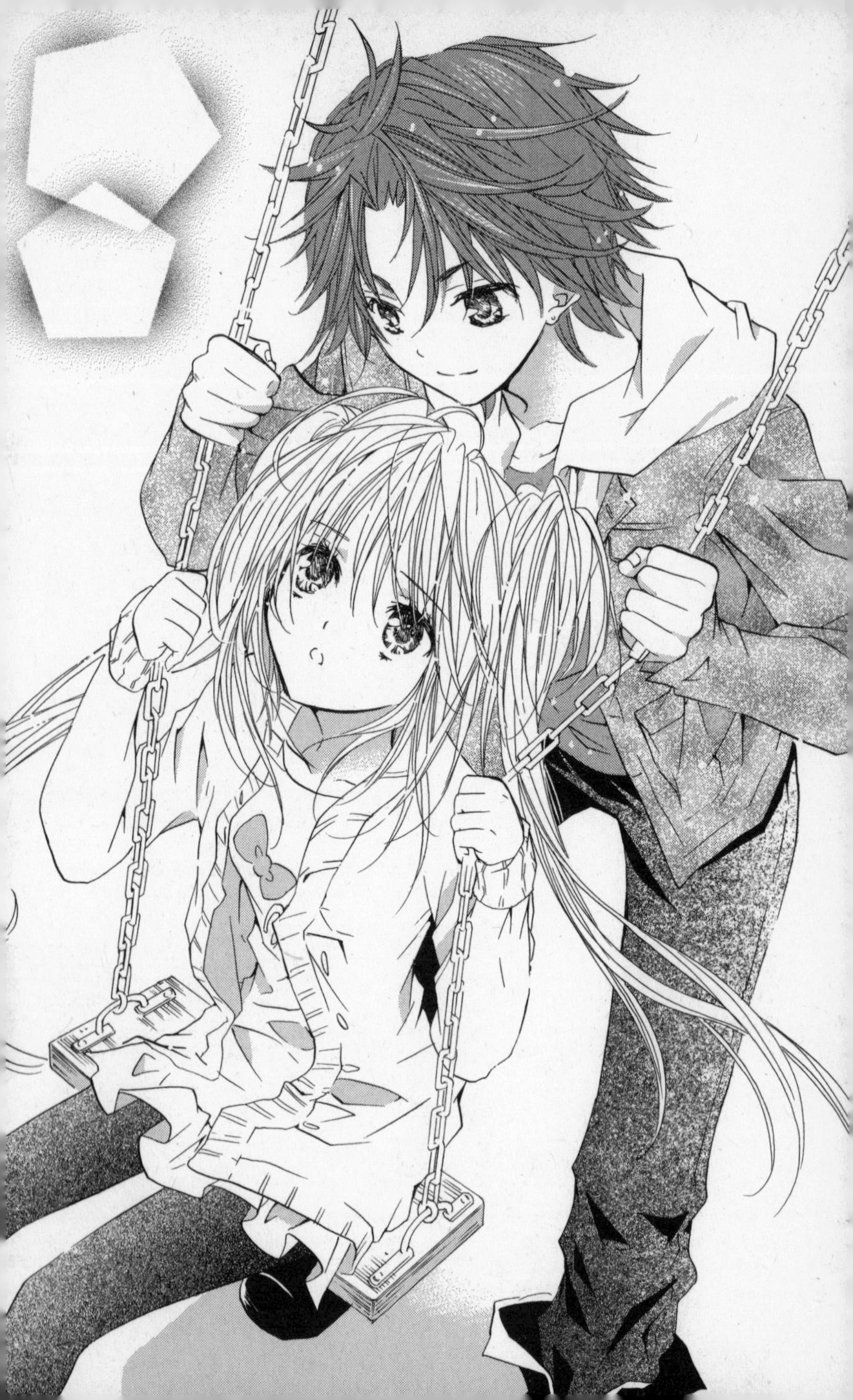

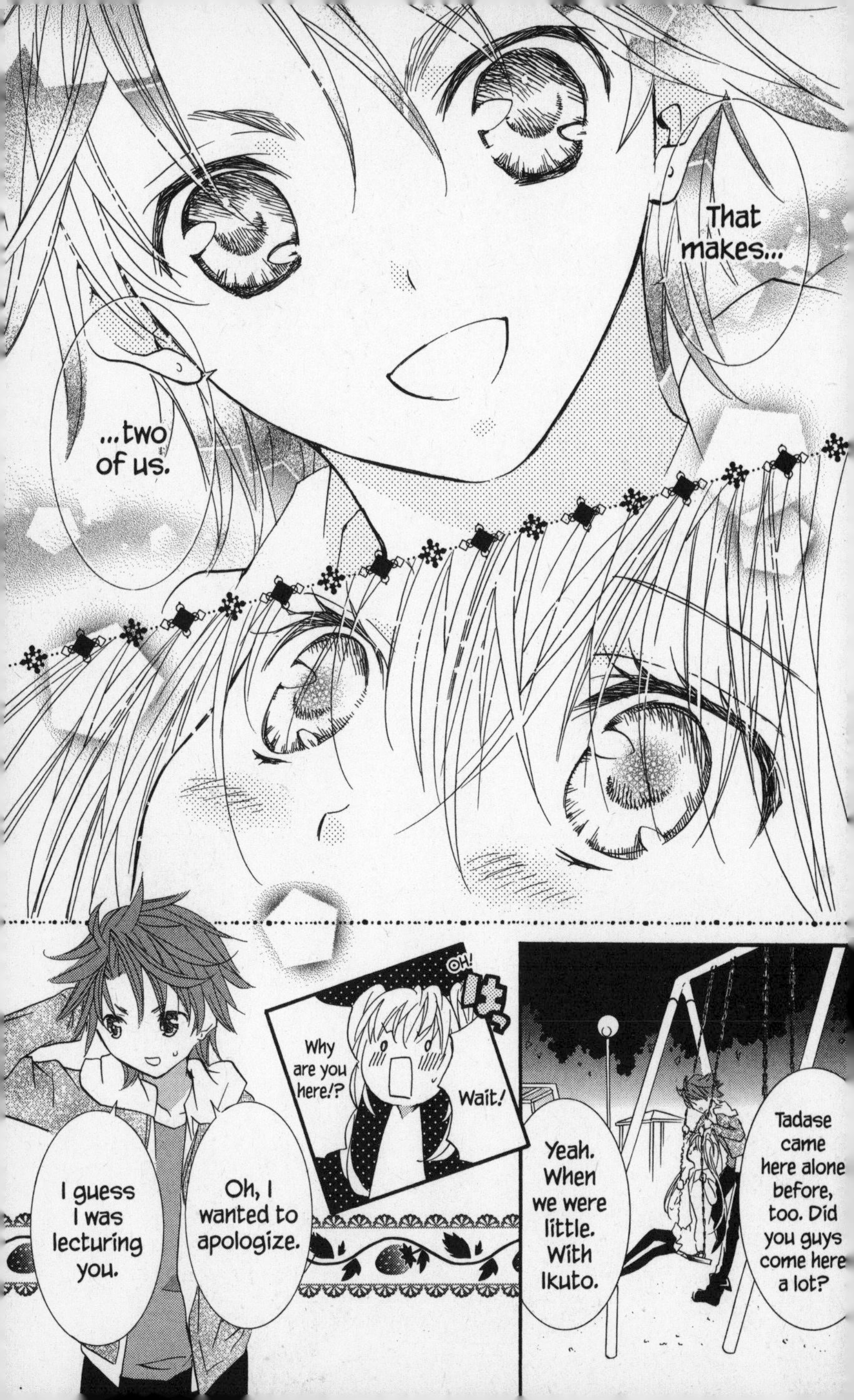
That makes...
...two of us.
Tadase came here alone before, too. Did you guys come here a lot?
Yeah. When we were little. With Ikuto.
OH!
Wait!
Why are you here!?
Oh, I wanted to apologize.
I guess I was lecturing you.

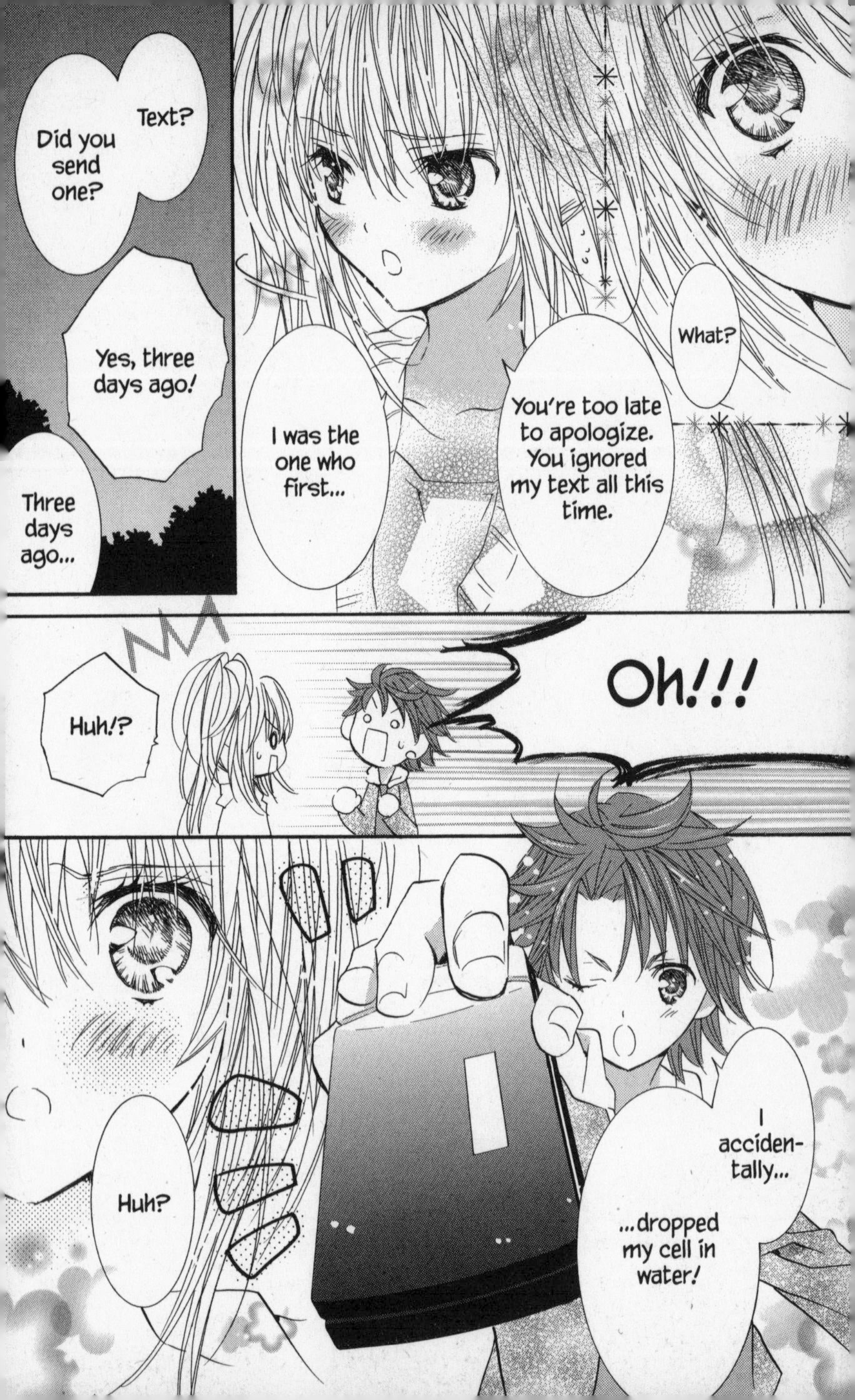
What?
You're too late to apologize. You ignored my text all this time.
I was the one who first...
Text? Did you send one?
Yes, three days ago!
Three days ago...
Oh!!!
Huh!?
I acciden-tally...
...dropped my cell in water!
Huh?

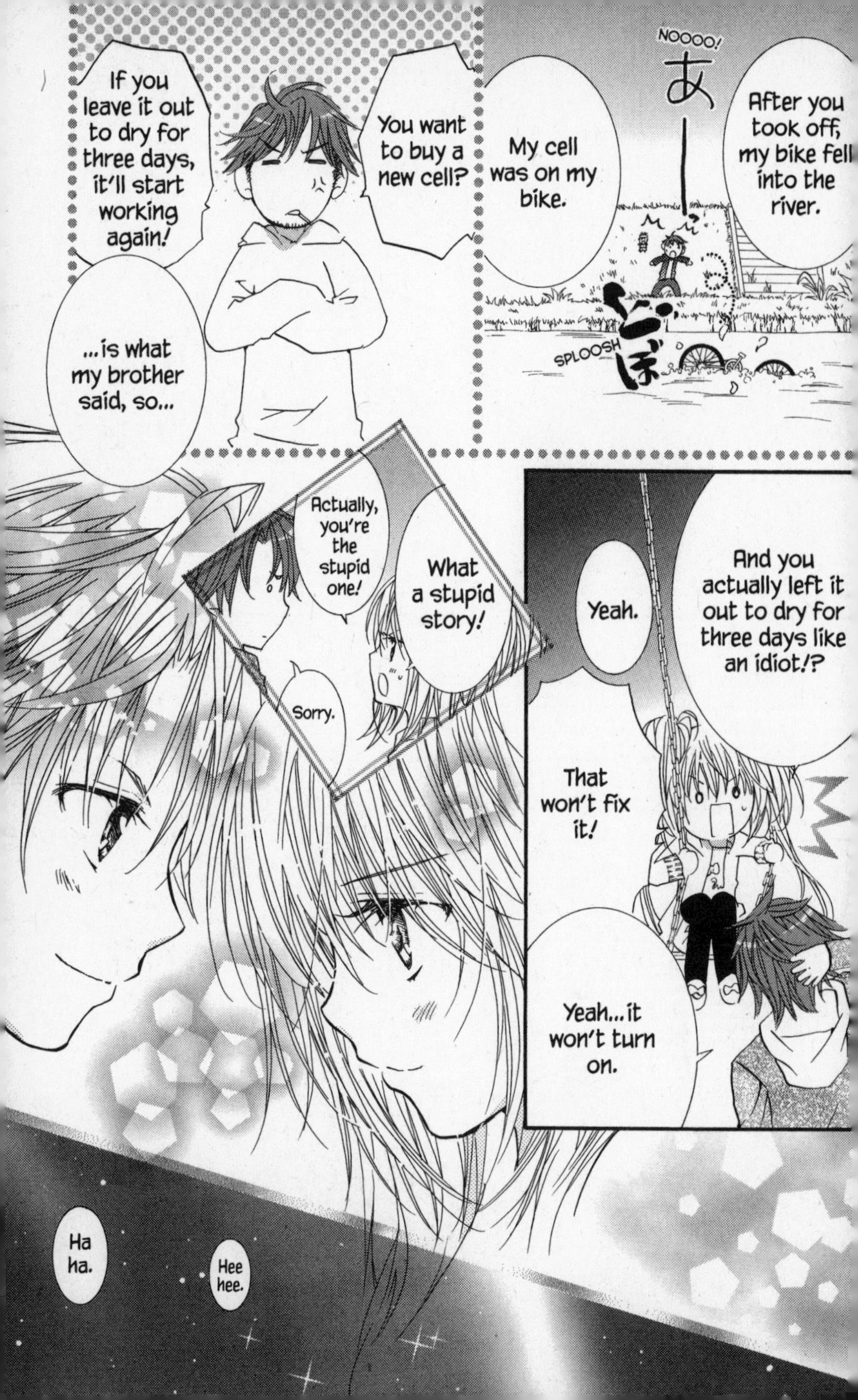

After you took off, my bike fell into the river.
NOOOO!
あー
SPLOOSH
どぼ
My cell was on my bike.
You want to buy a new cell?
If you leave it out to dry for three days, it'll start working again!
...is what my brother said, so...
And you actually left it out to dry for three days like an idiot!?
Yeah.
That won't fix it!
Yeah...it won't turn on.
What a stupid story!
Actually, you're the stupid one!
Sorry.
Ha ha.
Hee hee.

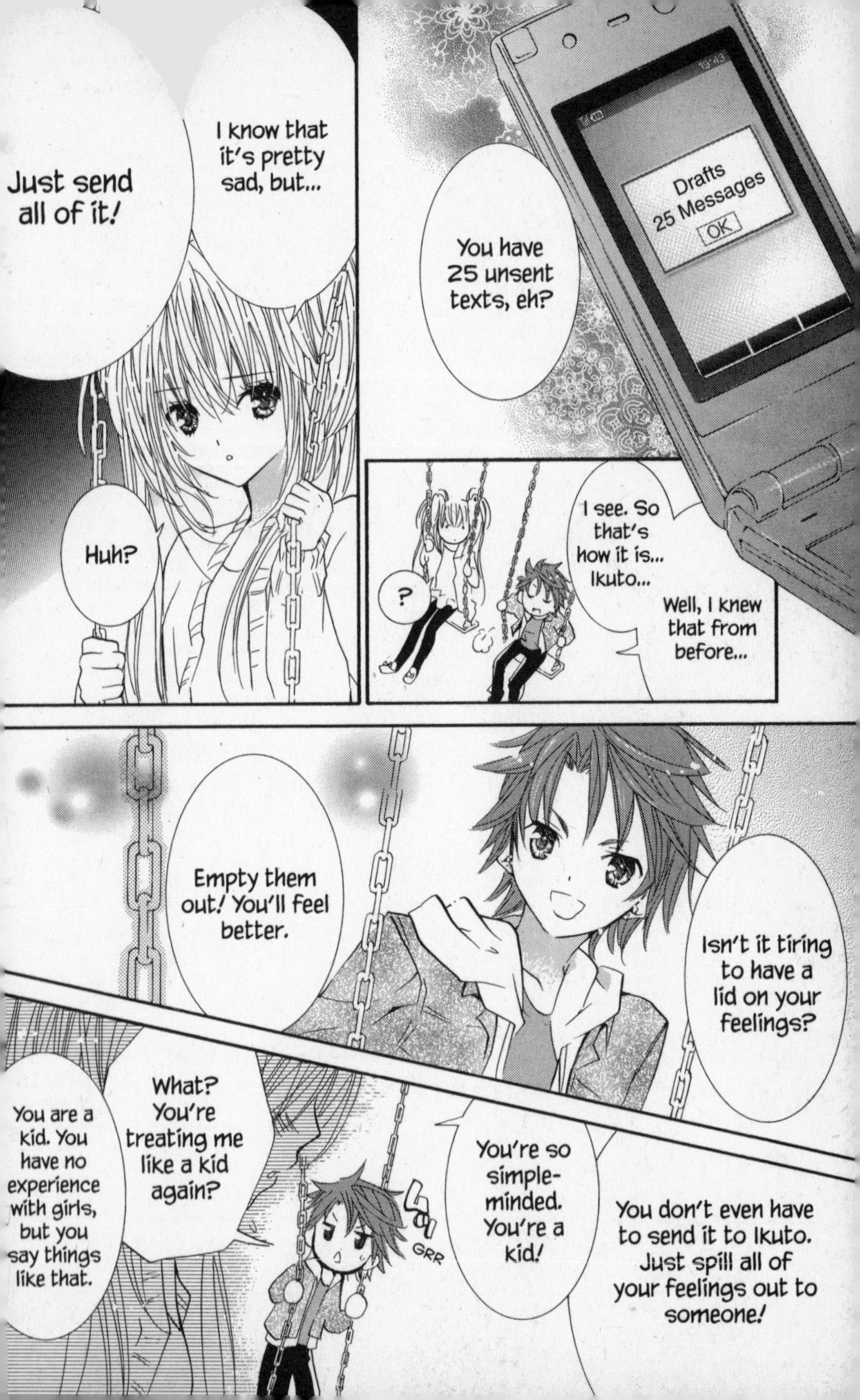
Drafts
25 Messages
OK
You have 25 unsent texts, eh?
I see. So that's how it is... Ikuto...
Well, I knew that from before...
?
I know that it's pretty sad, but...
Just send all of it!
Huh?
Isn't it tiring to have a lid on your feelings?
Empty them out! You'll feel better.
You don't even have to send it to Ikuto. Just spill all of your feelings out to someone!
You're so simple-minded. You're a kid!
GRR
What? You're treating me like a kid again?
You are a kid. You have no experience with girls, but you say things like that.

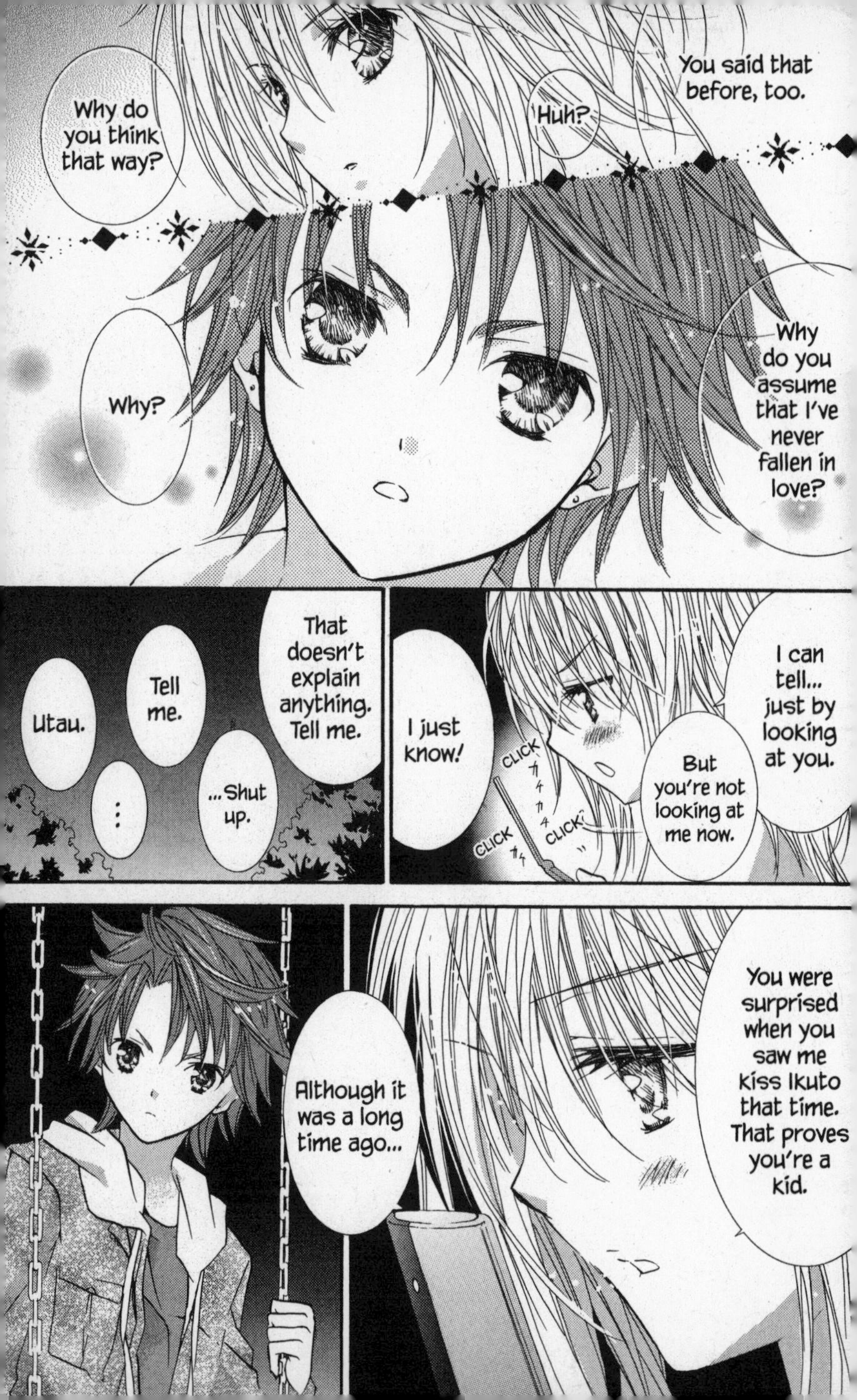
You said that before, too.
Huh?
Why do you think that way?
Why do you assume that I've never fallen in love?
Why?
I can tell... just by looking at you.
But you're not looking at me now.
CLICK
CLICK
CLICK
I just know!
That doesn't explain anything. Tell me.
Tell me.
...Shut up.
Utau.
...
You were surprised when you saw me kiss Ikuto that time. That proves you're a kid.
Although it was a long time ago...

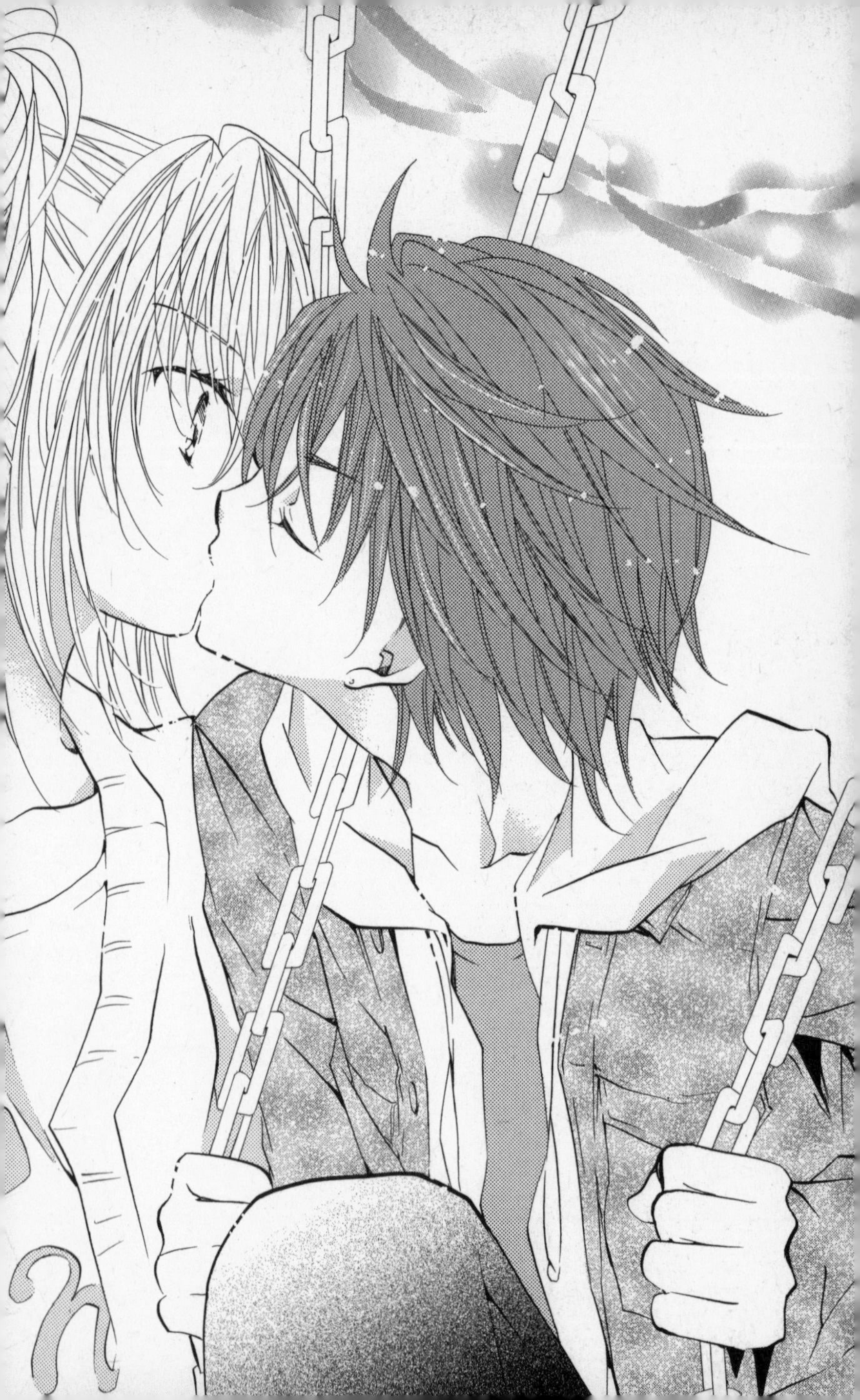

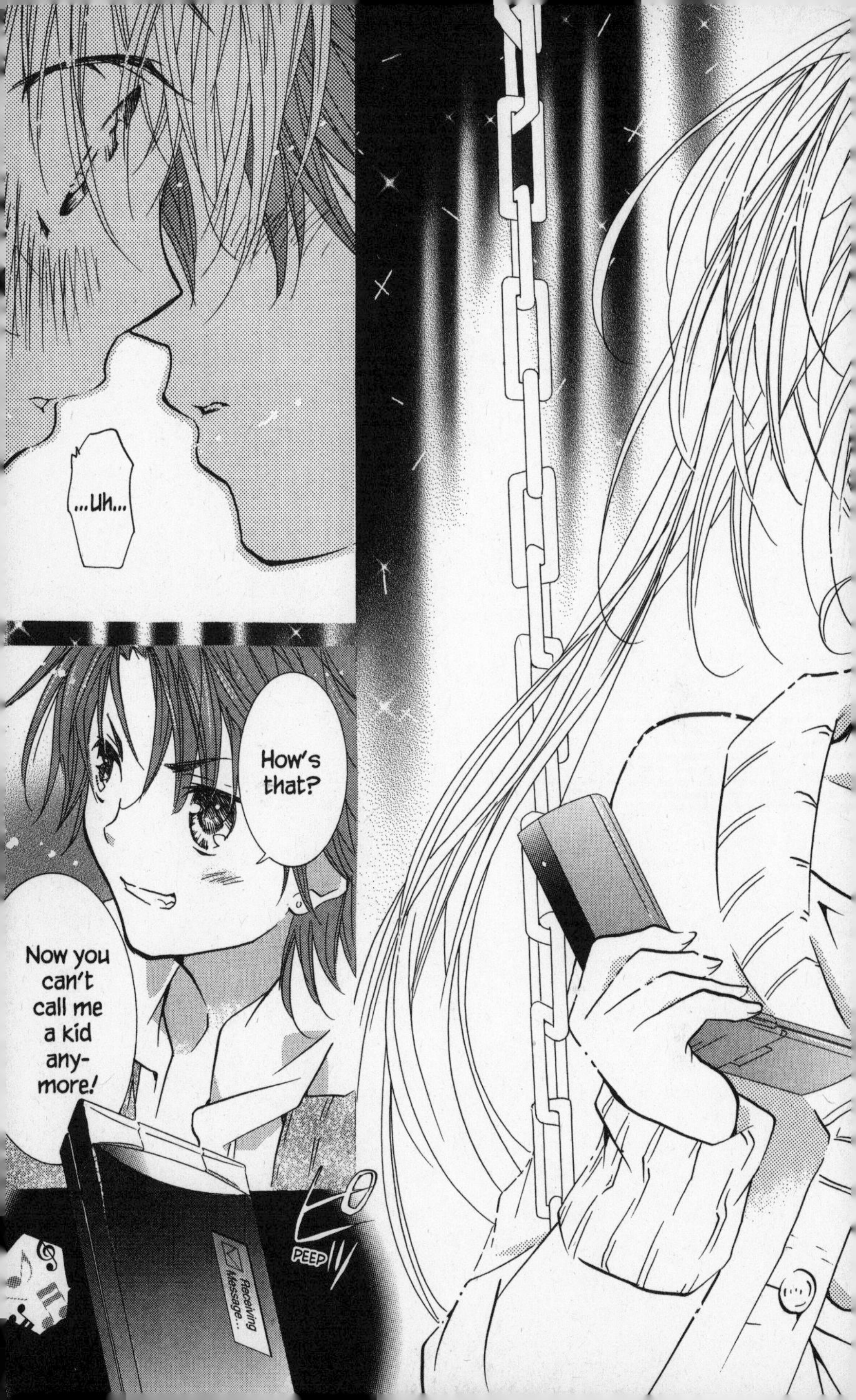
...uh...
How's that?
Now you can't call me a kid anymore!
PEEP
Receiving Message...

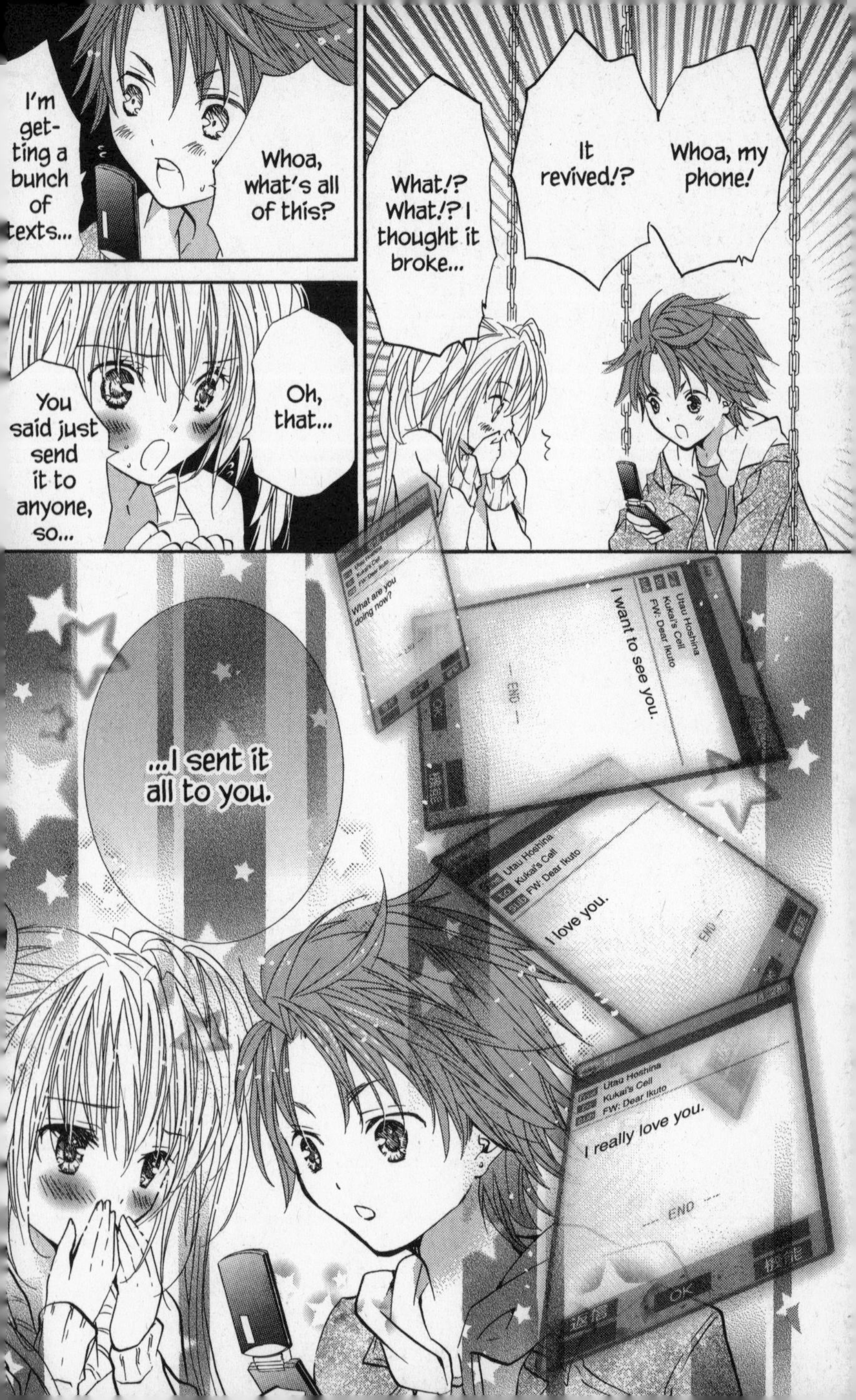
Whoa, my phone!
It revived!?
What!? What!? I thought it broke...
Whoa, what's all of this?
I'm get-ting a bunch of texts...
Oh, that...
You said just send it to anyone, so...
What are you doing now?
Utau Hoshina
Kukai's Cell
FW: Dear Ikuto
I want to see you.
— END —
...I sent it all to you.
Utau Hoshina
Kukai's Cell
FW: Dear Ikuto
I love you.
— END —
Utau Hoshina
Kukai's Cell
FW: Dear Ikuto
I really love you.
— END —
OK

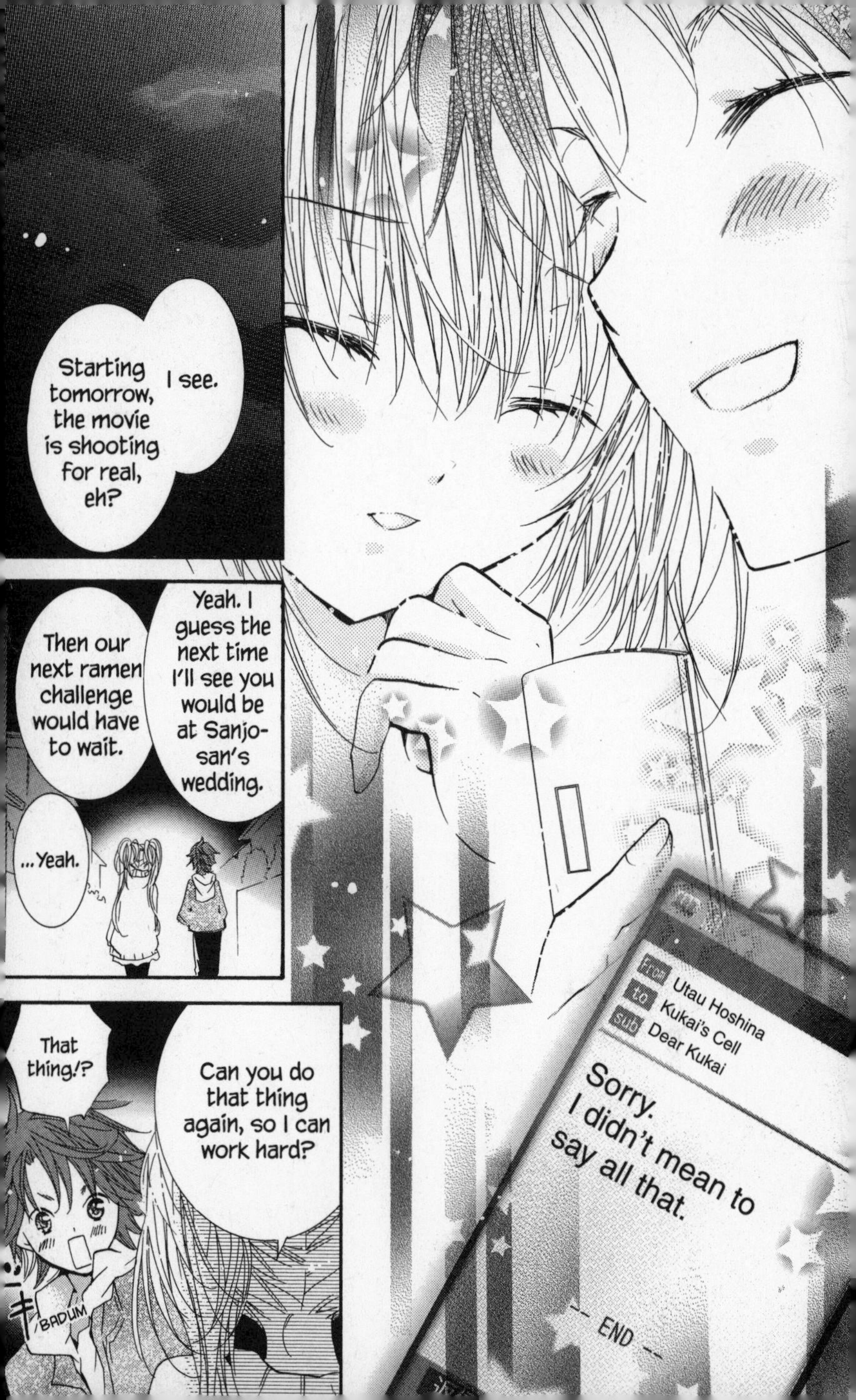

I see.
Starting tomorrow, the movie is shooting for real, eh?
Yeah. I guess the next time I'll see you would be at Sanjo-san's wedding.
Then our next ramen challenge would have to wait.
...Yeah.
Can you do that thing again, so I can work hard?
That thing!?
BADUM
From Utau Hoshina
to Kukai's Cell
sub Dear Kukai
Sorry. I didn't mean to say all that.
-- END --

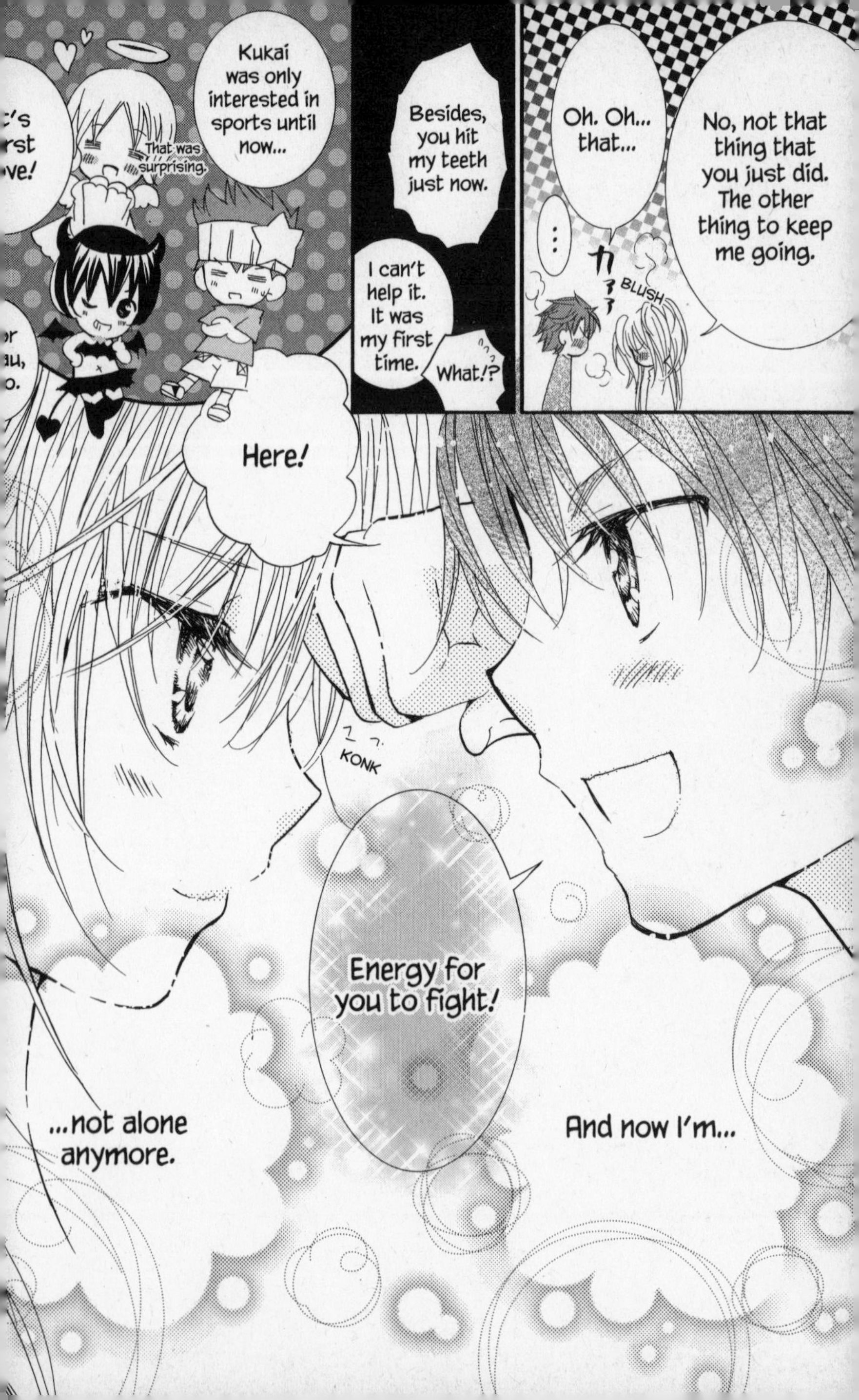
No, not that thing that you just did. The other thing to keep me going.
Oh. Oh... that...
...
BLUSH
Besides, you hit my teeth just now.
I can't help it. It was my first time.
What!?
Kukai was only interested in sports until now...
That was surprising.
Here!
KONK
Energy for you to fight!
And now I'm...
...not alone anymore.

Shugo Chara!

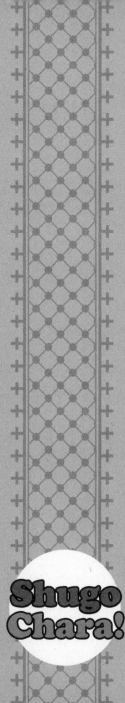

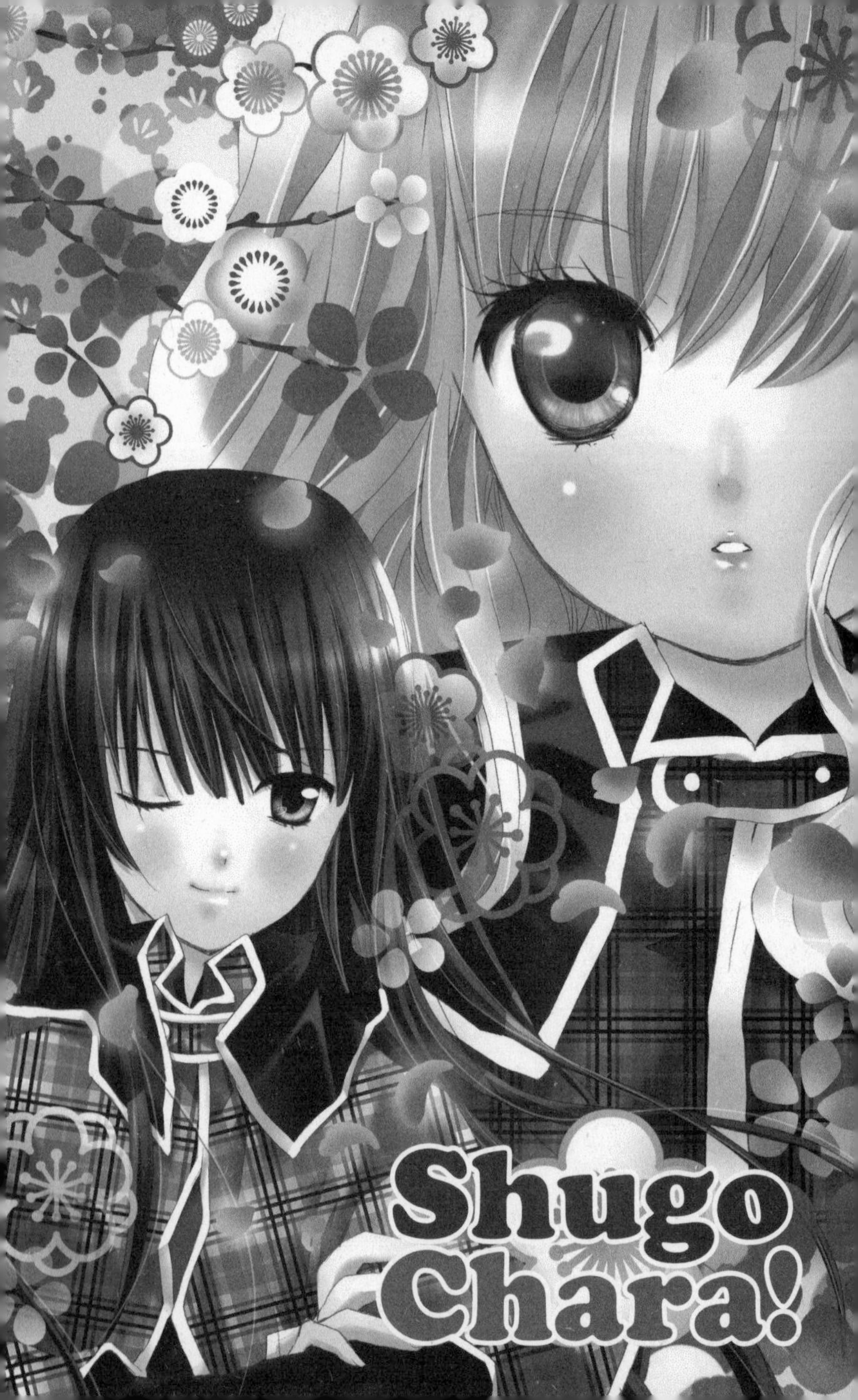
Shugo
Chara!

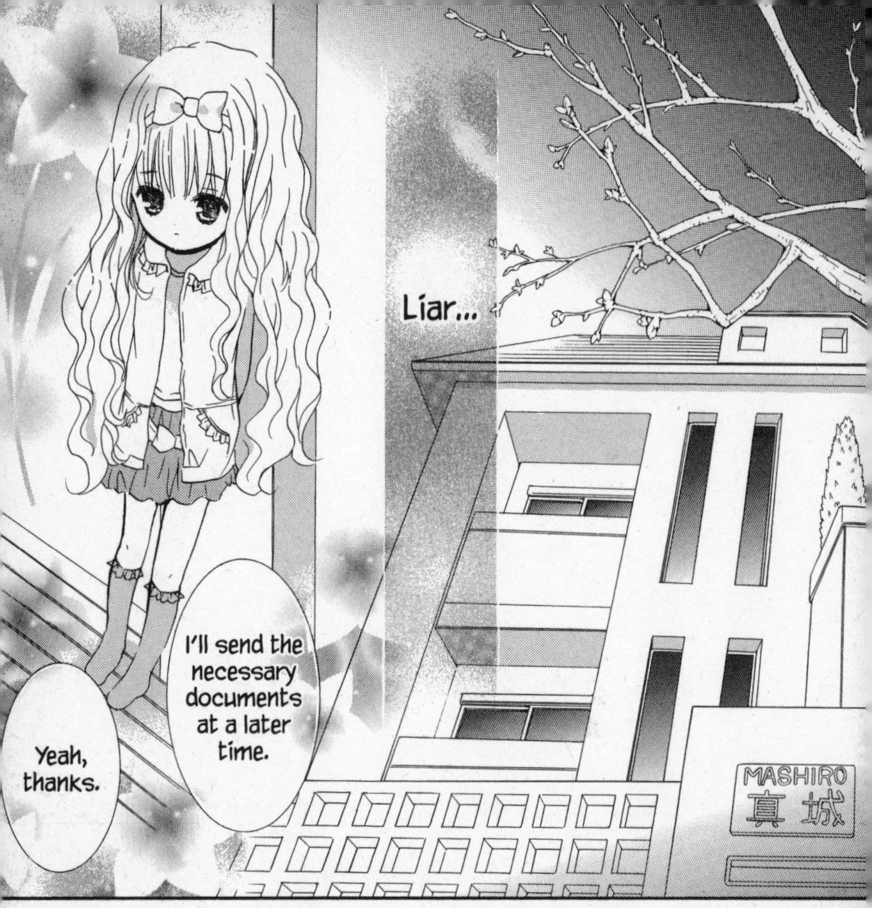
Liar...
I'll send the necessary documents at a later time.
Yeah, thanks.
MASHIRO
真城

Q1. How many siblings do you have? A1. Banri is an only child. I have two older brothers! Q2. What does Amu-chan's Character Transformation name "Amulet" mean? A2. It means "lucky charm." It sounds like something good will happen, right? Sort of...
Q3. What type of breed is Betty? A3. She is an Afghan Hound! They look so smart, don't they? Q4. If you were to write a letter to your future self, what would you write? A4. "Take care of your health," maybe...

For real...

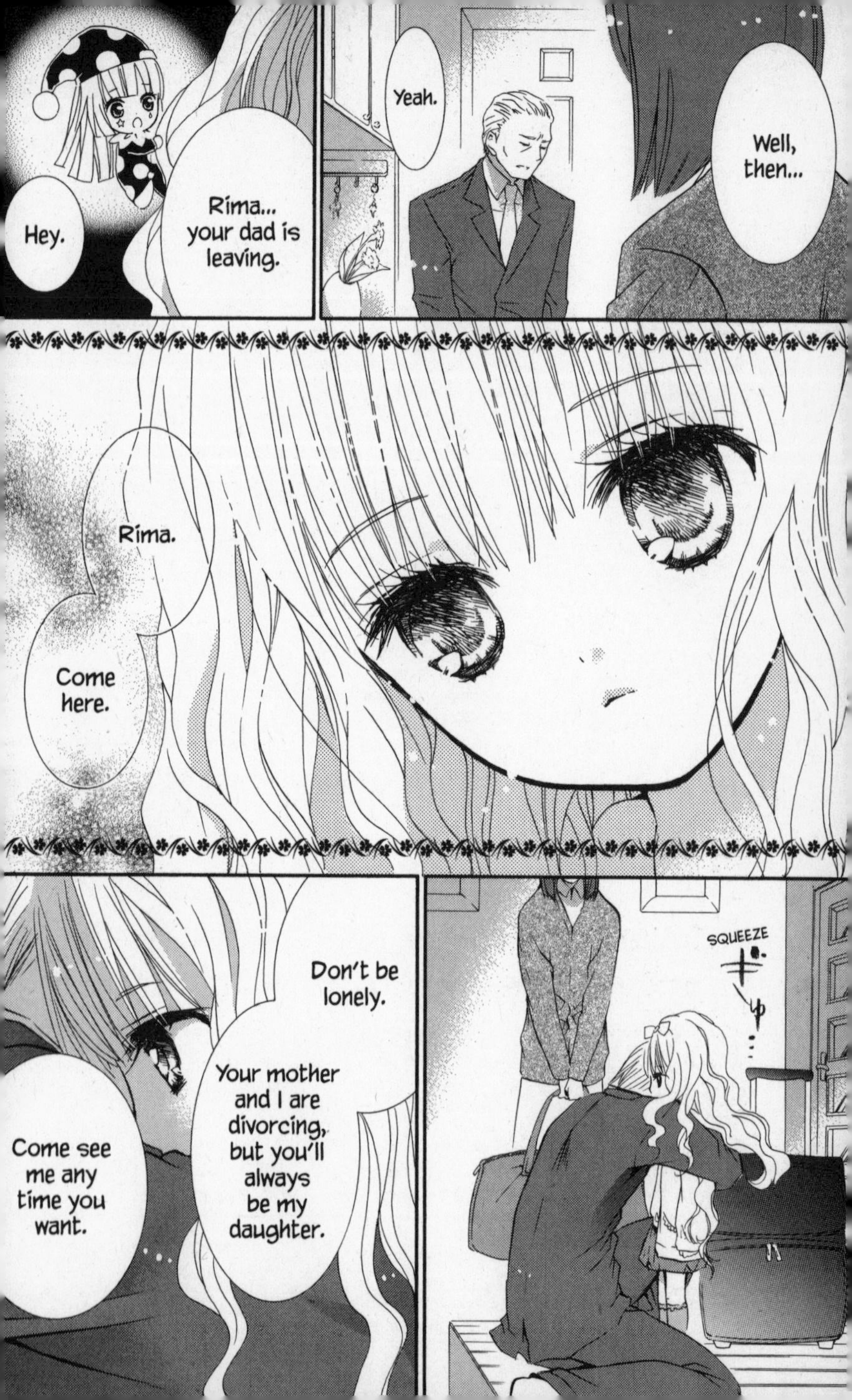
Well, then...
Yeah.
Rima... your dad is leaving.
Hey.
Rima.
Come here.
SQUEEZE
Don't be lonely.
Your mother and I are divorcing, but you'll always be my daughter.
Come see me any time you want.

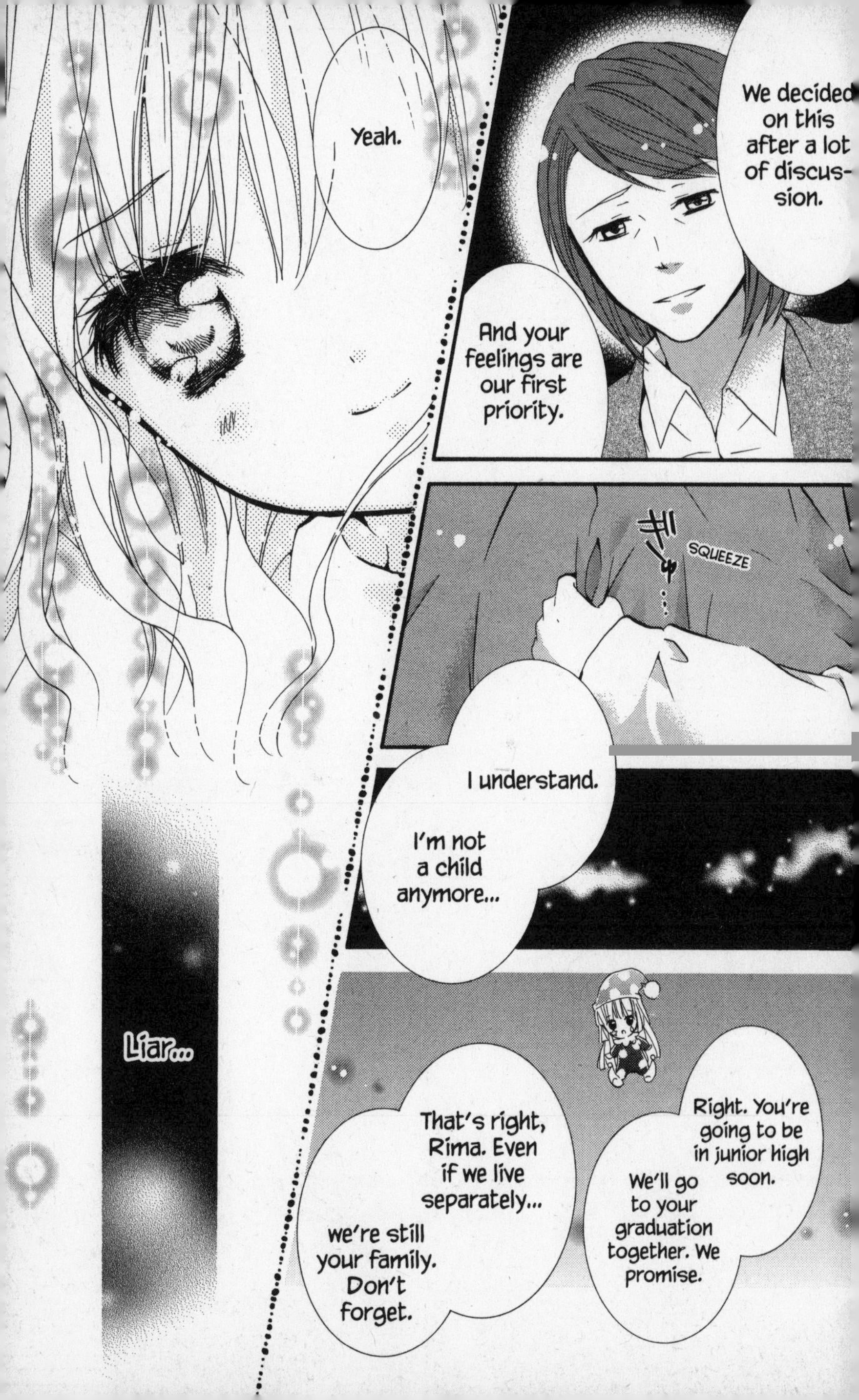

We decided on this after a lot of discus-sion.
And your feelings are our first priority.
SQUEEZE
I understand.
I'm not a child anymore...
Right. You're going to be in junior high soon.
We'll go to your graduation together. We promise.
That's right, Rima. Even if we live separately...
we're still your family. Don't forget.
Yeah.
Liar...

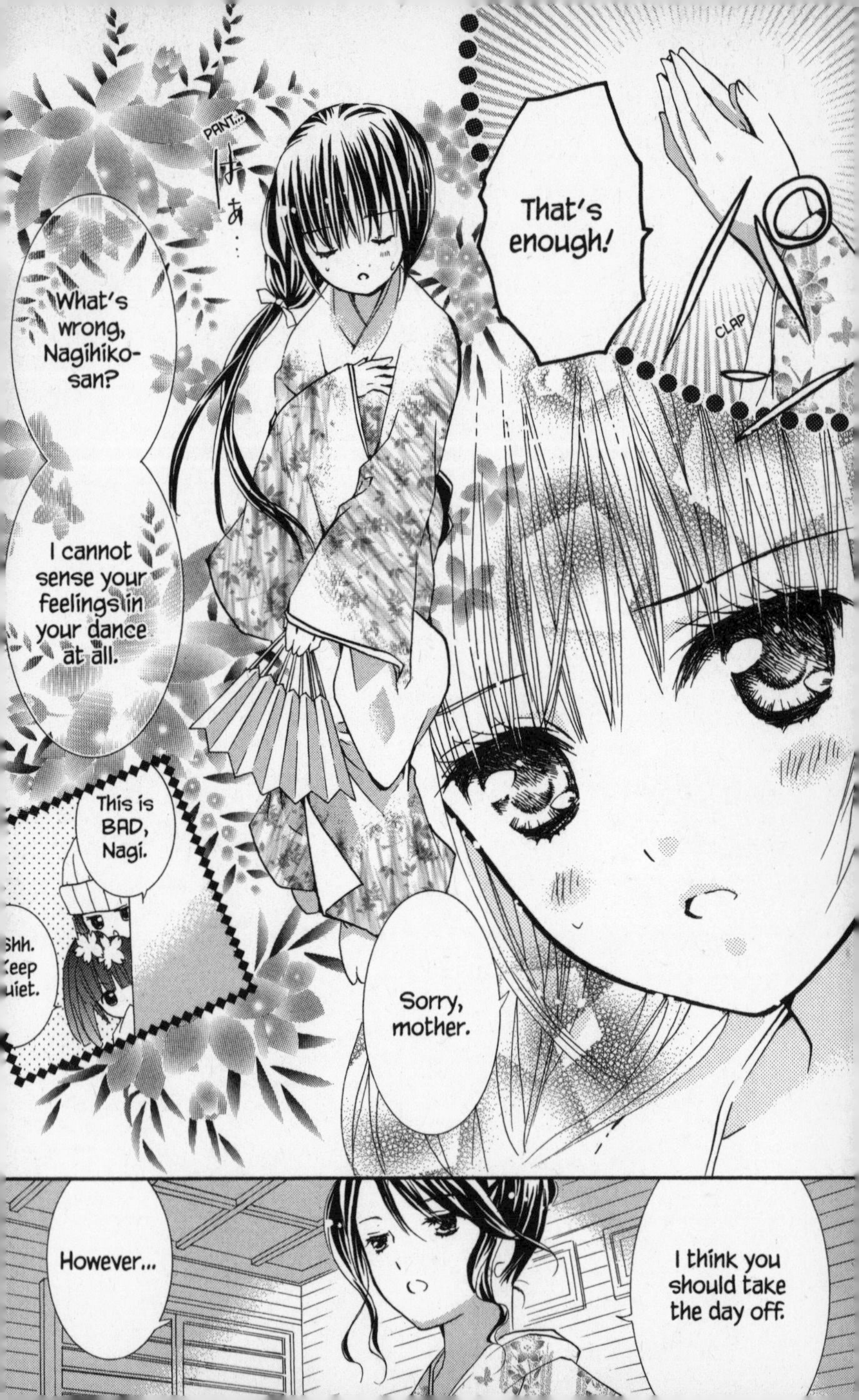
That's enough!
CLAP
PANT...
What's wrong, Nagihiko-san?
I cannot sense your feelings in your dance at all.
Sorry, mother.
This is BAD, Nagi.
Shh. Keep quiet.
I think you should take the day off.
However...

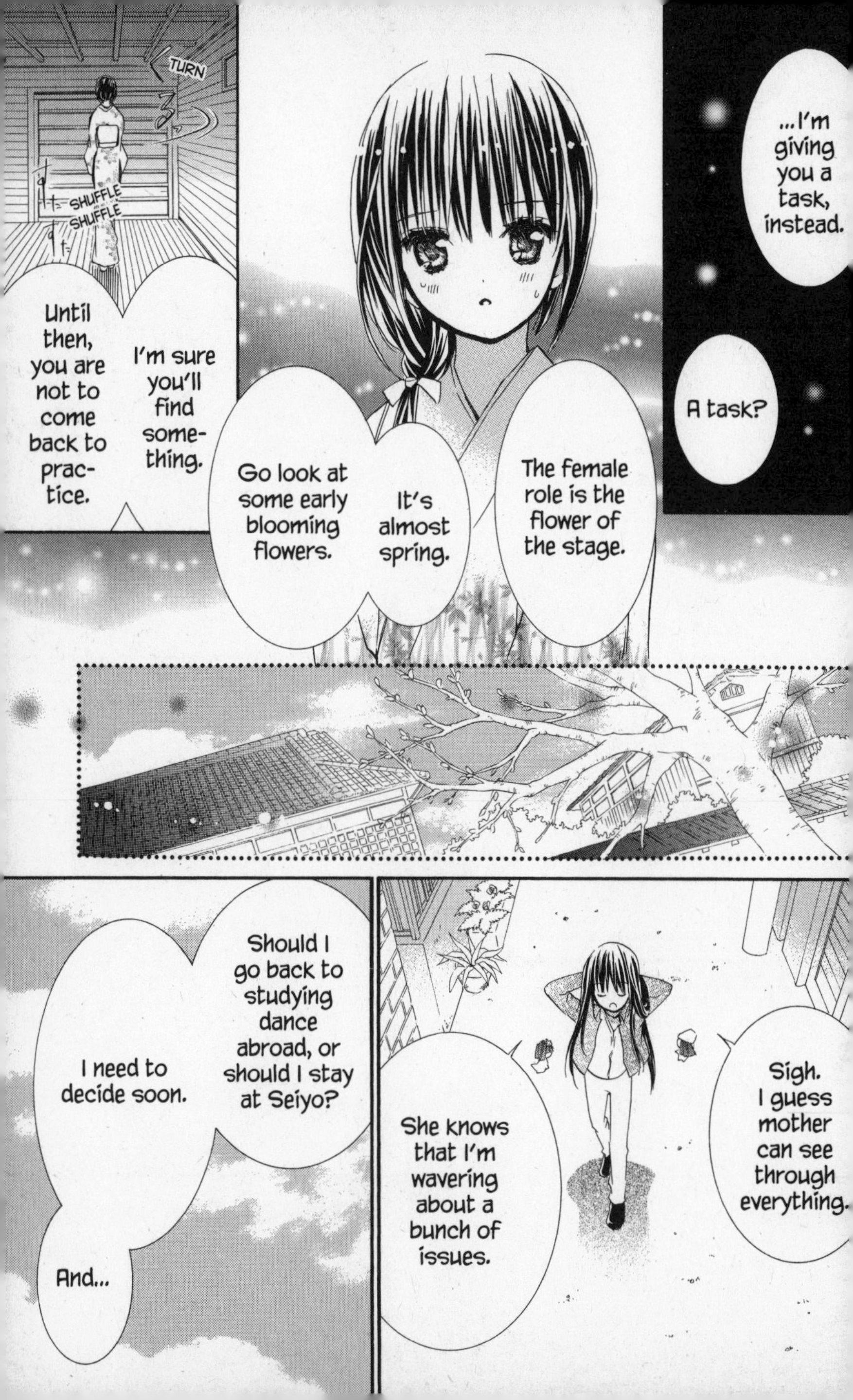
...I'm giving you a task, instead.
A task?
The female role is the flower of the stage.
It's almost spring.
Go look at some early blooming flowers.
TURN
SHUFFLE SHUFFLE
I'm sure you'll find some-thing.
Until then, you are not to come back to prac-tice.
Sigh. I guess mother can see through everything.
She knows that I'm wavering about a bunch of issues.
Should I go back to studying dance abroad, or should I stay at Seiyo?
I need to decide soon.
And...

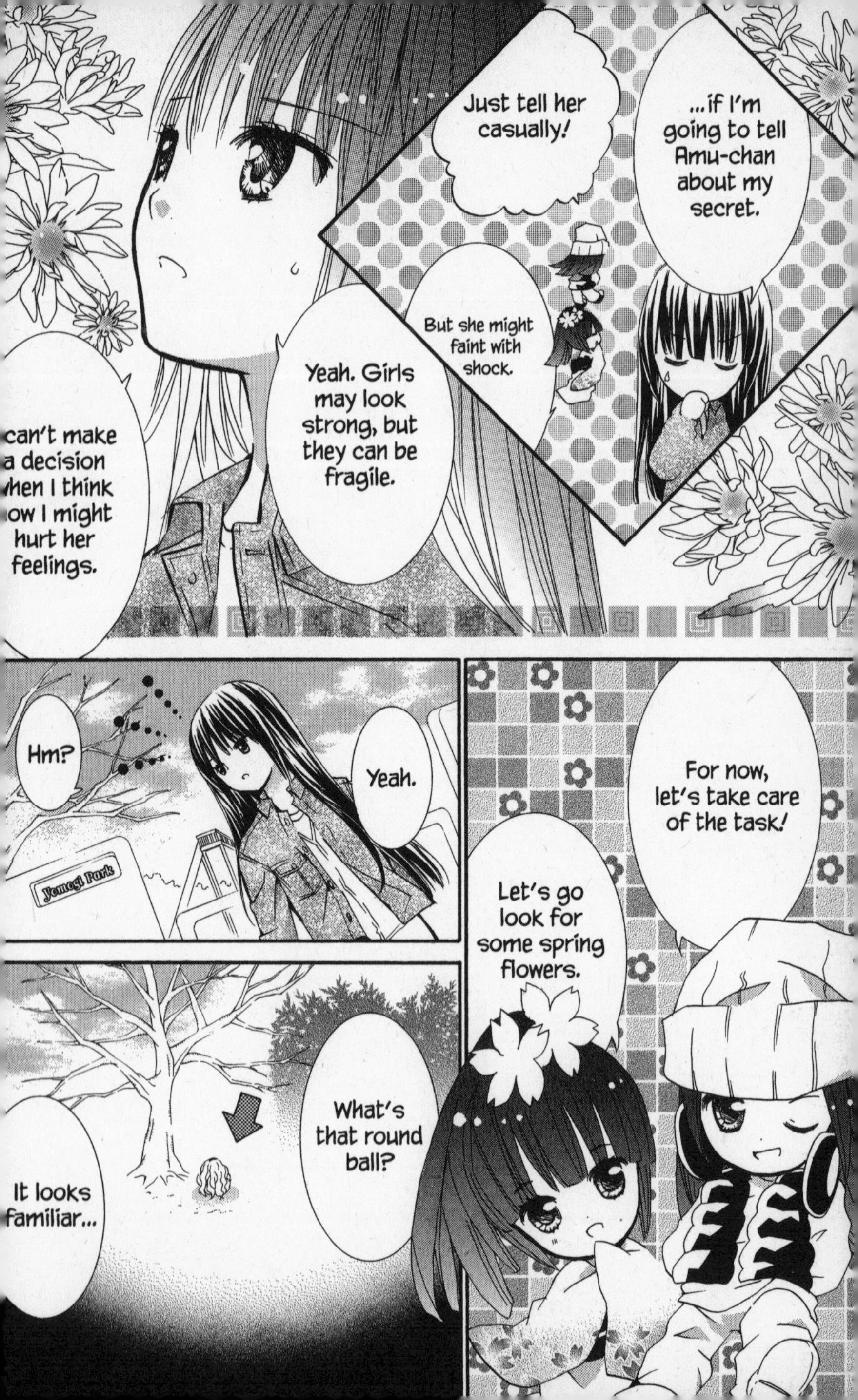
...if I'm going to tell Amu-chan about my secret.
Just tell her casually!
But she might faint with shock.
Yeah. Girls may look strong, but they can be fragile.
can't make a decision hen I think ow I might hurt her feelings.
For now, let's take care of the task!
Let's go look for some spring flowers.
Yeah.
Hm?
Yomogi Park
What's that round ball?
It looks familiar...

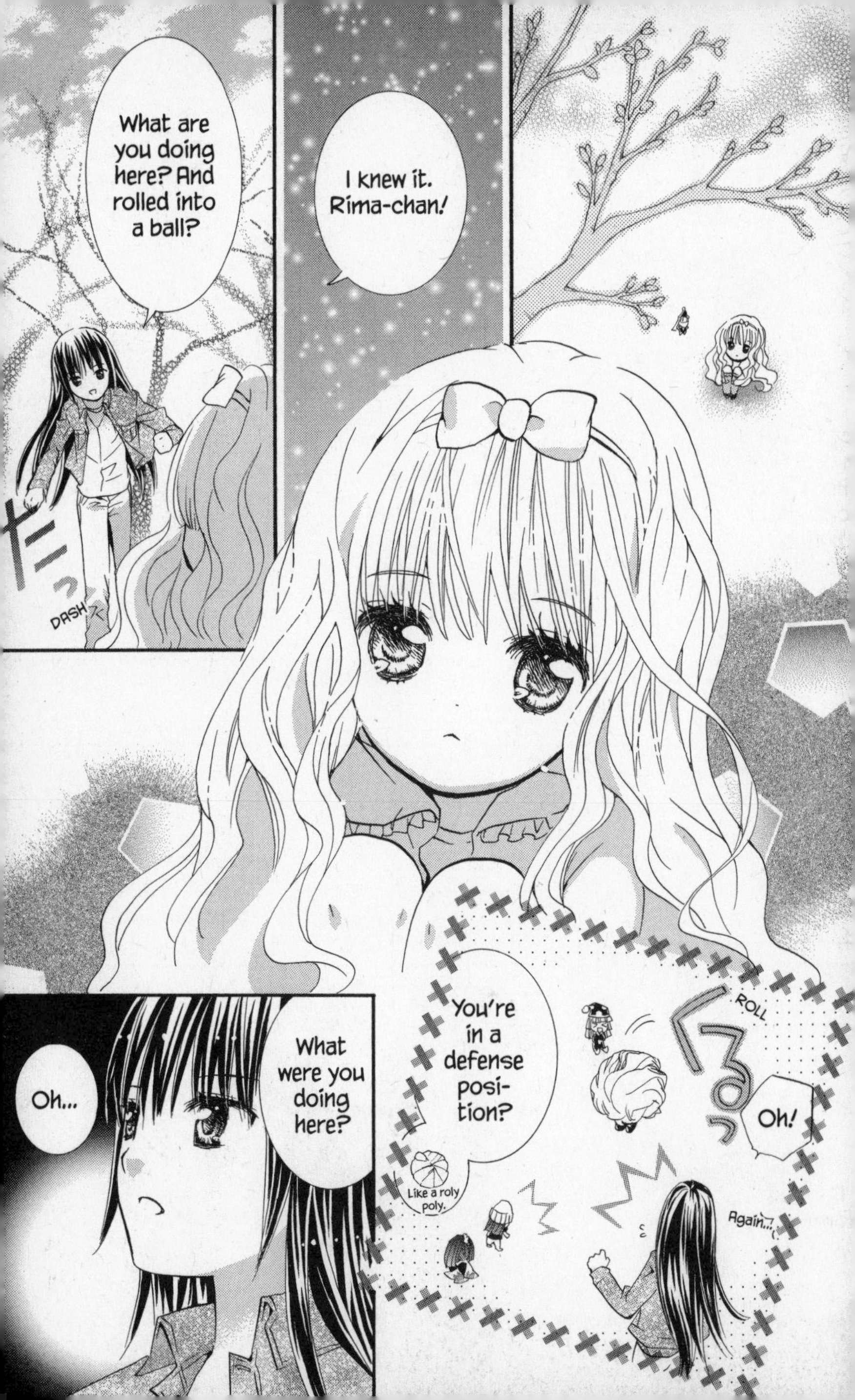
I knew it. Rima-chan!
What are you doing here? And rolled into a ball?
ダーっ
DASH
くるっ
ROLL
Oh!
You're in a defense position?
Again...!
Like a roly poly.
What were you doing here?
Oh...

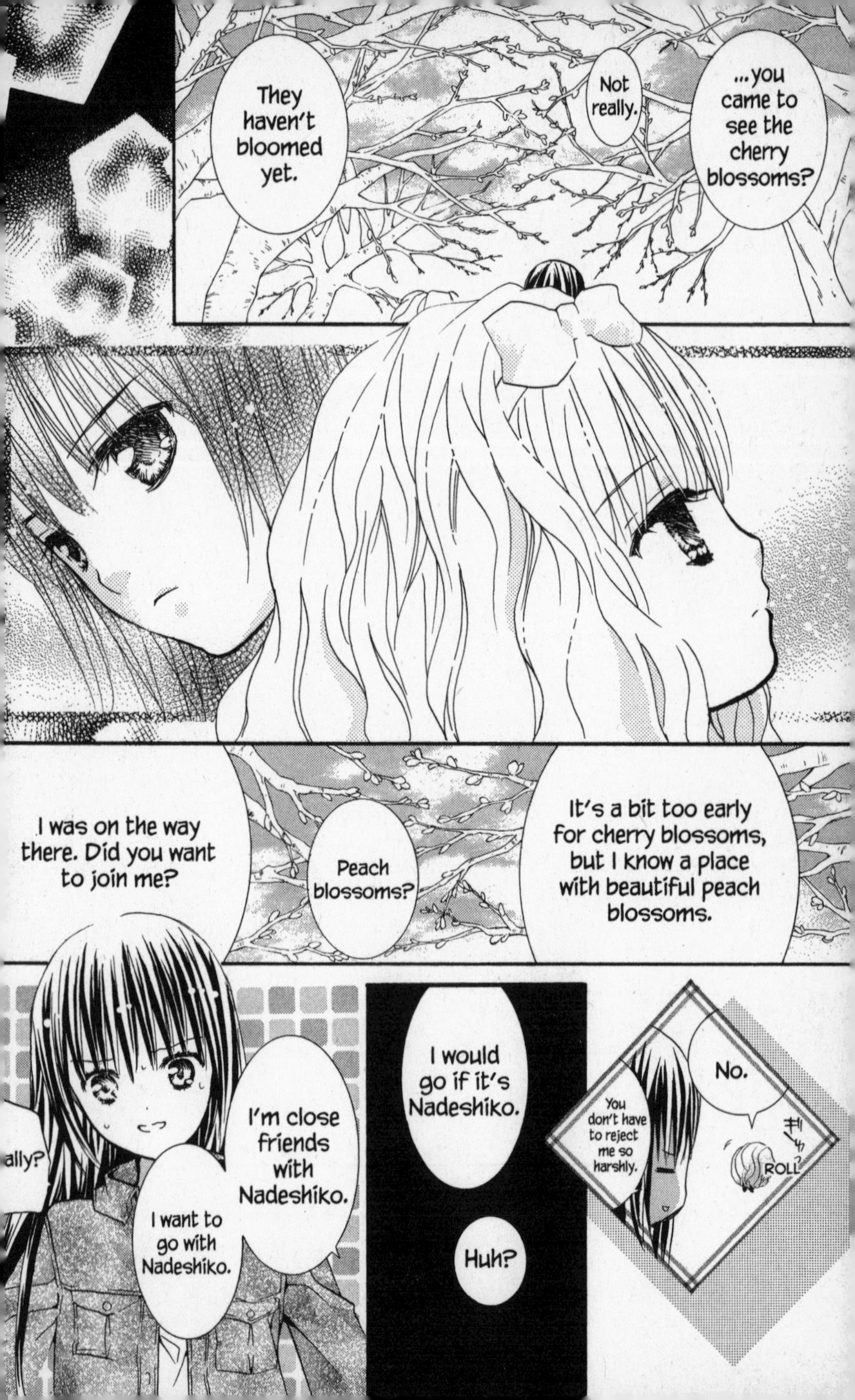
...you came to see the cherry blossoms?
Not really.
They haven't bloomed yet.
It's a bit too early for cherry blossoms, but I know a place with beautiful peach blossoms.
Peach blossoms?
I was on the way there. Did you want to join me?
No.
You don't have to reject me so harshly.
ROLL
I would go if it's Nadeshiko.
Huh?
I'm close friends with Nadeshiko.
ally?
I want to go with Nadeshiko.

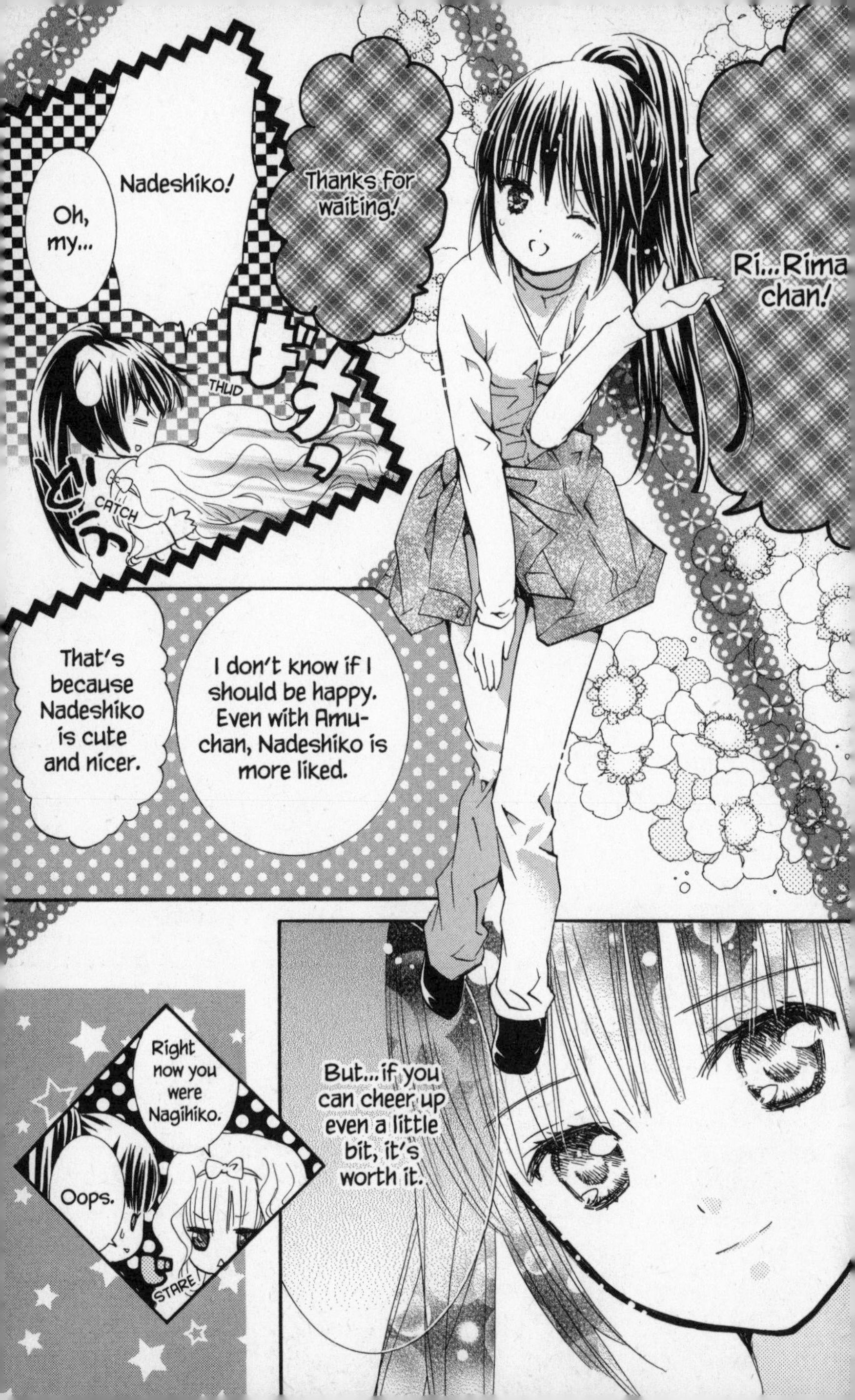
Ri...Rima chan!
Thanks for waiting!
Nadeshiko!
Oh, my...
THUD
CATCH
I don't know if I should be happy. Even with Amu-chan, Nadeshiko is more liked.
That's because Nadeshiko is cute and nicer.
But...if you can cheer up even a little bit, it's worth it.
Right now you were Nagihiko.
Oops.
STARE

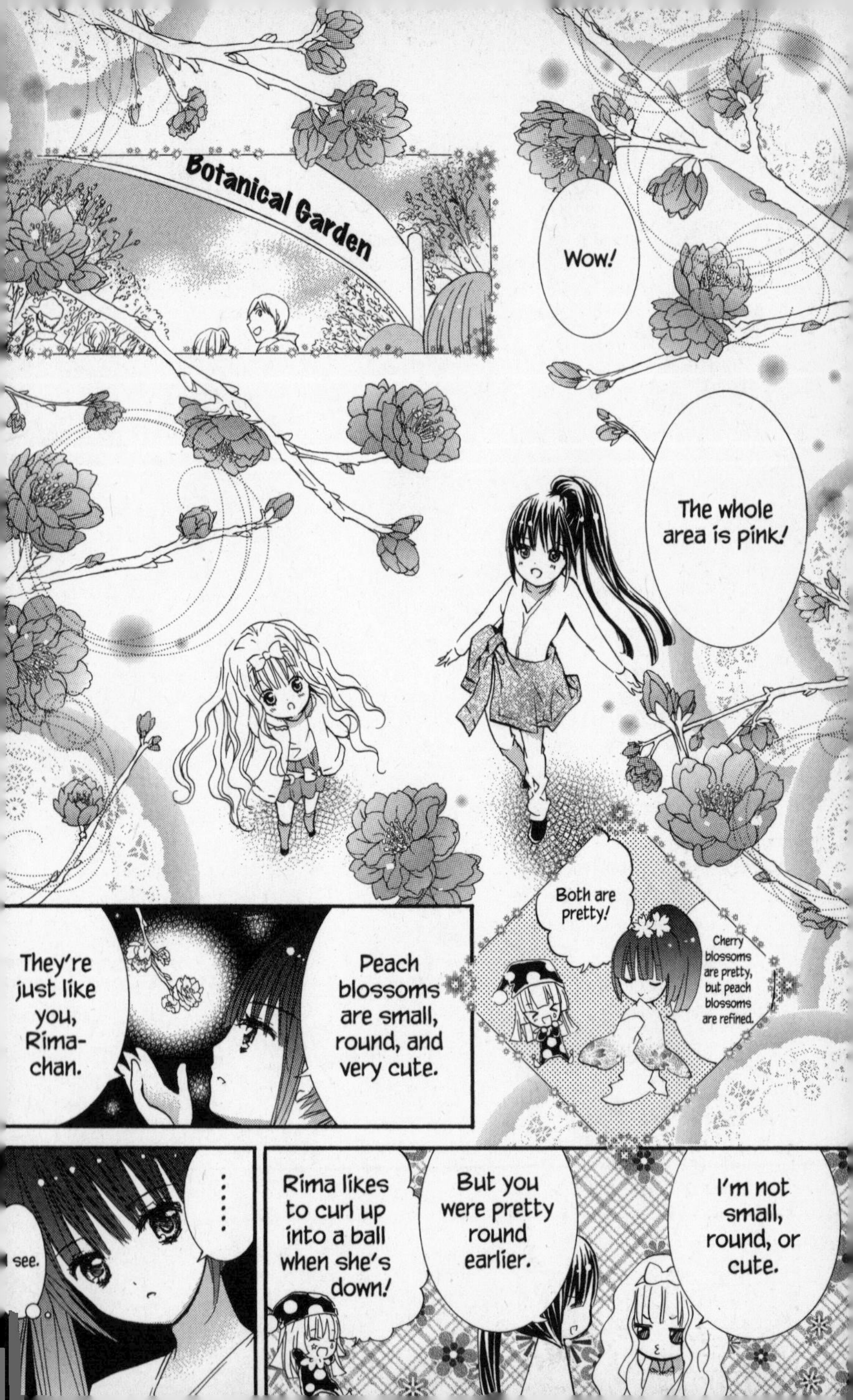
Wow!
The whole area is pink!
Botanical Garden
Both are pretty!
Cherry blossoms are pretty, but peach blossoms are refined.
Peach blossoms are small, round, and very cute.
They're just like you, Rima-chan.
I'm not small, round, or cute.
But you were pretty round earlier.
Rima likes to curl up into a ball when she's down!
......
see.

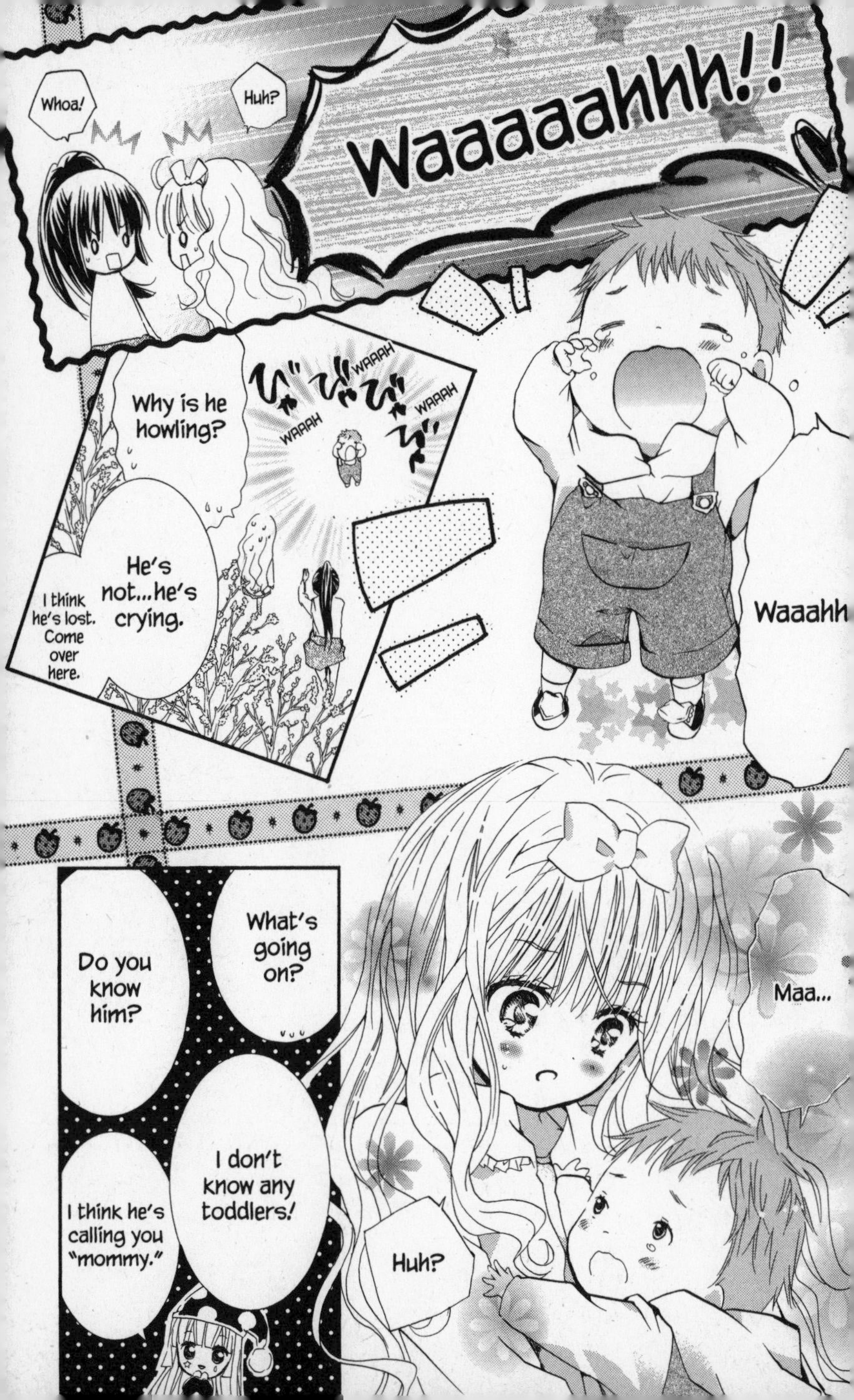
Waaaaahhh!!
Huh?
Whoa!
Waaahh
WAAAH
WAAAH
WAAAH
Why is he howling?
He's not...he's crying.
I think he's lost. Come over here.
Maa...
Huh?
What's going on?
Do you know him?
I don't know any toddlers!
I think he's calling you "mommy."

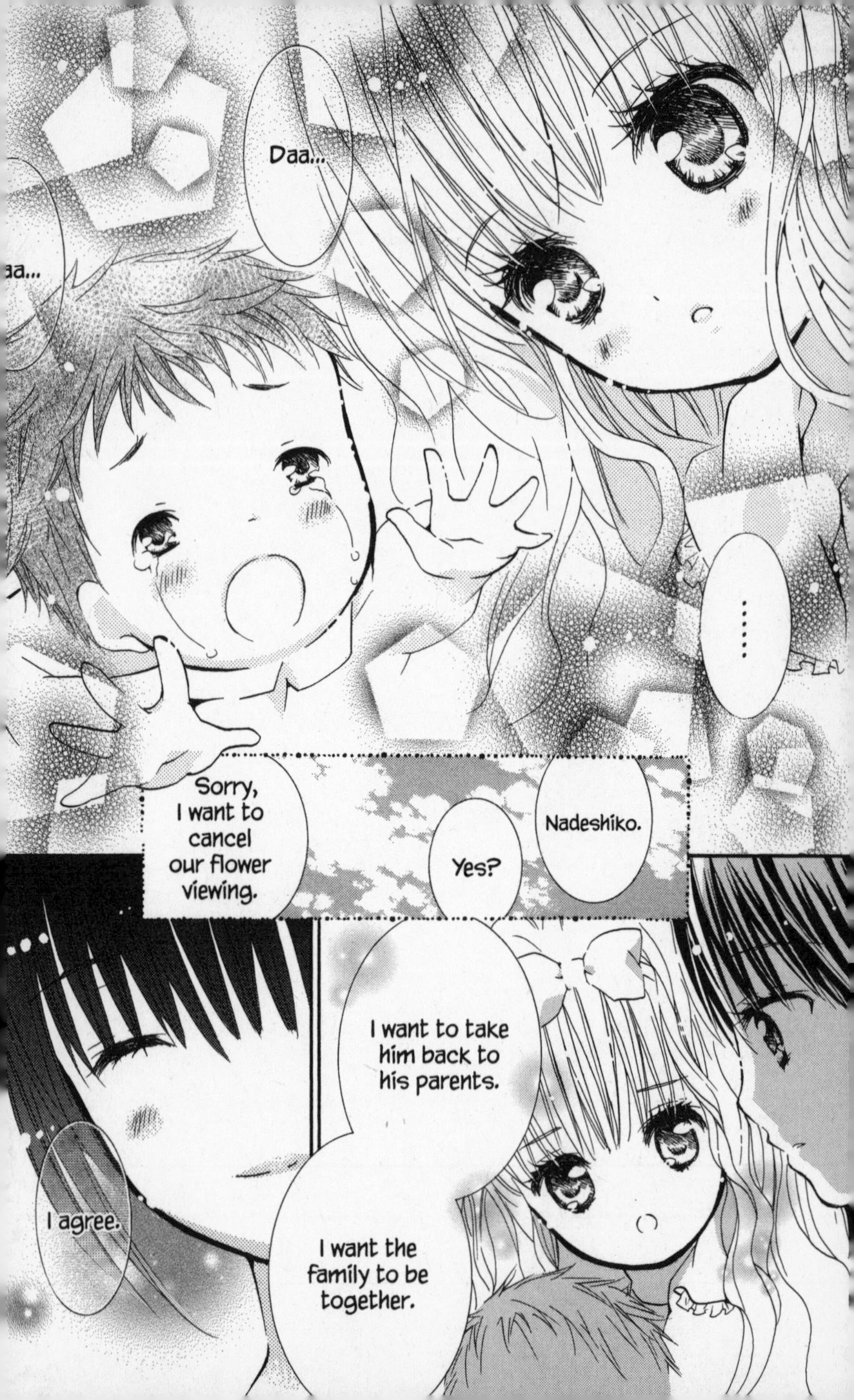
Daa...
aa...
......
Nadeshiko.
Yes?
Sorry, I want to cancel our flower viewing.
I want to take him back to his parents.
I want the family to be together.
I agree.

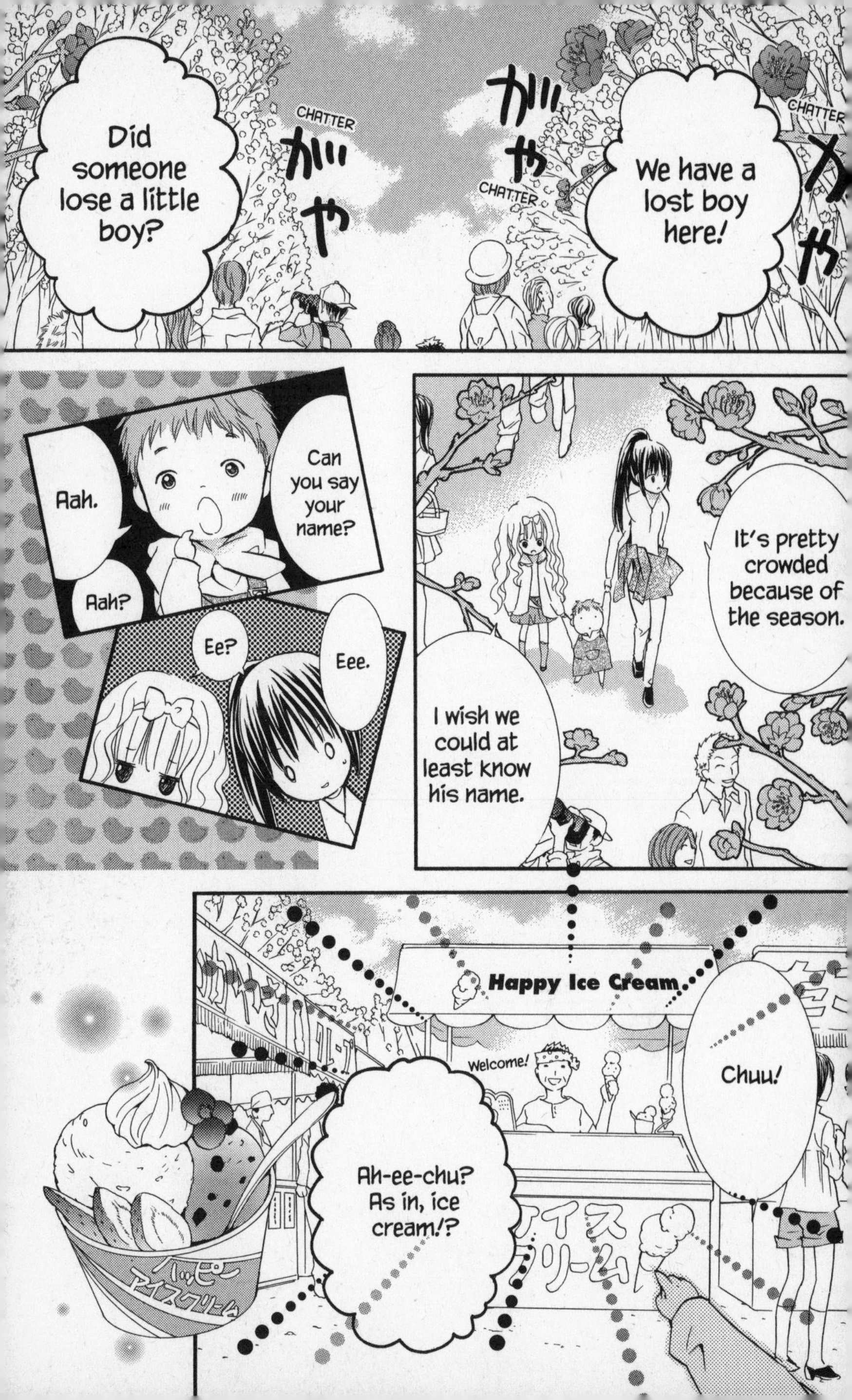
CHATTER
ガヤ
We have a lost boy here!
CHATTER
ガヤ
CHATTER
ガヤ
Did someone lose a little boy?
It's pretty crowded because of the season.
I wish we could at least know his name.
Can you say your name?
Aah.
Aah?
Eee.
Ee?
Happy Ice Cream
Chuu!
Welcome!
Ah-ee-chu? As in, ice cream!?
アイスクリーム
ハッピーアイスクリーム

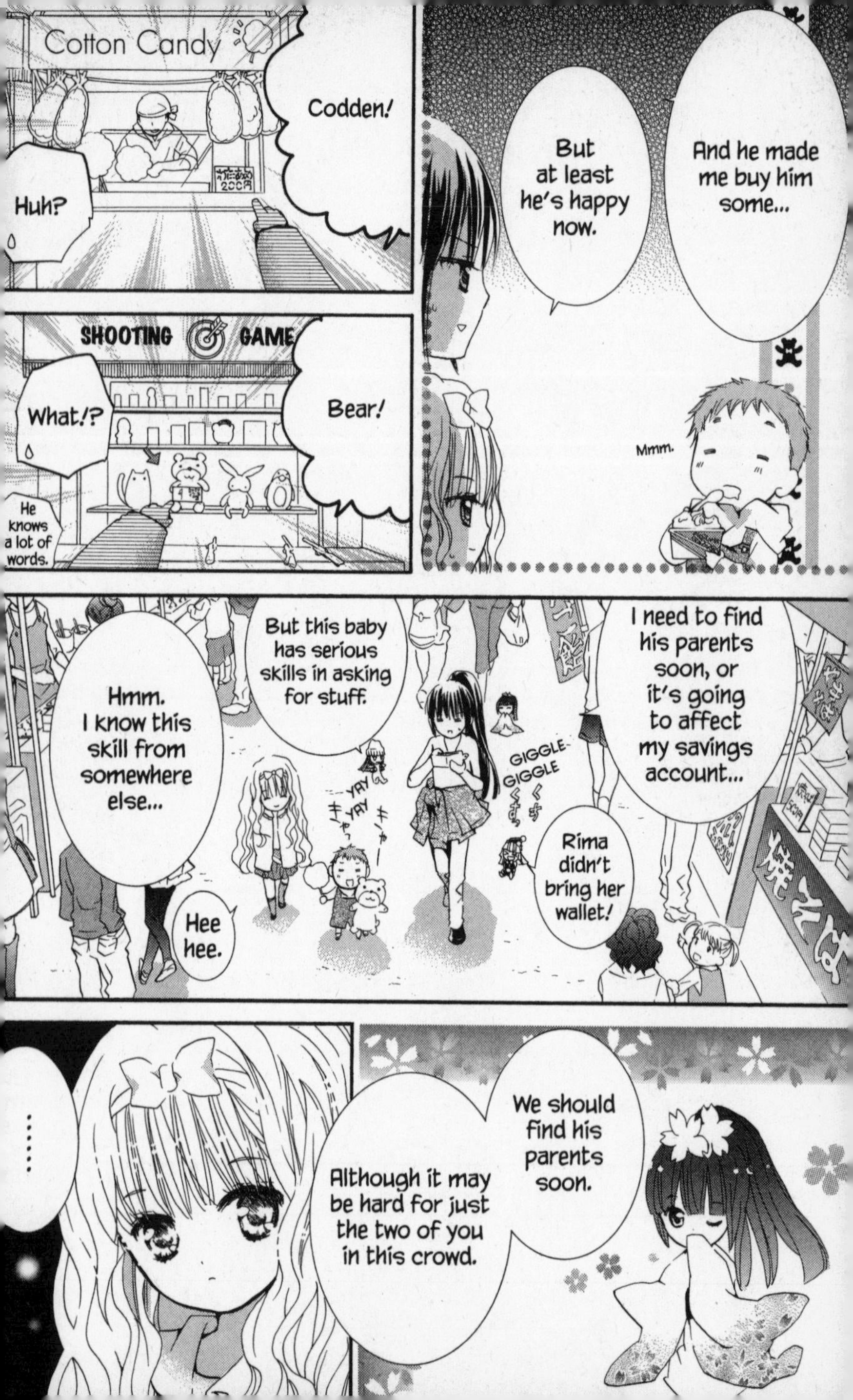
And he made me buy him some...
But at least he's happy now.
Mmm.
Cotton Candy
Codden!
Huh?
SHOOTING GAME
Bear!
What!?
He knows a lot of words.
I need to find his parents soon, or it's going to affect my savings account...
Rima didn't bring her wallet!
GIGGLE GIGGLE
But this baby has serious skills in asking for stuff.
YAY YAY
Hmm. I know this skill from somewhere else...
Hee hee.
We should find his parents soon.
Although it may be hard for just the two of you in this crowd.
......

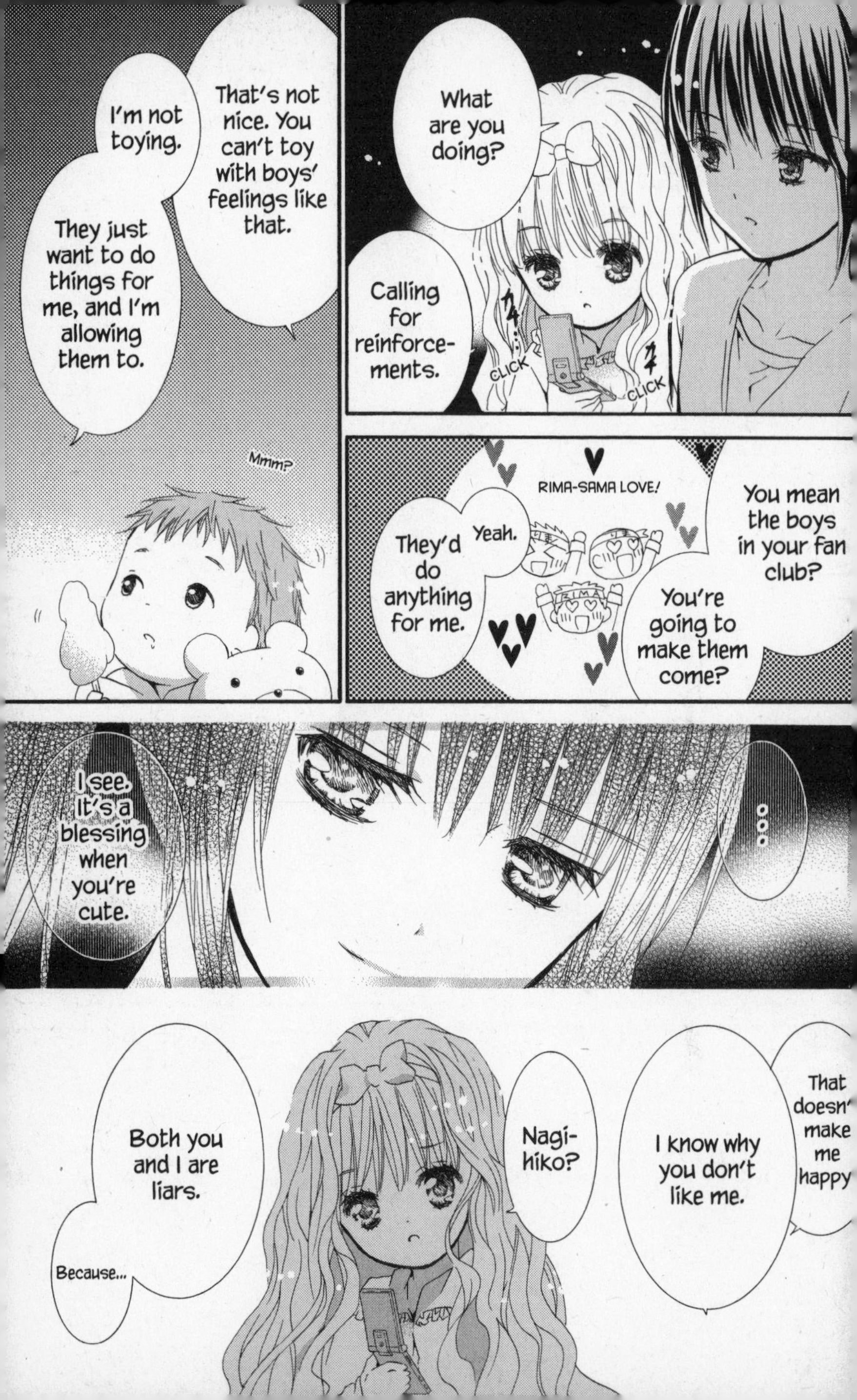
What are you doing?
Calling for reinforcements.
CLICK
CLICK
You mean the boys in your fan club?
RIMA-SAMA LOVE!
Yeah.
You're going to make them come?
They'd do anything for me.
That's not nice. You can't toy with boys' feelings like that.
I'm not toying.
They just want to do things for me, and I'm allowing them to.
Mmm?
...
I see. It's a blessing when you're cute.
That doesn't make me happy
I know why you don't like me.
Nagi-hiko?
Both you and I are liars.
Because...

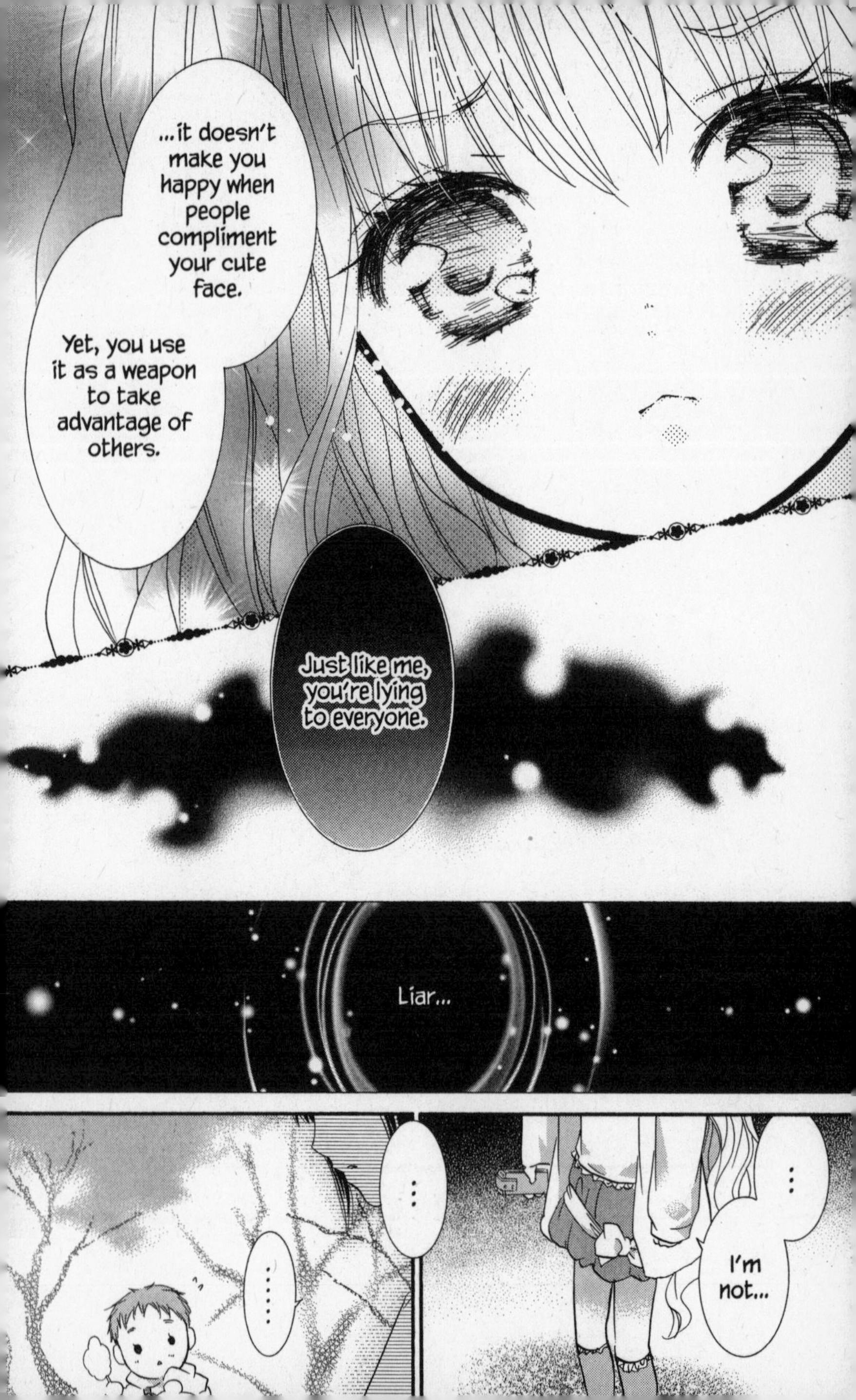
...it doesn't make you happy when people compliment your cute face.
Yet, you use it as a weapon to take advantage of others.
Just like me, you're lying to everyone.
Liar...
...
I'm not...
...
......

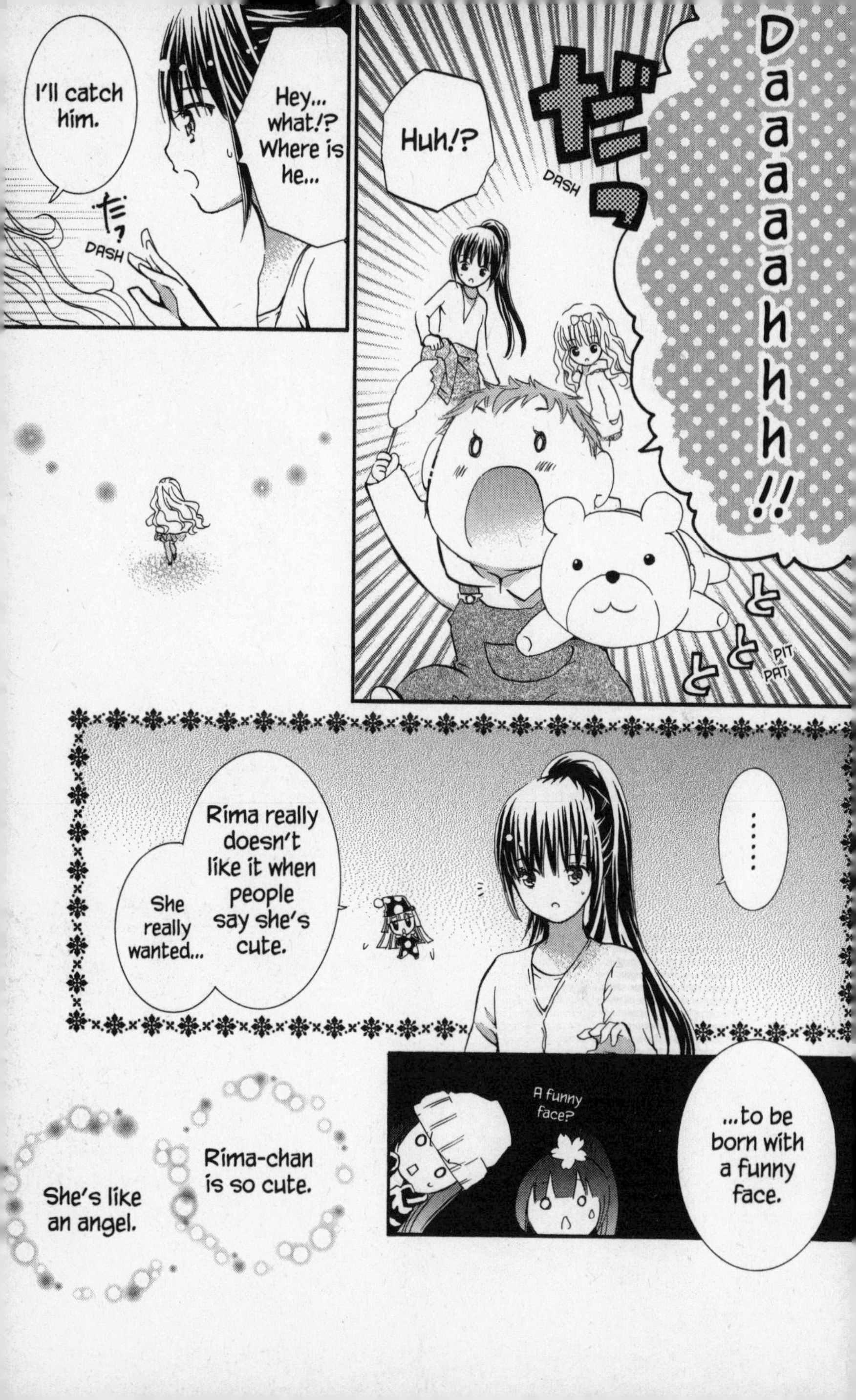
Daaaaahhh!!
DASH
Huh!?
PIT PAT
Hey... what!? Where is he...
I'll catch him.
DASH
......
Rima really doesn't like it when people say she's cute.
She really wanted...
...to be born with a funny face.
A funny face?
Rima-chan is so cute.
She's like an angel.

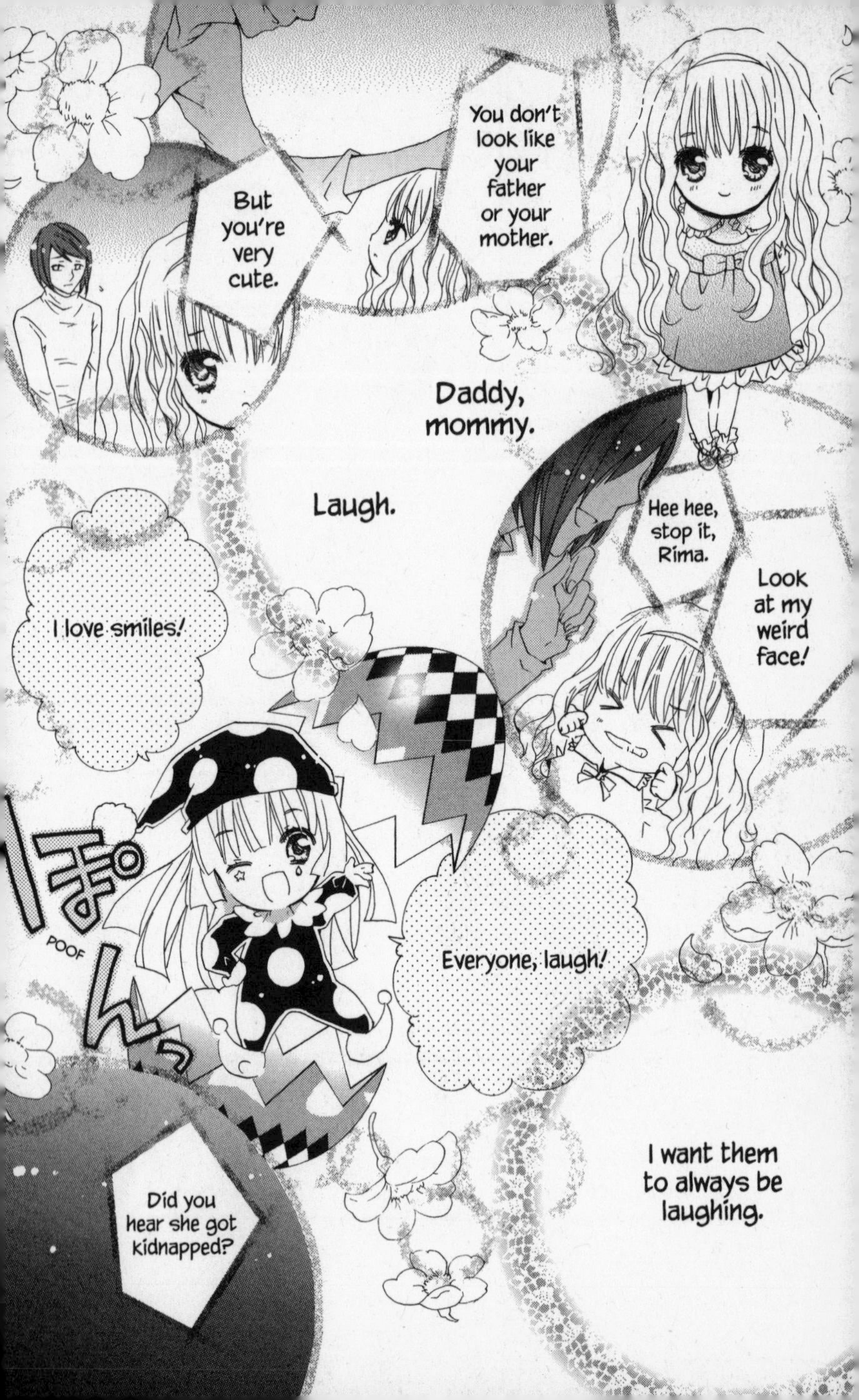
You don't look like your father or your mother.
But you're very cute.
Daddy, mommy.
Laugh.
Look at my weird face!
Hee hee, stop it, Rima.
I love smiles!
Everyone, laugh!
ぽん
POOF
I want them to always be laughing.
Did you hear she got kidnapped?

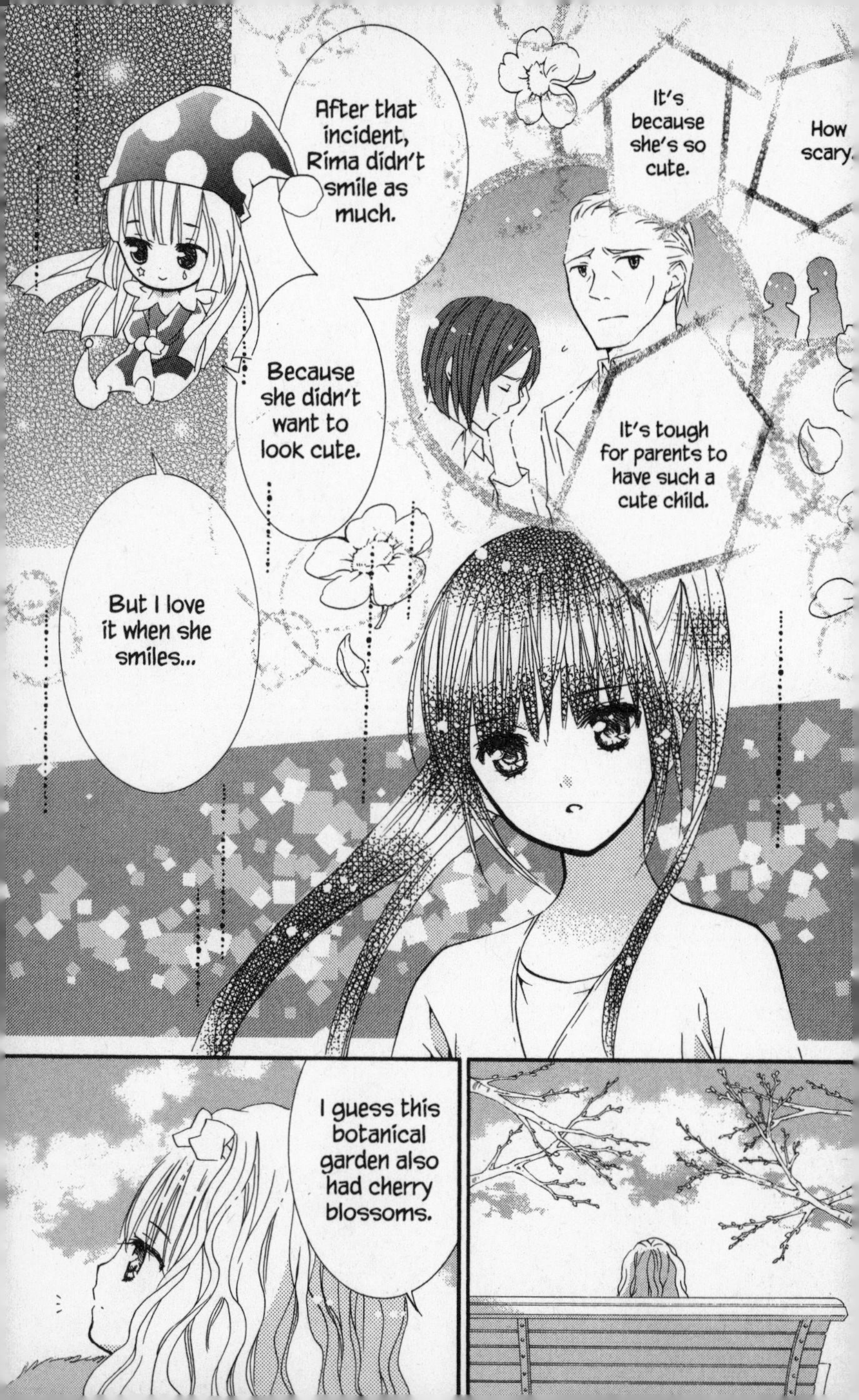
How scary.
It's because she's so cute.
It's tough for parents to have such a cute child.
After that incident, Rima didn't smile as much.
Because she didn't want to look cute.
But I love it when she smiles...
I guess this botanical garden also had cherry blossoms.

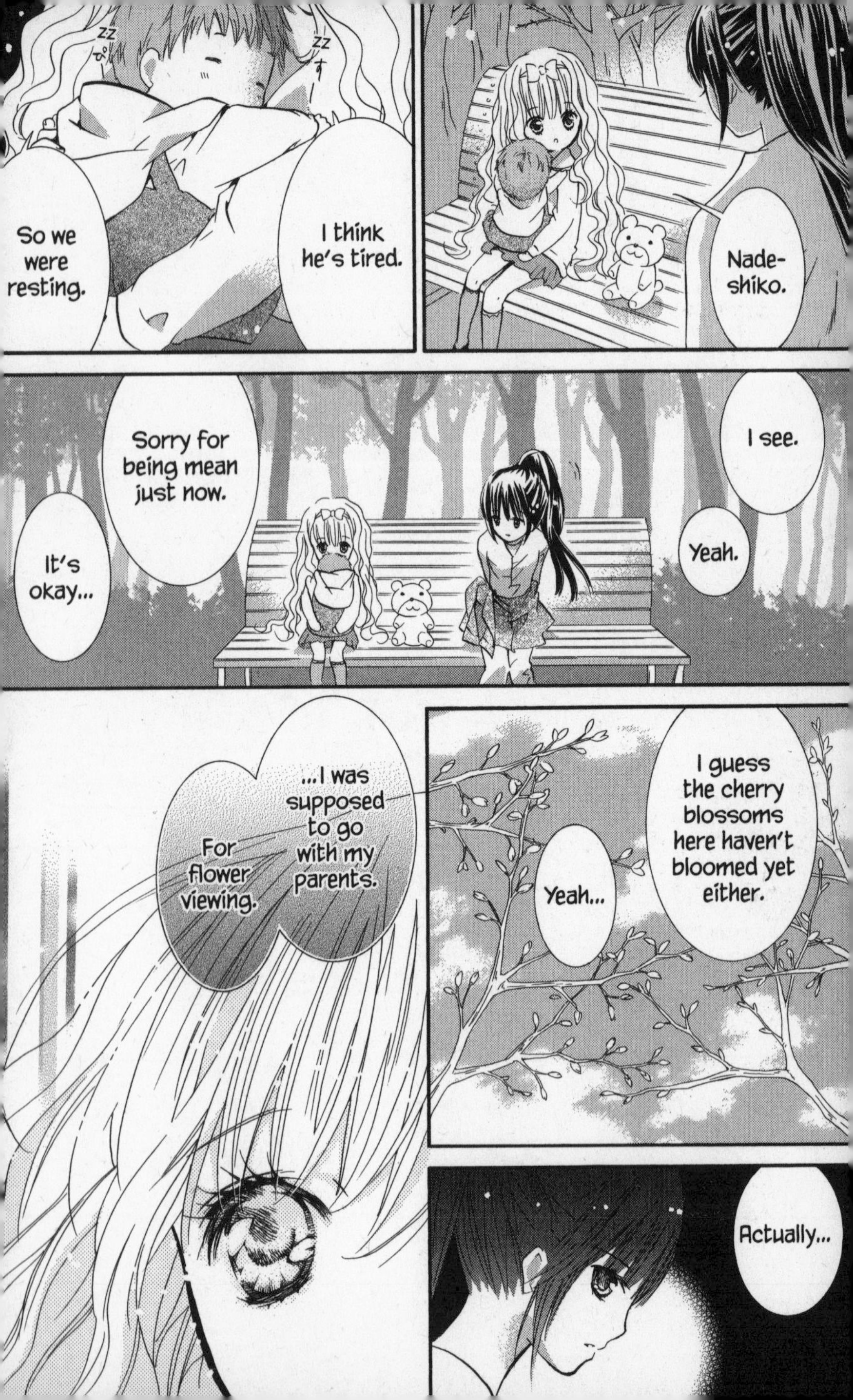
Nade-shiko.
zz
ぴ
zz
す
I think he's tired.
So we were resting.
I see.
Yeah.
Sorry for being mean just now.
It's okay...
I guess the cherry blossoms here haven't bloomed yet either.
Yeah...
Actually...
...I was supposed to go with my parents.
For flower viewing.

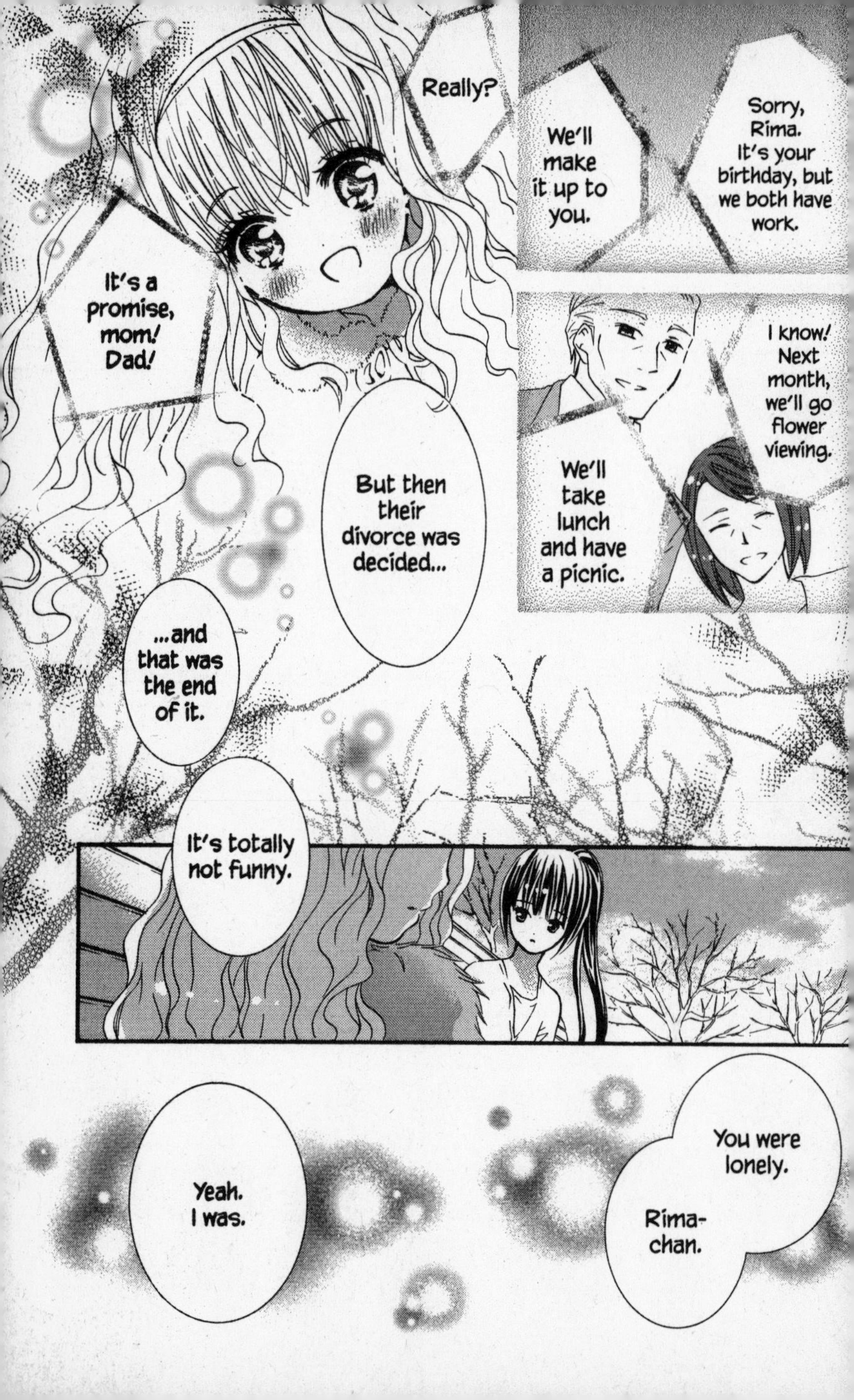
Sorry, Rima. It's your birthday, but we both have work.
We'll make it up to you.
I know! Next month, we'll go flower viewing.
We'll take lunch and have a picnic.
Really?
It's a promise, mom! Dad!
But then their divorce was decided...
...and that was the end of it.
It's totally not funny.
You were lonely.
Rima-chan.
Yeah. I was.

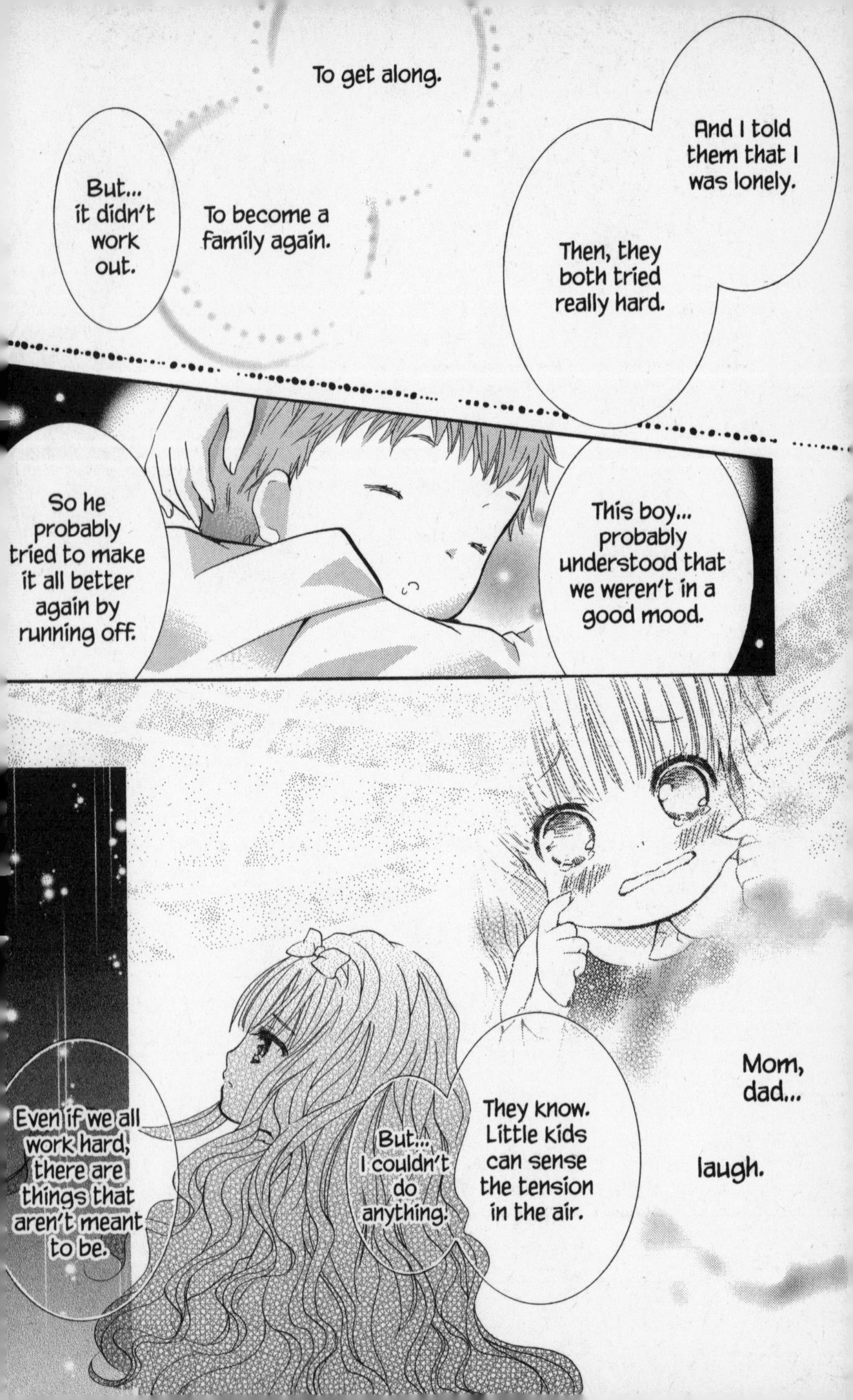
And I told them that I was lonely.
Then, they both tried really hard.
To get along.
To become a family again.
But... it didn't work out.
This boy... probably understood that we weren't in a good mood.
So he probably tried to make it all better again by running off.
Mom, dad...
laugh.
They know. Little kids can sense the tension in the air.
But... I couldn't do anything.
Even if we all work hard, there are things that aren't meant to be.

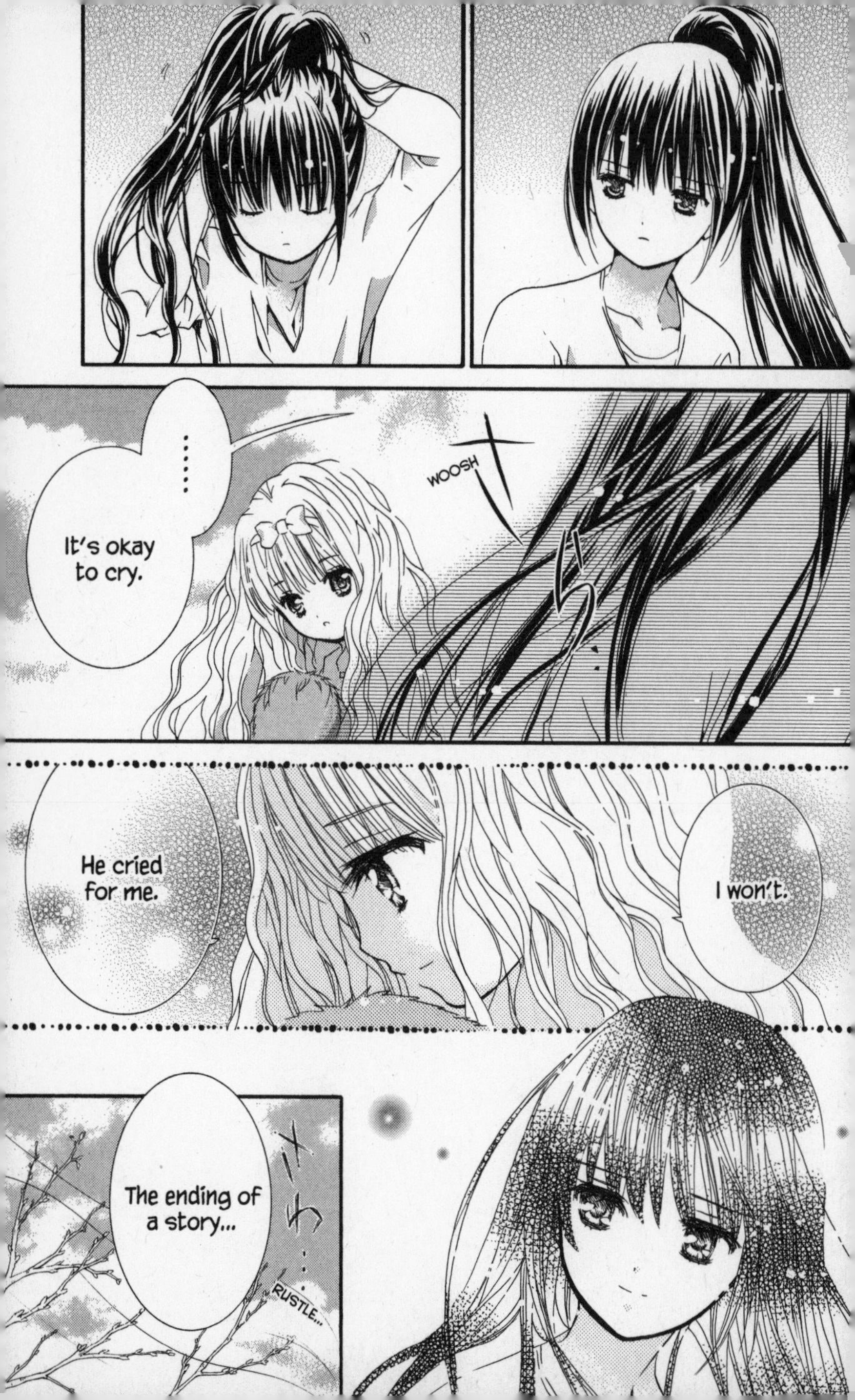
WOOSH
.....
It's okay to cry.
I won't.
He cried for me.
The ending of a story...
RUSTLE...

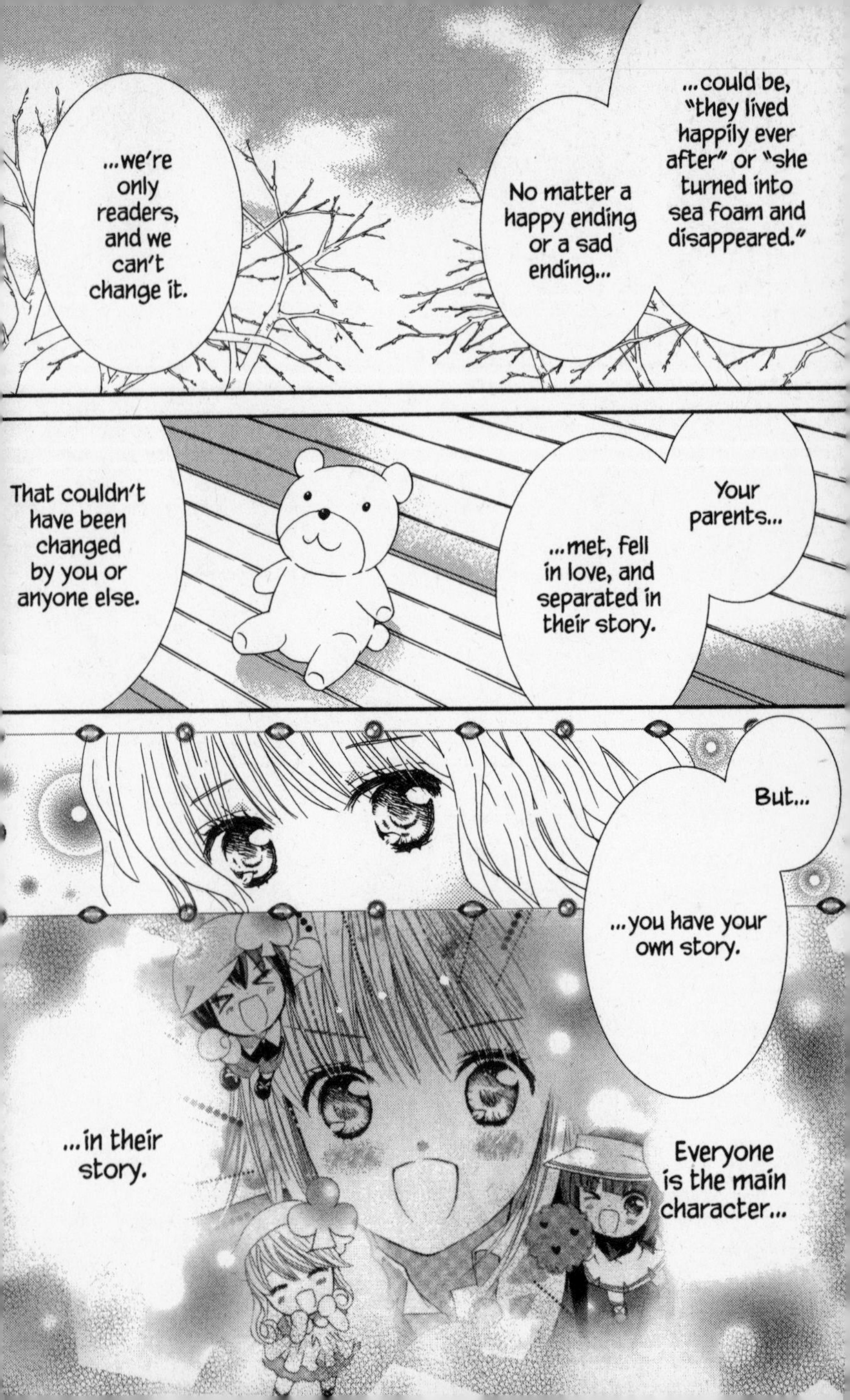
...could be, "they lived happily ever after" or "she turned into sea foam and disappeared."
No matter a happy ending or a sad ending...
...we're only readers, and we can't change it.
Your parents...
...met, fell in love, and separated in their story.
That couldn't have been changed by you or anyone else.
But...
...you have your own story.
Everyone is the main character...
...in their story.

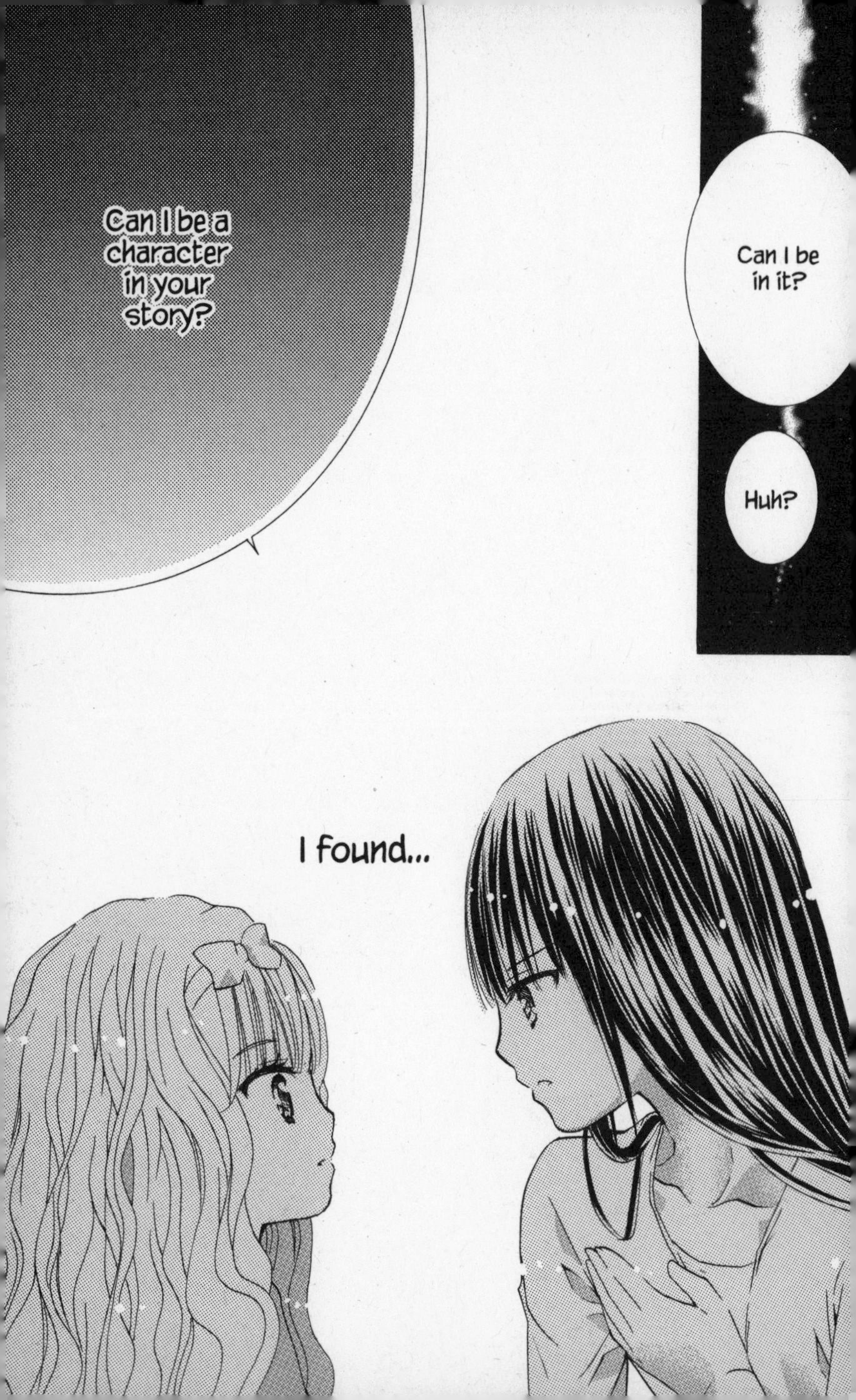
Can I be in it?
Huh?
Can I be a character in your story?
I found...

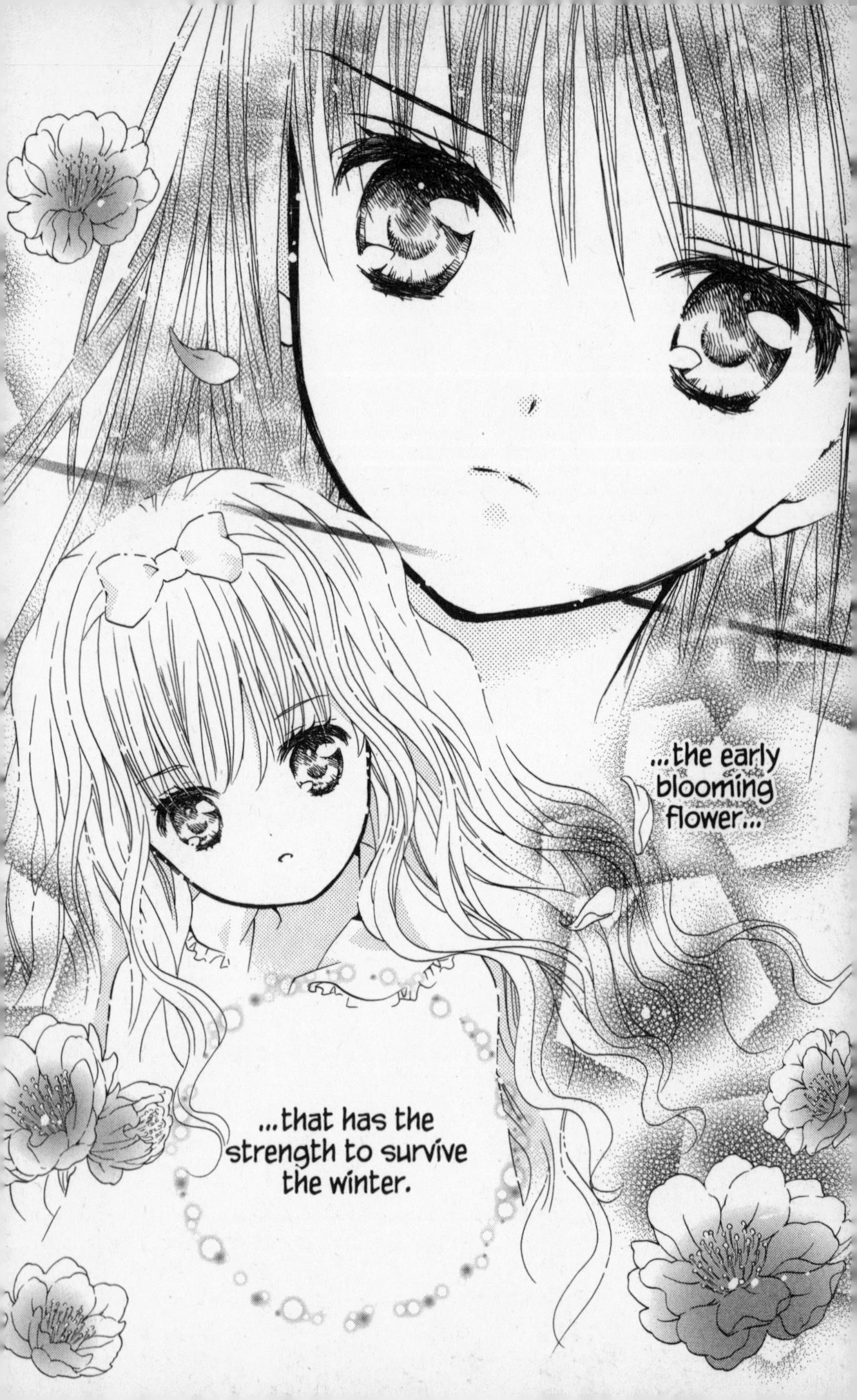
...the early blooming flower...
...that has the strength to survive the winter.

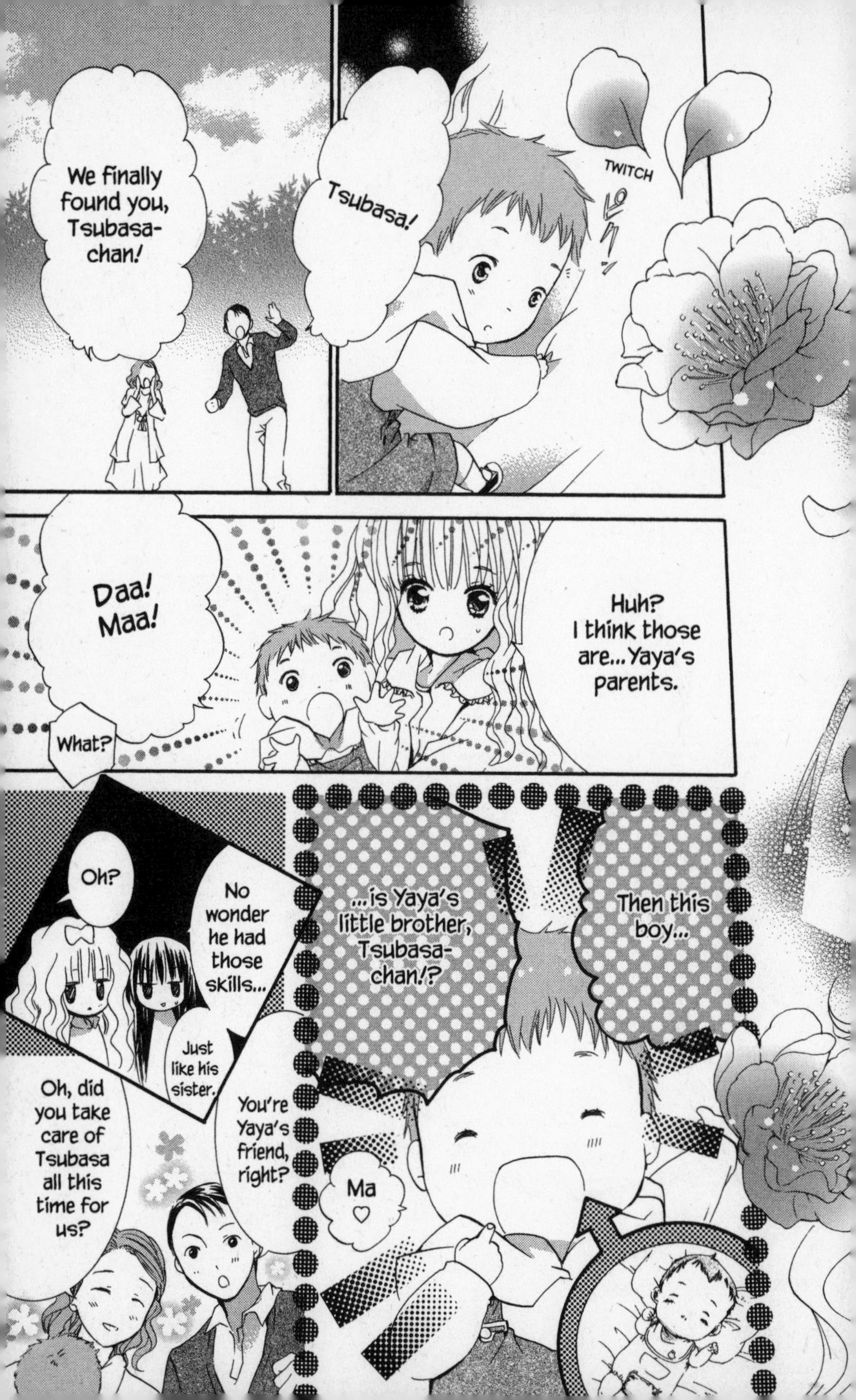
TWITCH
Tsubasa!
We finally found you, Tsubasa-chan!
Huh? I think those are...Yaya's parents.
Daa! Maa!
What?
Then this boy...
...is Yaya's little brother, Tsubasa-chan!?
Ma ♡
Oh?
No wonder he had those skills...
Just like his sister.
You're Yaya's friend, right?
Oh, did you take care of Tsubasa all this time for us?

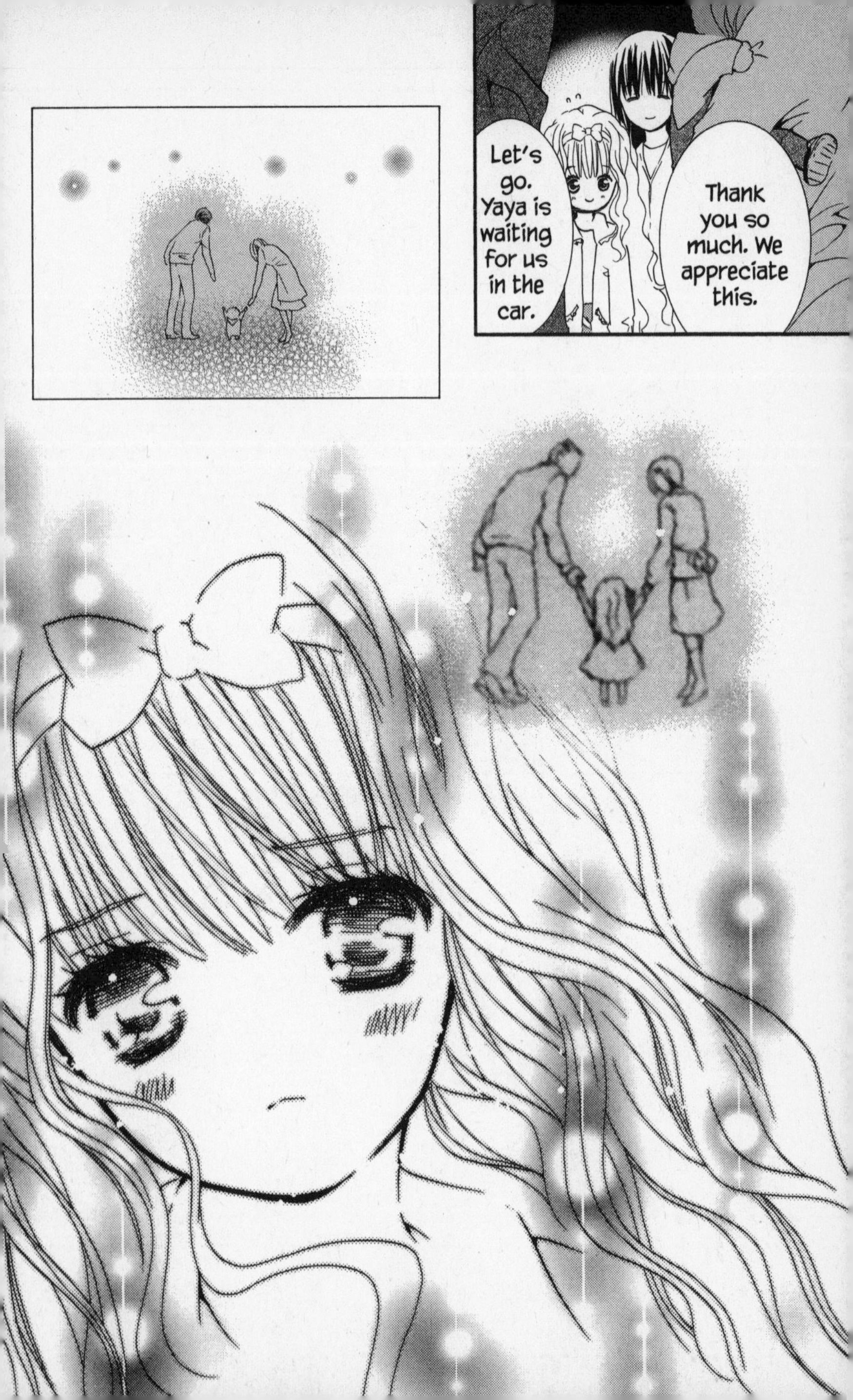
Thank you so much. We appreciate this.
Let's go. Yaya is waiting for us in the car.

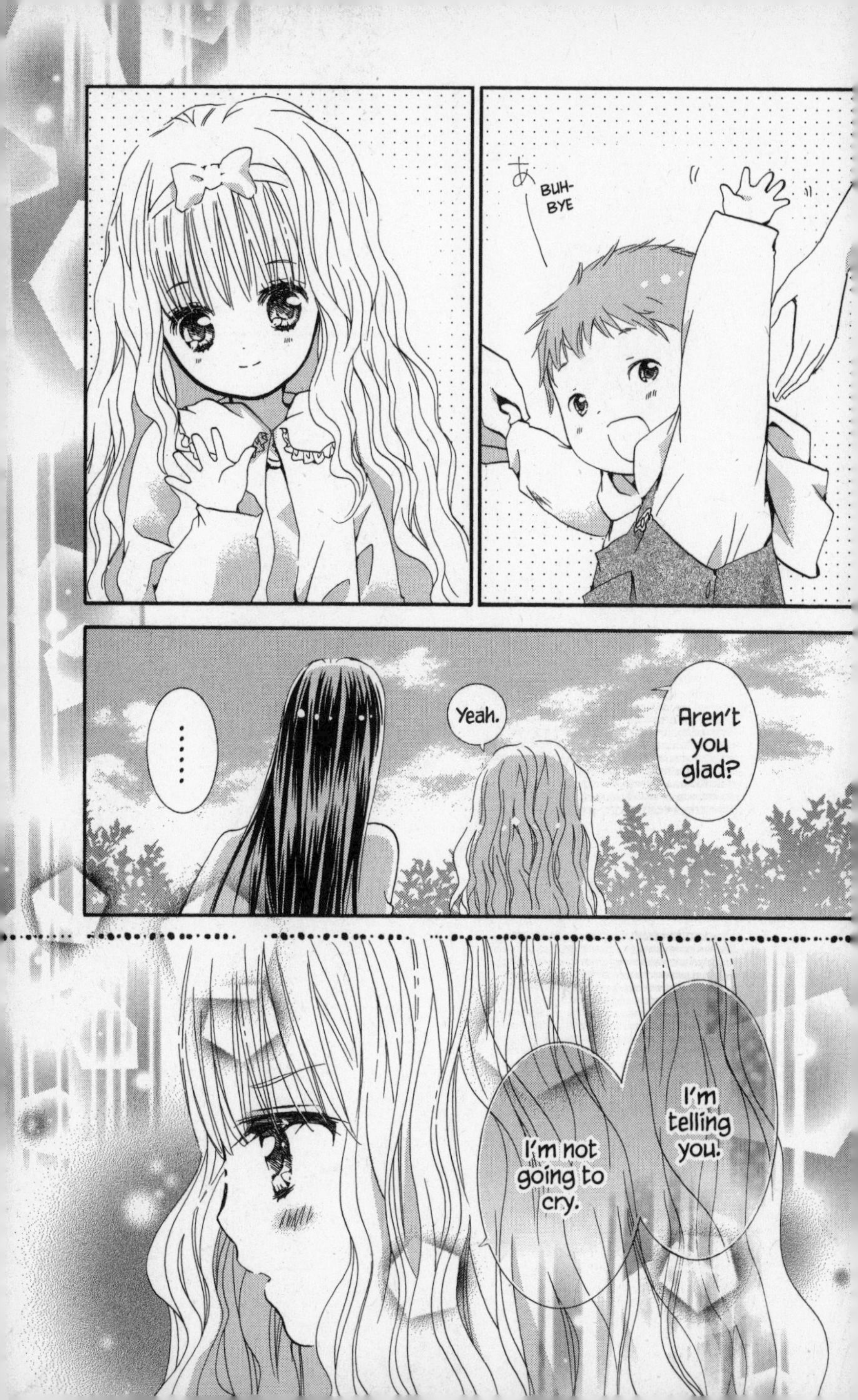
あ
BUH-BYE
Aren't you glad?
Yeah.
......
I'm telling you.
I'm not going to cry.

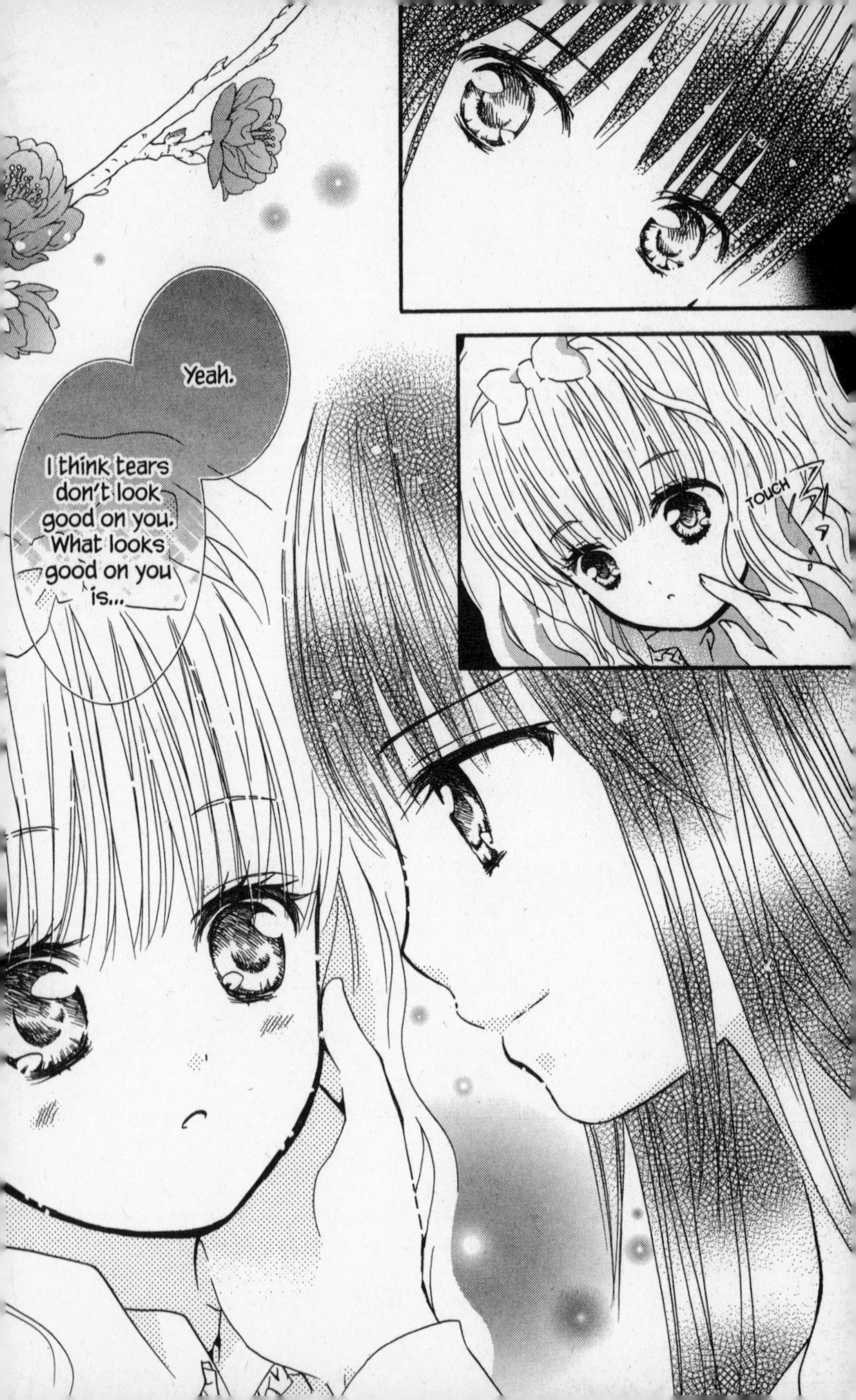
TOUCH
Yeah.
I think tears don't look good on you. What looks good on you is...

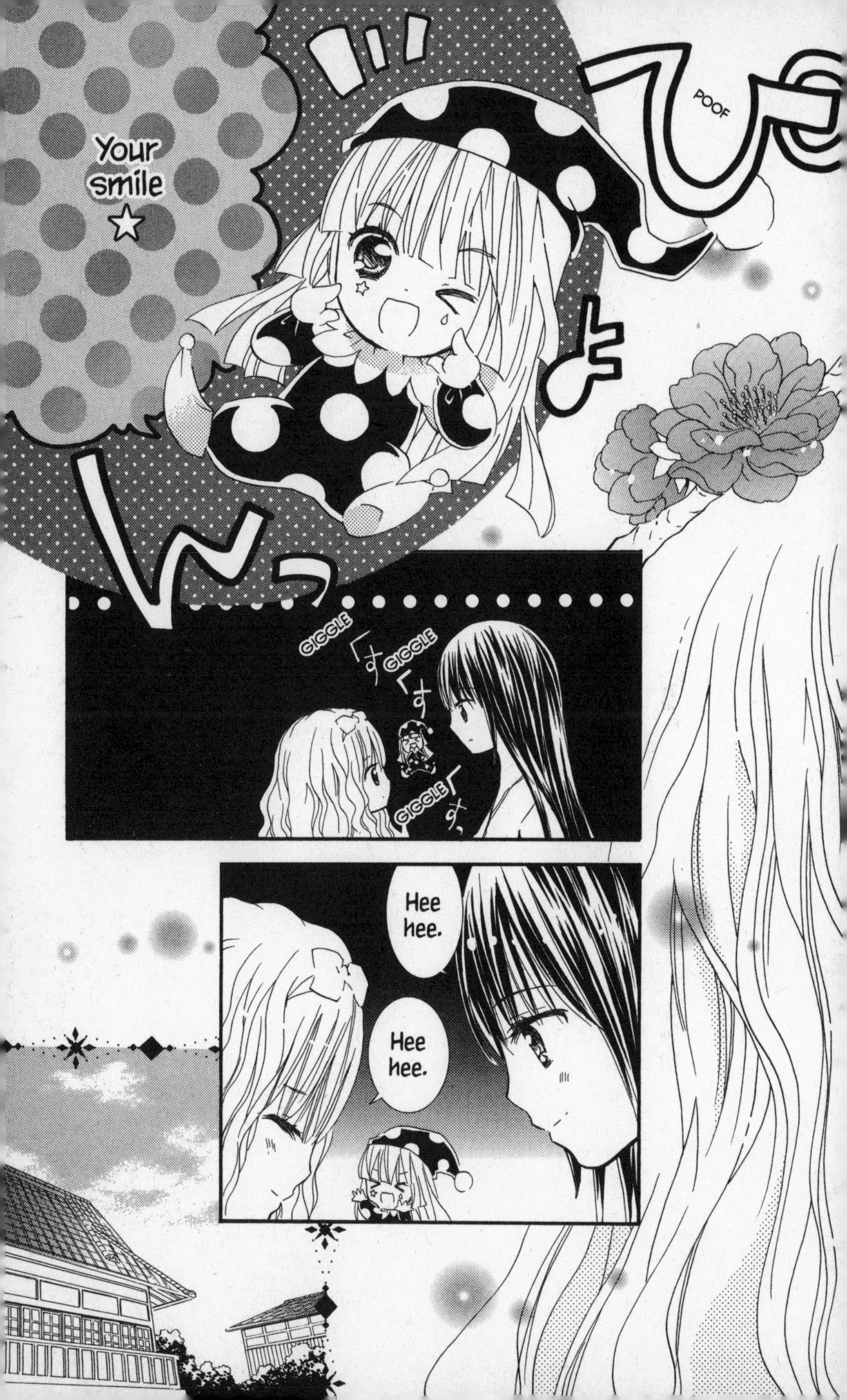

POOF
ぽんっ
Your smile ☆
GIGGLE くす
GIGGLE くす
GIGGLE くす
Hee hee.
Hee hee.

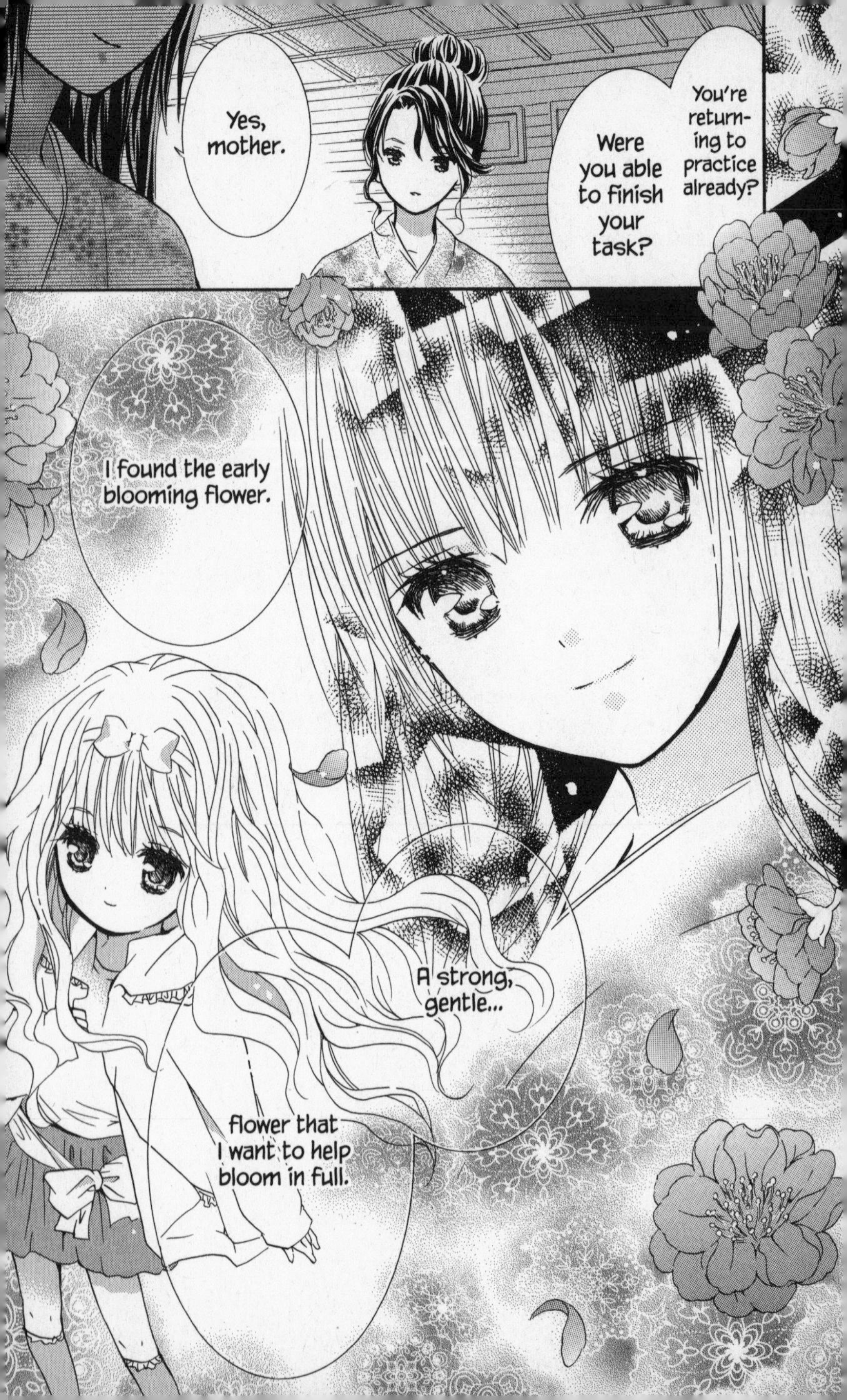
You're returning to practice already? Were you able to finish your task?
Yes, mother.
I found the early blooming flower.
A strong, gentle...
flower that I want to help bloom in full.

Shugo Chara!

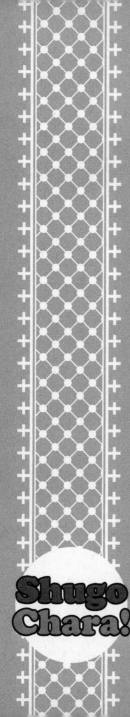

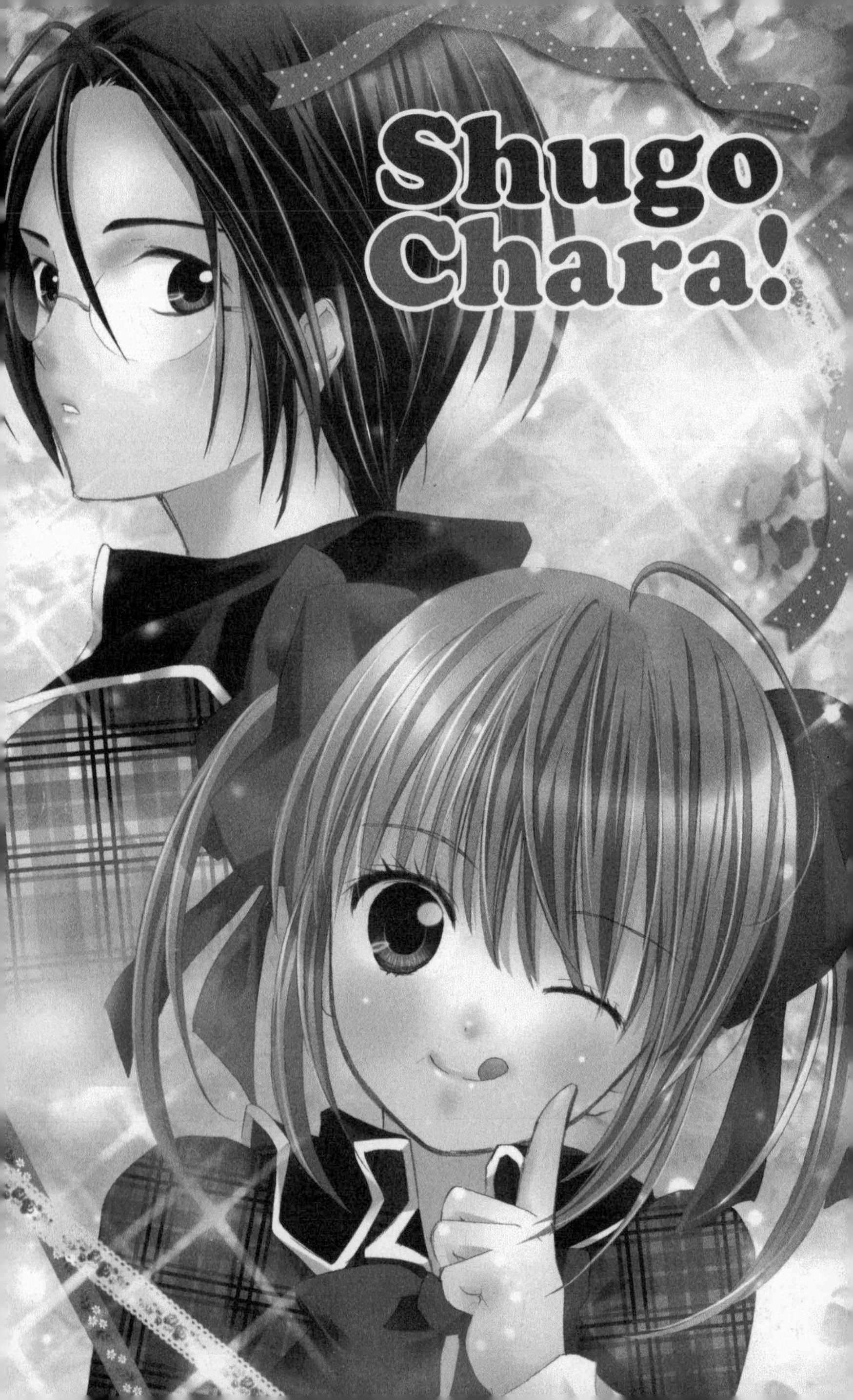
Shugo
Chara!

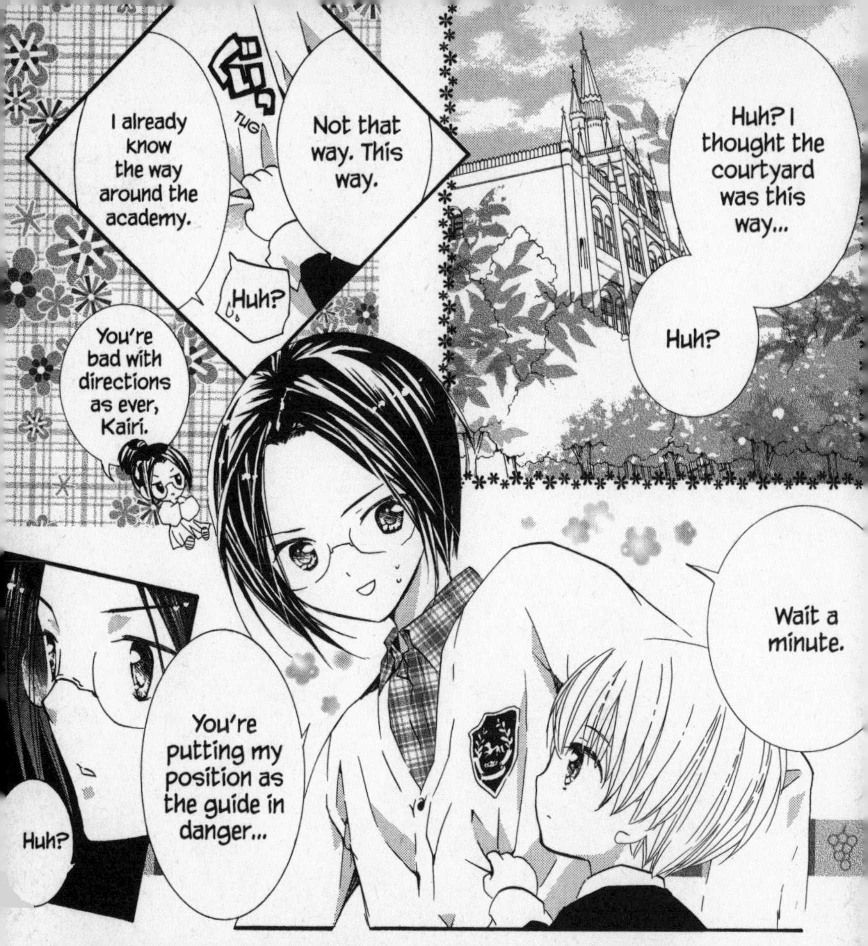
Huh? I thought the courtyard was this way...
Huh?
Not that way. This way.
TUG
I already know the way around the academy.
Huh?
You're bad with directions as ever, Kairi.
Wait a minute.
You're putting my position as the guide in danger...
Huh?

Q5. Where did you get the names for El and Il? A5. They come from ANGEL and DEVIL ♡ It would be fun if those two were my Guardian Characters... Although they might be fighting most of the time. Okay, so we saved the announcement for last. I'm sure everyone couldn't sleep over it! We're announcing the name for this thing ! Oh, you didn't lose sleep over it? Oh, okay... Anyway...to the announcement!!

GO!

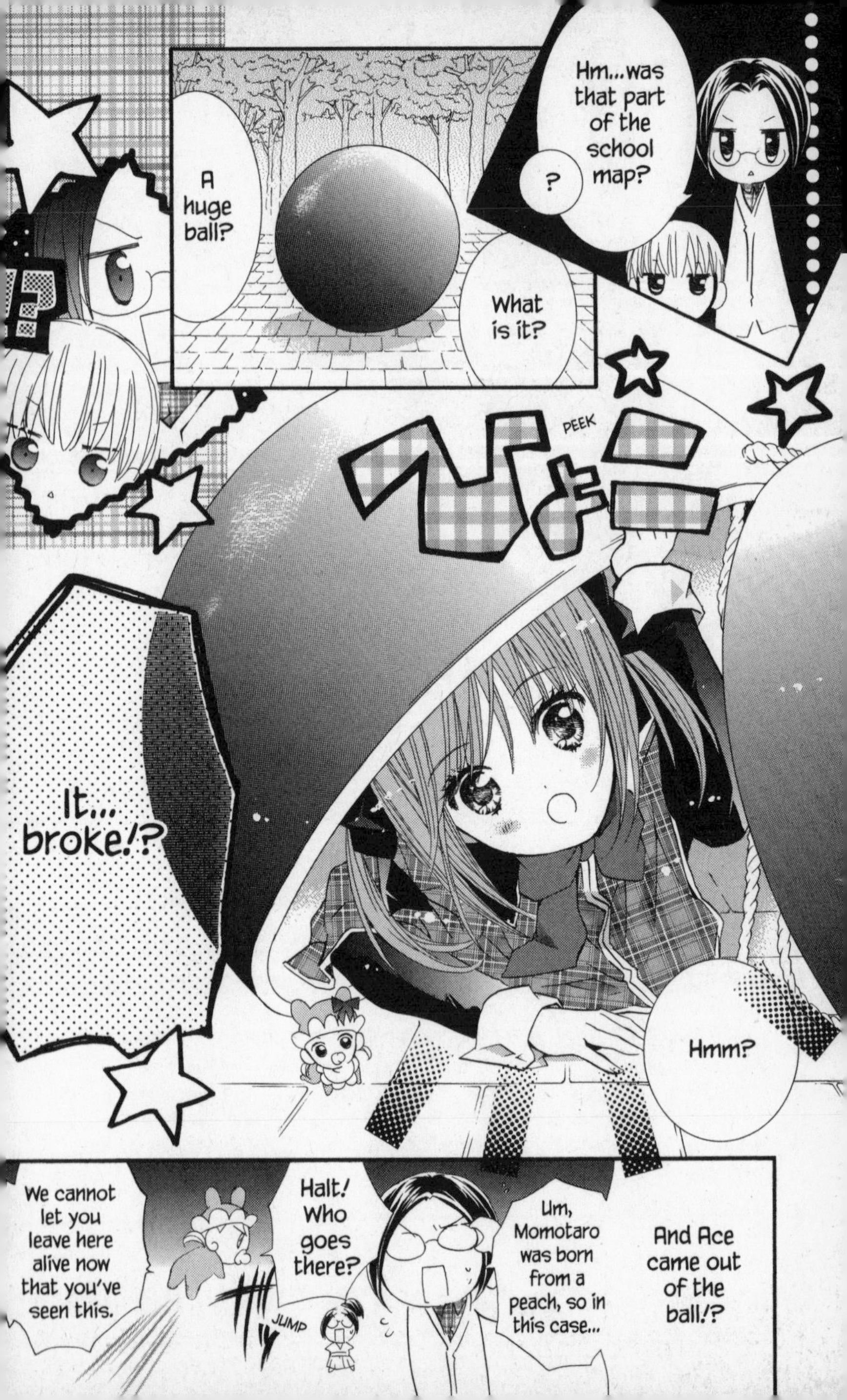
Hm...was that part of the school map?
?
What is it?
A huge ball?
PEEK
Hmm?
It... broke!?
And Ace came out of the ball!?
Um, Momotaro was born from a peach, so in this case...
Halt! Who goes there?
JUMP
We cannot let you leave here alive now that you've seen this.

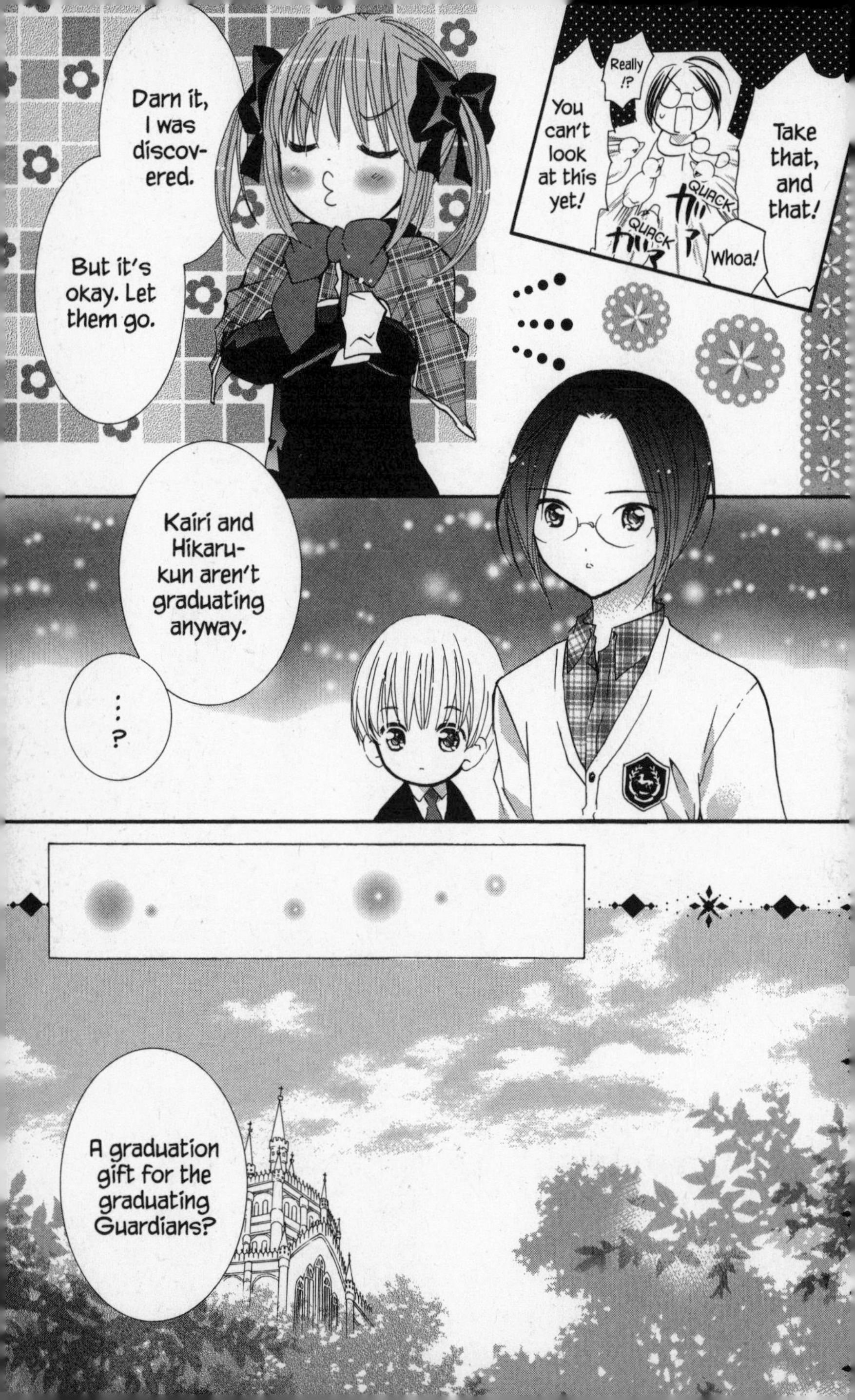
Take that, and that!
Really !?
You can't look at this yet!
QUACK
QUACK
Whoa!
....
Darn it, I was discov-ered.
But it's okay. Let them go.
Kairi and Hikaru-kun aren't graduating anyway.
...?
A graduation gift for the graduating Guardians?

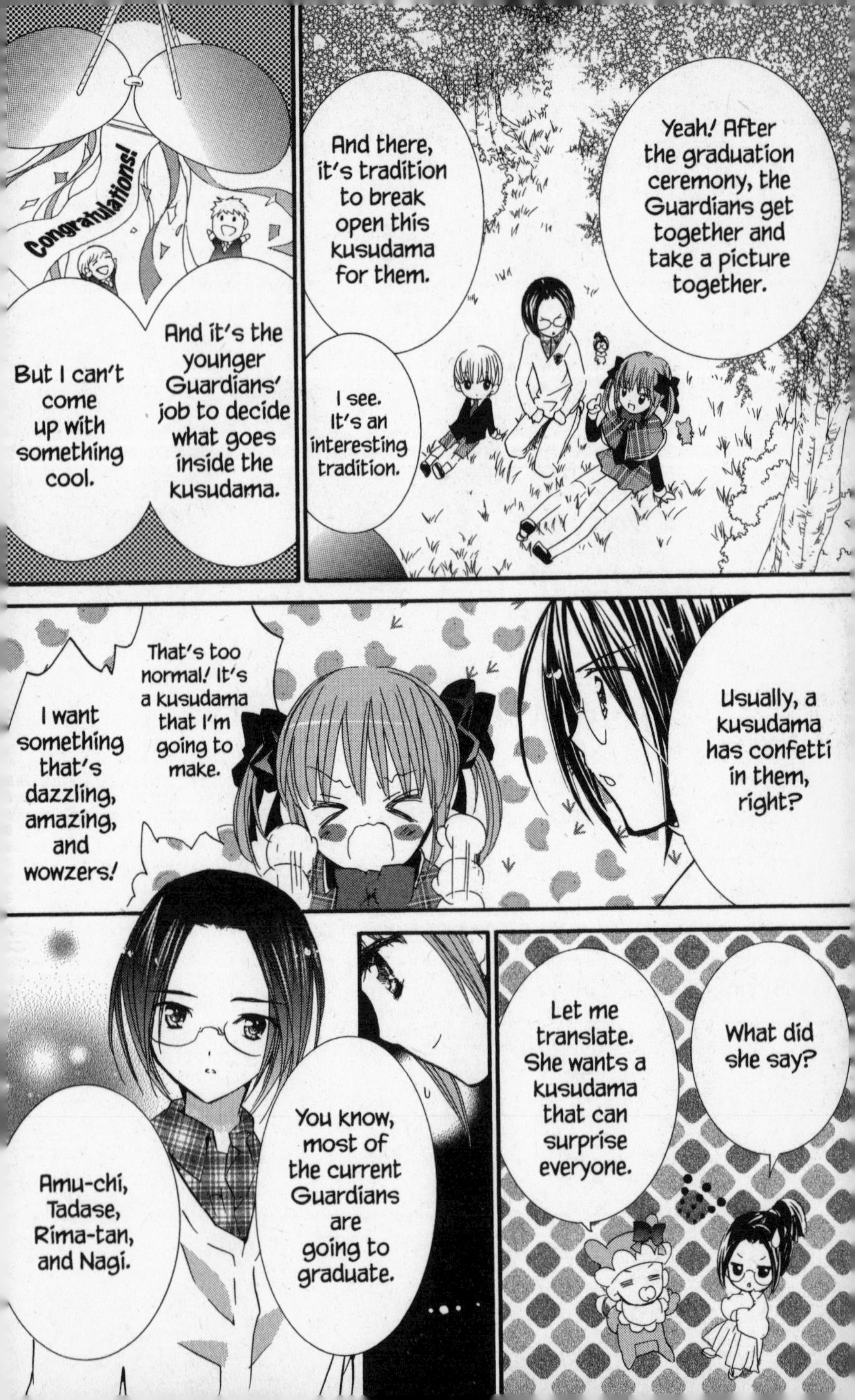
Yeah! After the graduation ceremony, the Guardians get together and take a picture together.
And there, it's tradition to break open this kusudama for them.
I see. It's an interesting tradition.
Congratulations!
And it's the younger Guardians' job to decide what goes inside the kusudama.
But I can't come up with something cool.
Usually, a kusudama has confetti in them, right?
That's too normal! It's a kusudama that I'm going to make.
I want something that's dazzling, amazing, and wowzers!
What did she say?
Let me translate. She wants a kusudama that can surprise everyone.
You know, most of the current Guardians are going to graduate.
Amu-chi, Tadase, Rima-tan, and Nagi.

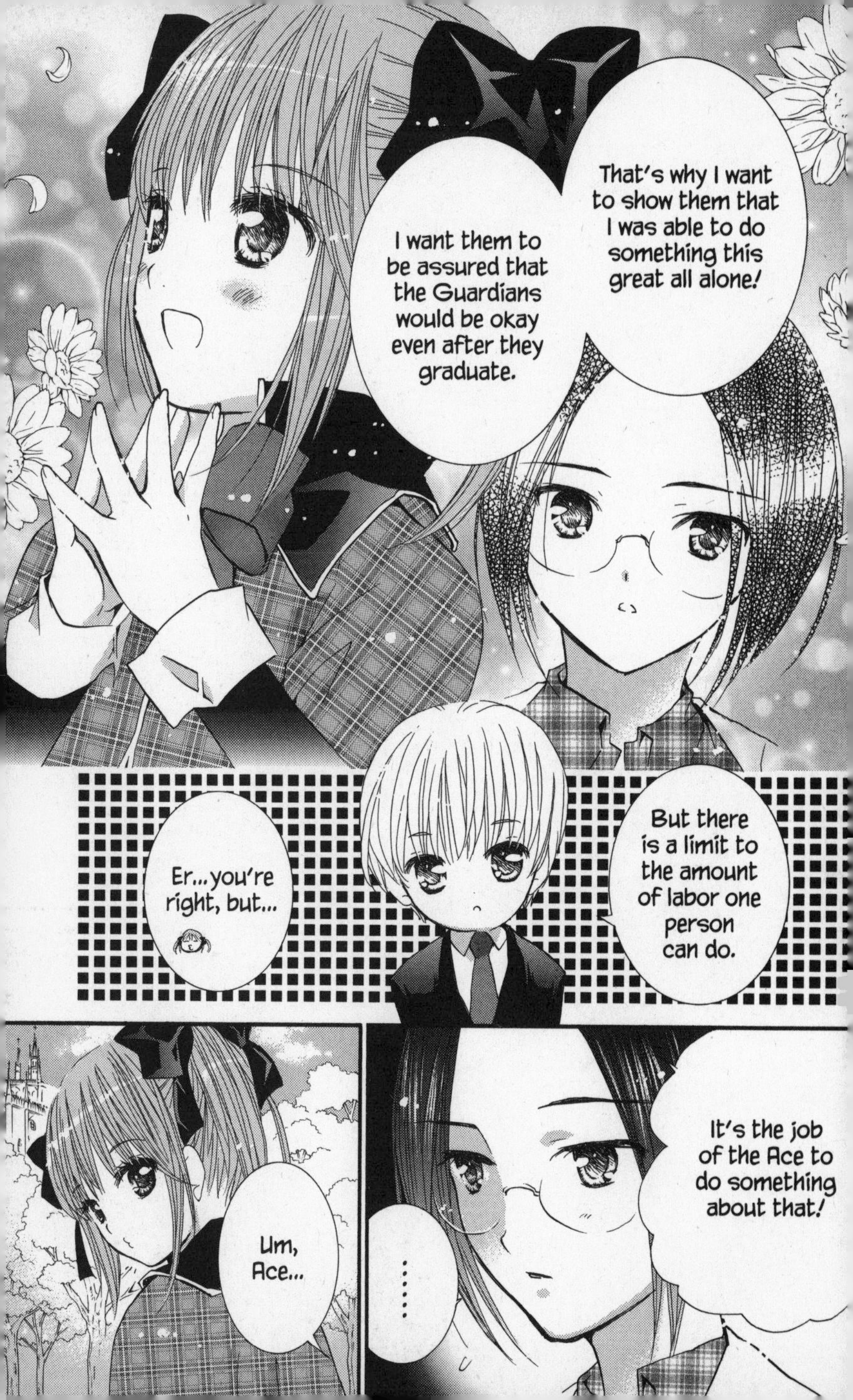
That's why I want to show them that I was able to do something this great all alone!
I want them to be assured that the Guardians would be okay even after they graduate.
But there is a limit to the amount of labor one person can do.
Er...you're right, but...
It's the job of the Ace to do something about that!
......
Um, Ace...

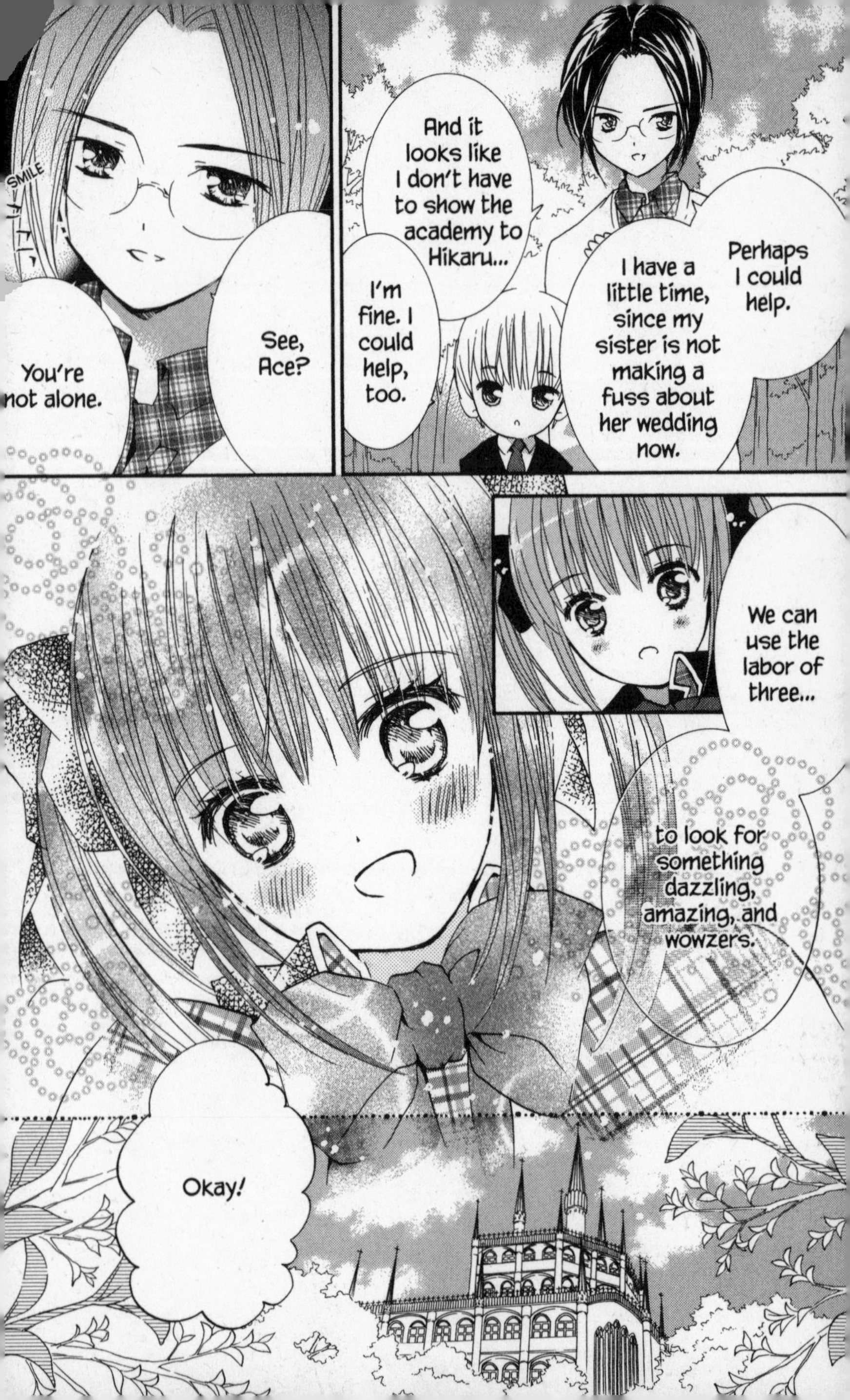
Perhaps I could help.
I have a little time, since my sister is not making a fuss about her wedding now.
And it looks like I don't have to show the academy to Hikaru...
I'm fine. I could help, too.
See, Ace?
SMILE
You're not alone.
We can use the labor of three...
to look for something dazzling, amazing, and wowzers.
Okay!

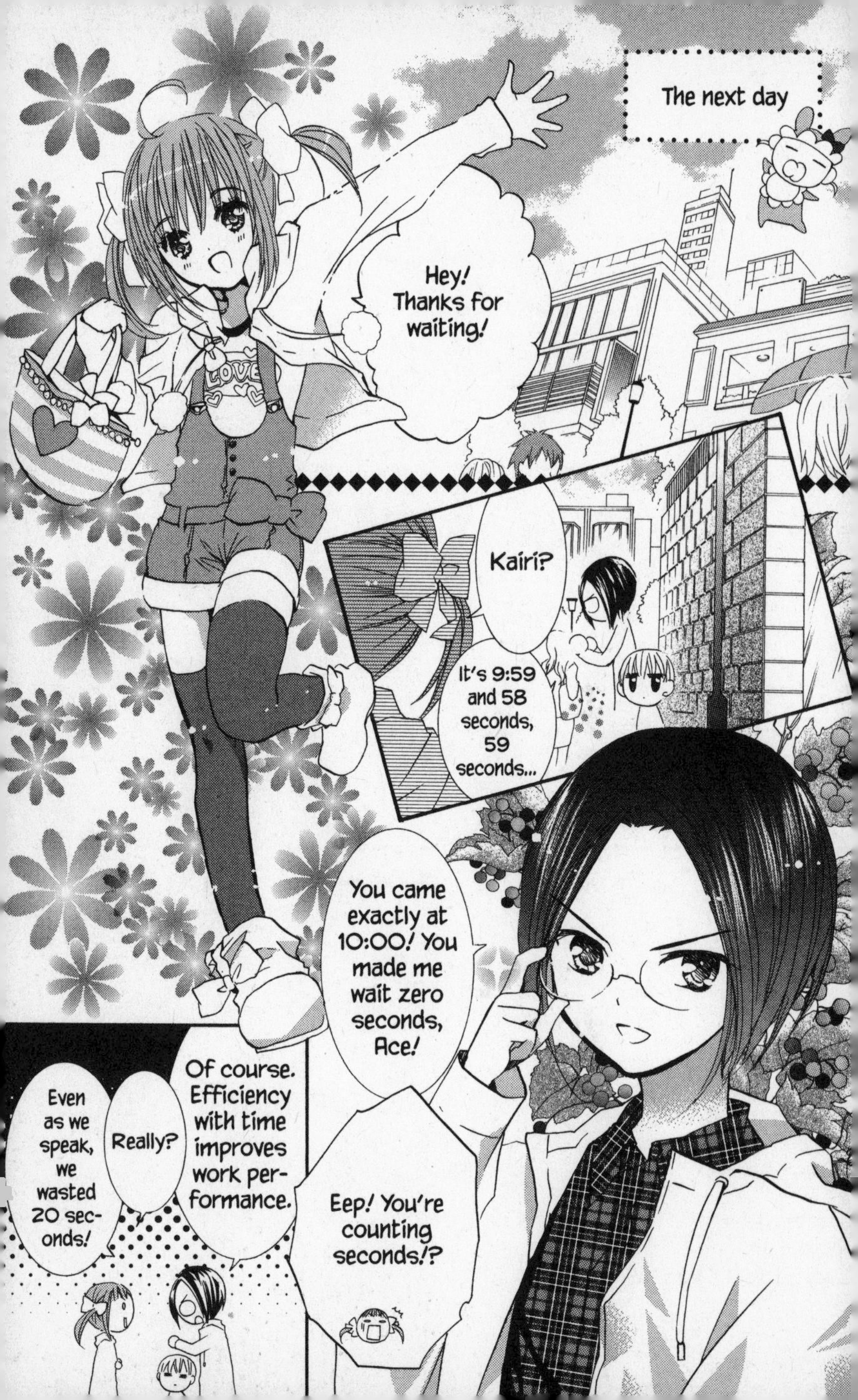
The next day
Hey! Thanks for waiting!
Kairi?
It's 9:59 and 58 seconds, 59 seconds...
You came exactly at 10:00! You made me wait zero seconds, Ace!
Eep! You're counting seconds!?
Of course. Efficiency with time improves work performance.
Really?
Even as we speak, we wasted 20 seconds!

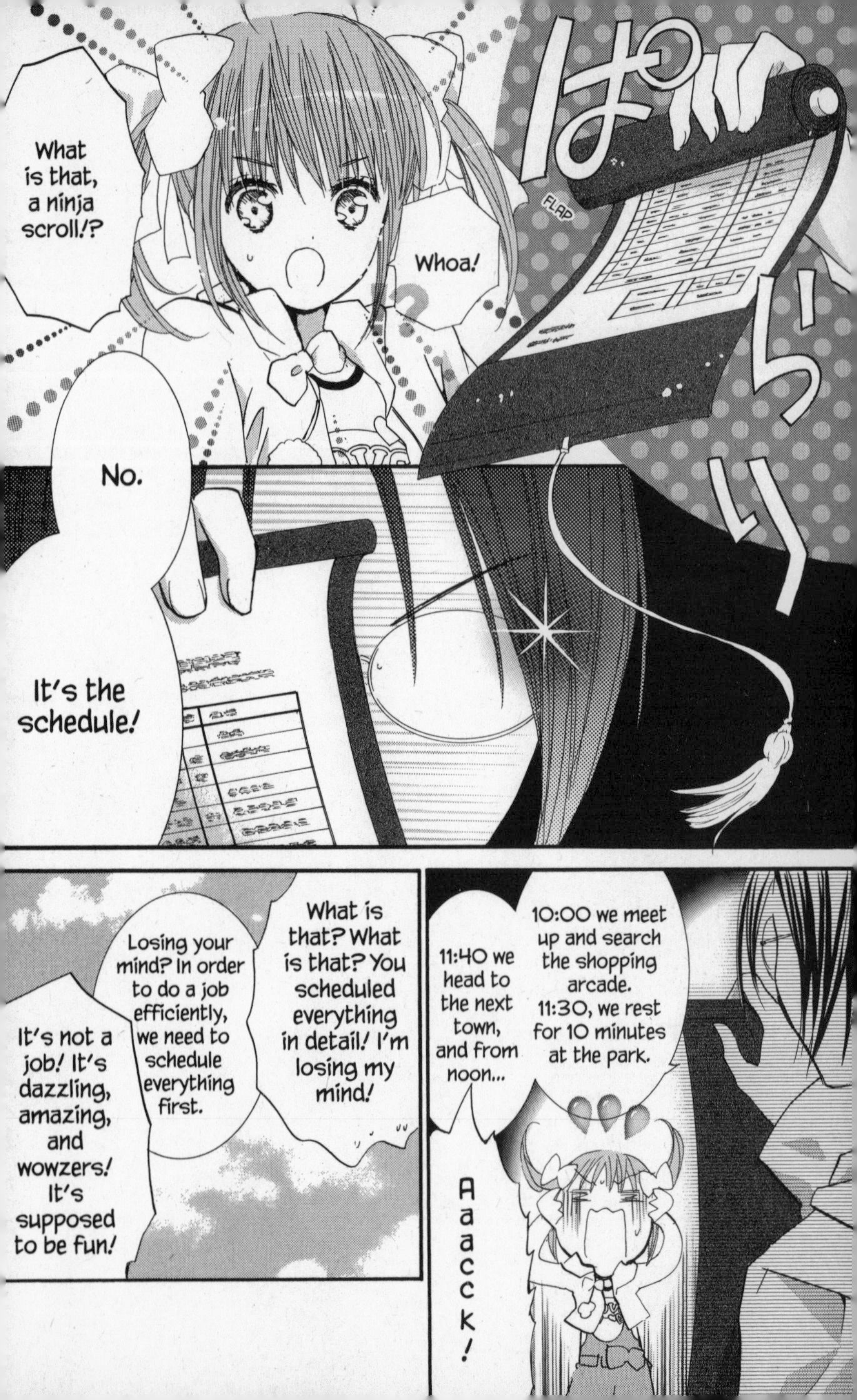

ぱらり
FLAP
Whoa!
What is that, a ninja scroll!?
No.
It's the schedule!
10:00 we meet up and search the shopping arcade. 11:30, we rest for 10 minutes at the park.
11:40 we head to the next town, and from noon...
Aaacck!
What is that? What is that? You scheduled everything in detail! I'm losing my mind!
Losing your mind? In order to do a job efficiently, we need to schedule everything first.
It's not a job! It's dazzling, amazing, and wowzers! It's supposed to be fun!

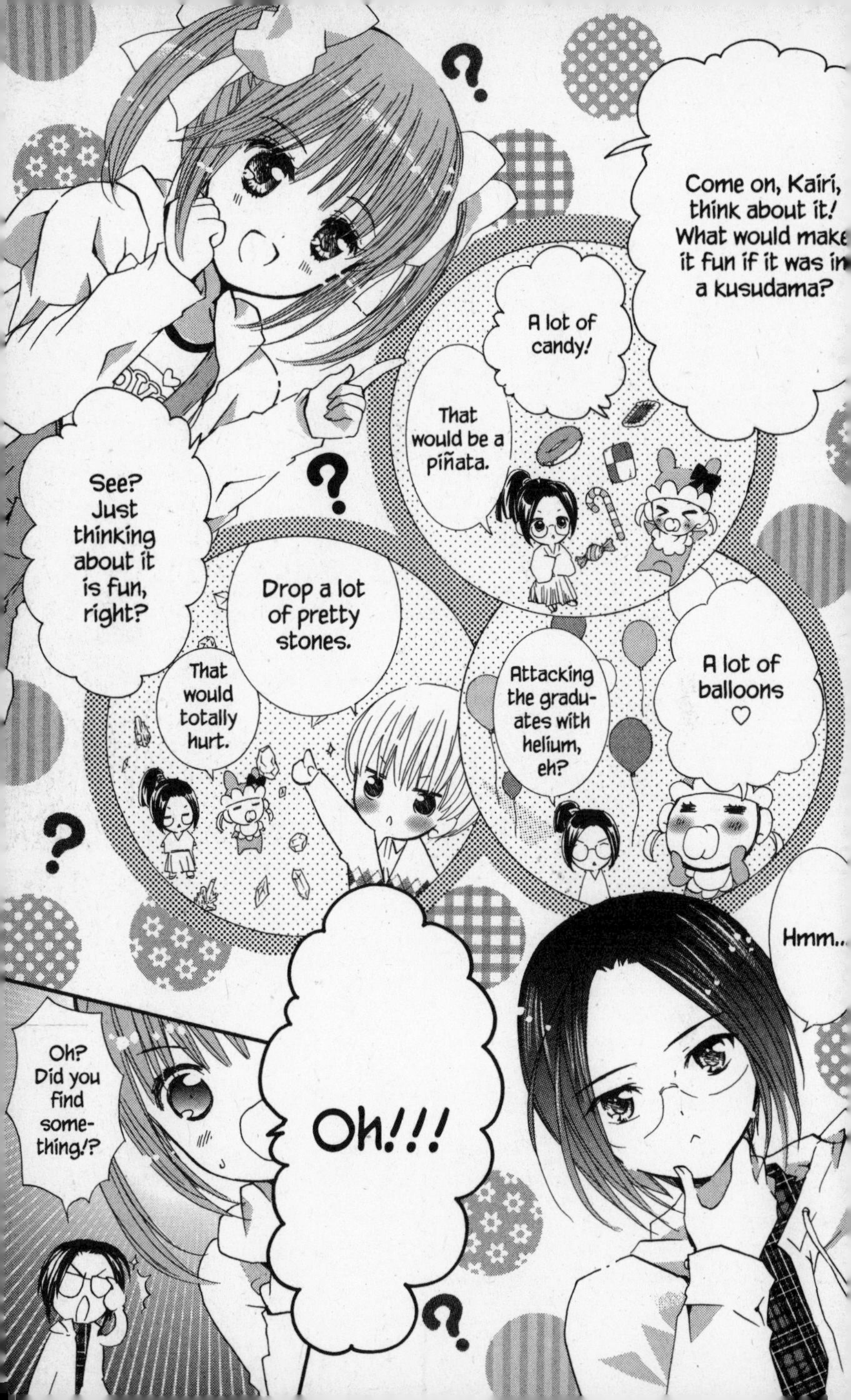

Come on, Kairi, think about it! What would make it fun if it was in a kusudama?
A lot of candy!
That would be a piñata.
A lot of balloons ♡
Attacking the graduates with helium, eh?
Drop a lot of pretty stones.
That would totally hurt.
See? Just thinking about it is fun, right?
Hmm...
Oh!!!
Oh? Did you find something!?

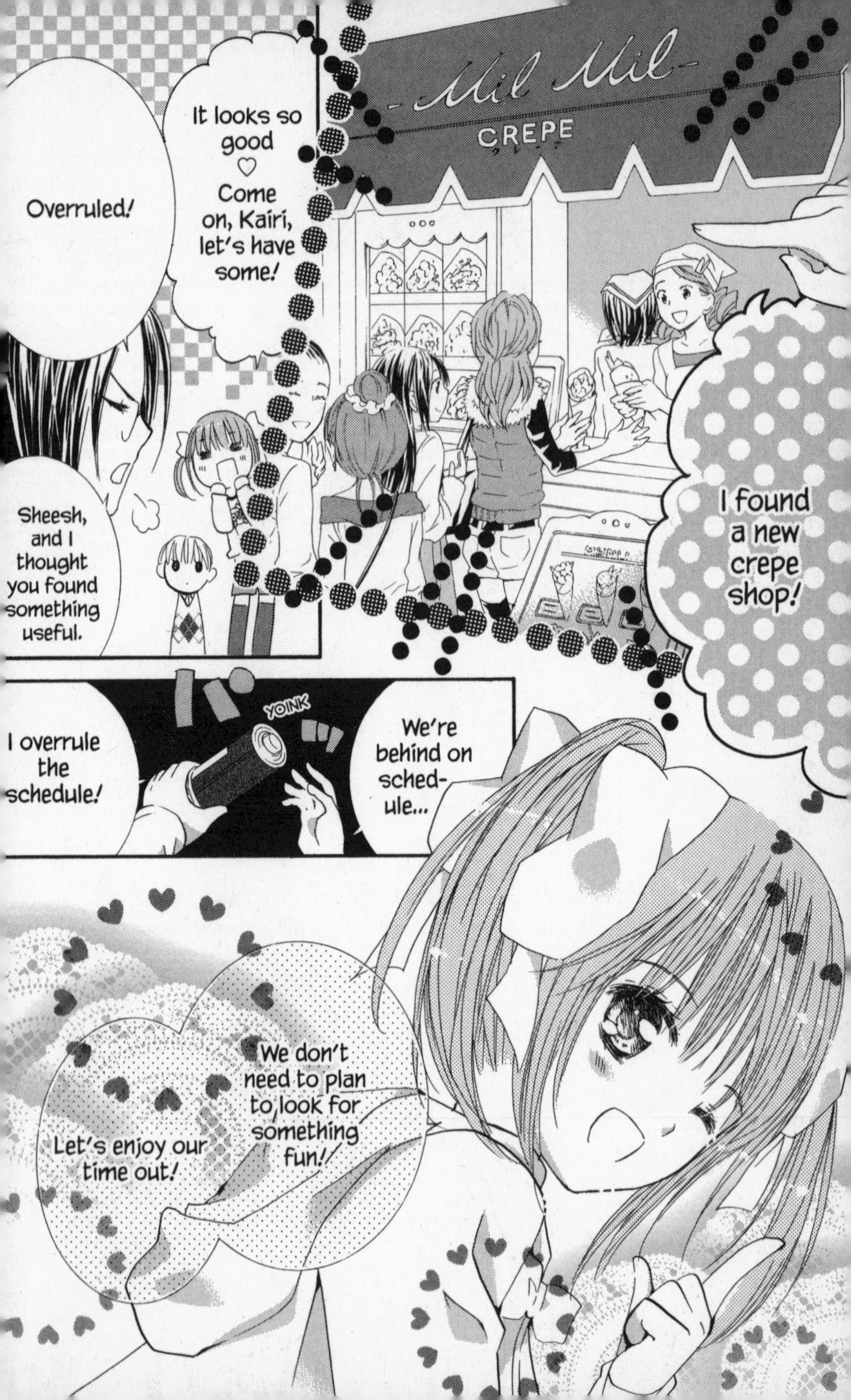
Mil Mil
CREPE
I found a new crepe shop!
It looks so good ♡ Come on, Kairi, let's have some!
Overruled!
Sheesh, and I thought you found something useful.
We're behind on schedule...
YOINK
I overrule the schedule!
We don't need to plan to look for something fun!
Let's enjoy our time out!

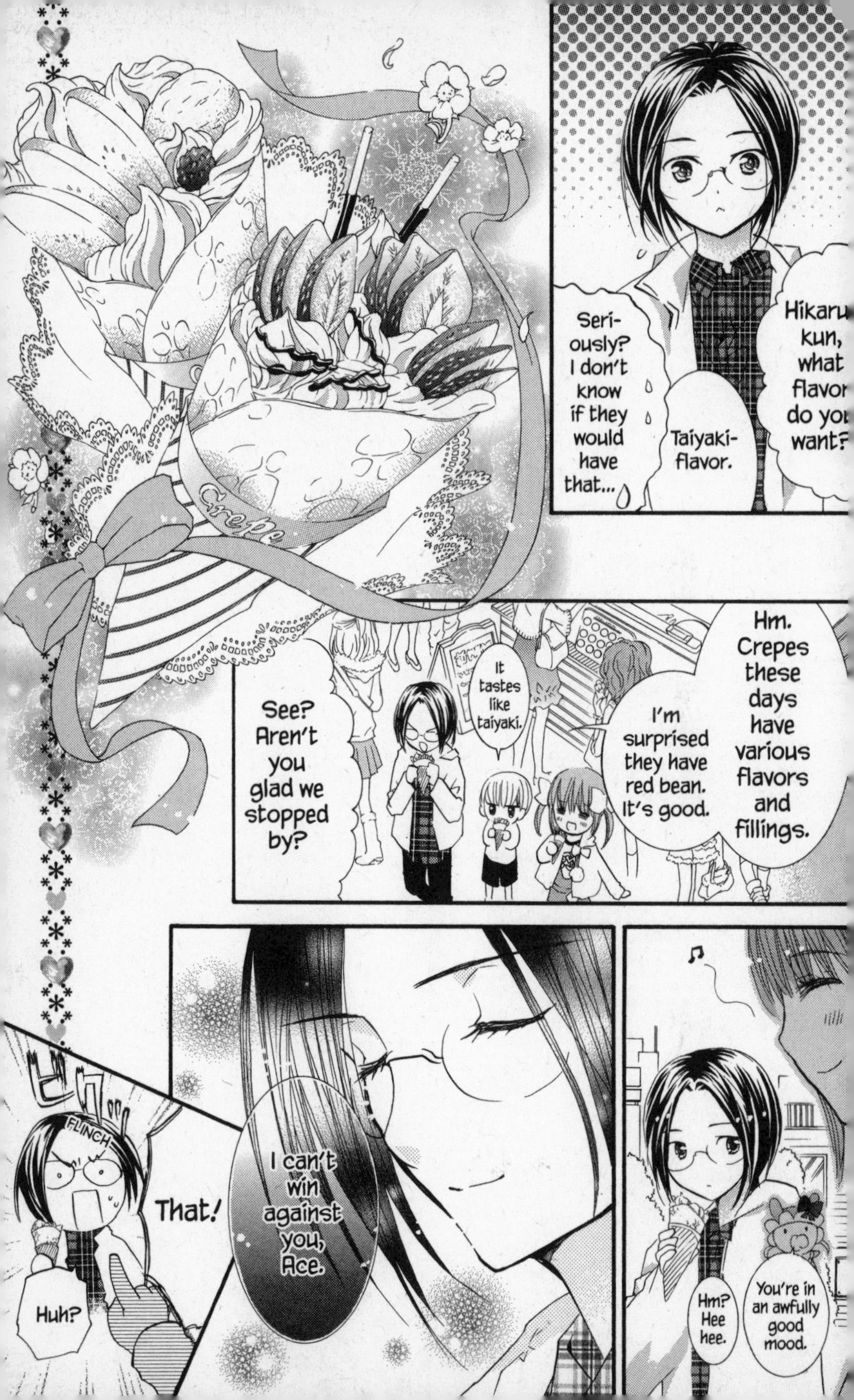
Hikaru kun, what flavor do you want?
Taiyaki-flavor.
Seri-ously? I don't know if they would have that...
Crepe
Hm. Crepes these days have various flavors and fillings.
I'm surprised they have red bean. It's good.
It tastes like taiyaki.
See? Aren't you glad we stopped by?
You're in an awfully good mood.
Hm? Hee hee.
I can't win against you, Ace.
FLINCH
That!
Huh?

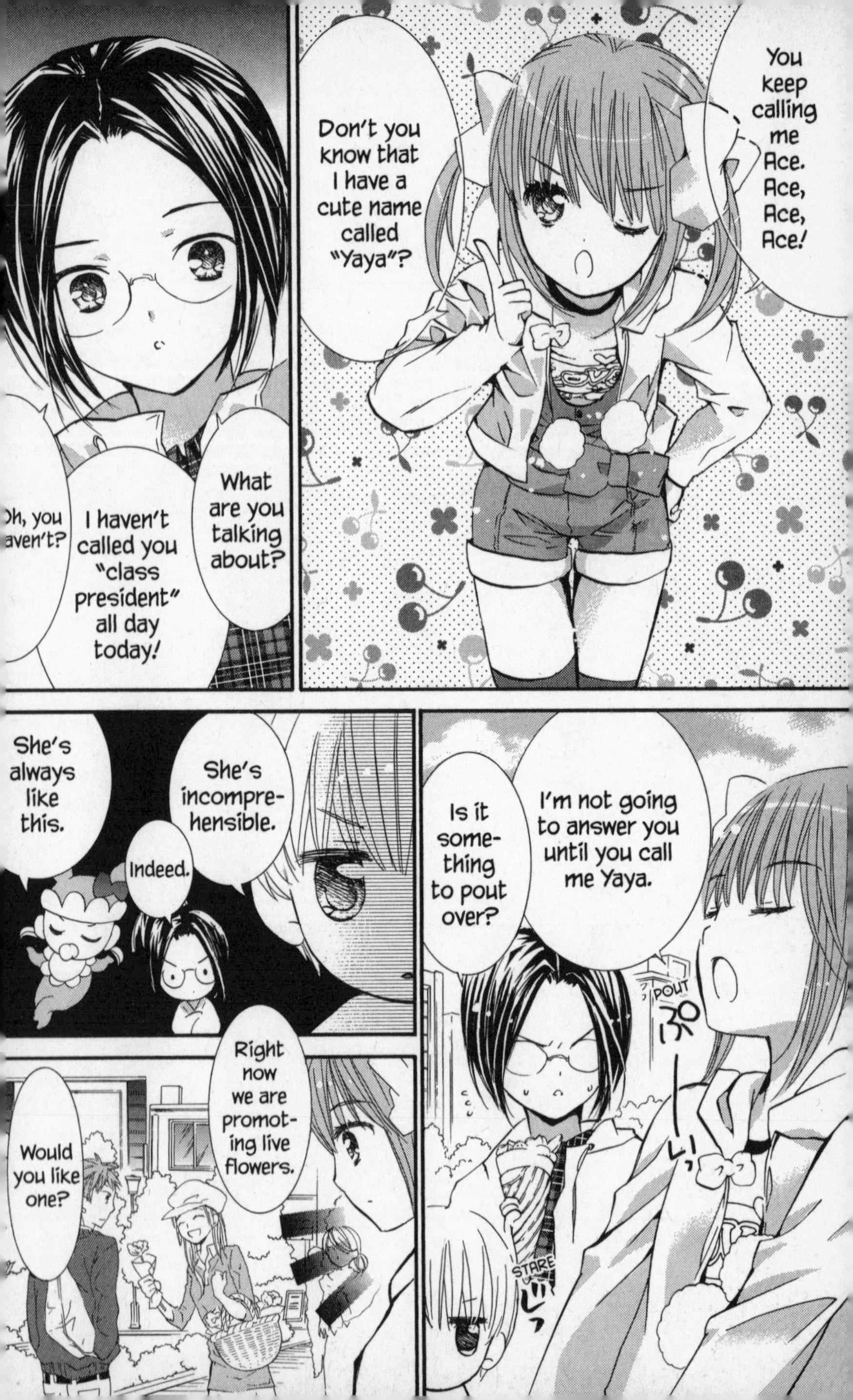
You keep calling me Ace. Ace, Ace, Ace!
Don't you know that I have a cute name called "Yaya"?
What are you talking about?
I haven't called you "class president" all day today!
h, you aven't?
I'm not going to answer you until you call me Yaya.
Is it something to pout over?
POUT
STARE
She's incomprehensible.
Indeed.
She's always like this.
Right now we are promoting live flowers.
Would you like one?

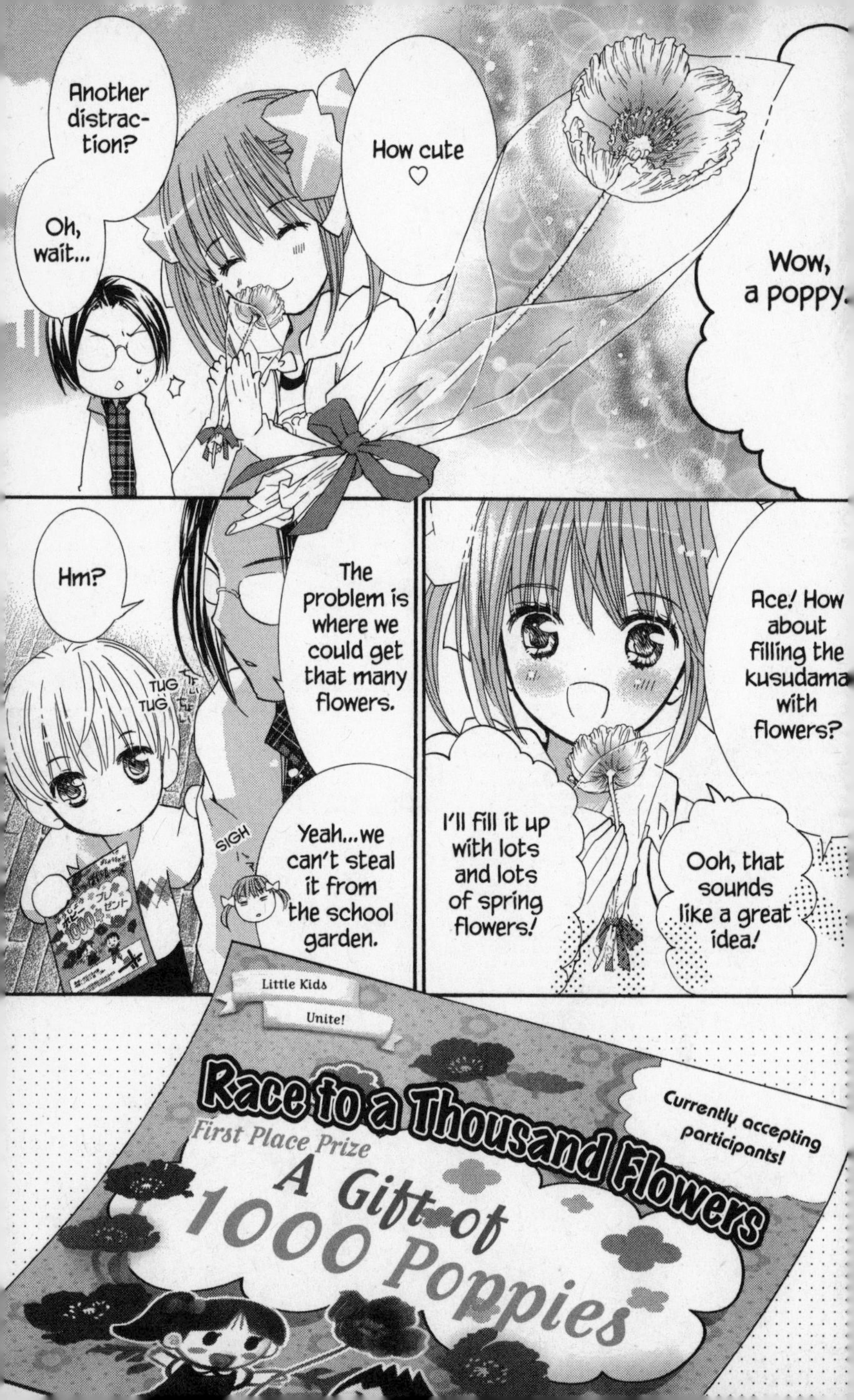
Wow, a poppy.
How cute ♡
Another distraction?
Oh, wait...
Ace! How about filling the kusudama with flowers?
Ooh, that sounds like a great idea!
I'll fill it up with lots and lots of spring flowers!
The problem is where we could get that many flowers.
Hm?
TUG TUG
Yeah...we can't steal it from the school garden.
SIGH
Little Kids
Unite!
Race to a Thousand Flowers
Currently accepting participants!
First Place Prize
A Gift of 1000 Poppies

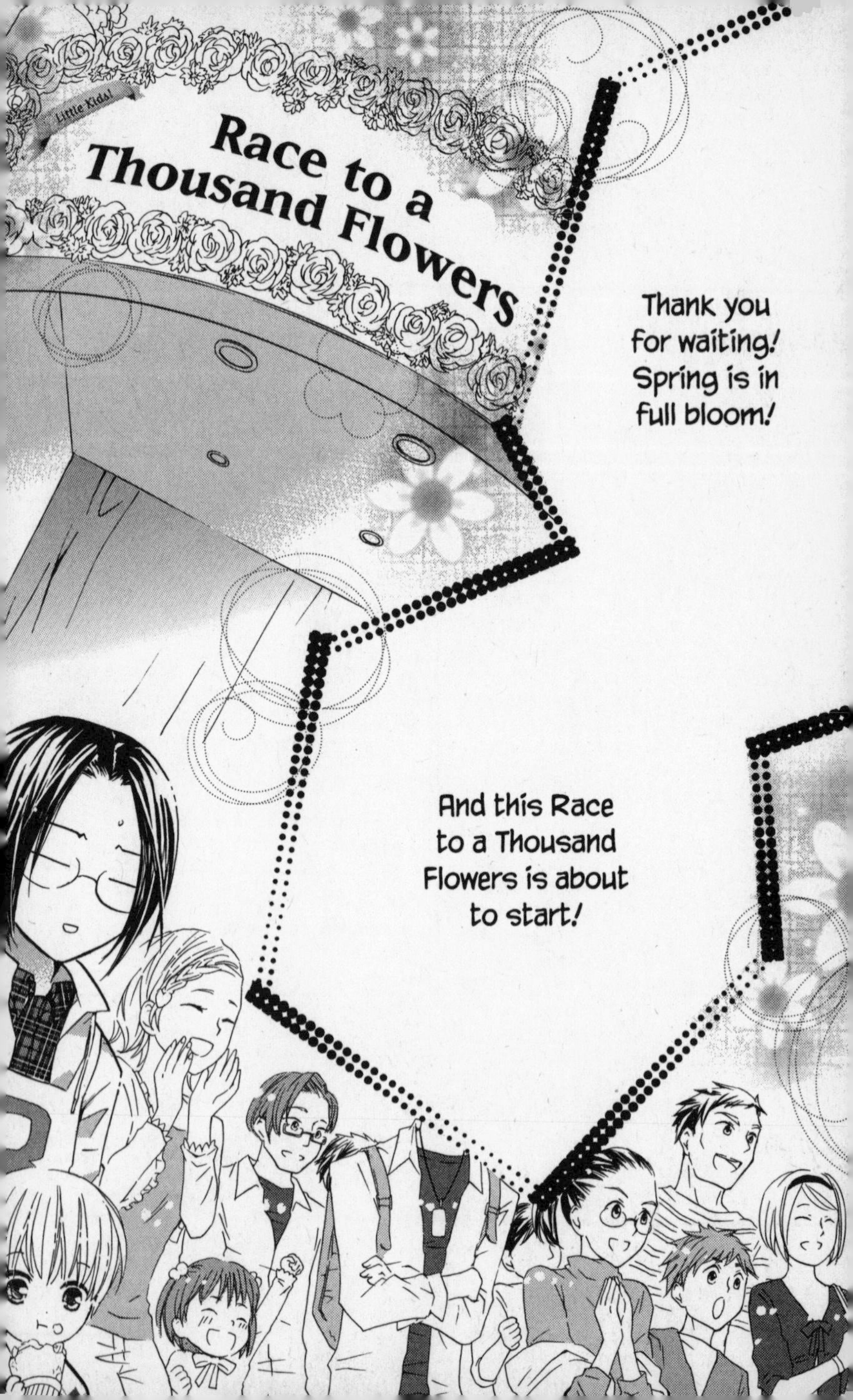
Little Kids!
Race to a Thousand Flowers
Thank you for waiting! Spring is in full bloom!
And this Race to a Thousand Flowers is about to start!

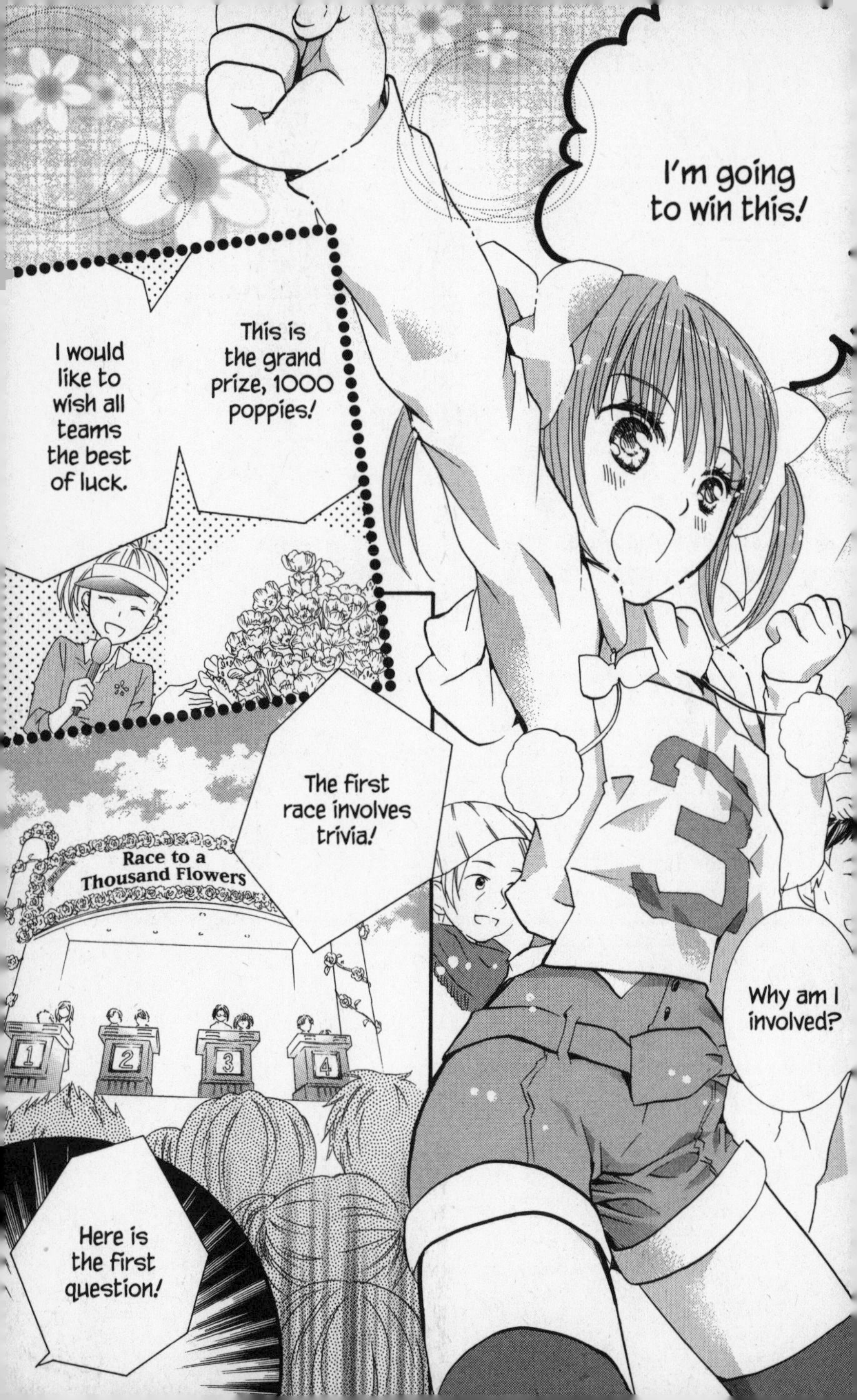
I'm going to win this!
Why am I involved?
This is the grand prize, 1000 poppies!
I would like to wish all teams the best of luck.
The first race involves trivia!
Race to a Thousand Flowers
1
2
3
4
Here is the first question!

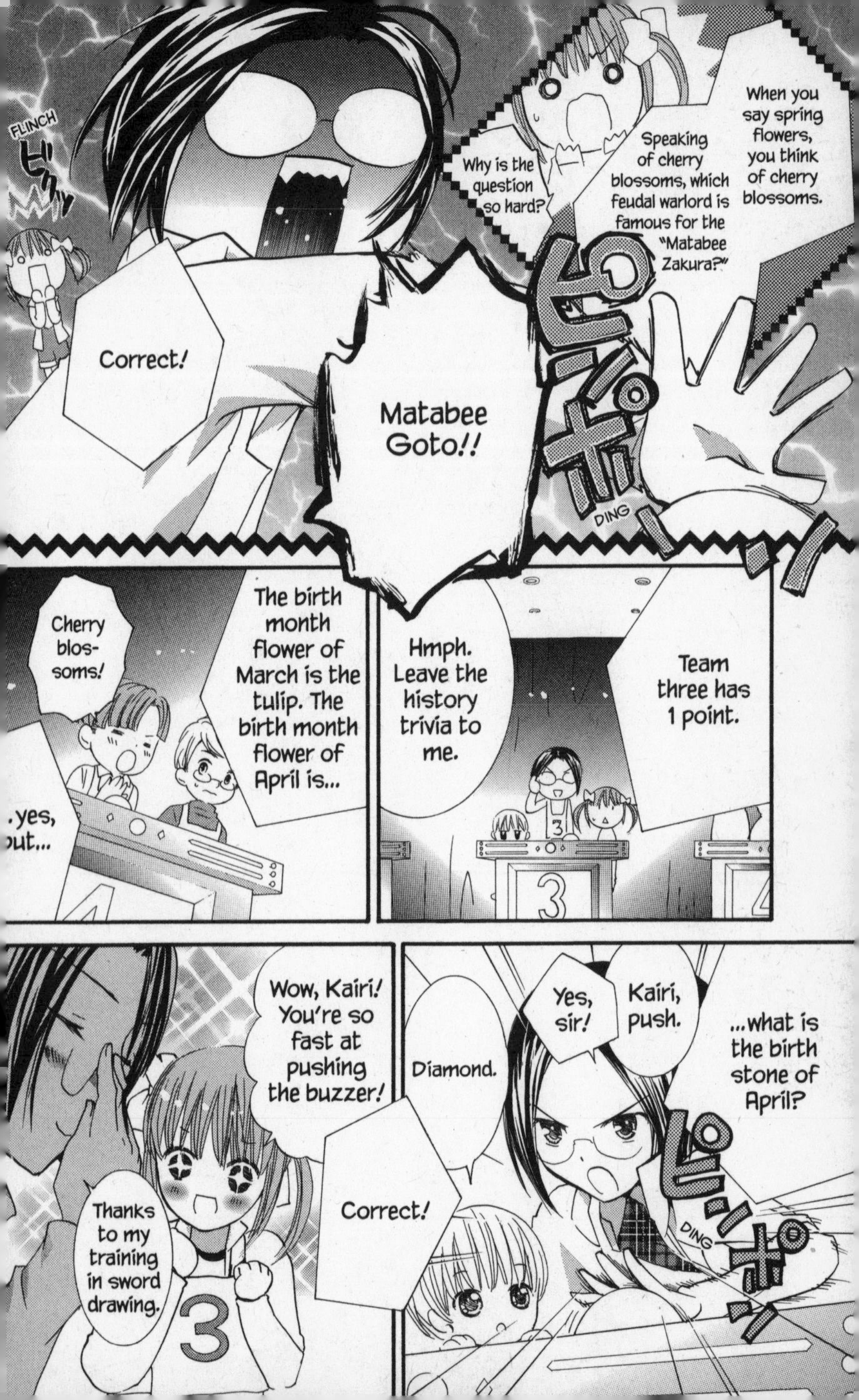
When you say spring flowers, you think of cherry blossoms.
Speaking of cherry blossoms, which feudal warlord is famous for the "Matabee Zakura?"
Why is the question so hard?
DING
Matabee Goto!!
FLINCH
Correct!
Team three has 1 point.
Hmph. Leave the history trivia to me.
The birth month flower of March is the tulip. The birth month flower of April is...
Cherry blos-soms!
. yes, ut...
...what is the birth stone of April?
DING
Kairi, push.
Yes, sir!
Diamond.
Correct!
Wow, Kairi! You're so fast at pushing the buzzer!
Thanks to my training in sword drawing.

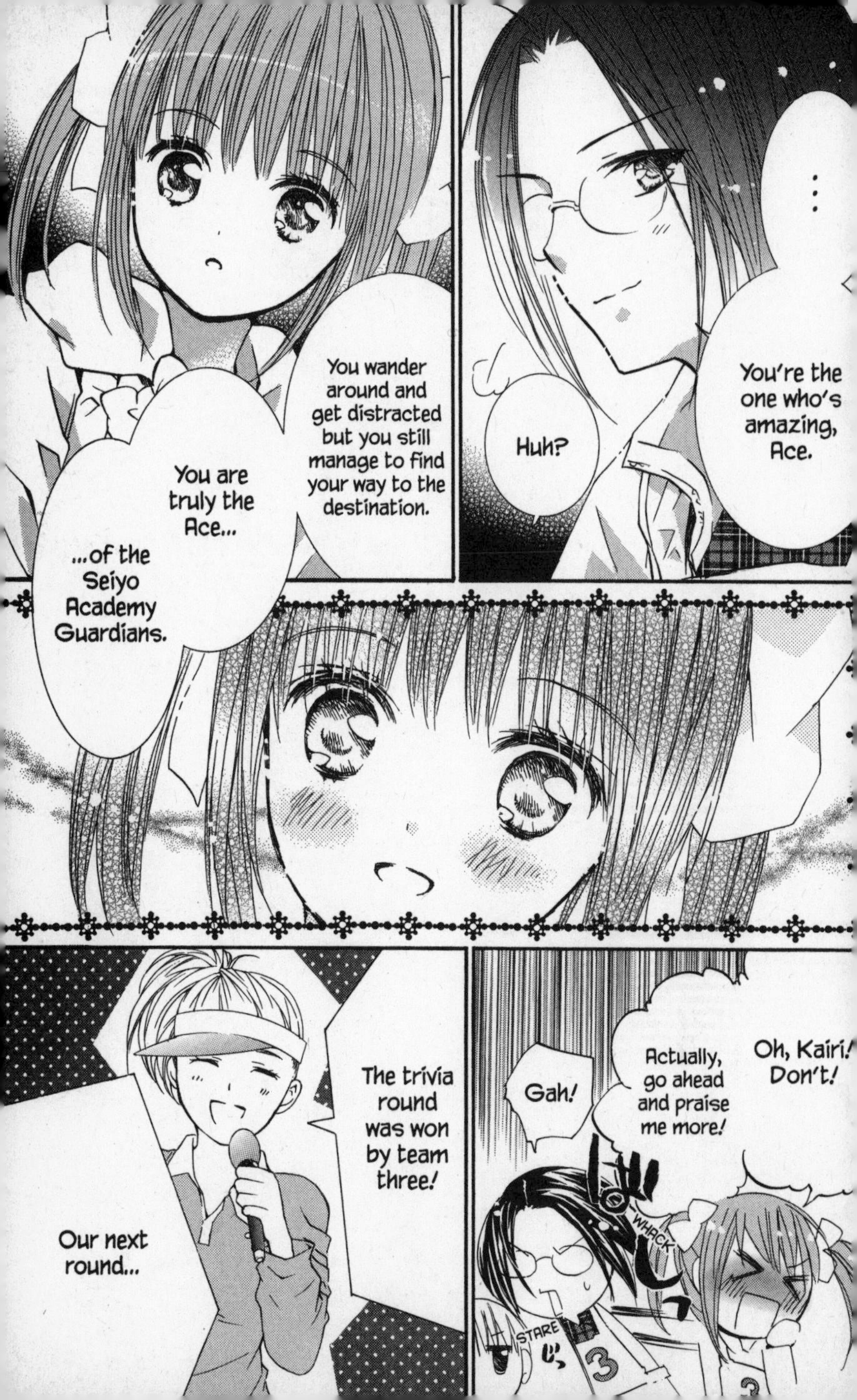
...
You're the one who's amazing, Ace.
Huh?
You wander around and get distracted but you still manage to find your way to the destination.
You are truly the Ace...
...of the Seiyo Academy Guardians.
Oh, Kairi! Don't!
Actually, go ahead and praise me more!
Gah!
WHACK
STARE
The trivia round was won by team three!
Our next round...

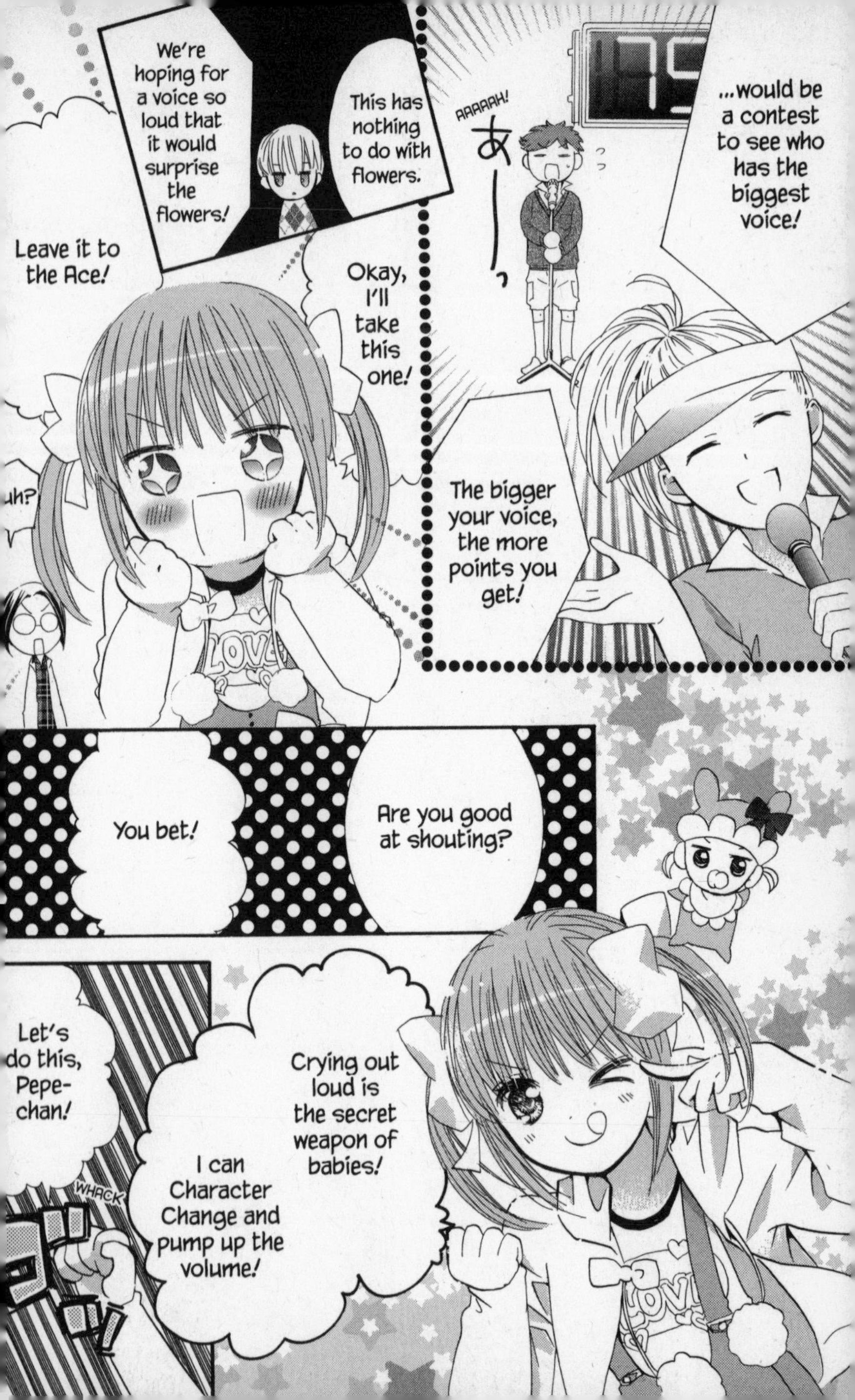
...would be a contest to see who has the biggest voice!
AAAAAH!
あー
The bigger your voice, the more points you get!
We're hoping for a voice so loud that it would surprise the flowers!
This has nothing to do with flowers.
Okay, I'll take this one!
Leave it to the Ace!
Are you good at shouting?
You bet!
Crying out loud is the secret weapon of babies!
I can Character Change and pump up the volume!
Let's do this, Pepe-chan!
WHACK

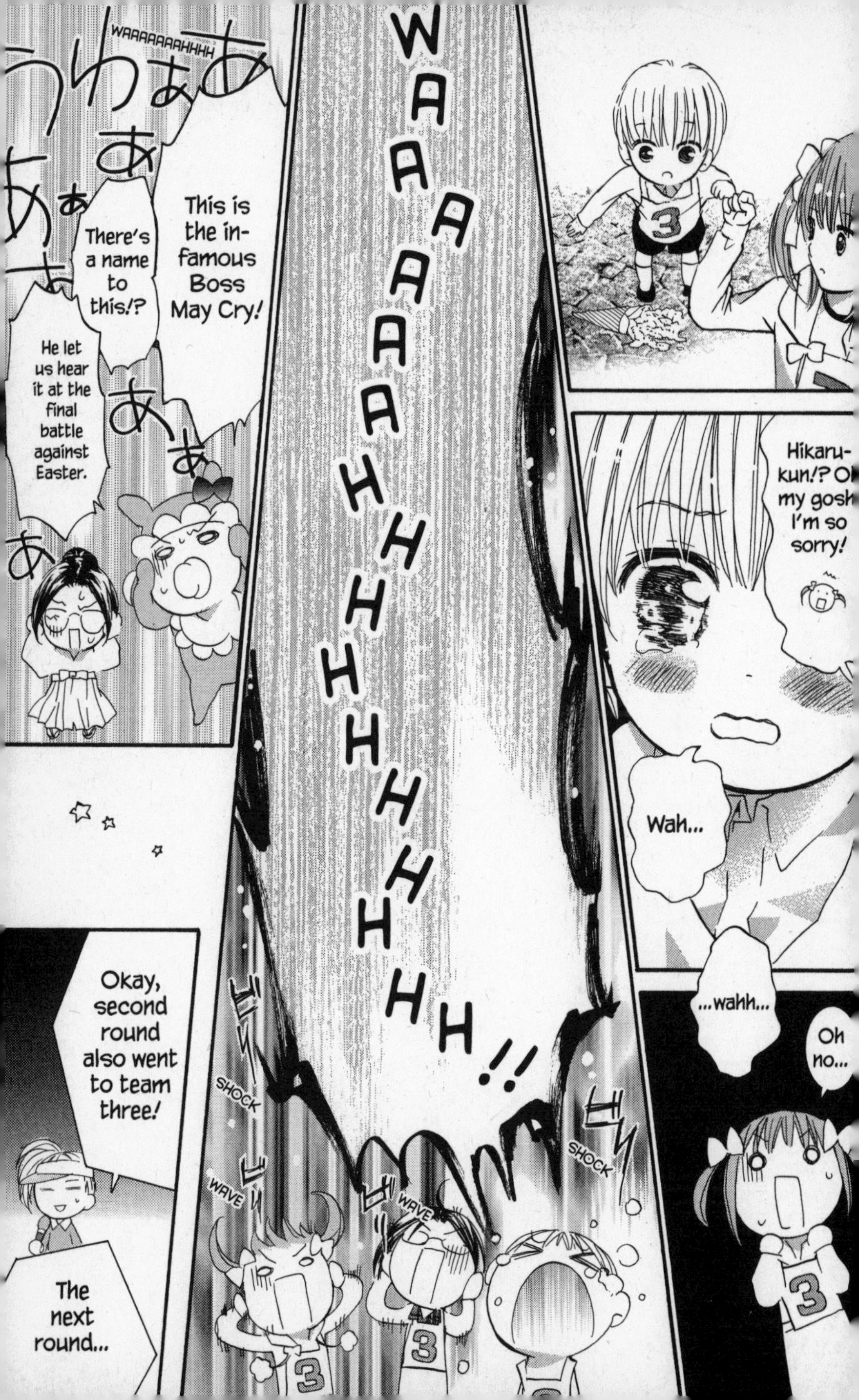
Hikaru-kun!? Oh my gosh I'm so sorry!
Wah...
...wahh...
Oh no...
WAAAAAAHHHHHHHHHH!!
SHOCK
WAVE
WAVE
SHOCK
WAAAAAAAAHHHH
This is the infamous Boss May Cry!
There's a name to this!?
He let us hear it at the final battle against Easter.
Okay, second round also went to team three!
The next round...

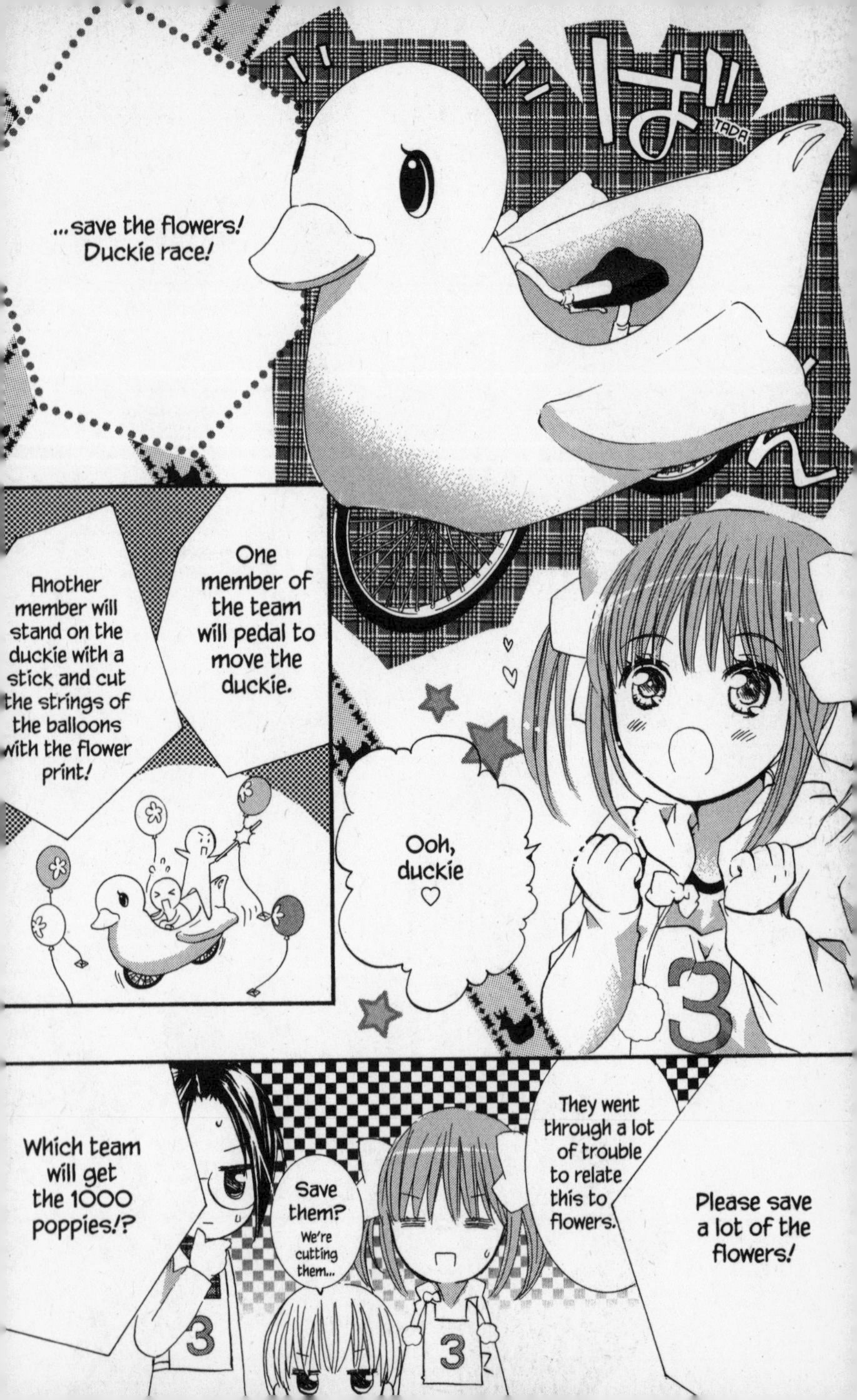
ぱ
TADA
...save the flowers! Duckie race!
One member of the team will pedal to move the duckie.
Another member will stand on the duckie with a stick and cut the strings of the balloons with the flower print!
Ooh, duckie ♡
Please save a lot of the flowers!
They went through a lot of trouble to relate this to flowers.
Save them? We're cutting them...
Which team will get the 1000 poppies!?

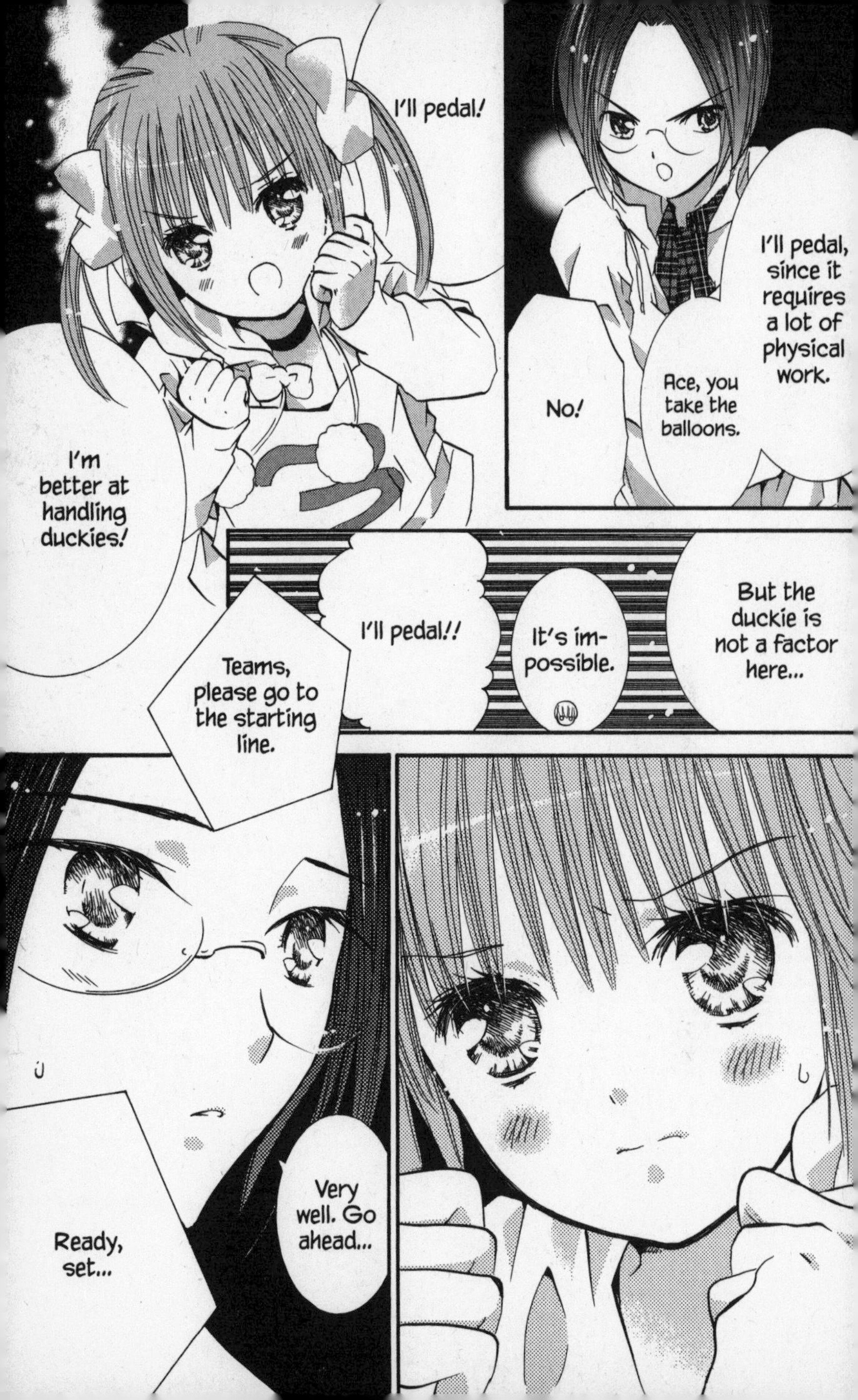
I'll pedal, since it requires a lot of physical work.
Ace, you take the balloons.
No!
I'll pedal!
I'm better at handling duckies!
But the duckie is not a factor here...
It's impossible.
I'll pedal!!
Teams, please go to the starting line.
Very well. Go ahead...
Ready, set...

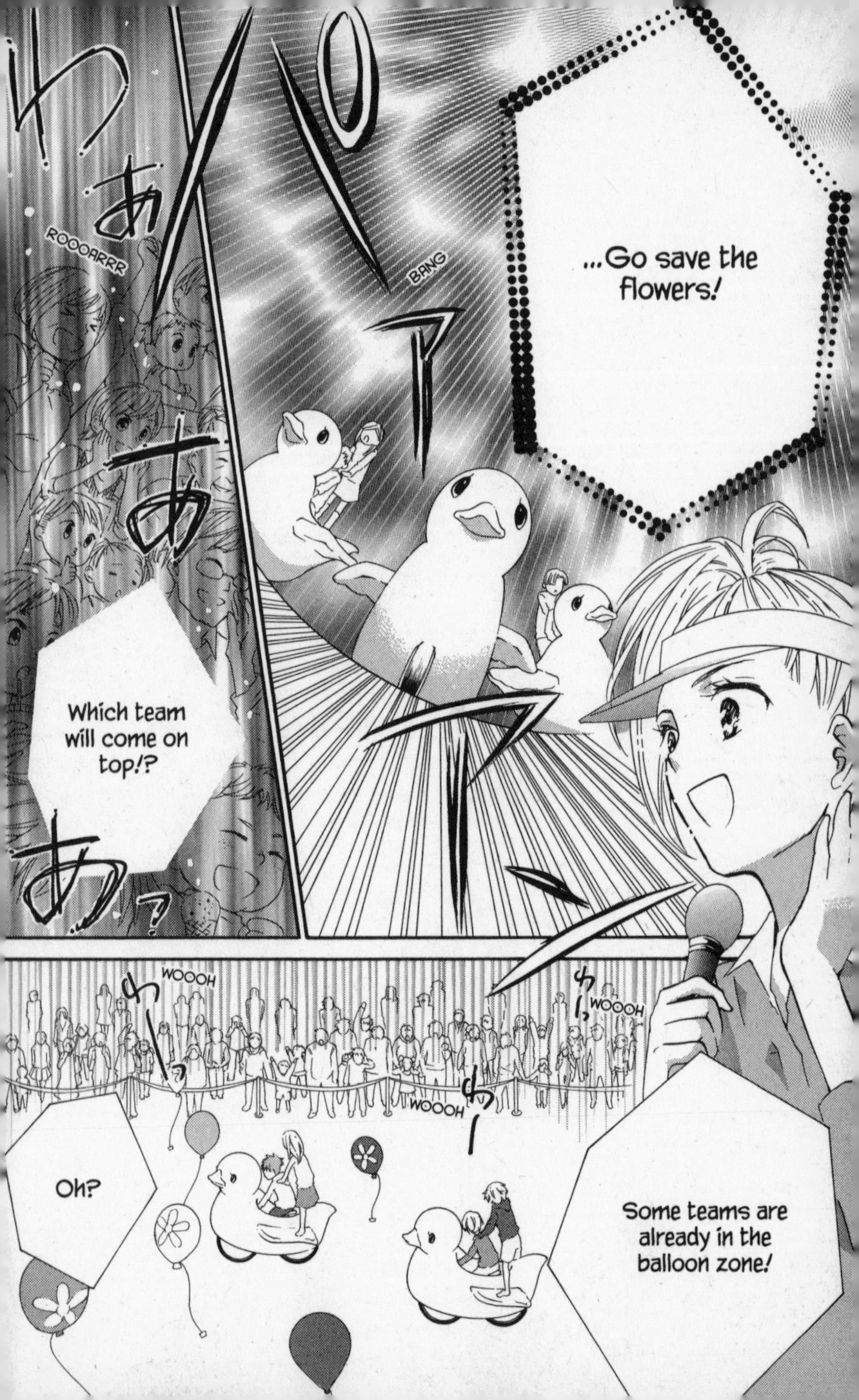
...Go save the flowers!
BANG
ROOOARRR
Which team will come on top!?
Some teams are already in the balloon zone!
WOOOH
WOOOH
WOOOH
Oh?

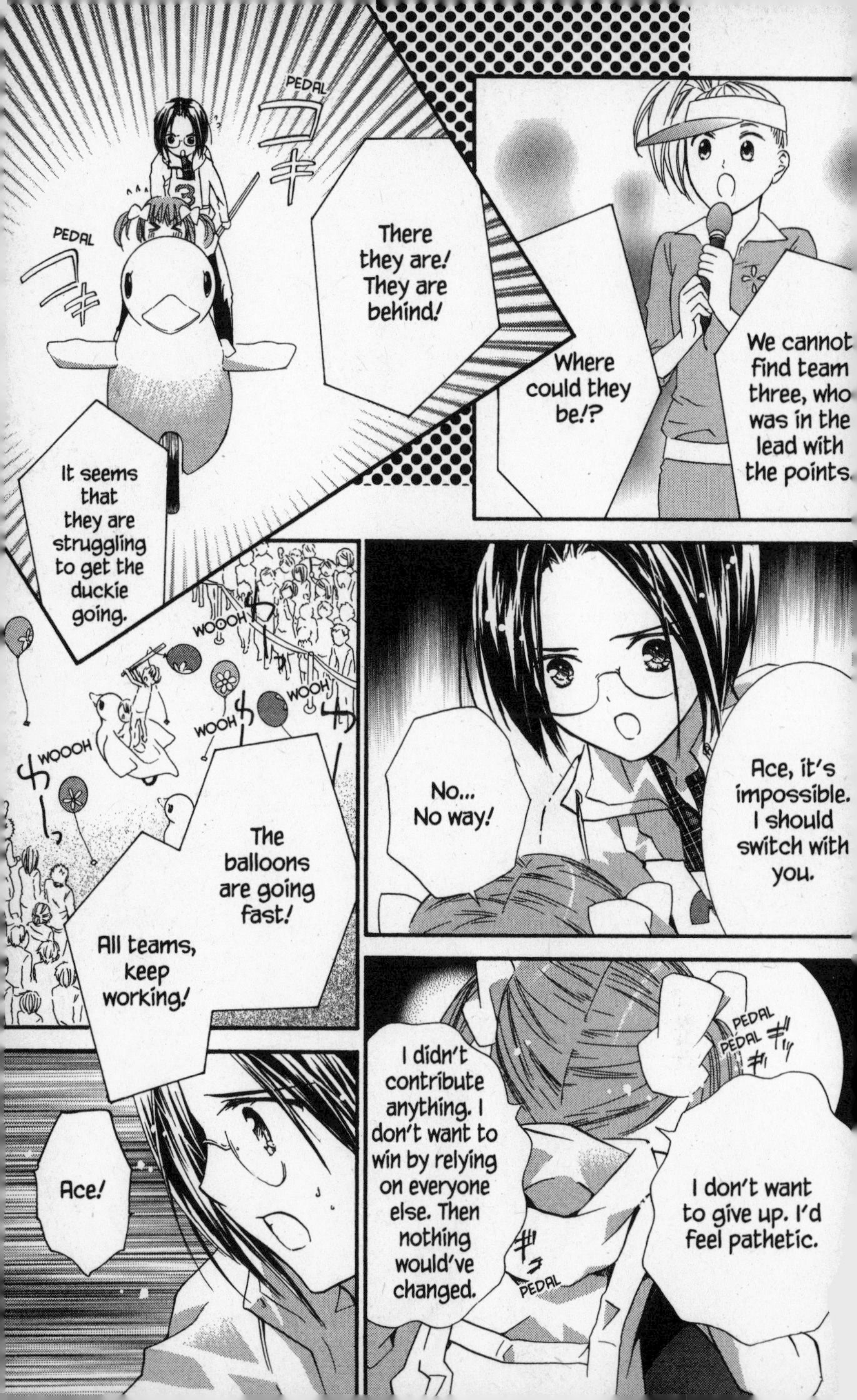
We cannot find team three, who was in the lead with the points.
Where could they be!?
There they are! They are behind!
PEDAL
PEDAL
It seems that they are struggling to get the duckie going.
Ace, it's impossible. I should switch with you.
No... No way!
WOOOH
WOOH
WOOH
WOOOH
The balloons are going fast!
All teams, keep working!
PEDAL
PEDAL
I don't want to give up. I'd feel pathetic.
I didn't contribute anything. I don't want to win by relying on everyone else. Then nothing would've changed.
PEDAL
Ace!

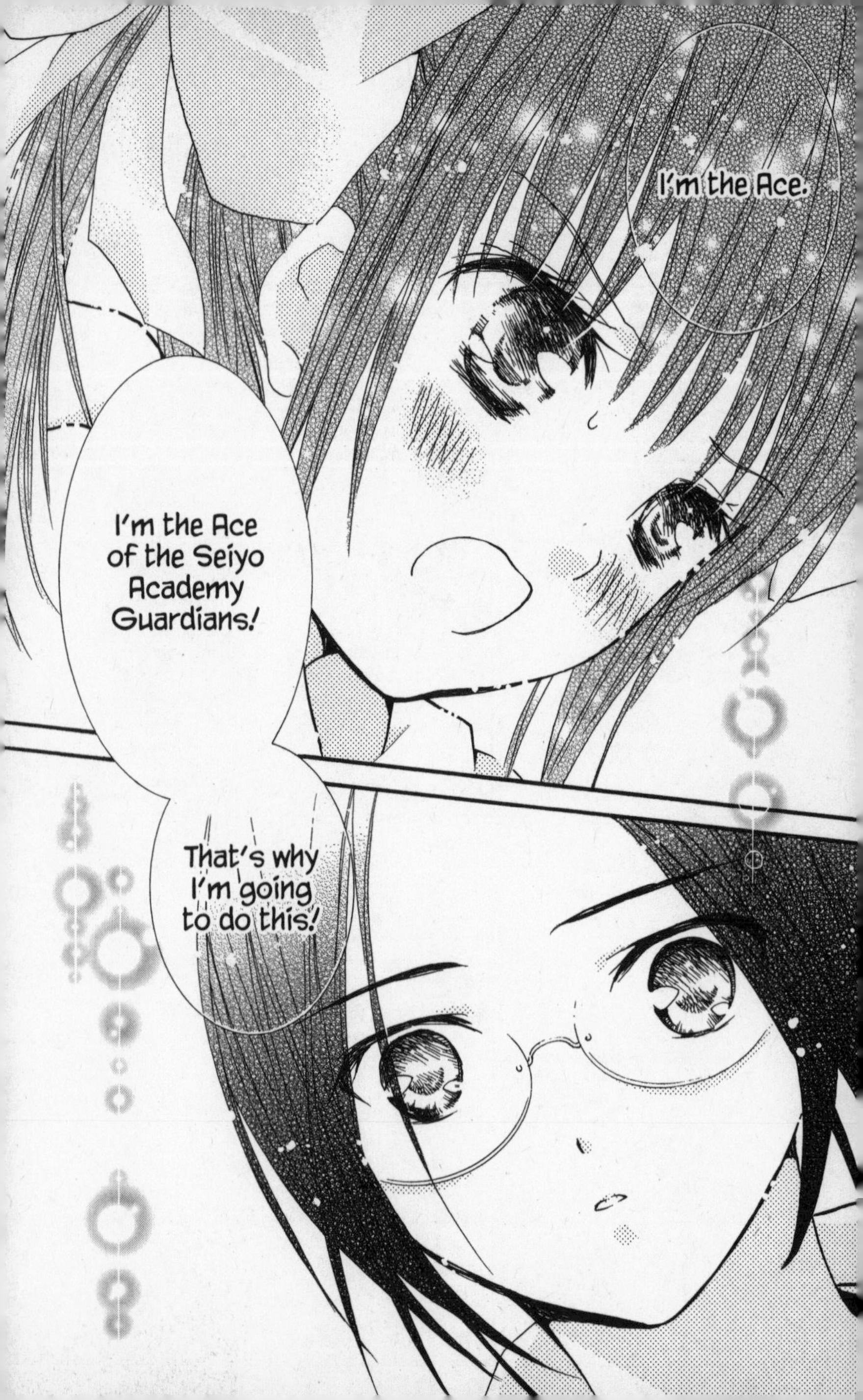
I'm the Ace.
I'm the Ace of the Seiyo Academy Guardians!
That's why I'm going to do this!

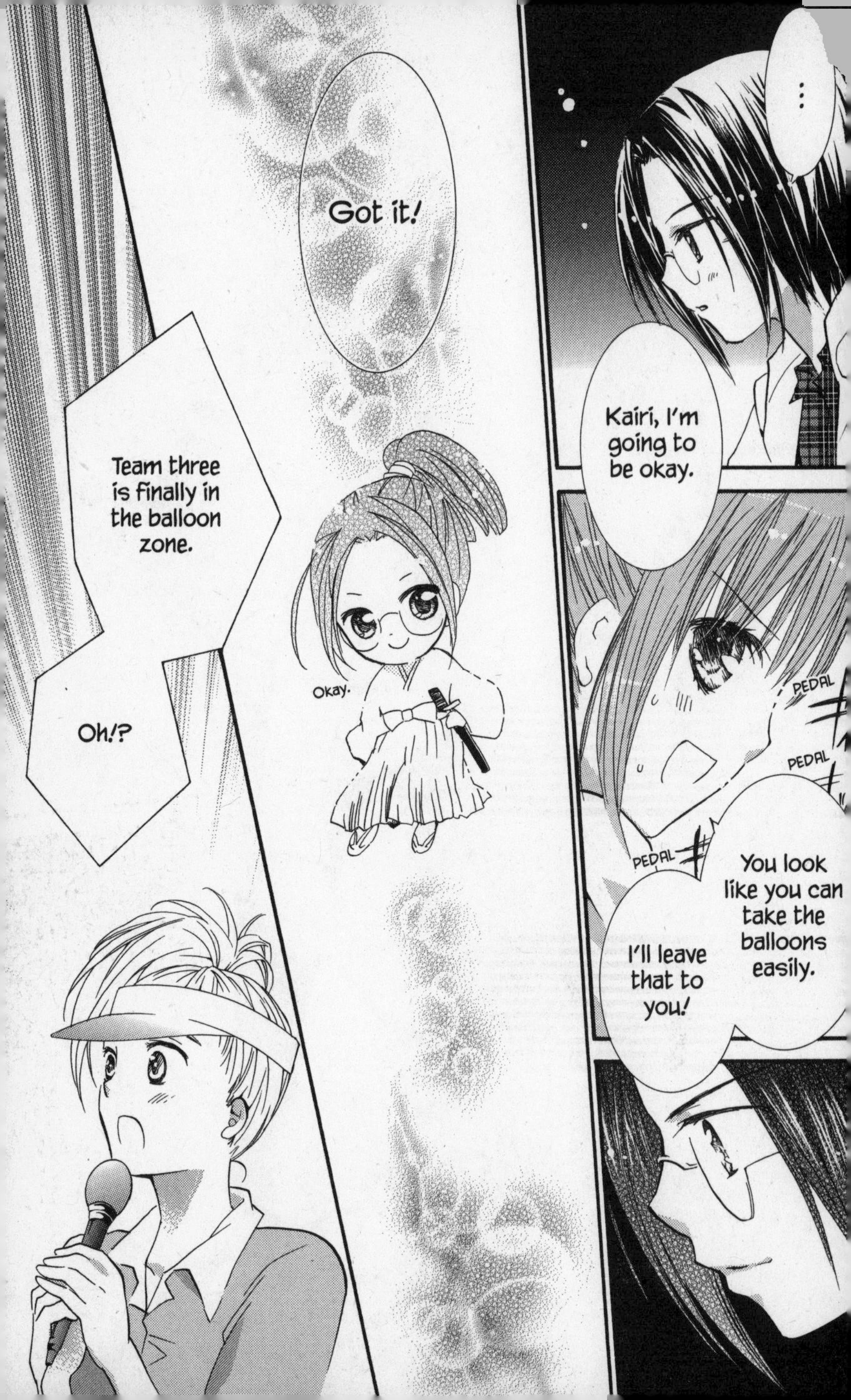
...
Kairi, I'm going to be okay.
PEDAL
PEDAL
PEDAL
You look like you can take the balloons easily.
I'll leave that to you!
Got it!
Okay.
Team three is finally in the balloon zone.
Oh!?

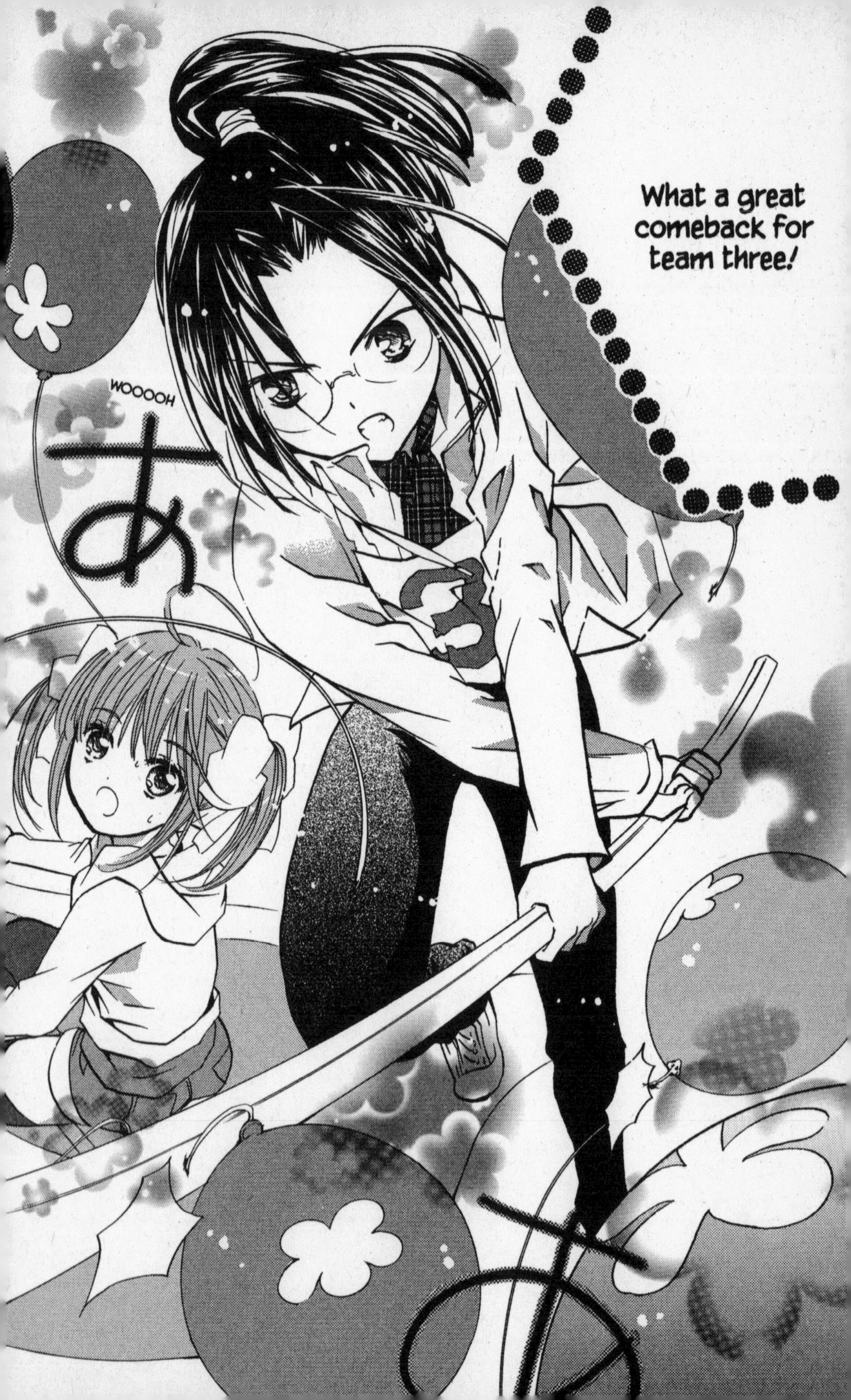
What a great comeback for team three!
WOOOOH
あ

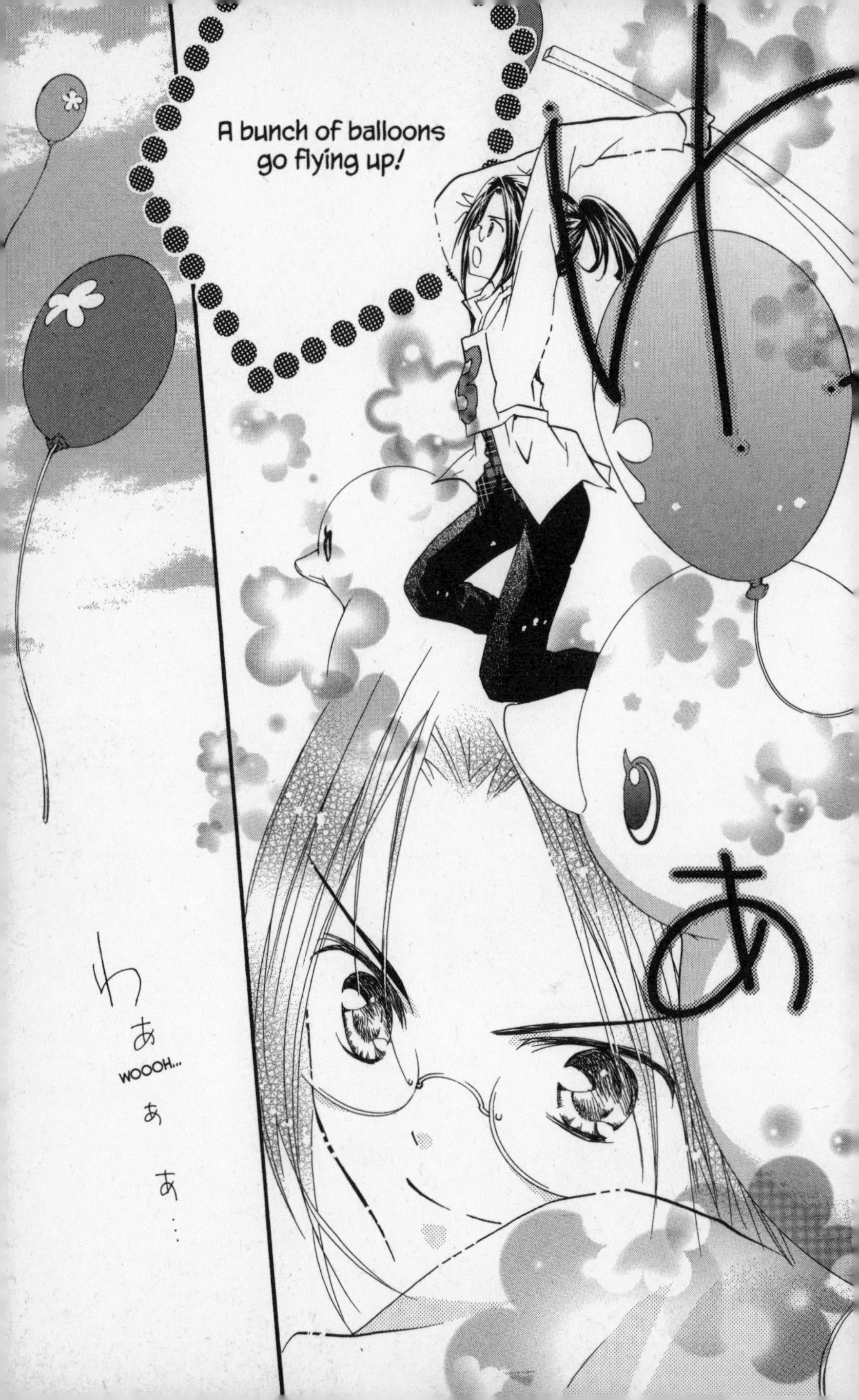
A bunch of balloons go flying up!
あ
わあああ…
WOOOH...

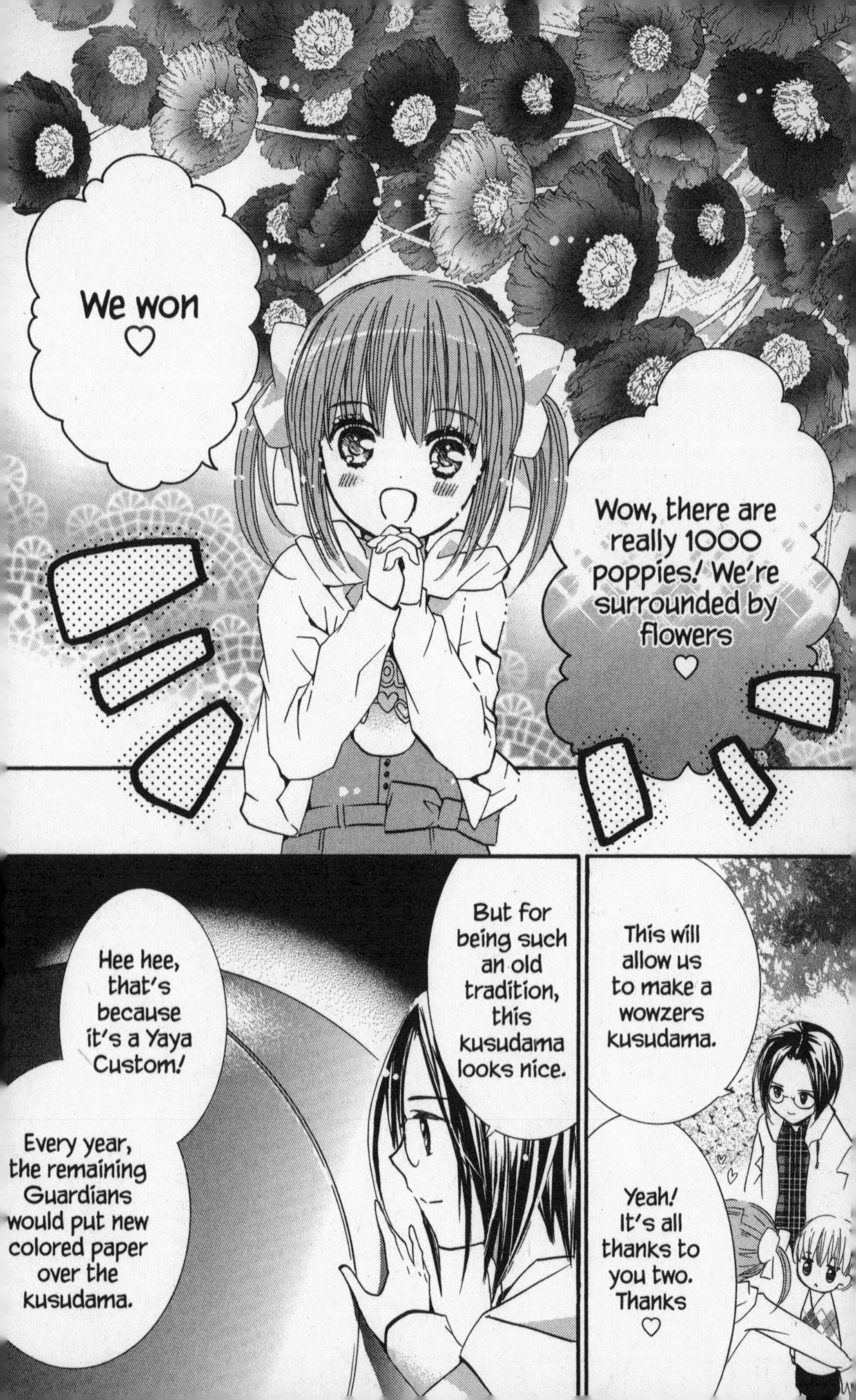
Wow, there are really 1000 poppies! We're surrounded by flowers ♡
We won ♡
This will allow us to make a wowzers kusudama.
Yeah! It's all thanks to you two. Thanks ♡
But for being such an old tradition, this kusudama looks nice.
Hee hee, that's because it's a Yaya Custom!
Every year, the remaining Guardians would put new colored paper over the kusudama.

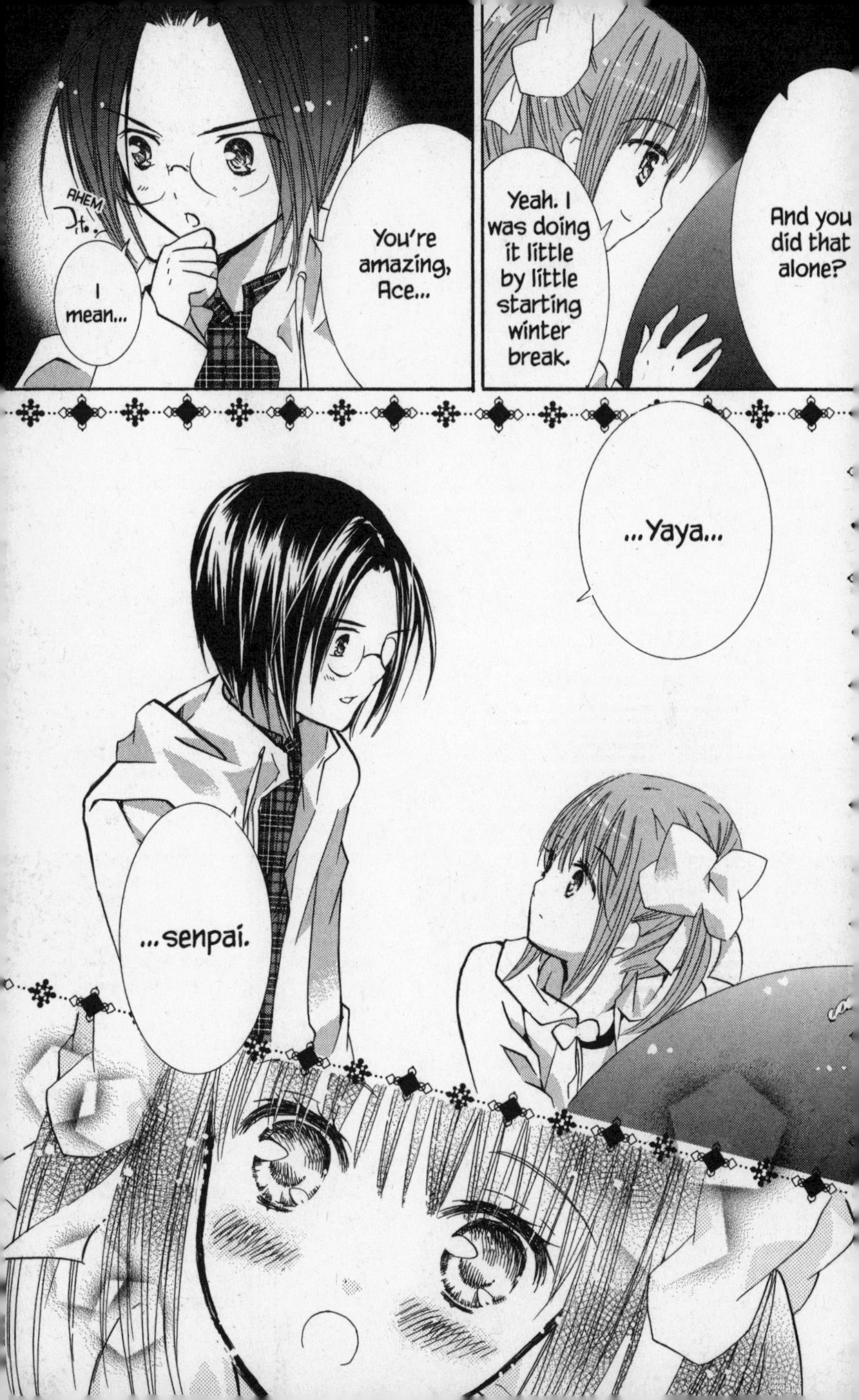
And you did that alone?
Yeah. I was doing it little by little starting winter break.
You're amazing, Ace...
AHEM
I mean...
...Yaya...
...senpai.

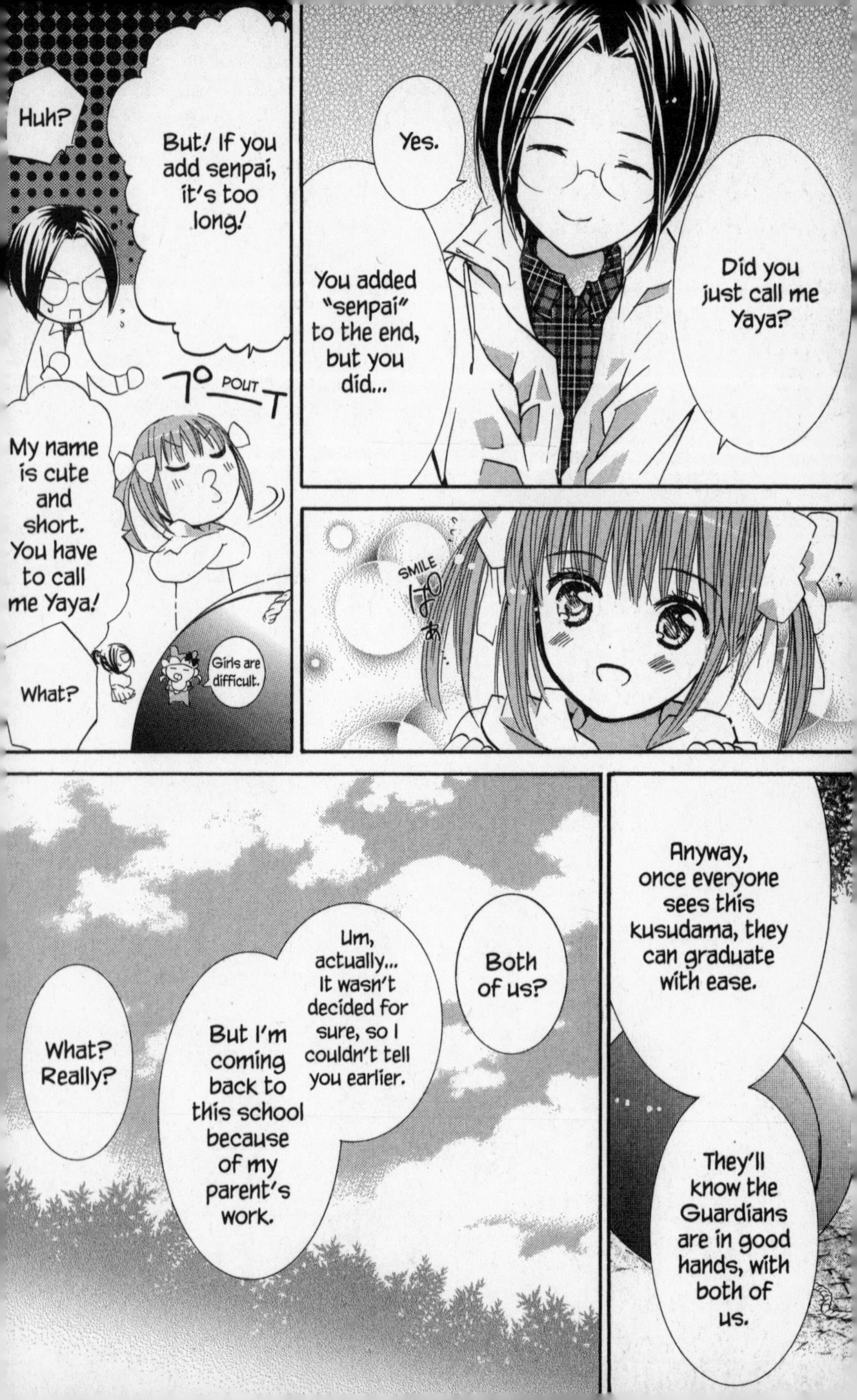
Did you just call me Yaya?
Yes.
You added "senpai" to the end, but you did...
SMILE
But! If you add senpai, it's too long!
Huh?
POUT
My name is cute and short. You have to call me Yaya!
Girls are difficult.
What?
Anyway, once everyone sees this kusudama, they can graduate with ease.
They'll know the Guardians are in good hands, with both of us.
Both of us?
Um, actually... It wasn't decided for sure, so I couldn't tell you earlier.
But I'm coming back to this school because of my parent's work.
What? Really?

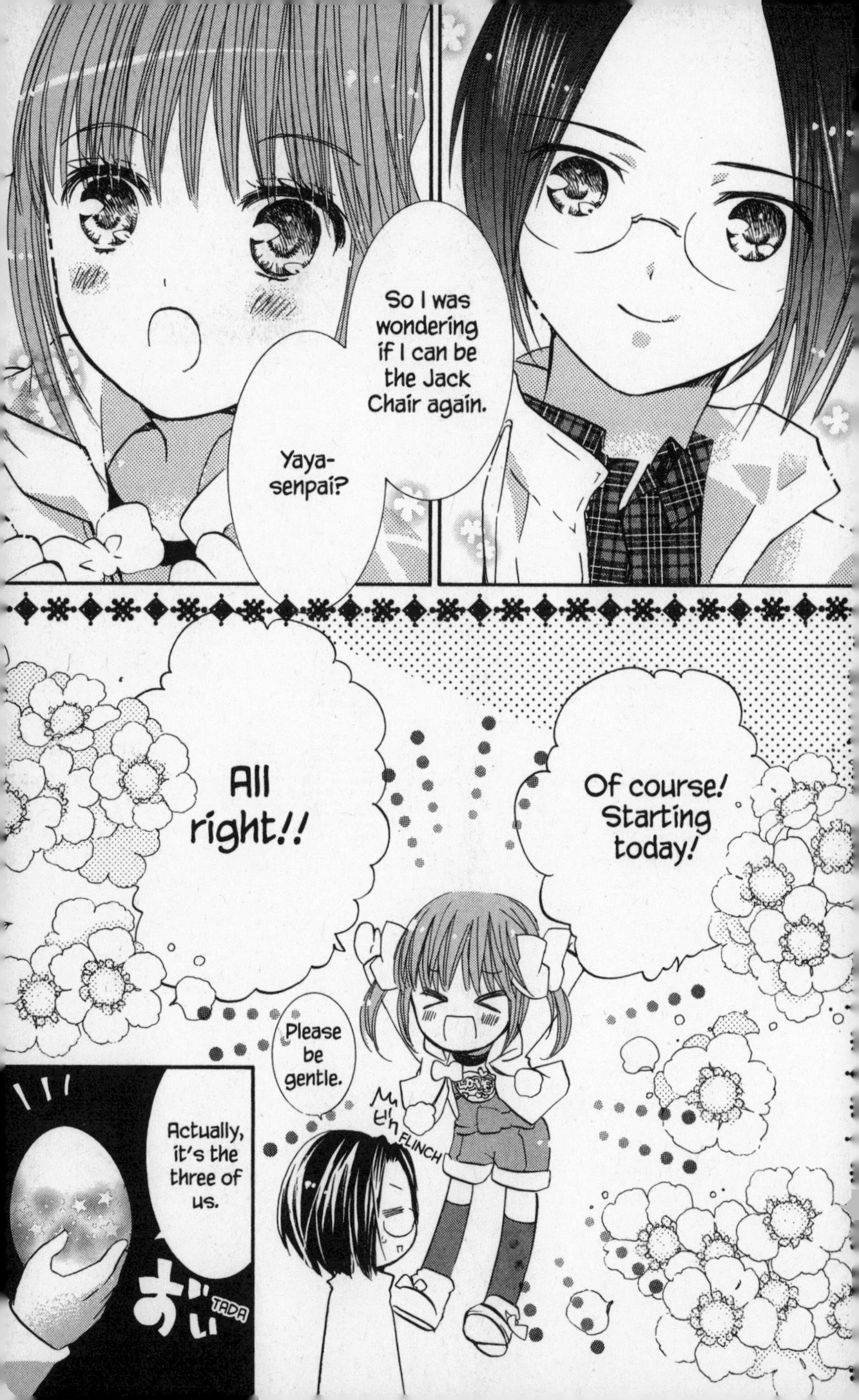
So I was wondering if I can be the Jack Chair again.
Yaya-senpai?
Of course! Starting today!
All right!!
Please be gentle.
FLINCH
Actually, it's the three of us.
TADA

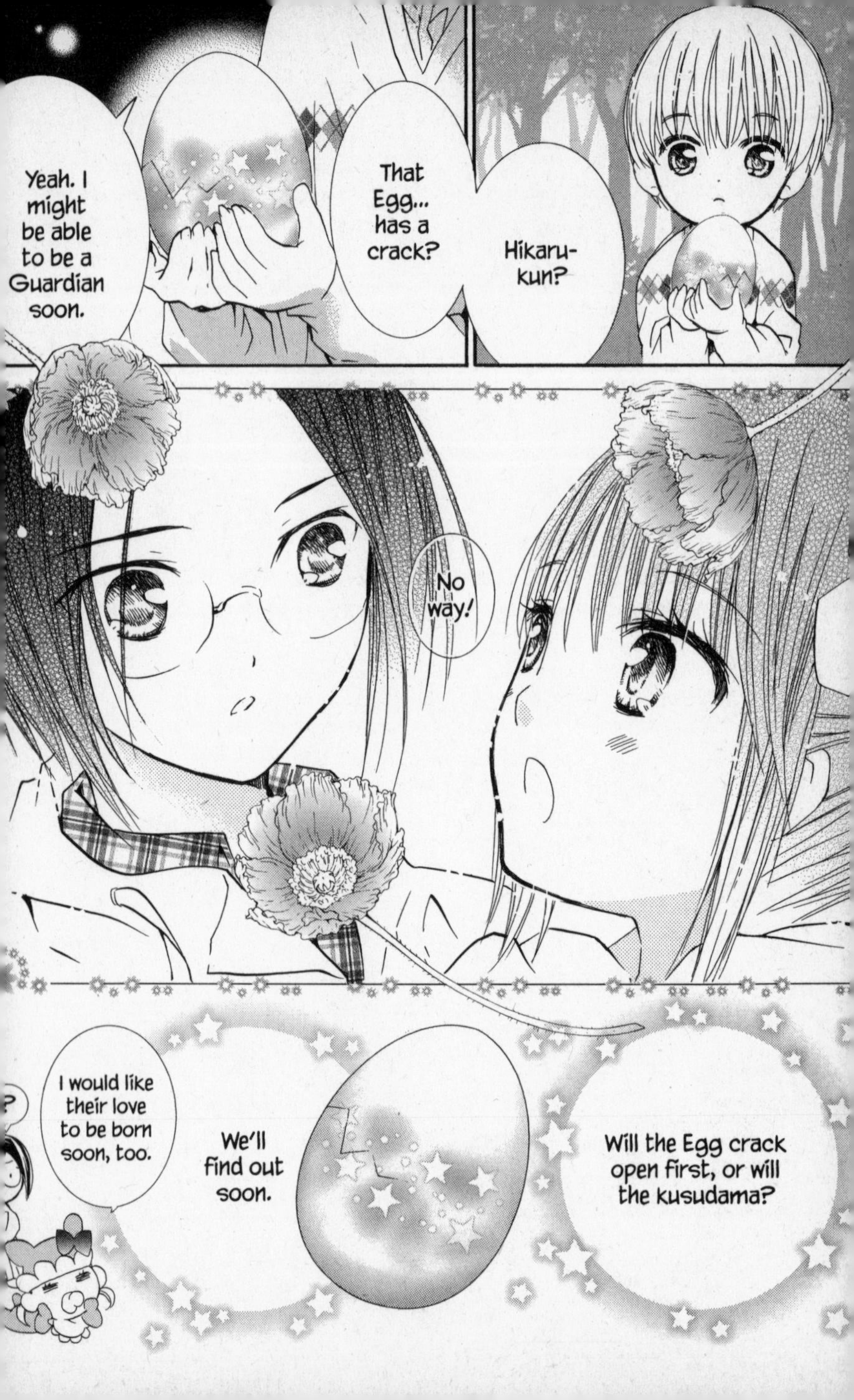
Hikaru-kun?
That Egg... has a crack?
Yeah. I might be able to be a Guardian soon.
No way!
Will the Egg crack open first, or will the kusudama?
We'll find out soon.
I would like their love to be born soon, too.
?

Shugo Chara!

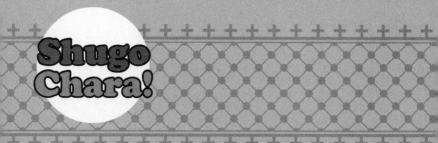

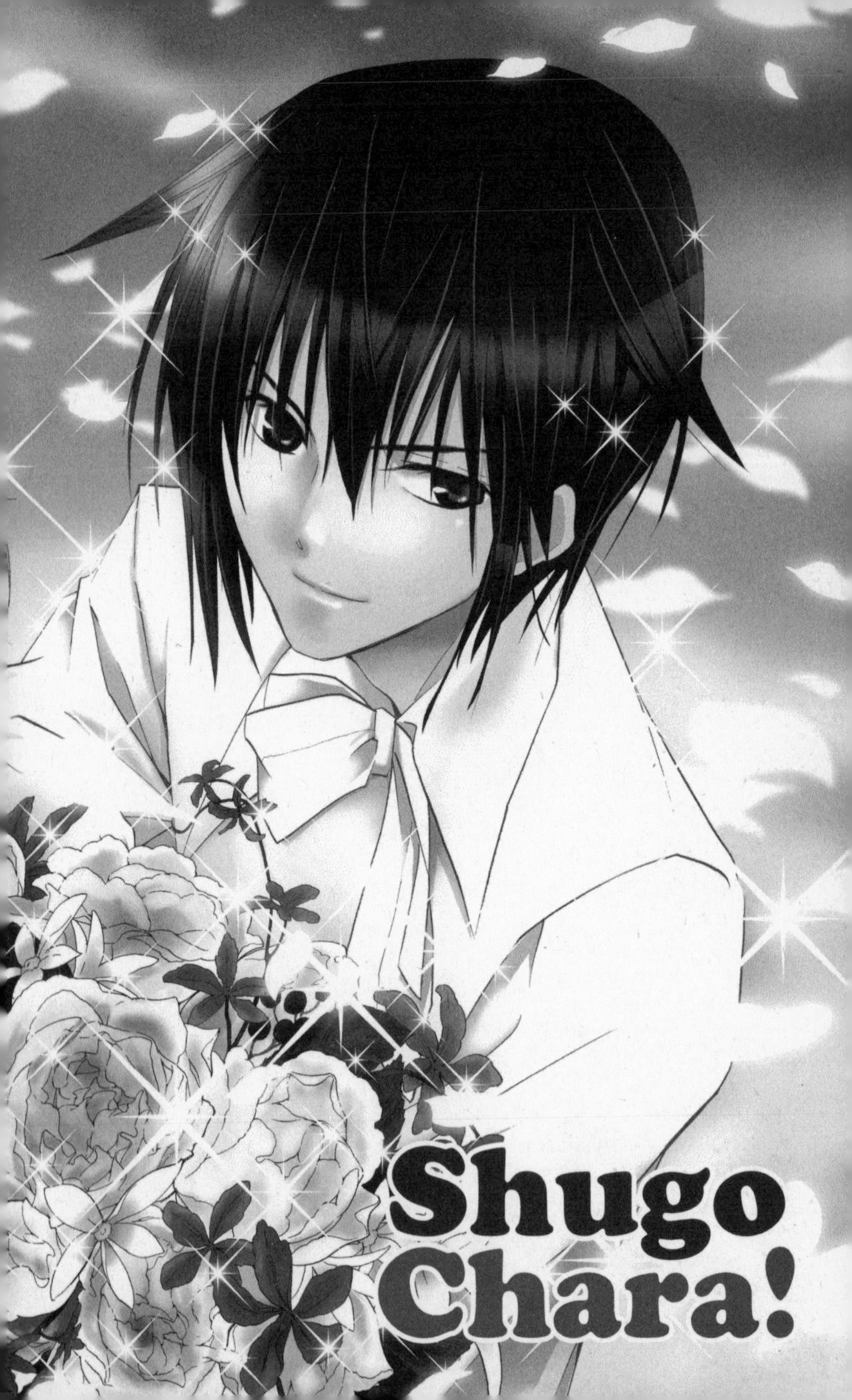
Shugo
Chara!

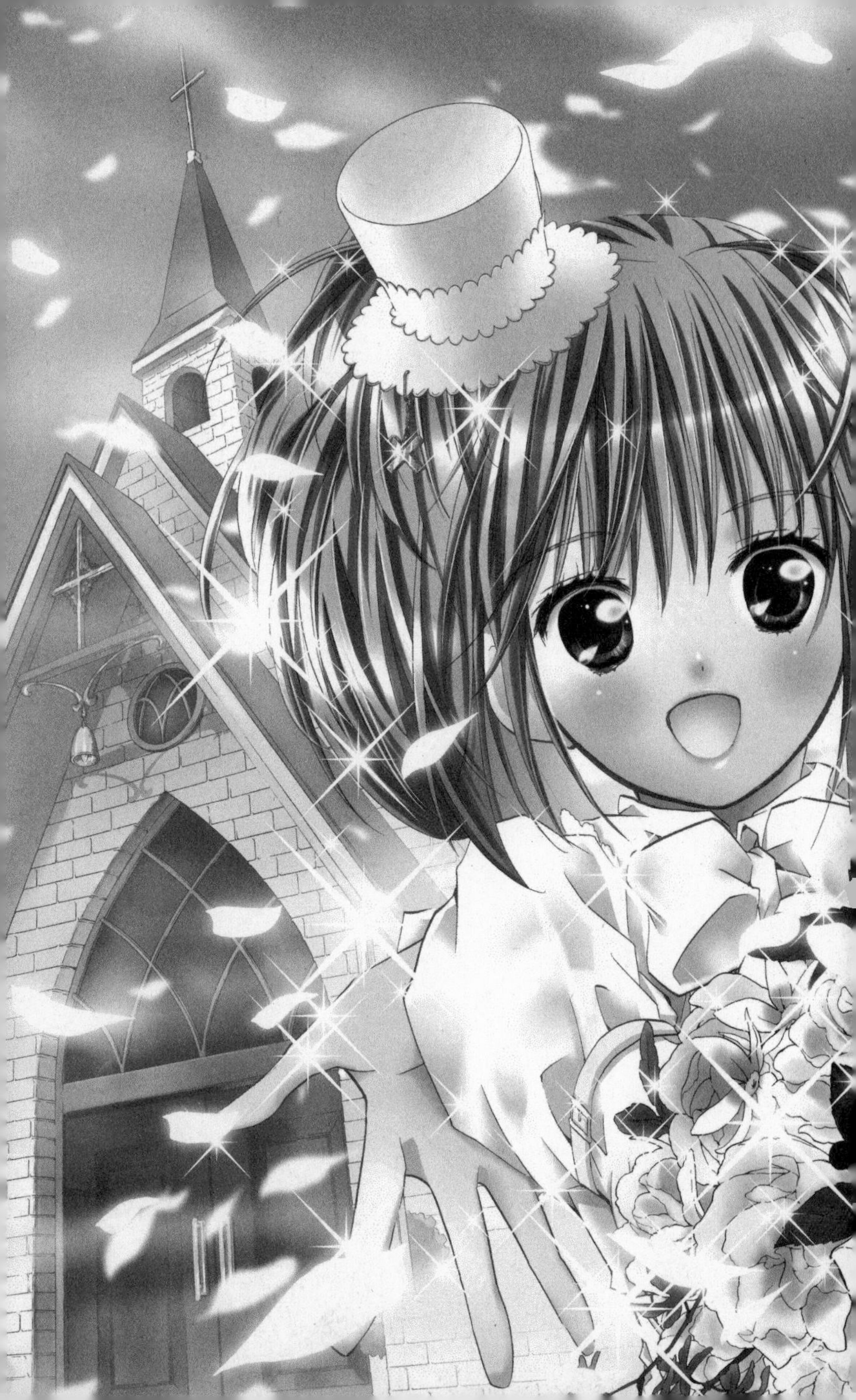

Shugo Chara!

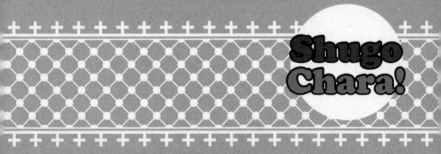

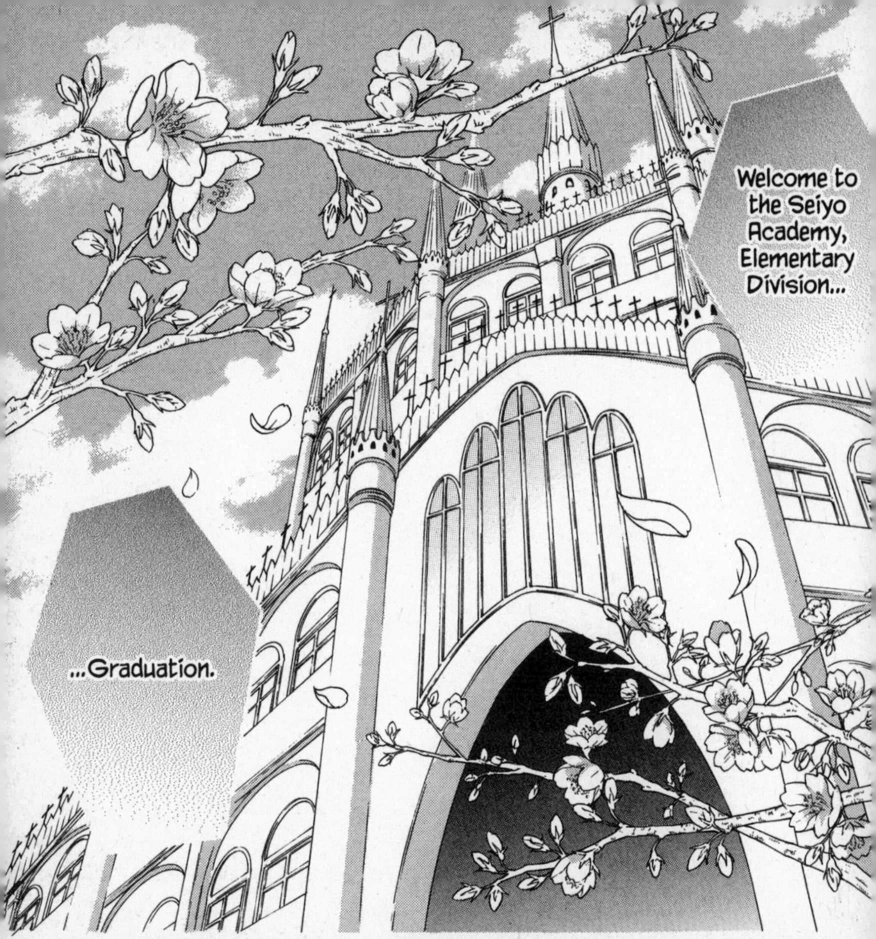
Welcome to the Seiyo Academy, Elementary Division...
...Graduation.

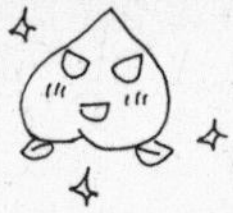

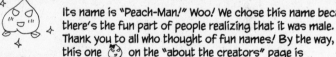

Its name is "Peach-Man!" Woo! We chose this name because there's the fun part of people realizing that it was male. Thank you to all who thought of fun names! By the way, this one on the "about the creators" page is Peach-Woman. What, there's two of them!? Yes, because there are two of us.

So this concludes our Q&A. Thank you so very much ♡♡♡ Please read our afterword!

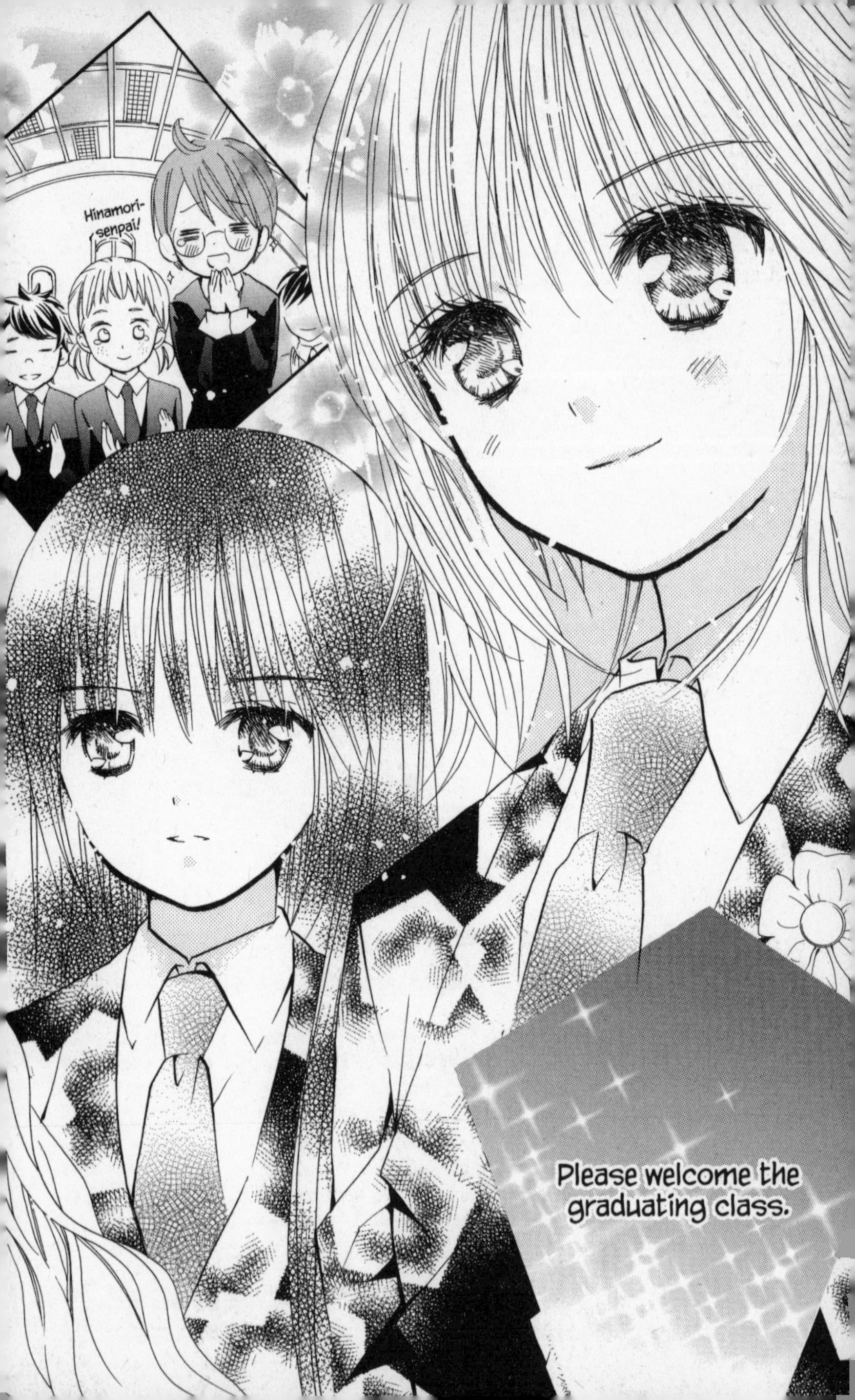
Hinamori-senpai!
Please welcome the graduating class.

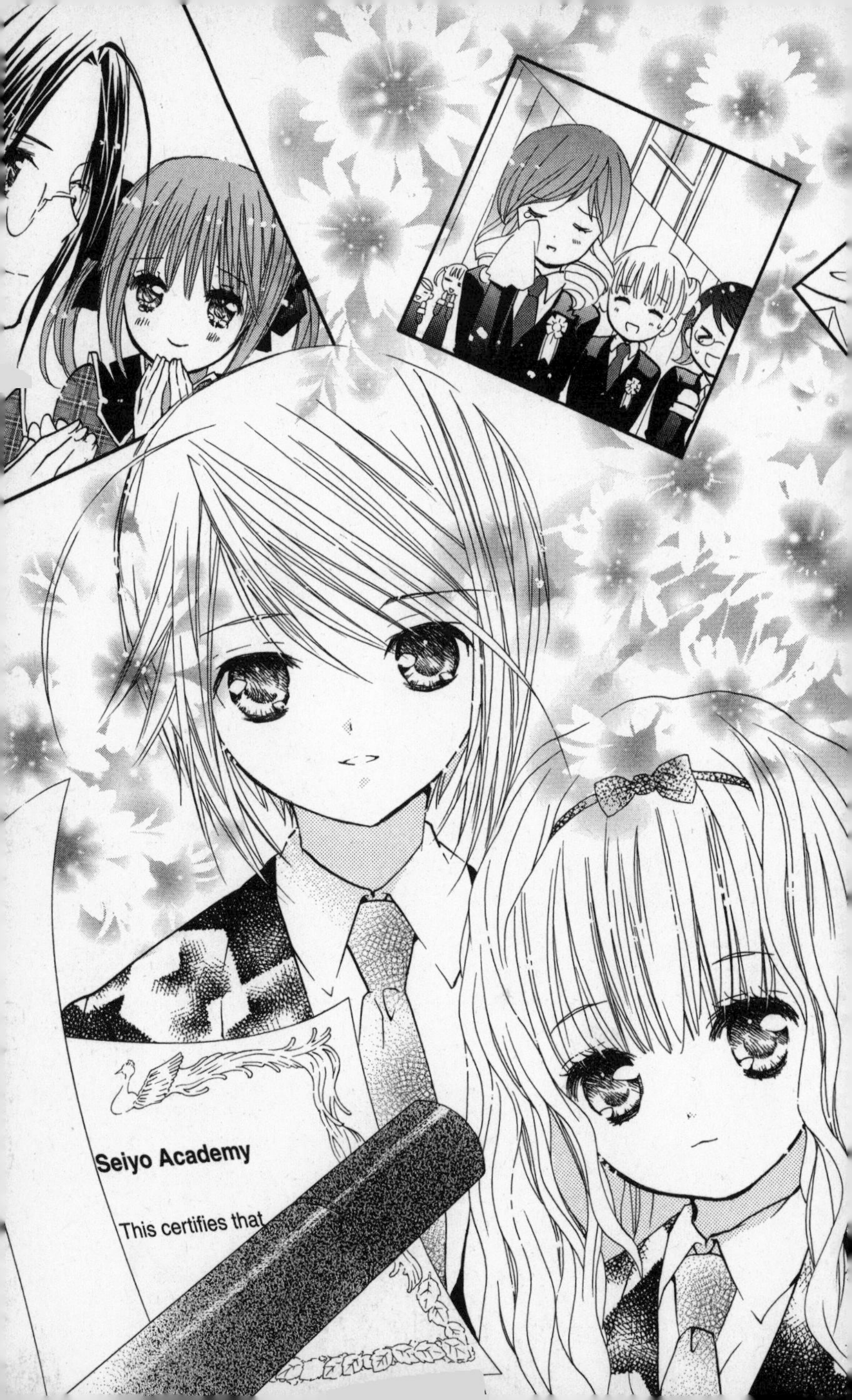
Seiyo Academy
This certifies that

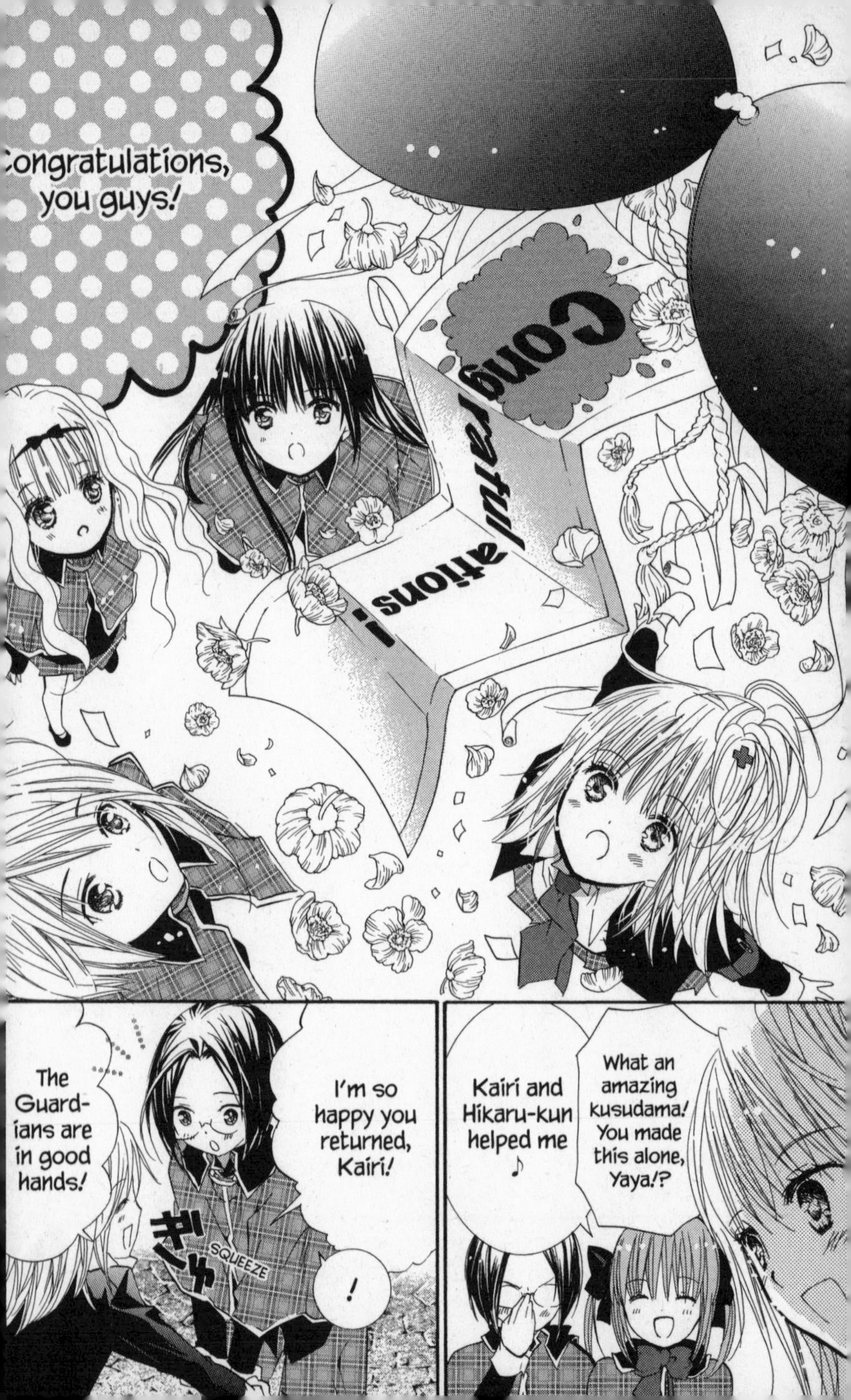
Congratulations, you guys!
Congratulations!
What an amazing kusudama! You made this alone, Yaya!?
Kairi and Hikaru-kun helped me ♪
I'm so happy you returned, Kairi!
The Guard-ians are in good hands!
SQUEEZE
!

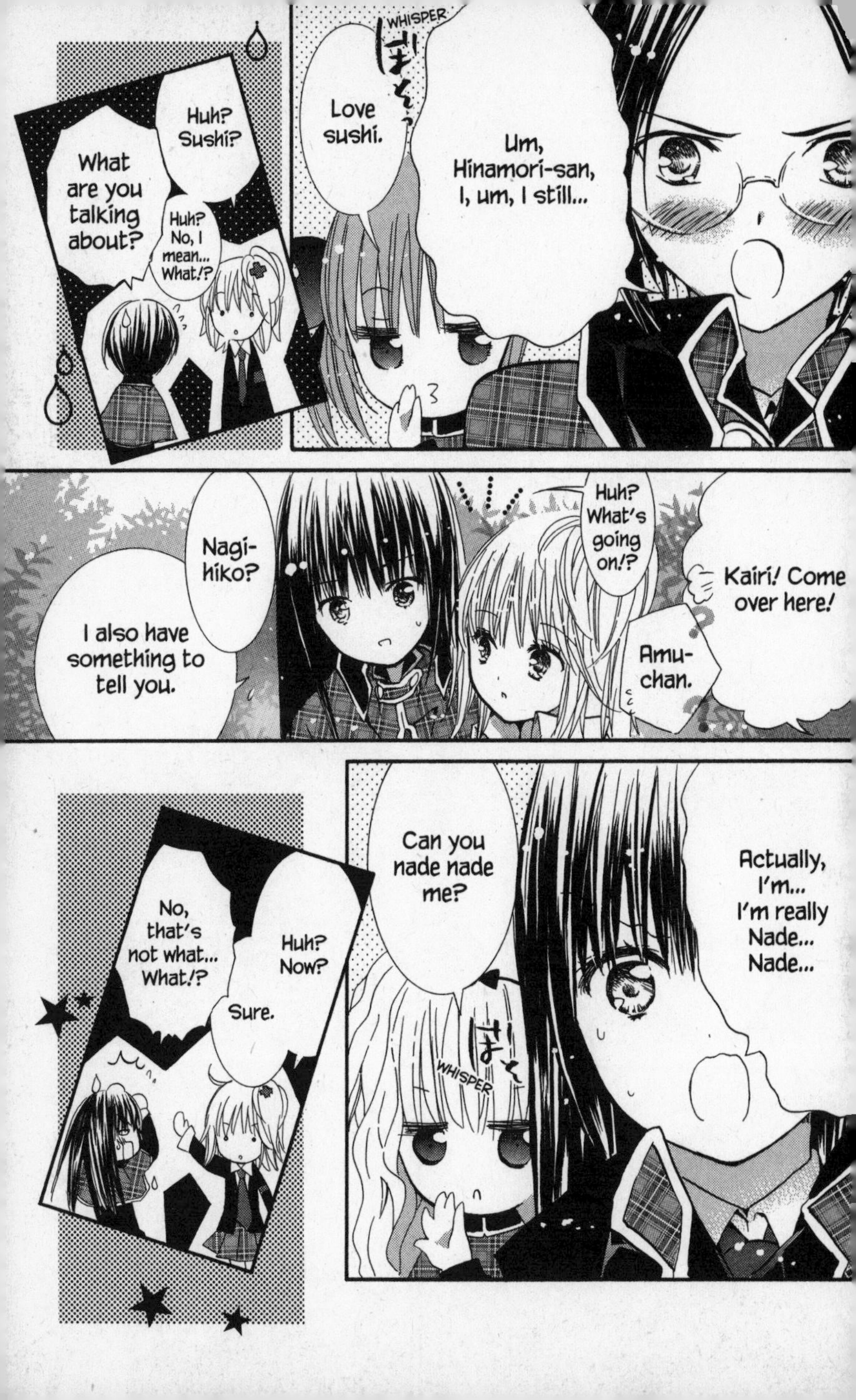
Um, Hinamori-san, I, um, I still...
WHISPER
ぼそっ
Love sushi.
Huh? Sushi?
What are you talking about?
Huh? No, I mean... What!?
Kairi! Come over here!
Amu-chan.
Huh? What's going on!?
Nagi-hiko?
I also have something to tell you.
Actually, I'm... I'm really Nade... Nade...
Can you nade nade me?
ぼそっ
WHISPER
Huh? Now?
Sure.
No, that's not what... What!?

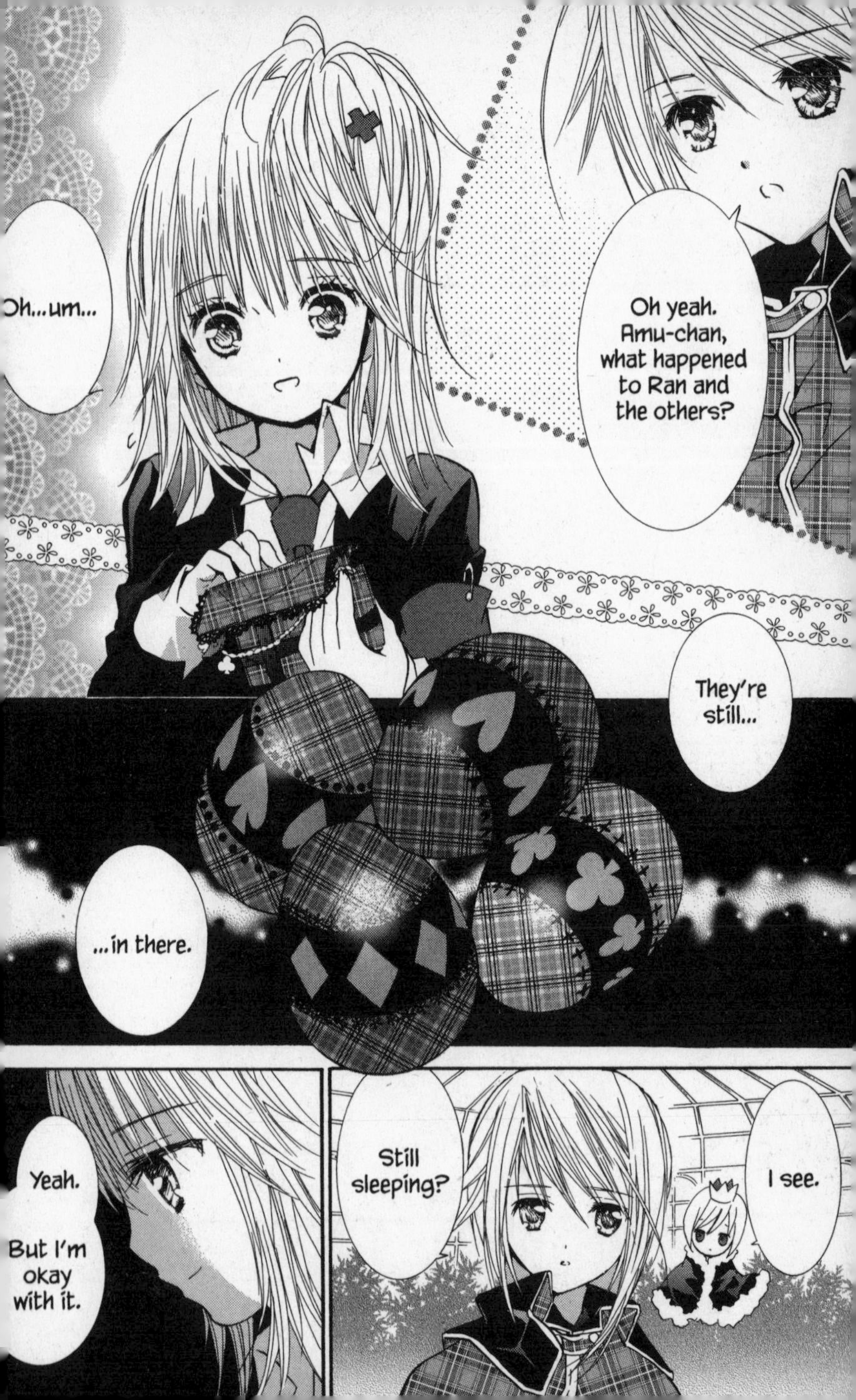
Oh yeah. Amu-chan, what happened to Ran and the others?
Oh...um...
They're still...
...in there.
I see.
Still sleeping?
Yeah.
But I'm okay with it.

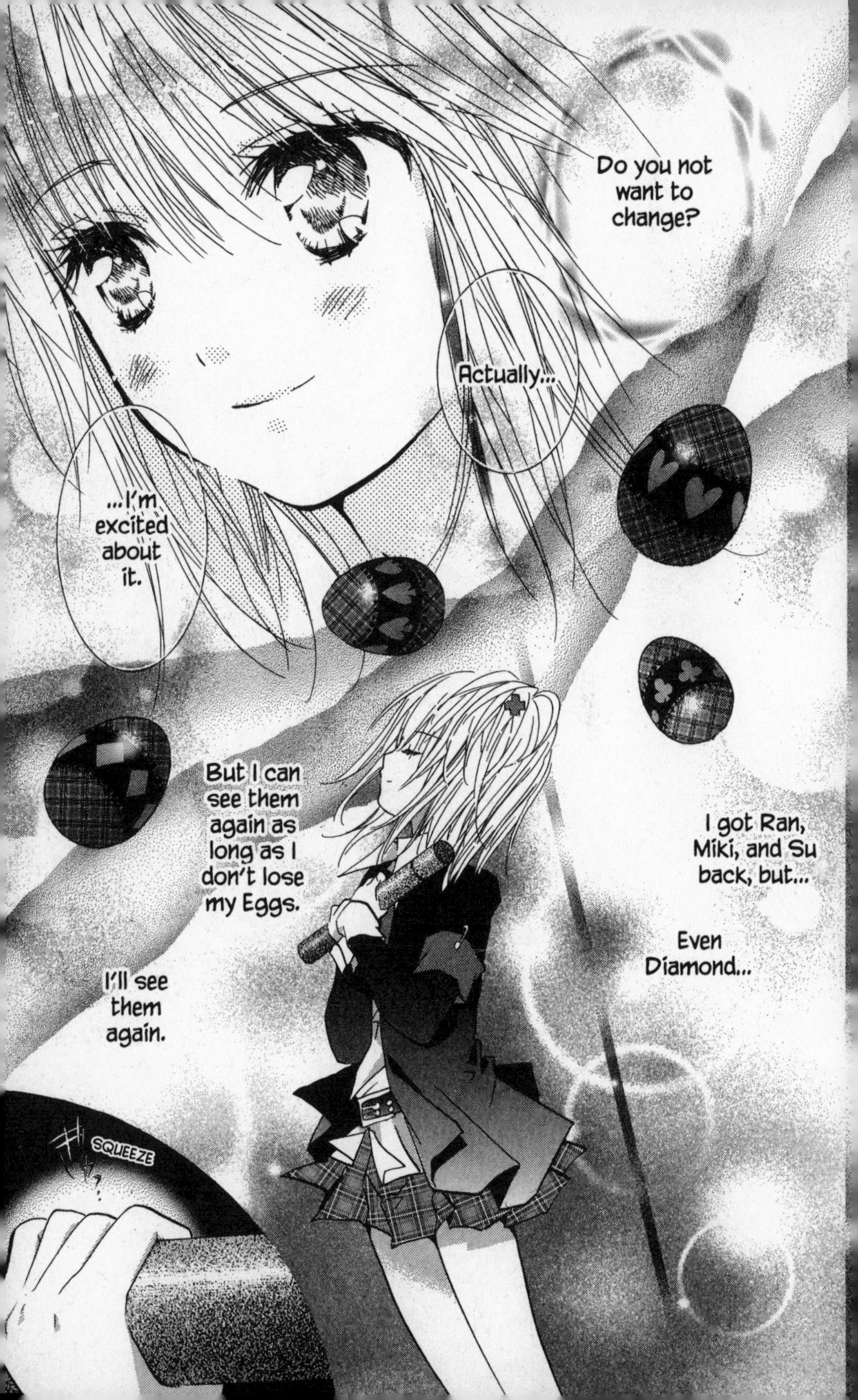
Do you not want to change?
Actually...
...I'm excited about it.
I got Ran, Miki, and Su back, but...
Even Diamond...
But I can see them again as long as I don't lose my Eggs.
I'll see them again.
SQUEEZE

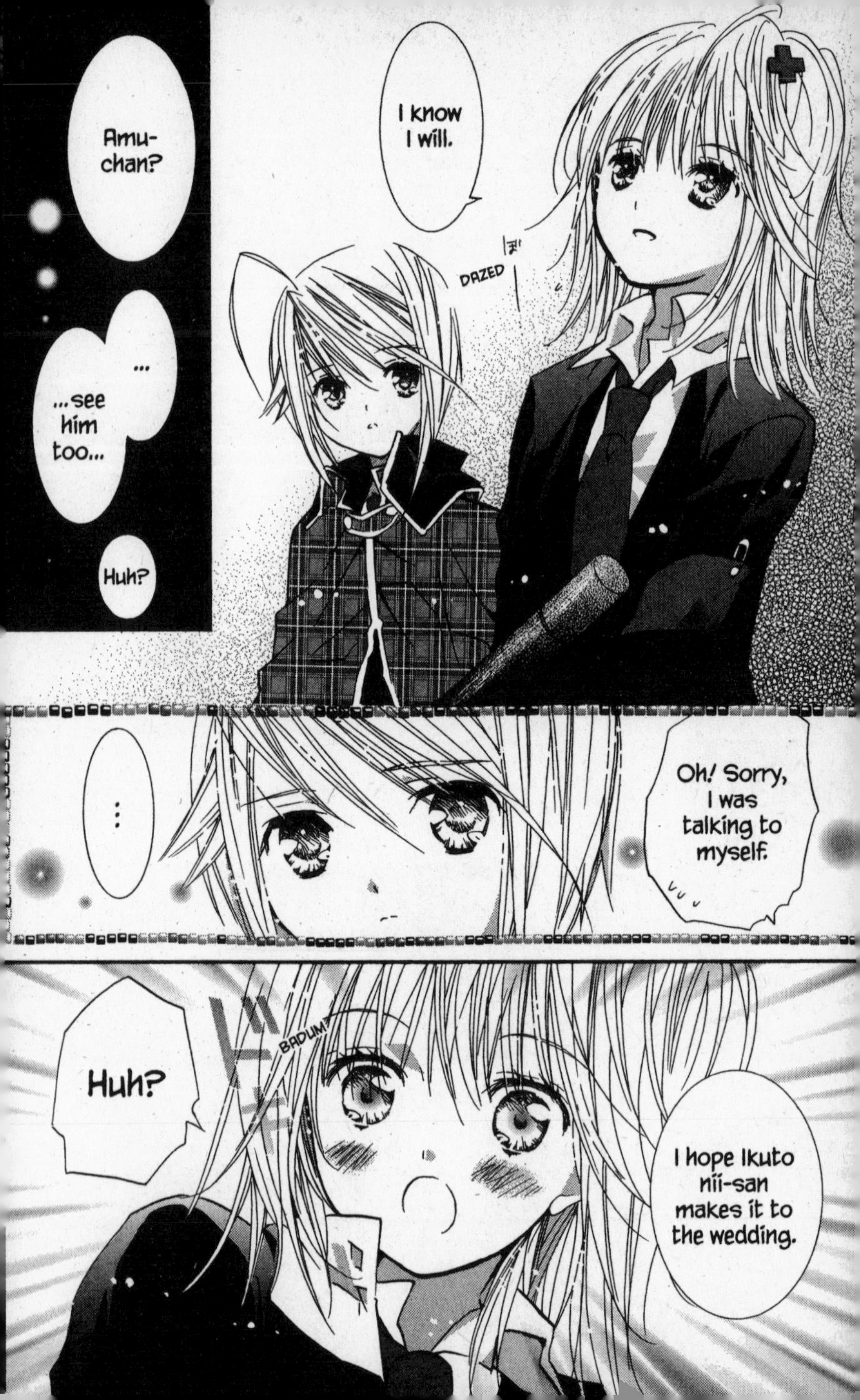
I know I will.
DAZED
Amu-chan?
...
...see him too...
Huh?
Oh! Sorry, I was talking to myself.
...
I hope Ikuto nii-san makes it to the wedding.
BADUM
Huh?

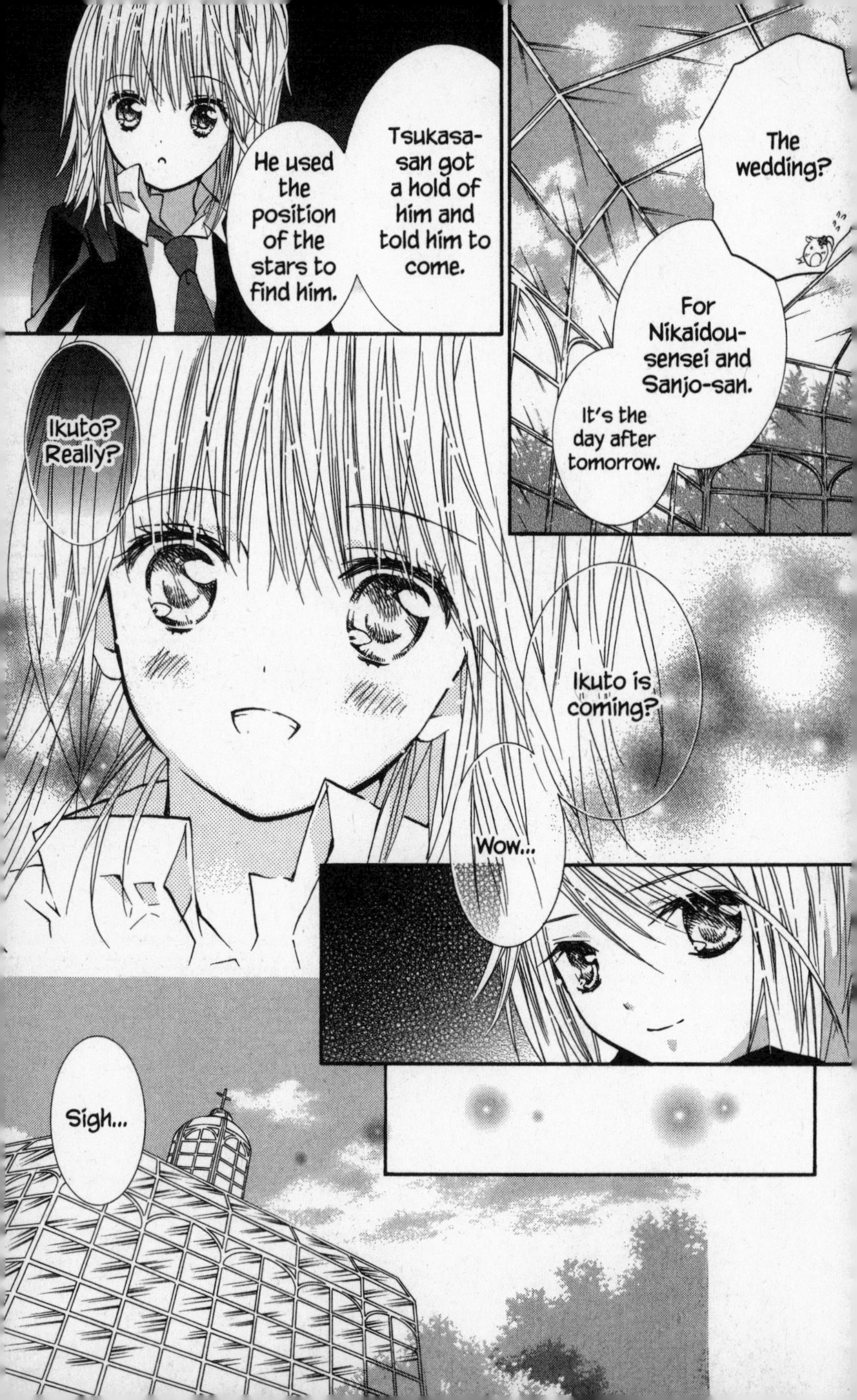
The wedding?
For Nikaidou-sensei and Sanjo-san.
It's the day after tomorrow.
Tsukasa-san got a hold of him and told him to come.
He used the position of the stars to find him.
Ikuto? Really?
Ikuto is coming?
Wow...
Sigh...

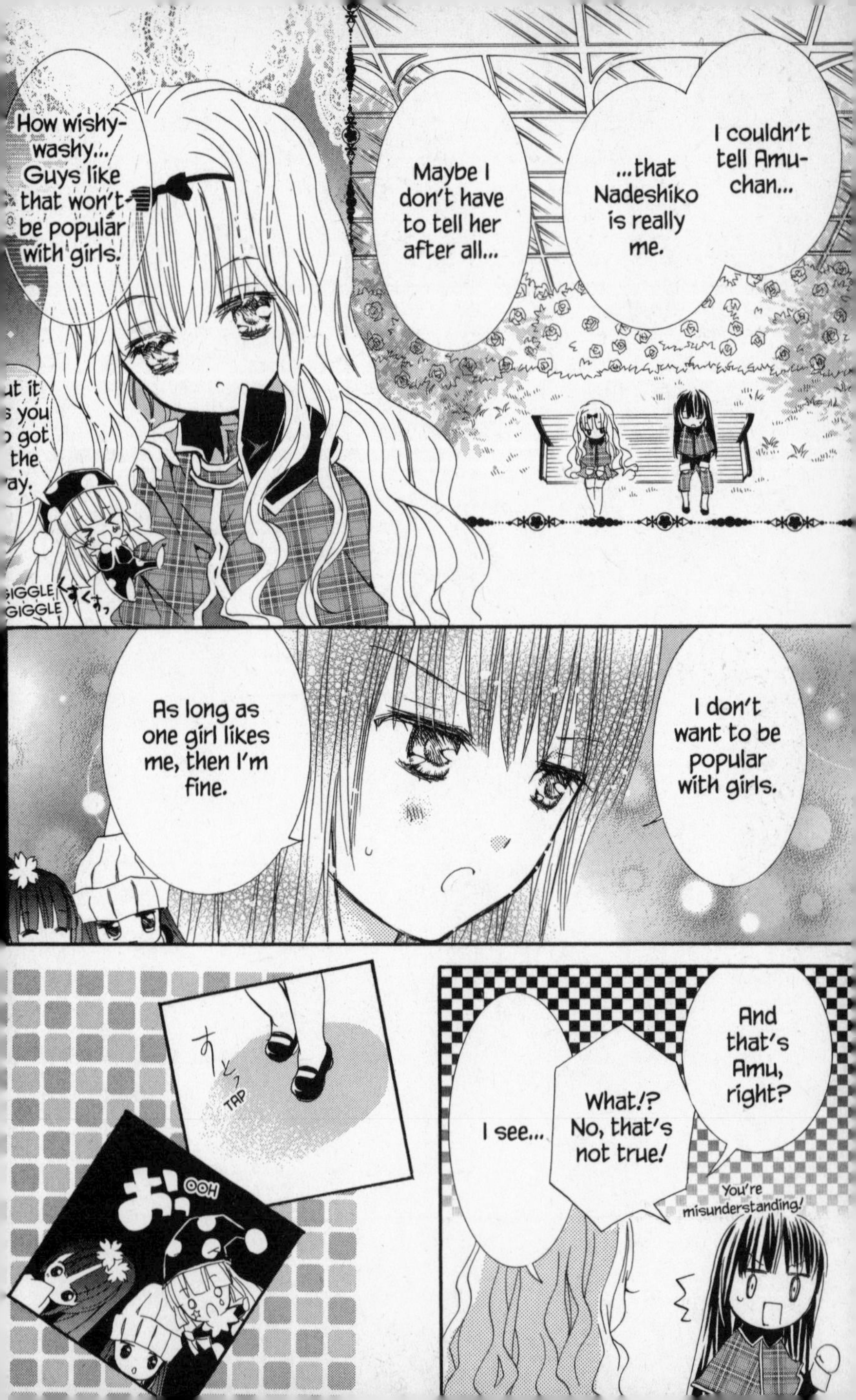
I couldn't tell Amu-chan...
...that Nadeshiko is really me.
Maybe I don't have to tell her after all...
How wishy-washy... Guys like that won't be popular with girls.
GIGGLE GIGGLE
くすくすっ
I don't want to be popular with girls.
As long as one girl likes me, then I'm fine.
And that's Amu, right?
What!? No, that's not true!
You're misunderstanding!
I see...
すとっ
TAP
おっ
OOH

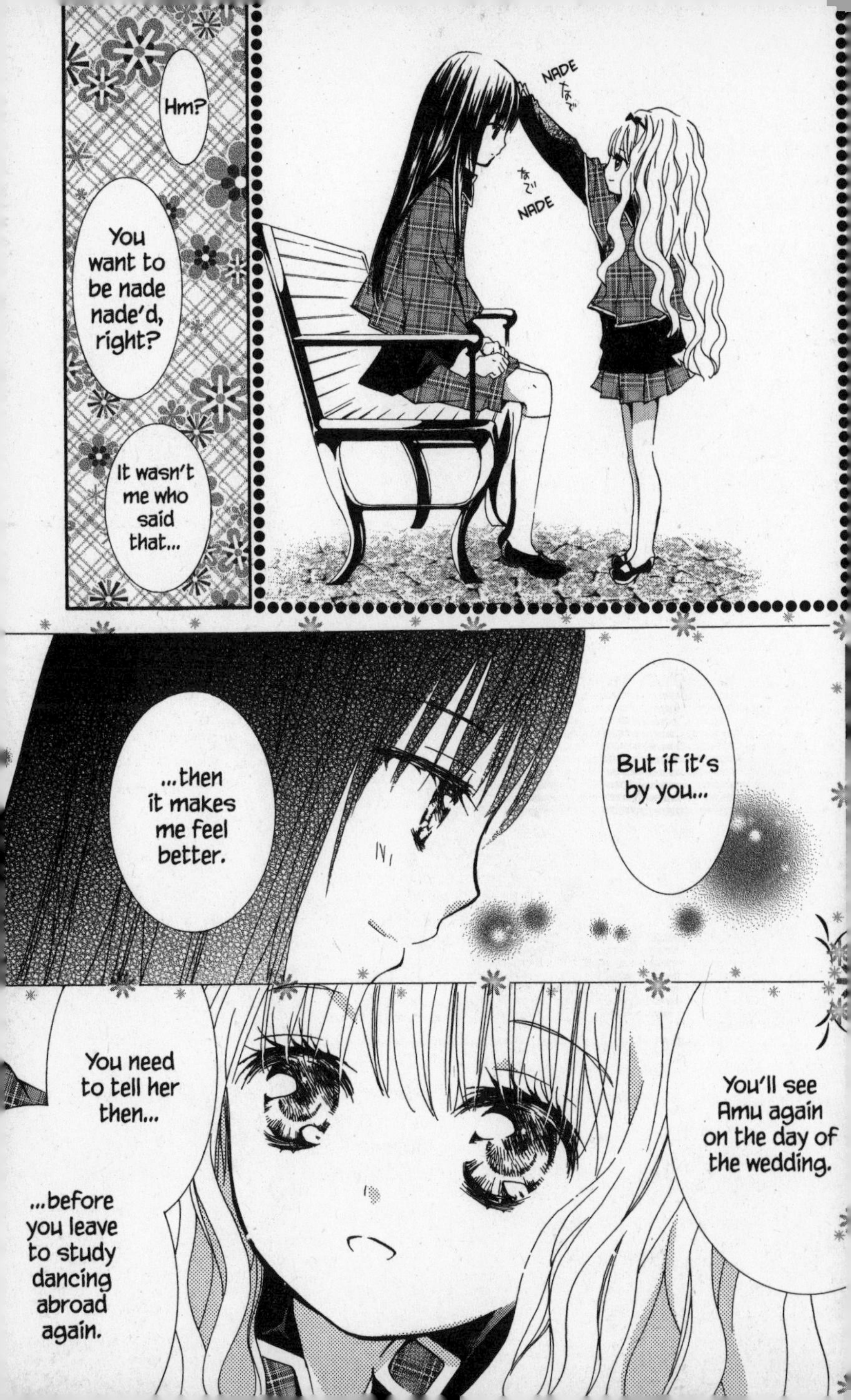
NADE なで
なで NADE
Hm?
You want to be nade nade'd, right?
It wasn't me who said that...
But if it's by you...
...then it makes me feel better.
You'll see Amu again on the day of the wedding.
You need to tell her then...
...before you leave to study dancing abroad again.

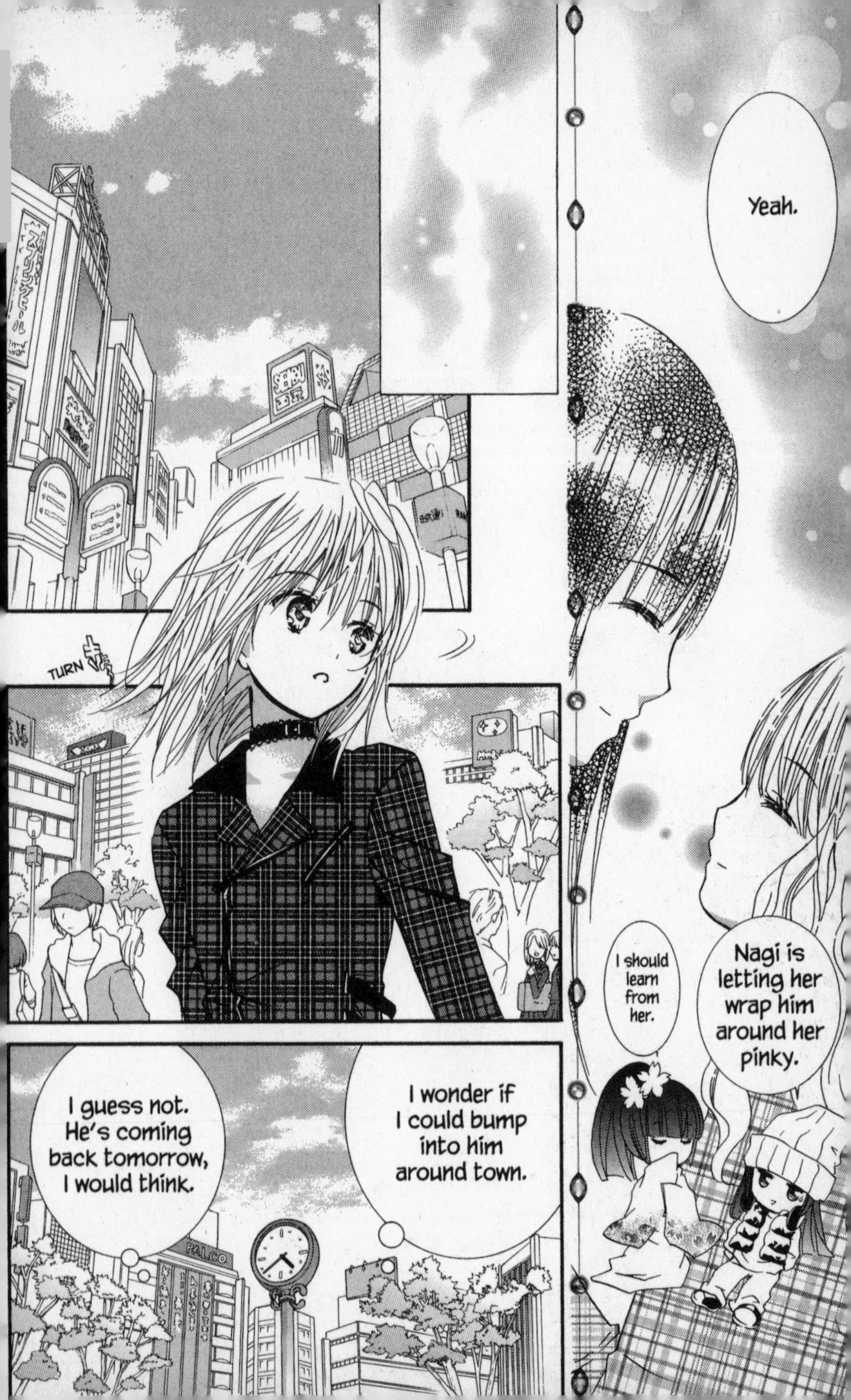
Yeah.
Nagi is letting her wrap him around her pinky.
I should learn from her.
TURN
I wonder if I could bump into him around town.
I guess not. He's coming back tomorrow, I would think.

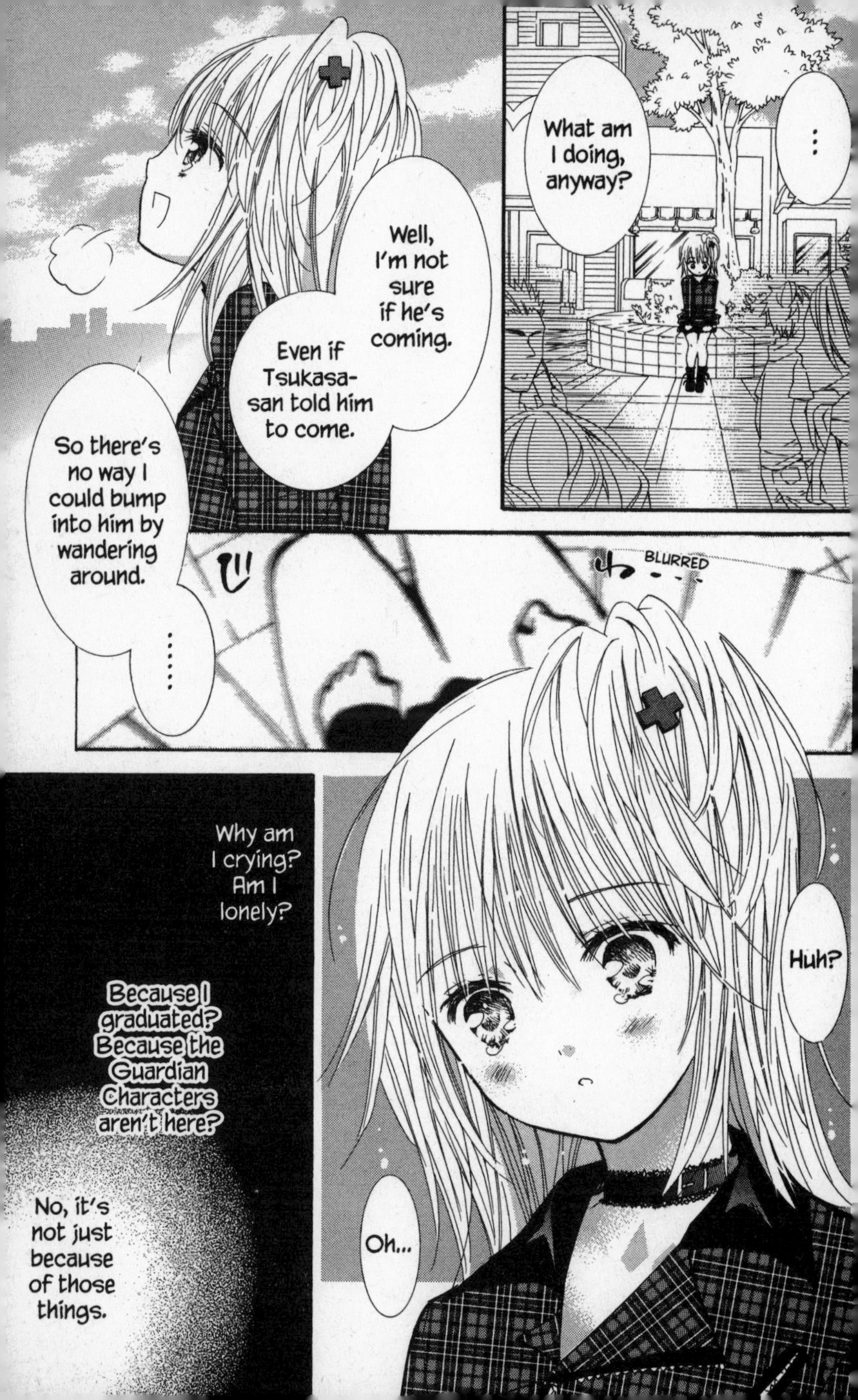

...
What am I doing, anyway?
Well, I'm not sure if he's coming.
Even if Tsukasa-san told him to come.
So there's no way I could bump into him by wandering around.
BLURRED
......
Huh?
Oh...
Why am I crying? Am I lonely?
Because I graduated? Because the Guardian Characters aren't here?
No, it's not just because of those things.

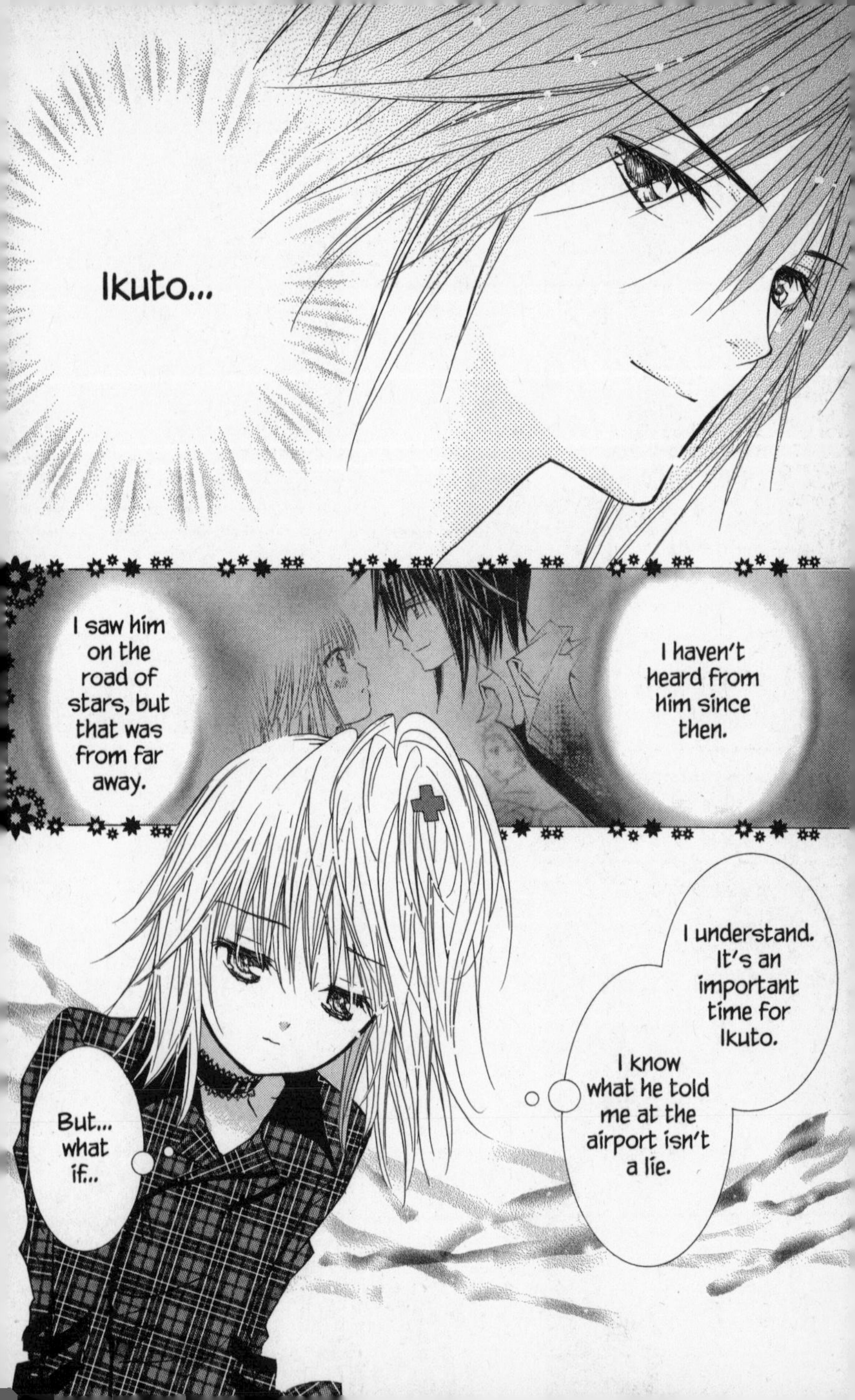
Ikuto...
I saw him on the road of stars, but that was from far away.
I haven't heard from him since then.
I understand. It's an important time for Ikuto.
I know what he told me at the airport isn't a lie.
But... what if...

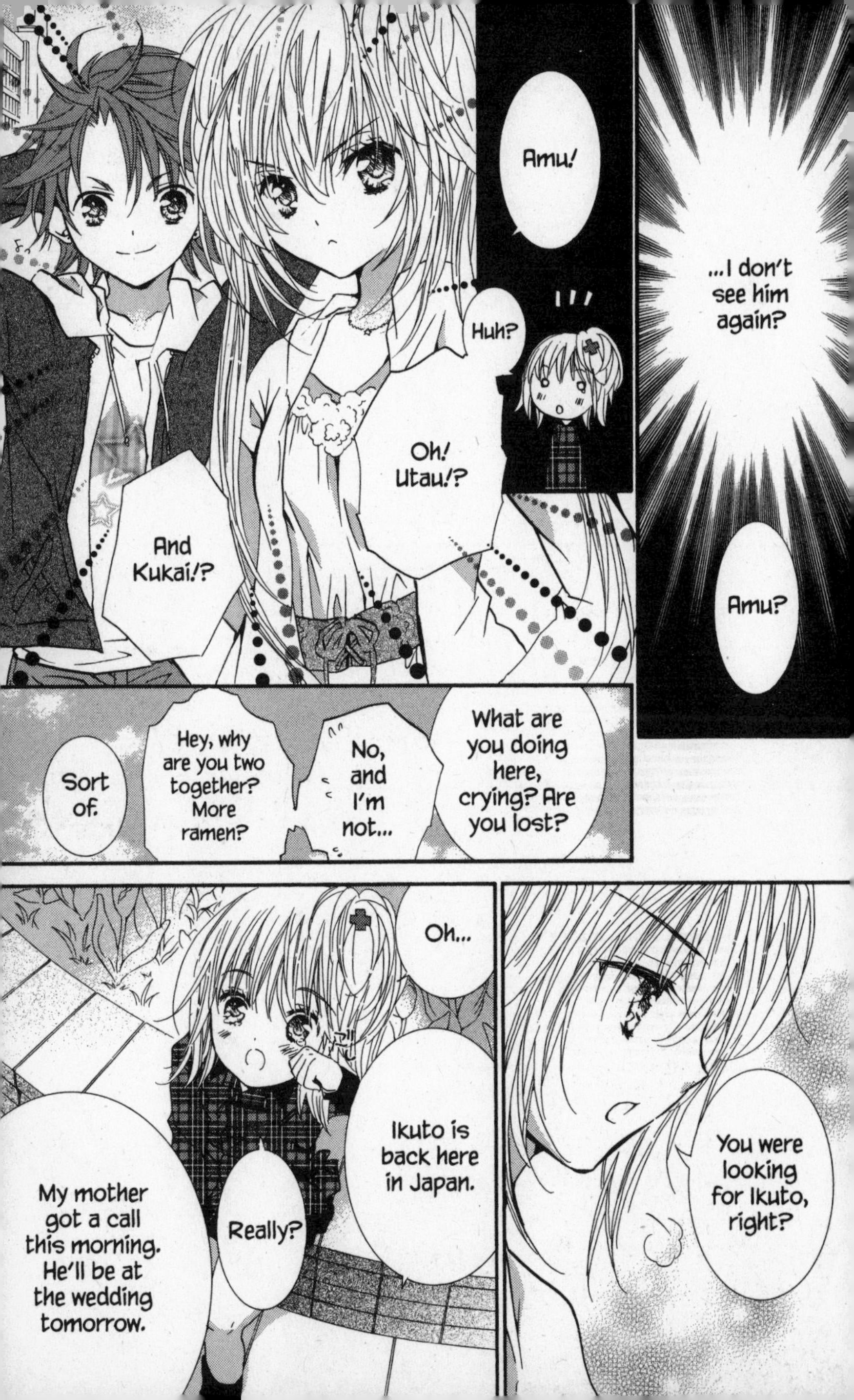

...I don't see him again?
Amu?
Amu!
Huh?
Oh! Utau!?
And Kukai!?
What are you doing here, crying? Are you lost?
No, and I'm not...
Hey, why are you two together? More ramen?
Sort of.
You were looking for Ikuto, right?
Oh...
Ikuto is back here in Japan.
Really?
My mother got a call this morning. He'll be at the wedding tomorrow.

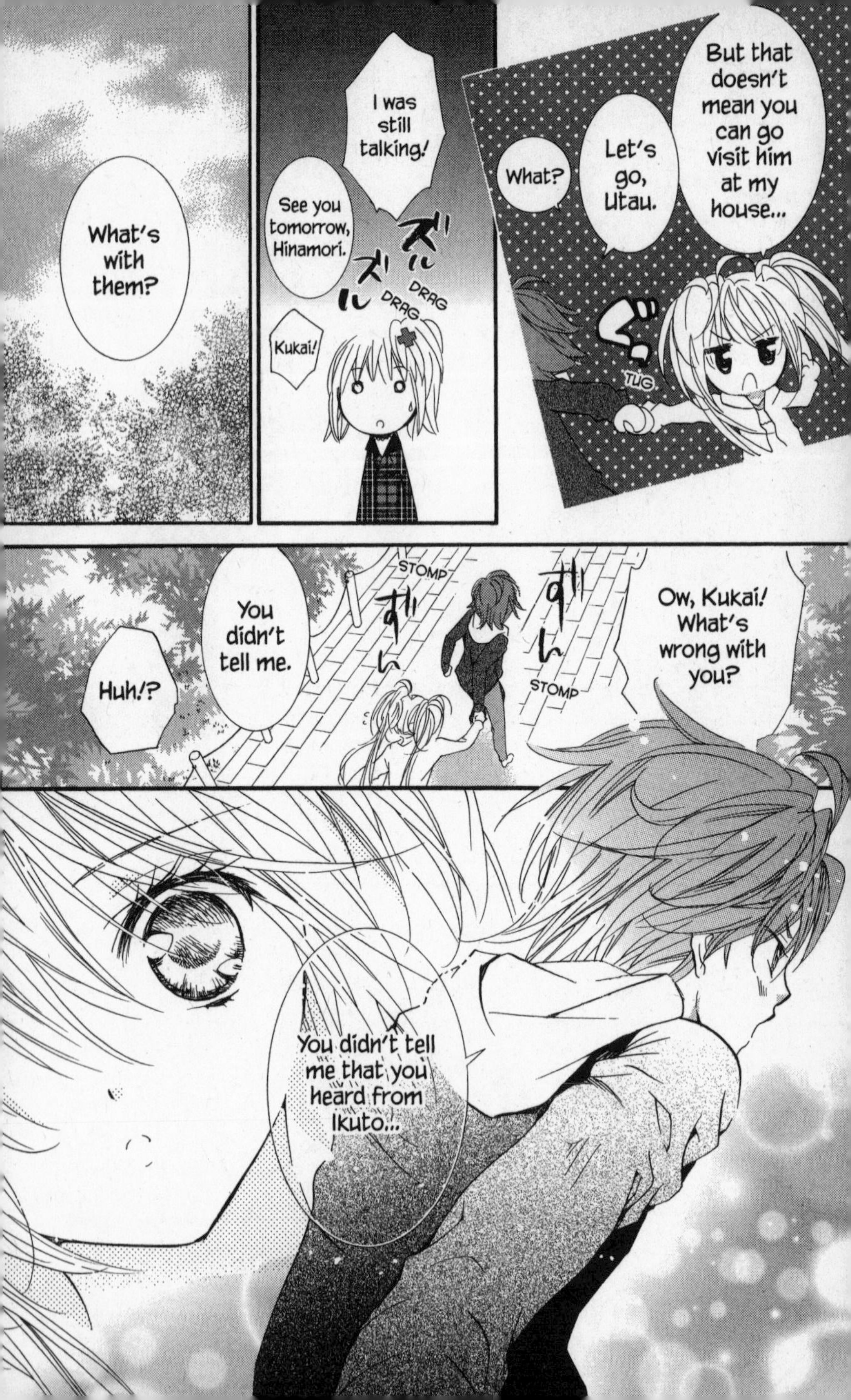
But that doesn't mean you can go visit him at my house...
Let's go, Utau.
What?
TUG
I was still talking!
See you tomorrow, Hinamori.
DRAG
DRAG
Kukai!
What's with them?
Ow, Kukai! What's wrong with you?
STOMP
STOMP
You didn't tell me.
Huh!?
You didn't tell me that you heard from Ikuto...

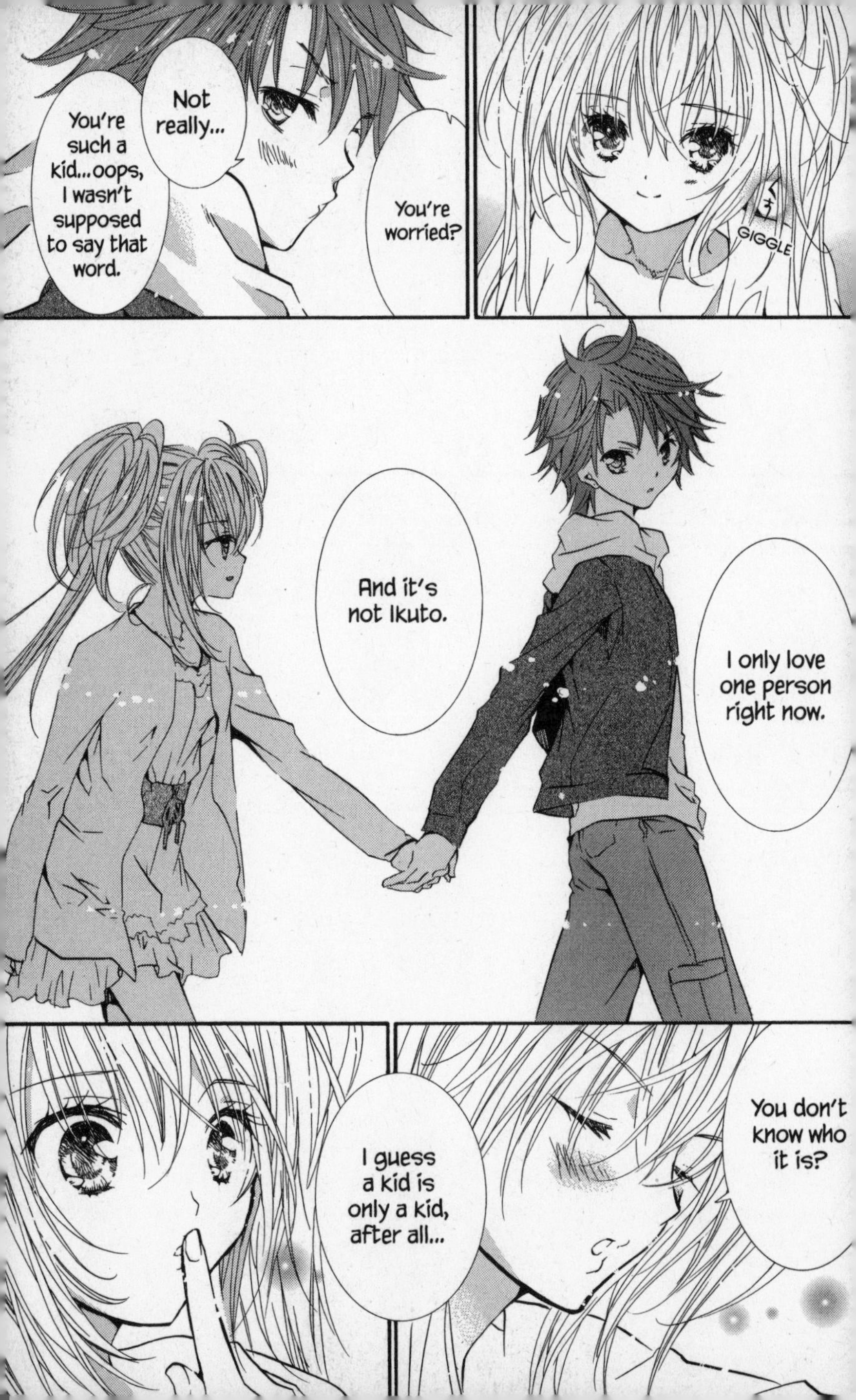
GIGGLE
You're worried?
Not really...
You're such a kid...oops, I wasn't supposed to say that word.
I only love one person right now.
And it's not Ikuto.
You don't know who it is?
I guess a kid is only a kid, after all...

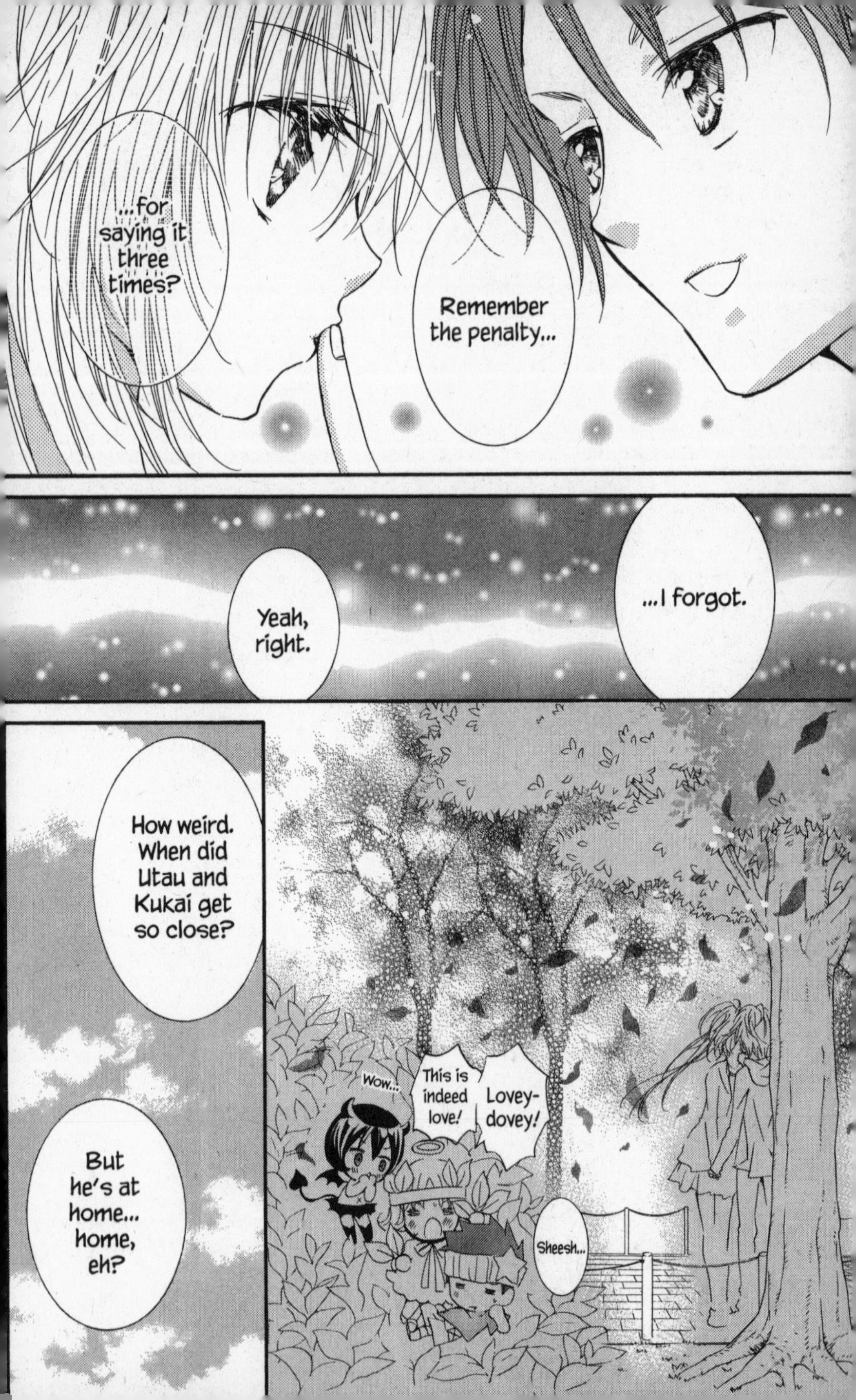
Remember the penalty...
...for saying it three times?
...I forgot.
Yeah, right.
Lovey-dovey!
This is indeed love!
Wow...
Sheesh...
How weird. When did Utau and Kukai get so close?
But he's at home... home, eh?

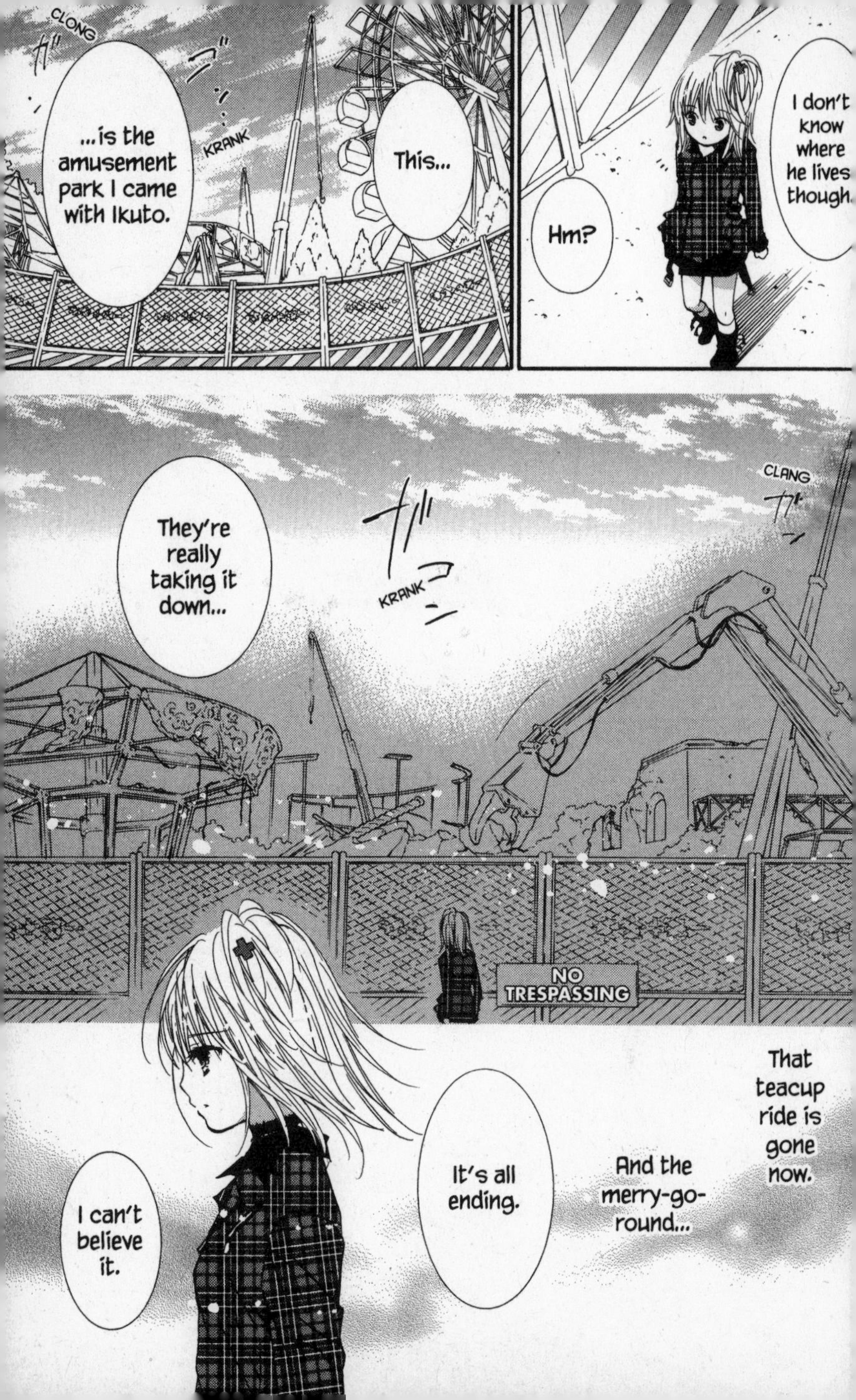
I don't know where he lives though.
Hm?
KRANK
This...
...is the amusement park I came with Ikuto.
CLONG
CLANG
KRANK
They're really taking it down...
NO TRESPASSING
That teacup ride is gone now.
And the merry-go-round...
It's all ending.
I can't believe it.

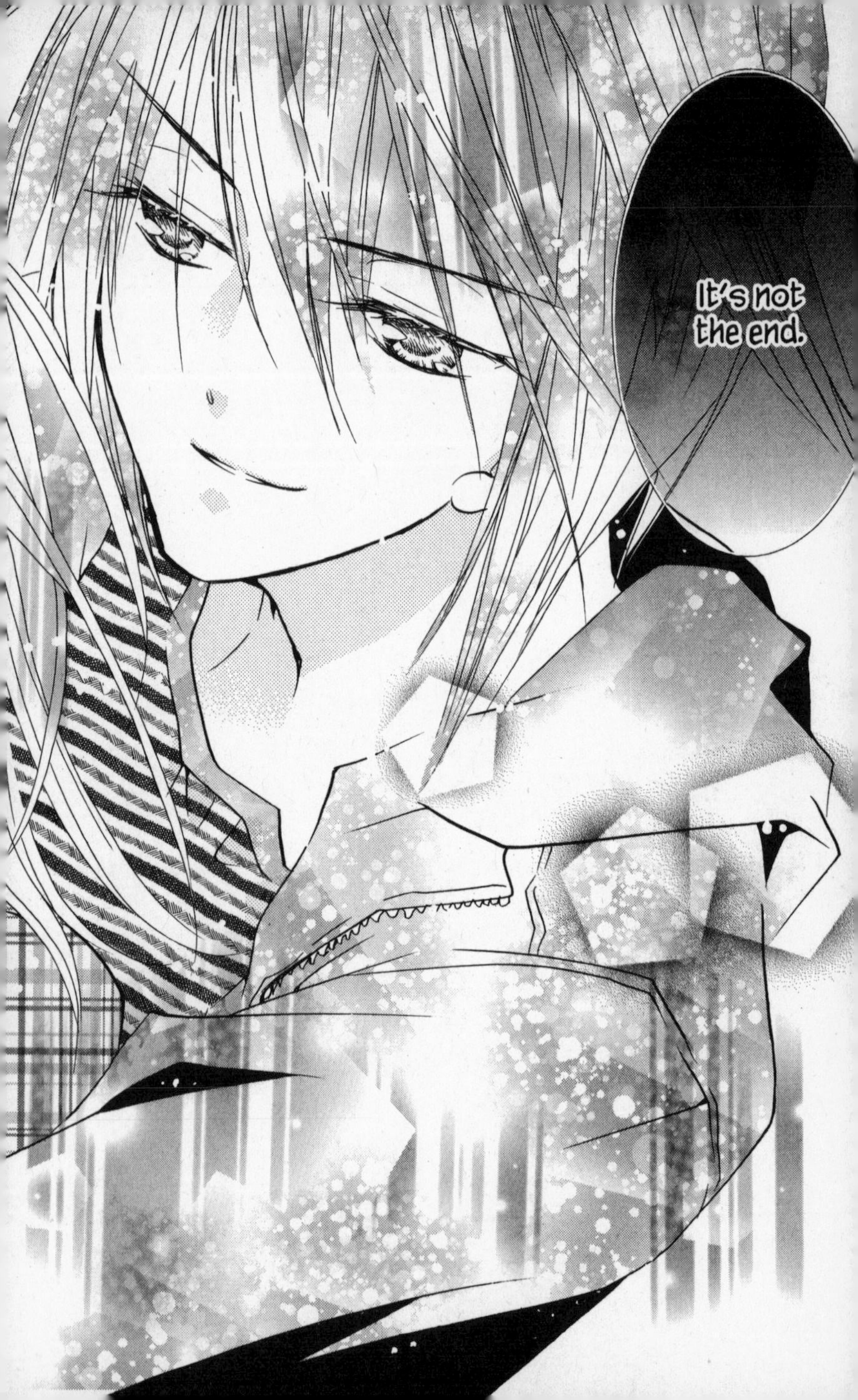
It's not the end.

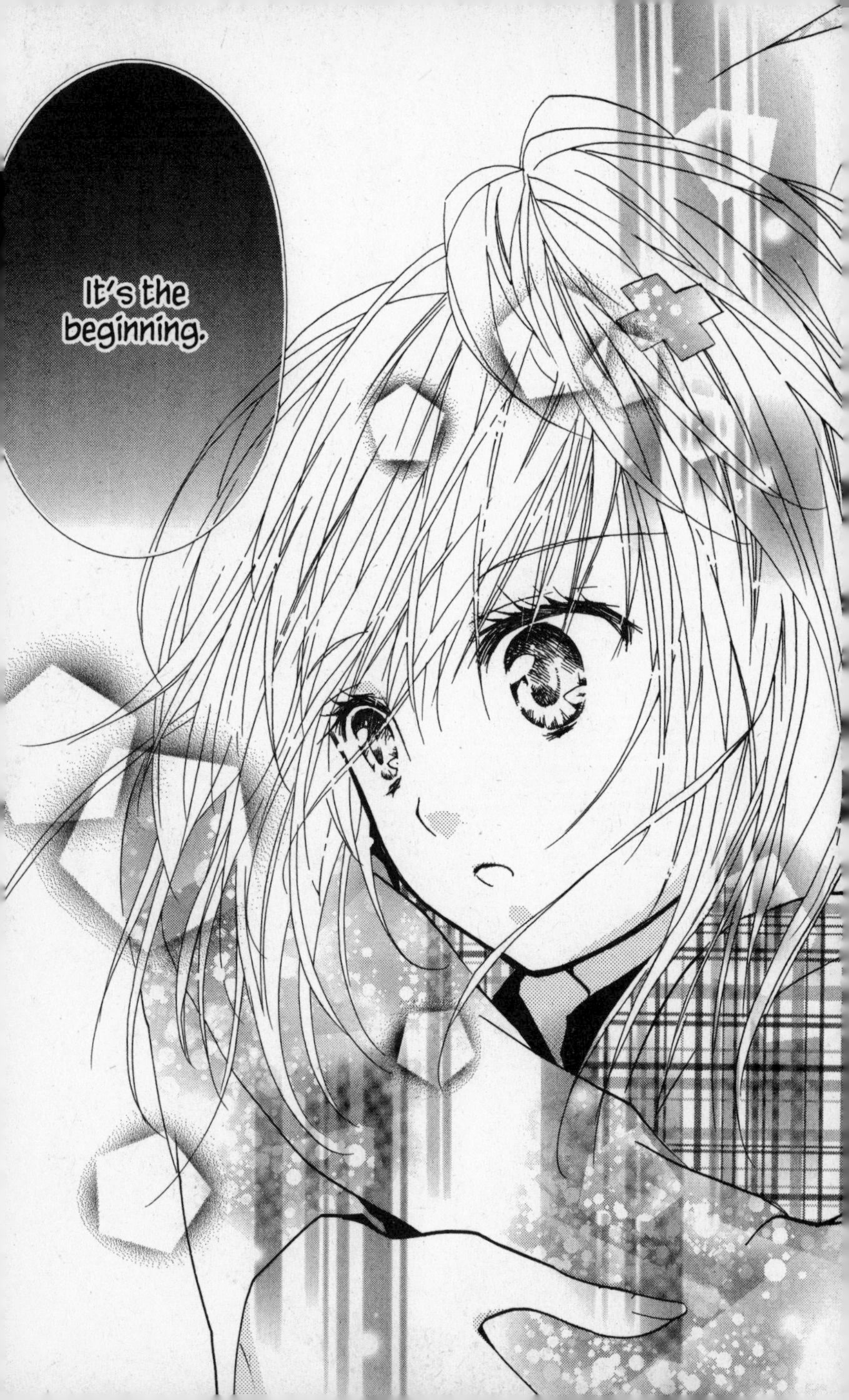
It's the beginning.

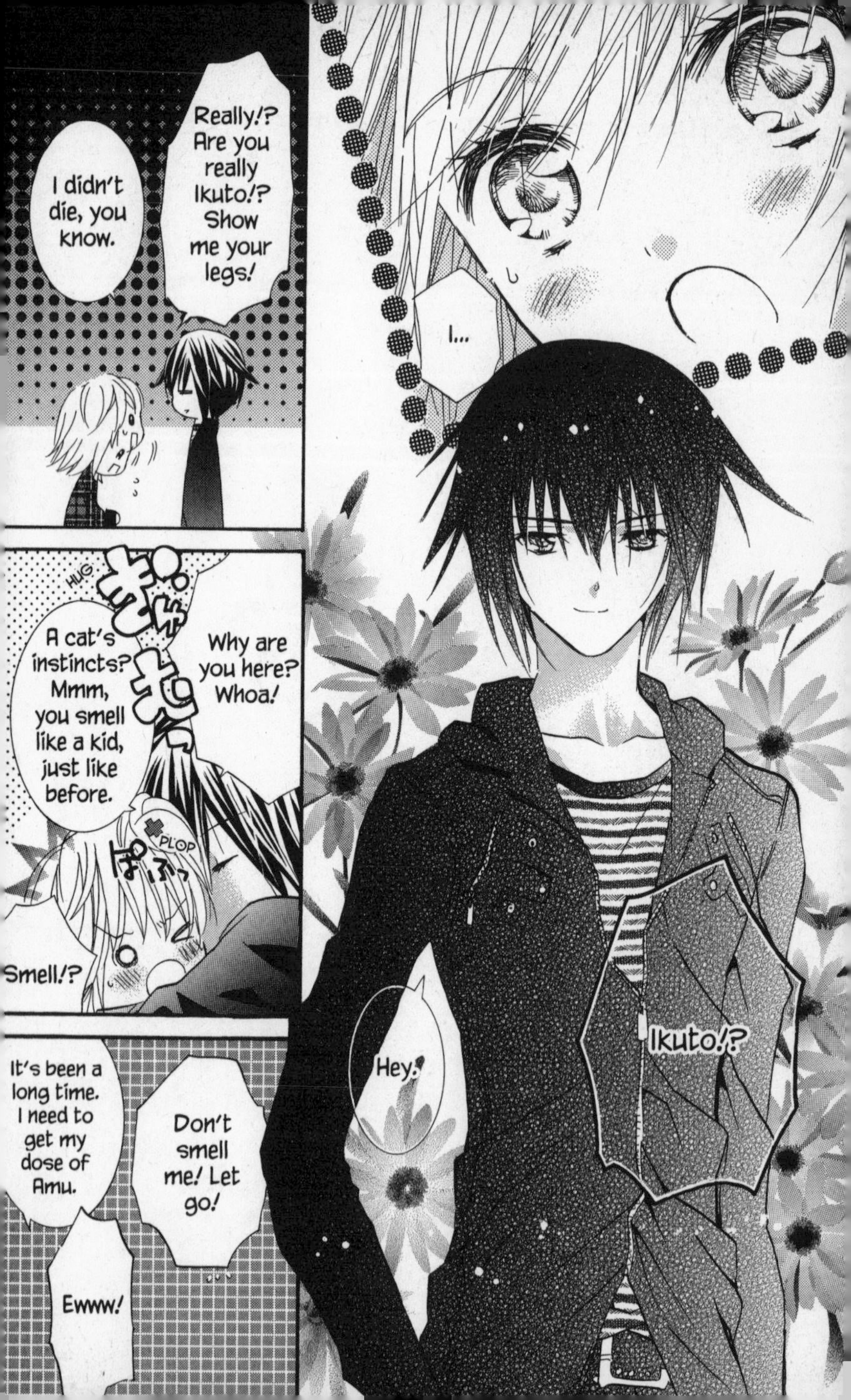
I...
Ikuto!?
Hey.
Really!? Are you really Ikuto!? Show me your legs!
I didn't die, you know.
Why are you here? Whoa!
HUG
A cat's instincts? Mmm, you smell like a kid, just like before.
PLOP
Smell!?
Don't smell me! Let go!
It's been a long time. I need to get my dose of Amu.
Ewww!

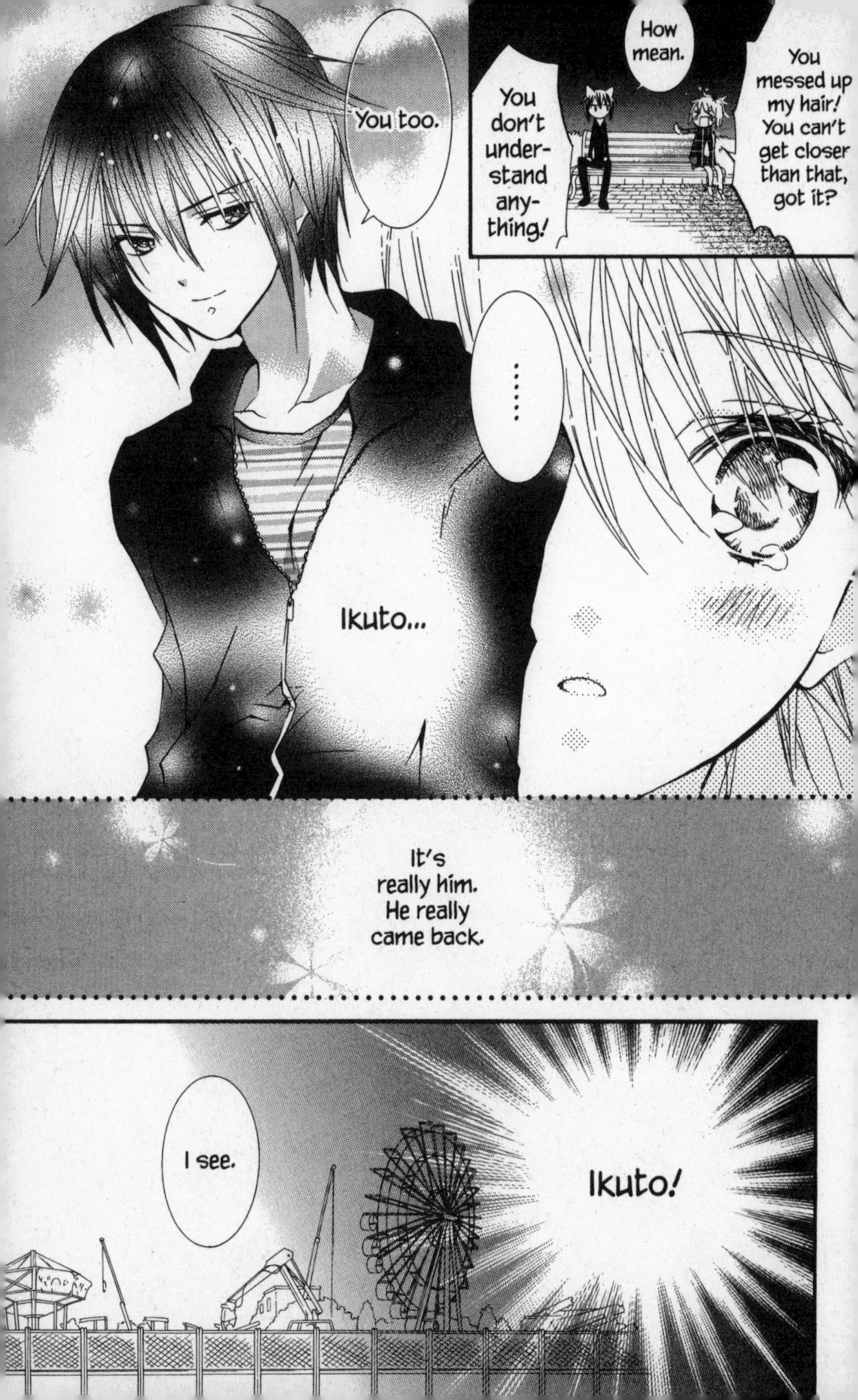
You messed up my hair! You can't get closer than that, got it?
How mean.
You don't understand anything!
You too.
......
Ikuto...
It's really him. He really came back.
Ikuto!
I see.

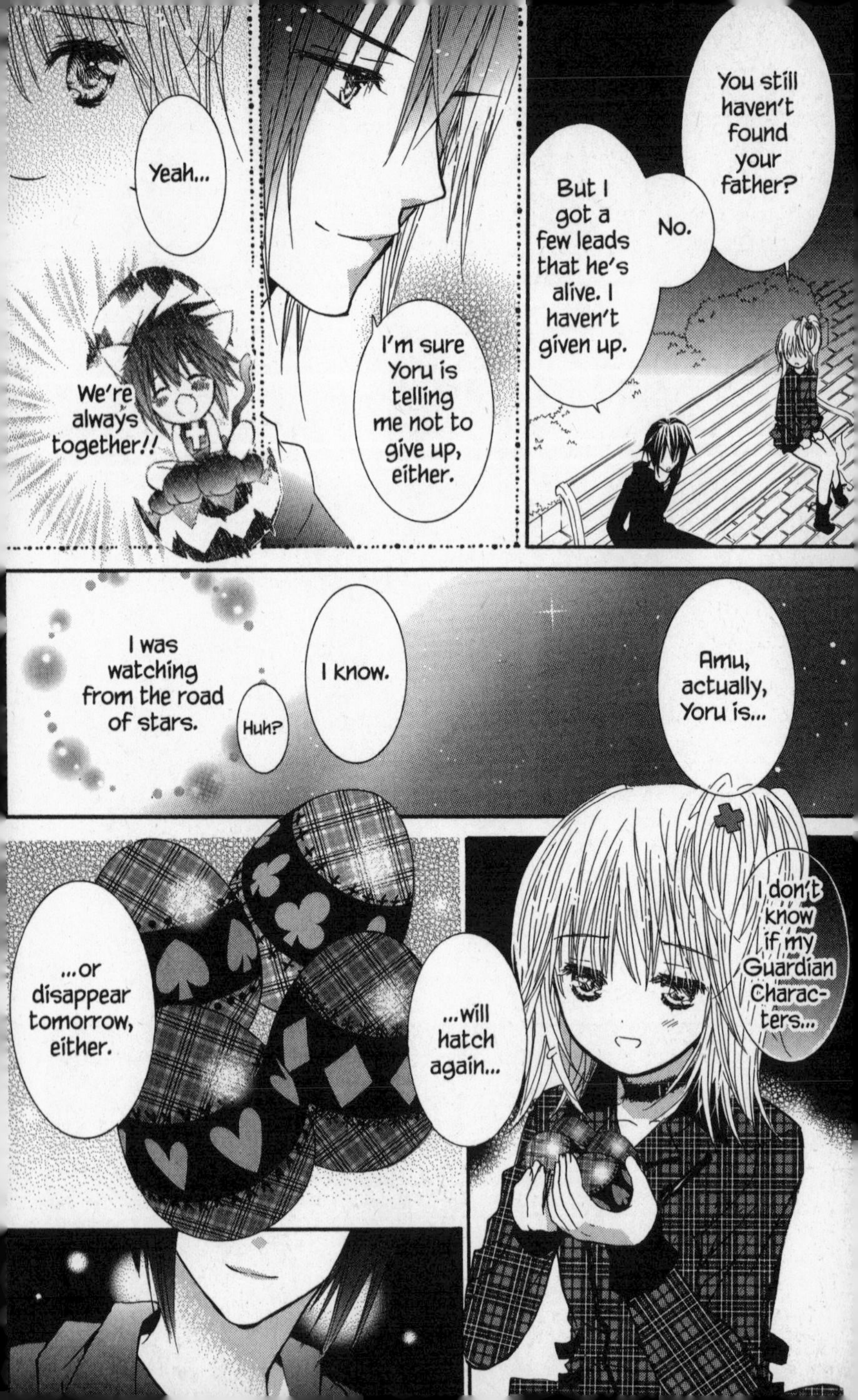
You still haven't found your father?
No.
But I got a few leads that he's alive. I haven't given up.
I'm sure Yoru is telling me not to give up, either.
Yeah...
We're always together!!
Amu, actually, Yoru is...
I know.
Huh?
I was watching from the road of stars.
I don't know if my Guardian Characters...
...will hatch again...
...or disappear tomorrow, either.

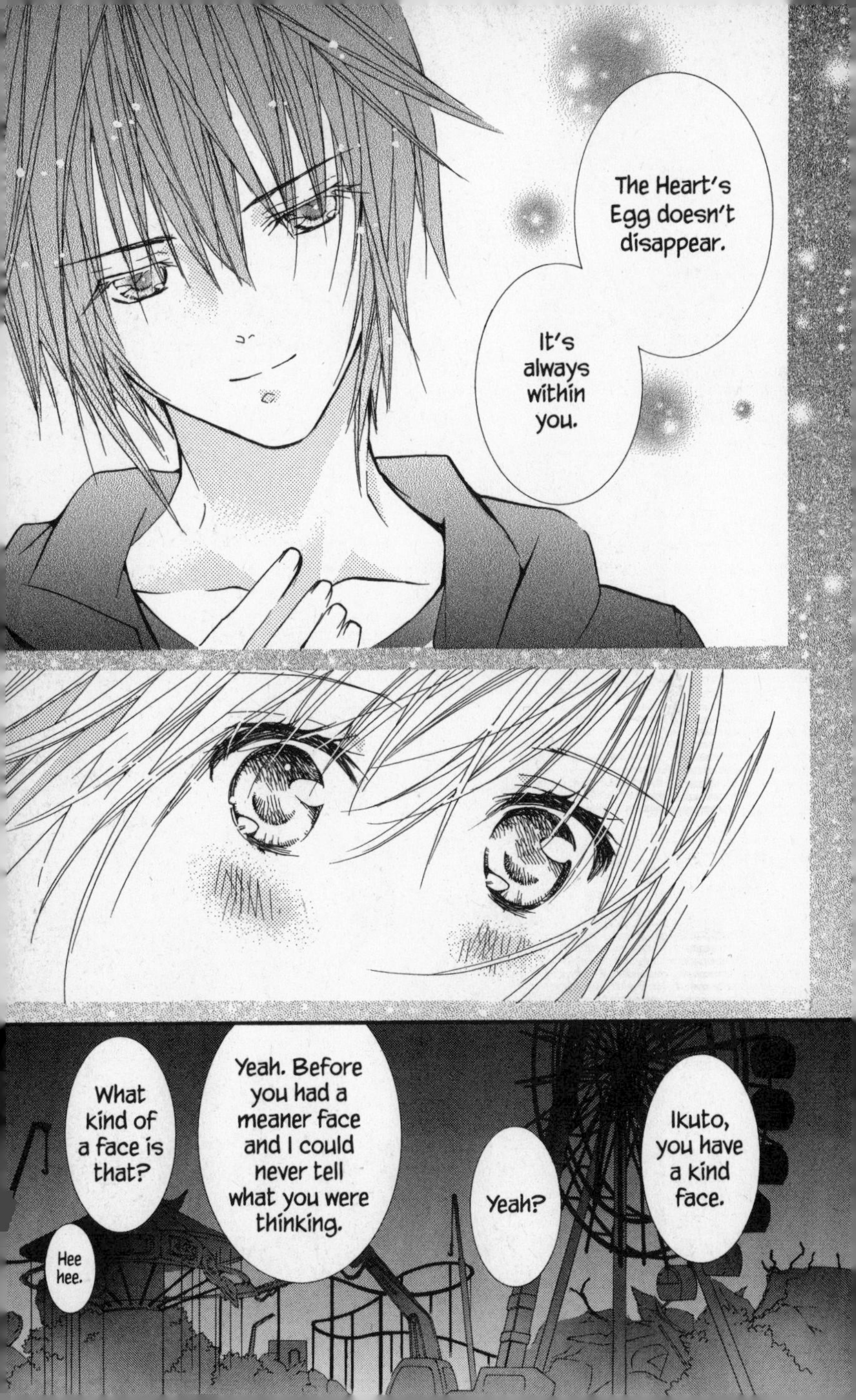
The Heart's Egg doesn't disappear.
It's always within you.
Ikuto, you have a kind face.
Yeah?
Yeah. Before you had a meaner face and I could never tell what you were thinking.
What kind of a face is that?
Hee hee.

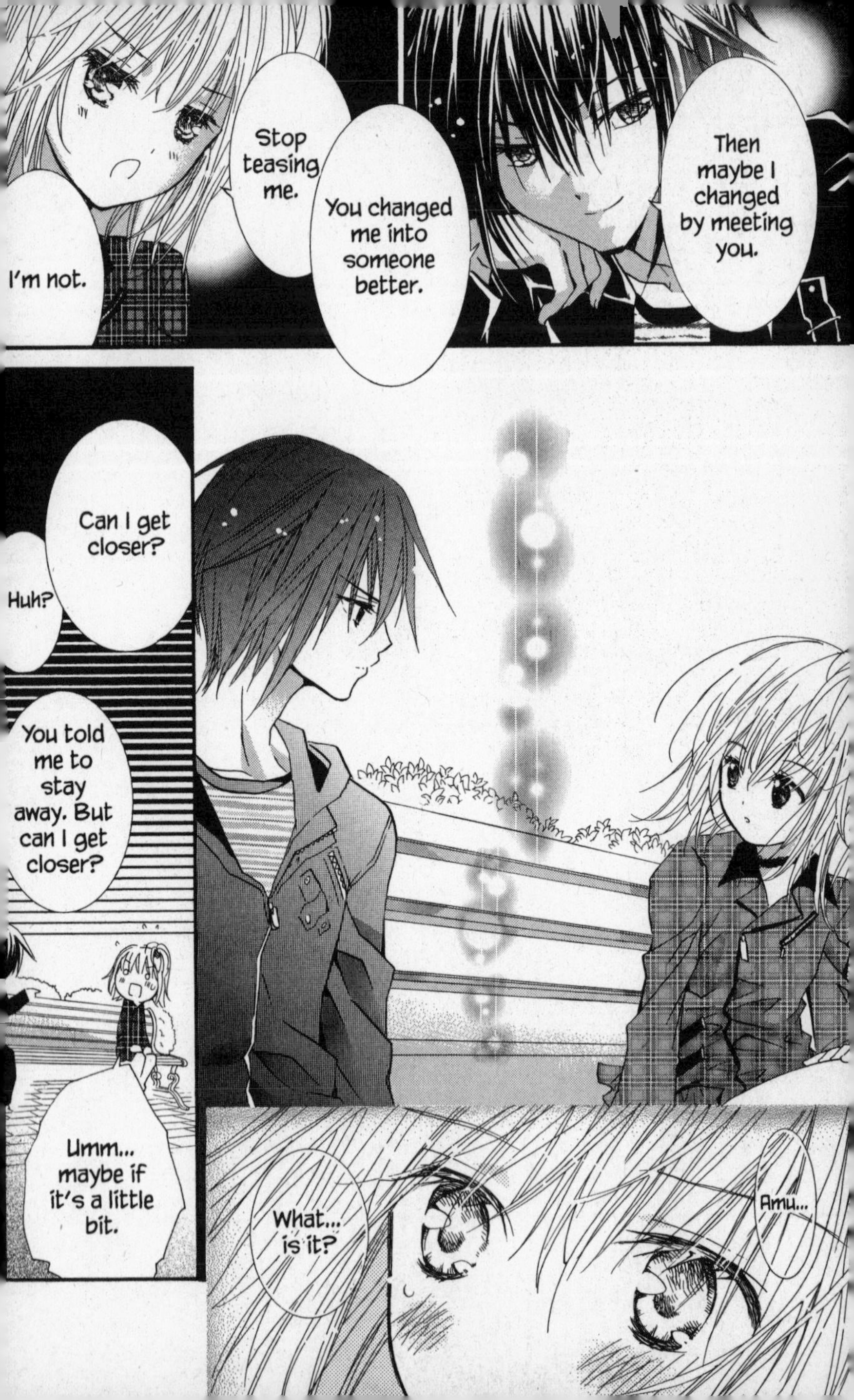
Then maybe I changed by meeting you.
You changed me into someone better.
Stop teasing me.
I'm not.
Can I get closer?
Huh?
You told me to stay away. But can I get closer?
Umm... maybe if it's a little bit.
Amu...
What... is it?

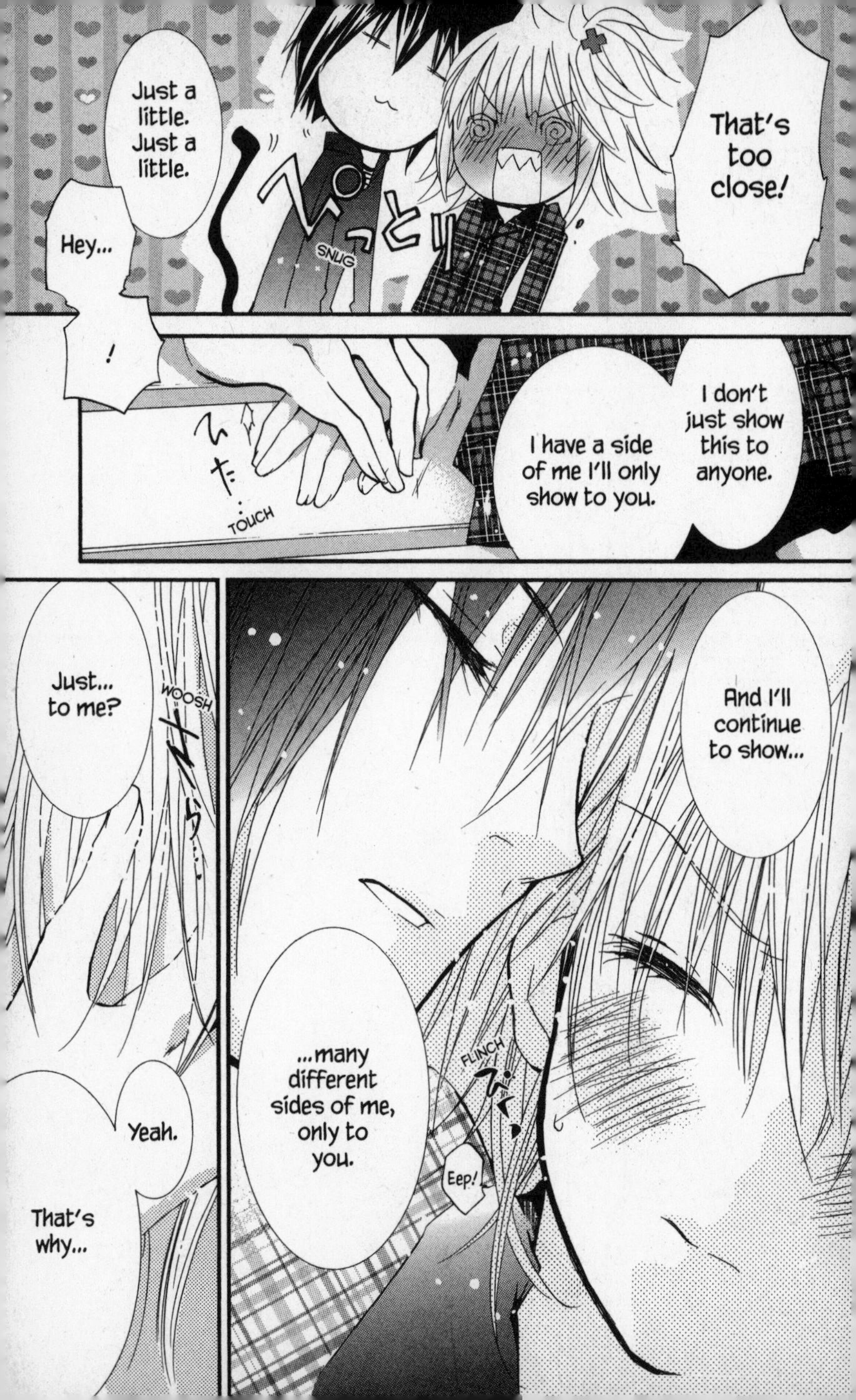

That's too close!
Just a little. Just a little.
SNUG
Hey...
I don't just show this to anyone.
I have a side of me I'll only show to you.
!
TOUCH
And I'll continue to show...
...many different sides of me, only to you.
FLINCH
Eep!
Just... to me?
WOOSH
Yeah.
That's why...

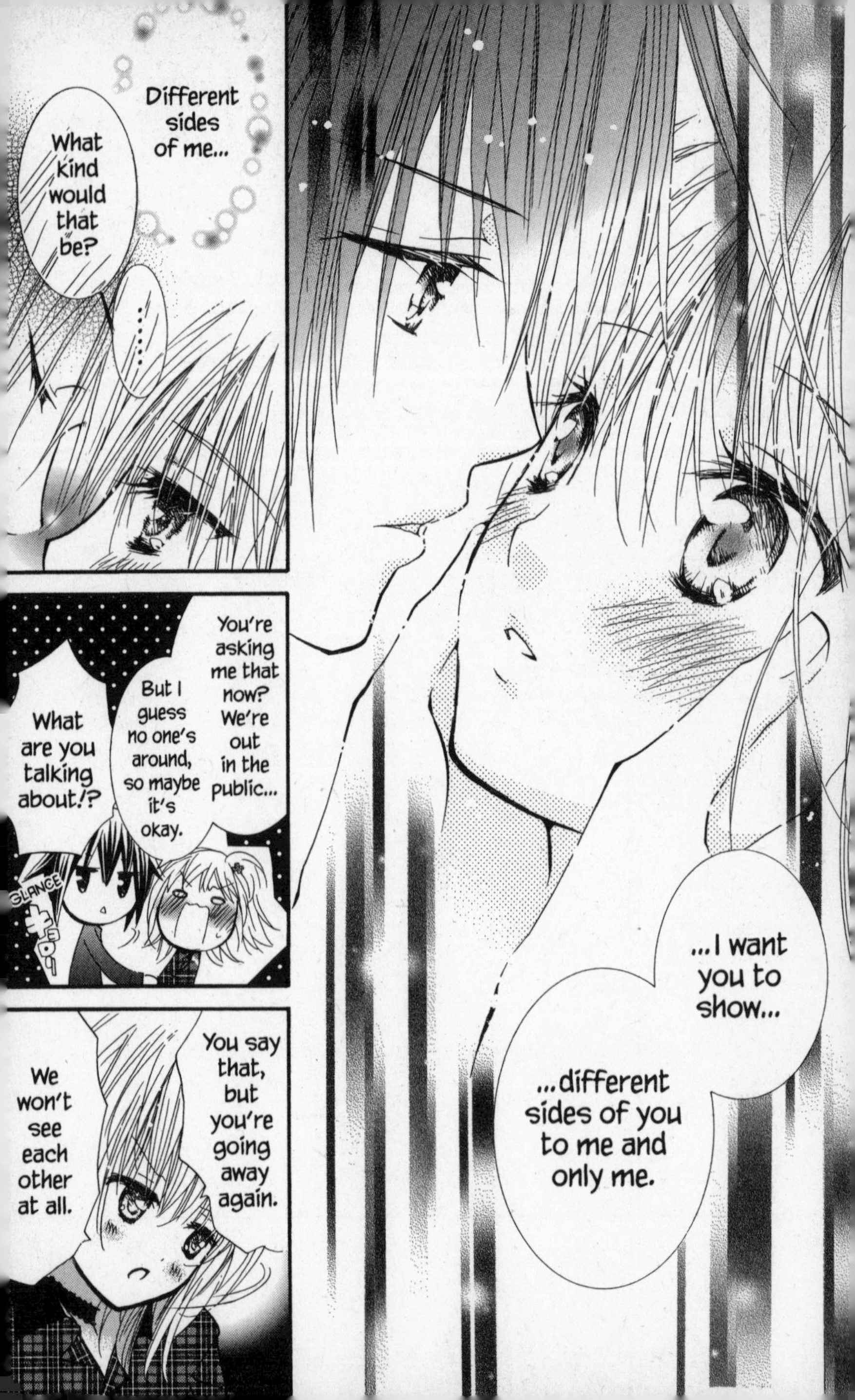
...I want you to show...
...different sides of you to me and only me.
Different sides of me...
What kind would that be?
......
You're asking me that now? We're out in the public...
But I guess no one's around, so maybe it's okay.
What are you talking about!?
GLANCE
You say that, but you're going away again.
We won't see each other at all.

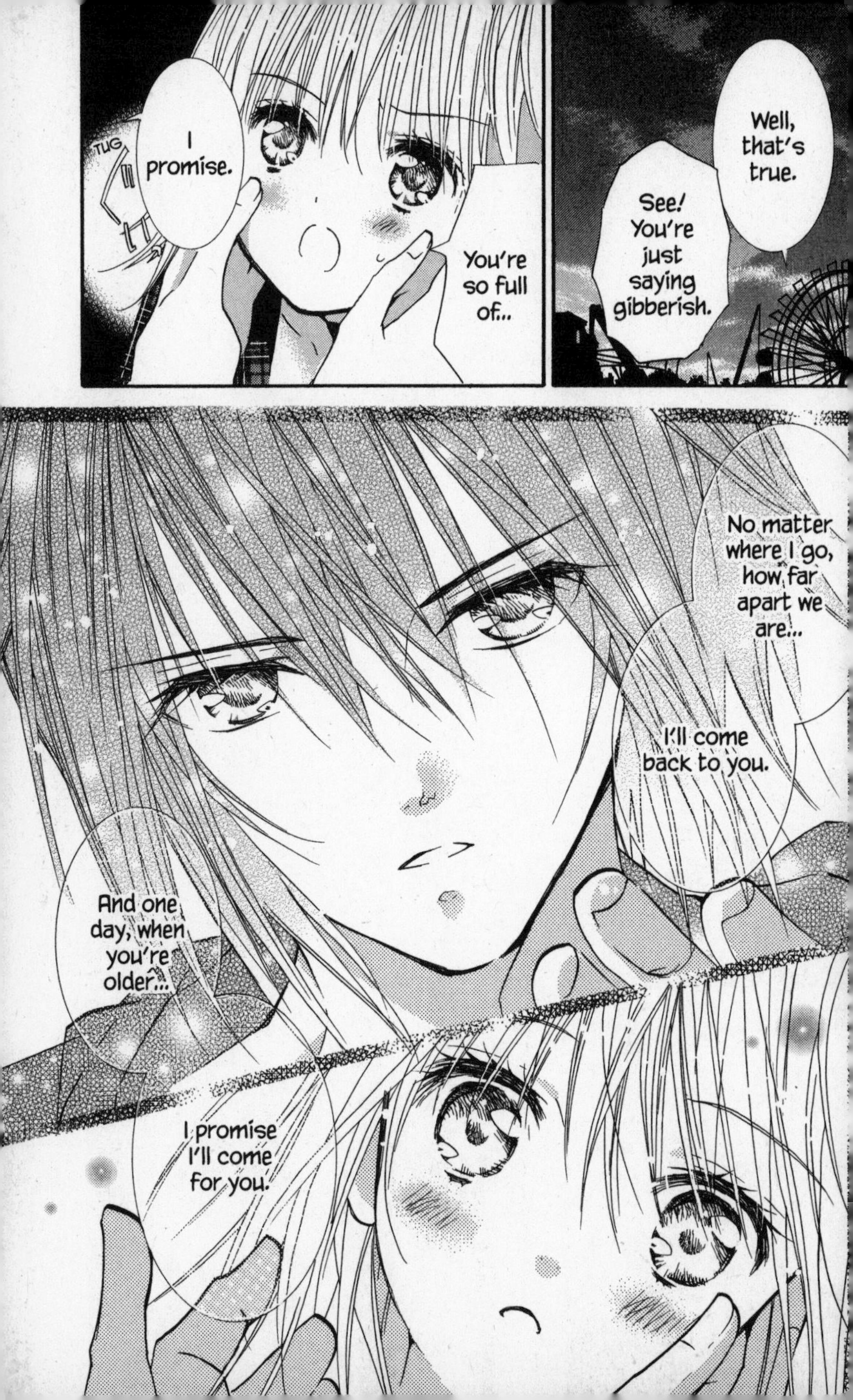
Well, that's true.
See! You're just saying gibberish.
You're so full of...
I promise.
TUG
No matter where I go, how far apart we are...
I'll come back to you.
And one day, when you're older...
I promise I'll come for you.

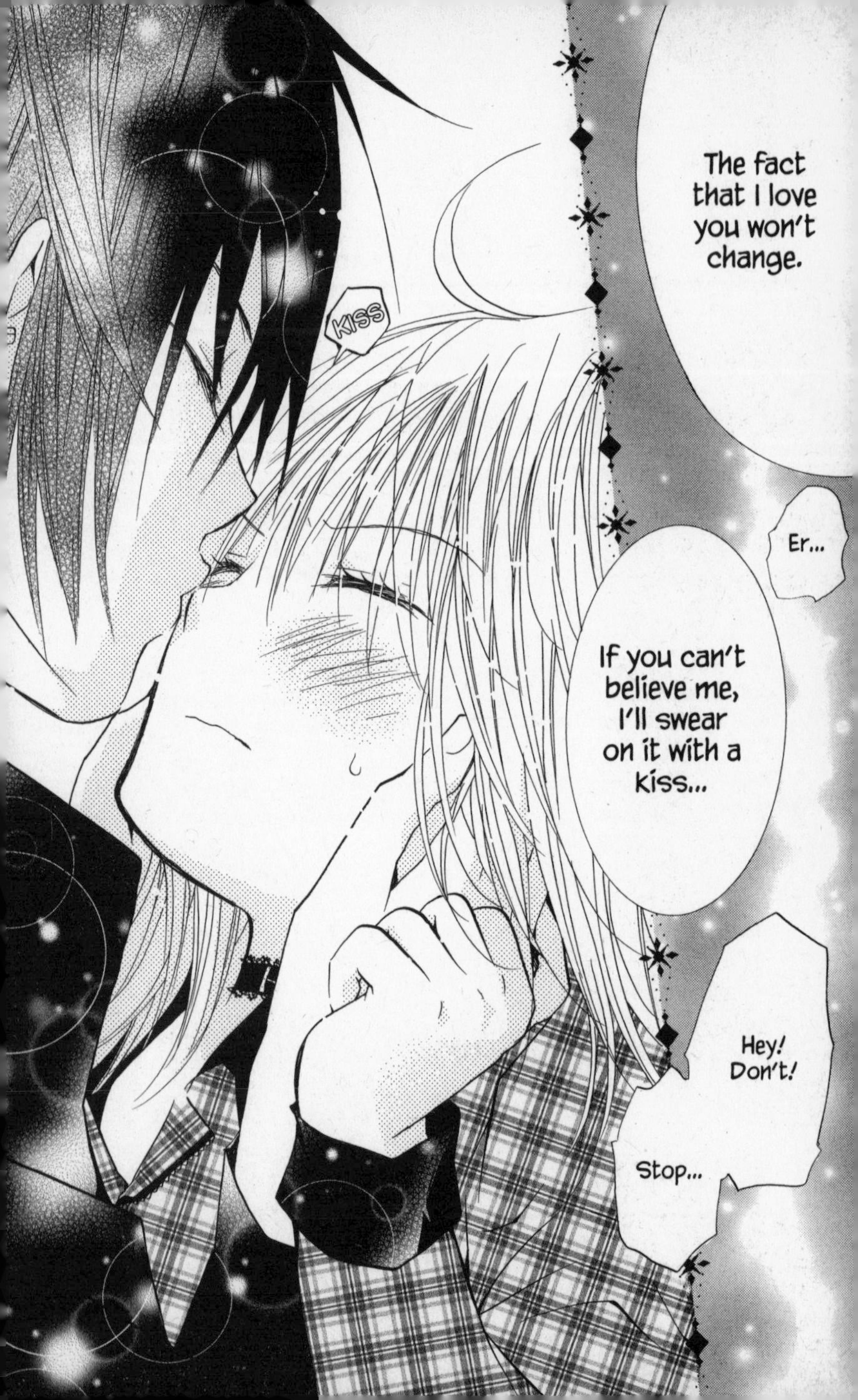
The fact that I love you won't change.
KISS
Er...
If you can't believe me, I'll swear on it with a kiss...
Hey! Don't!
Stop...

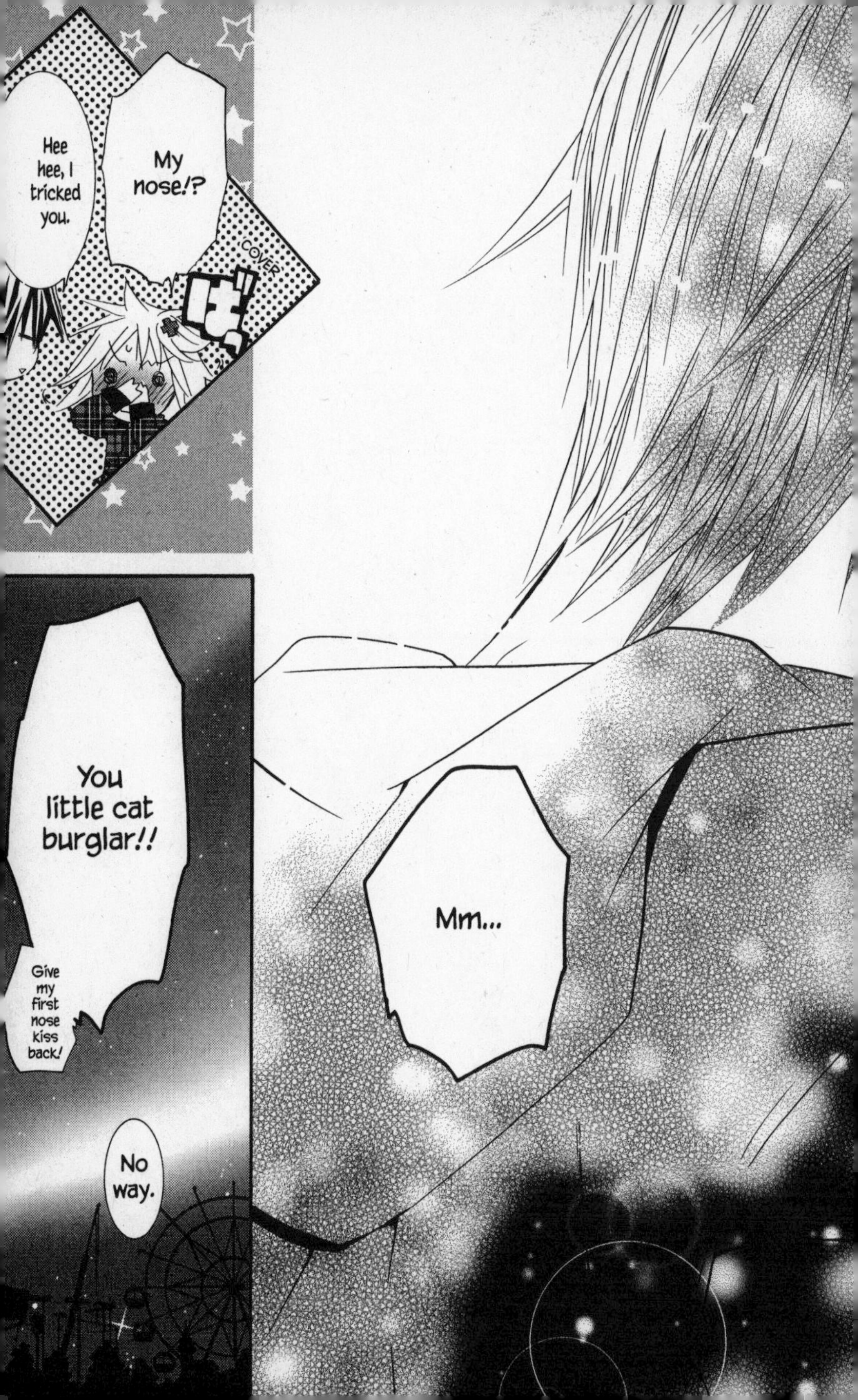
Mm...
My nose!?
Hee hee, I tricked you.
COVER
You little cat burglar!!
Give my first nose kiss back!
No way.

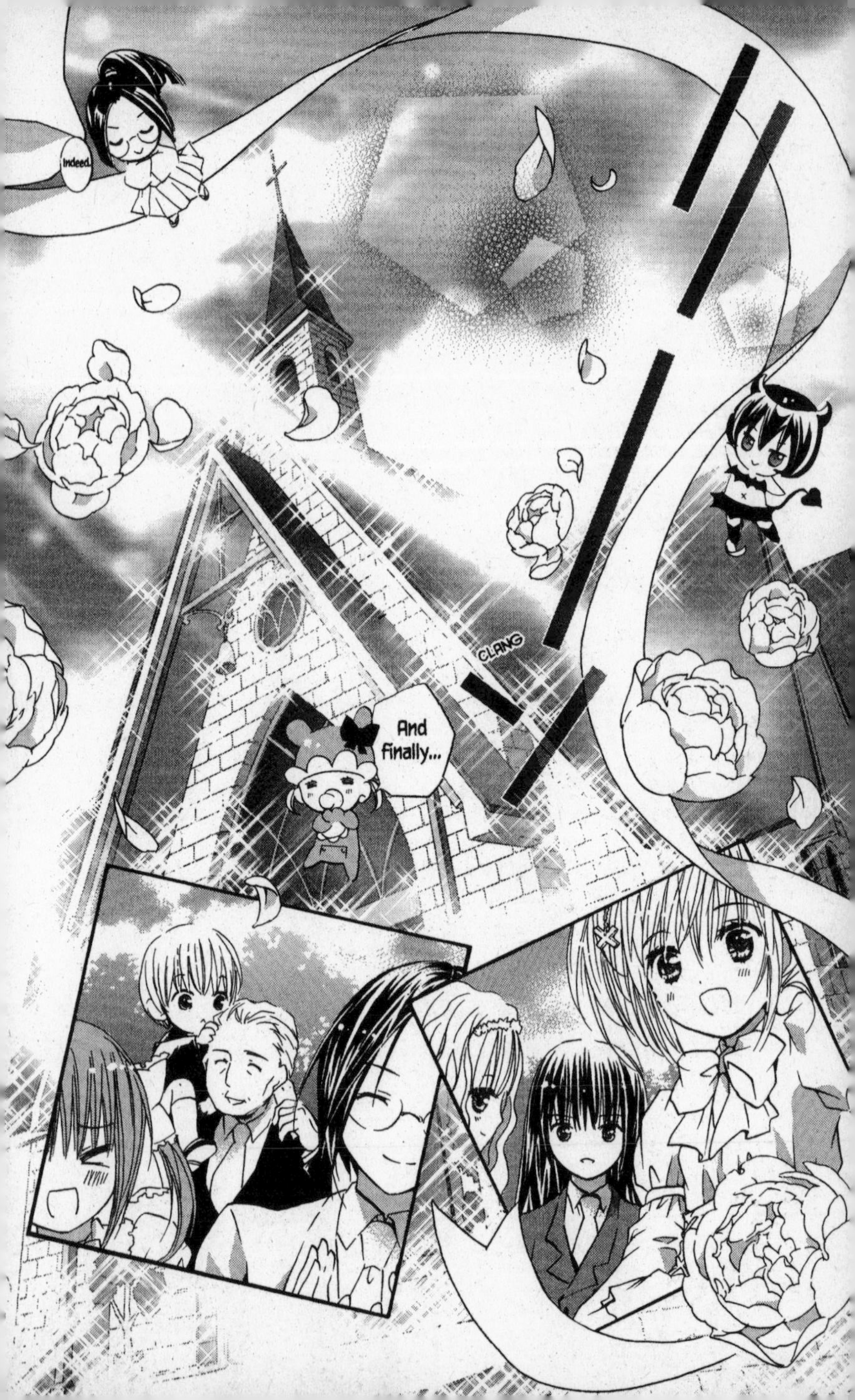
Indeed.
And finally...
CLANG

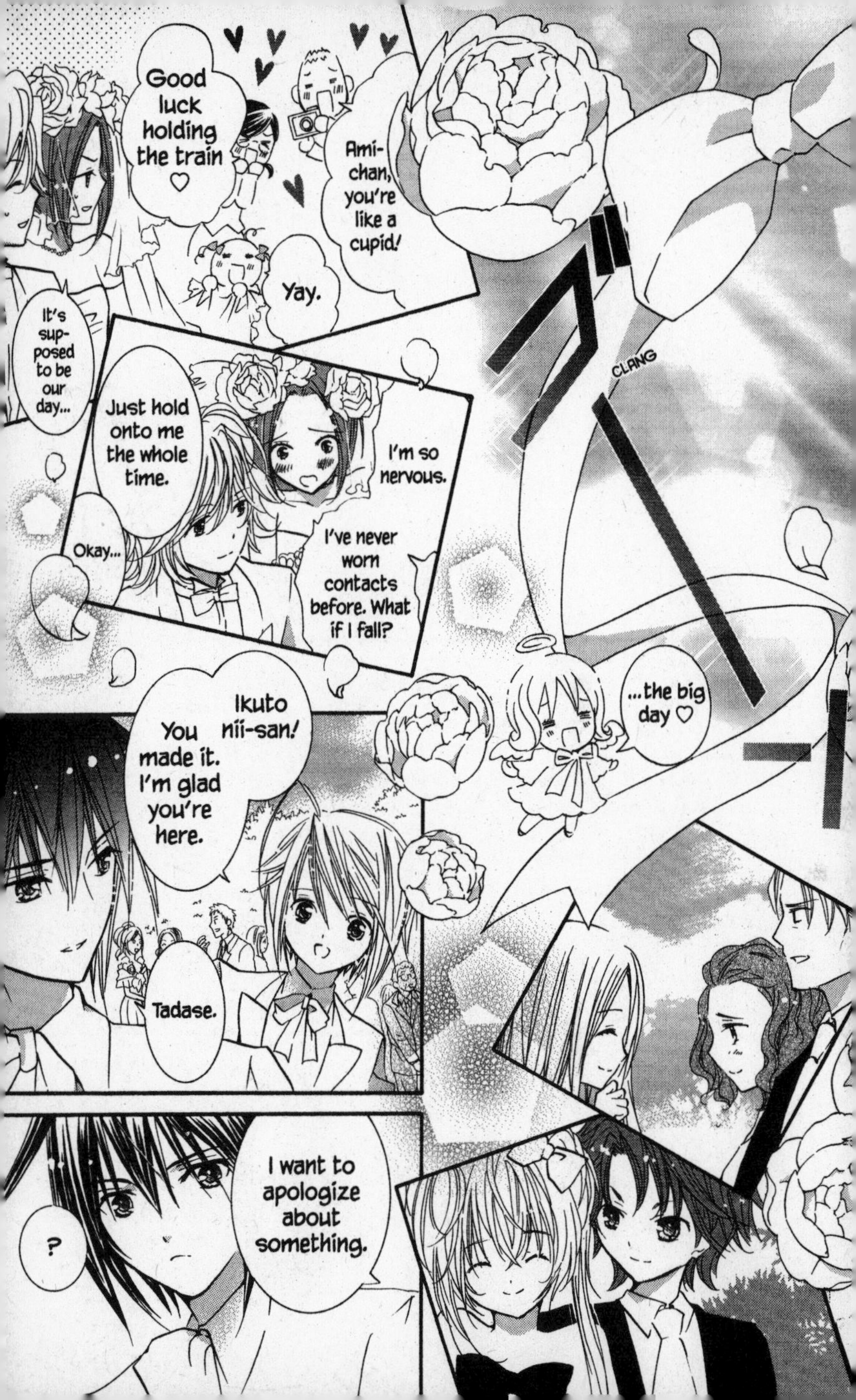
CLANG
...the big day ♡
Ami-chan, you're like a cupid!
Good luck holding the train ♡
Yay.
It's sup-posed to be our day...
I'm so nervous.
Just hold onto me the whole time.
I've never worn contacts before. What if I fall?
Okay...
Ikuto nii-san!
You made it. I'm glad you're here.
Tadase.
I want to apologize about something.
?

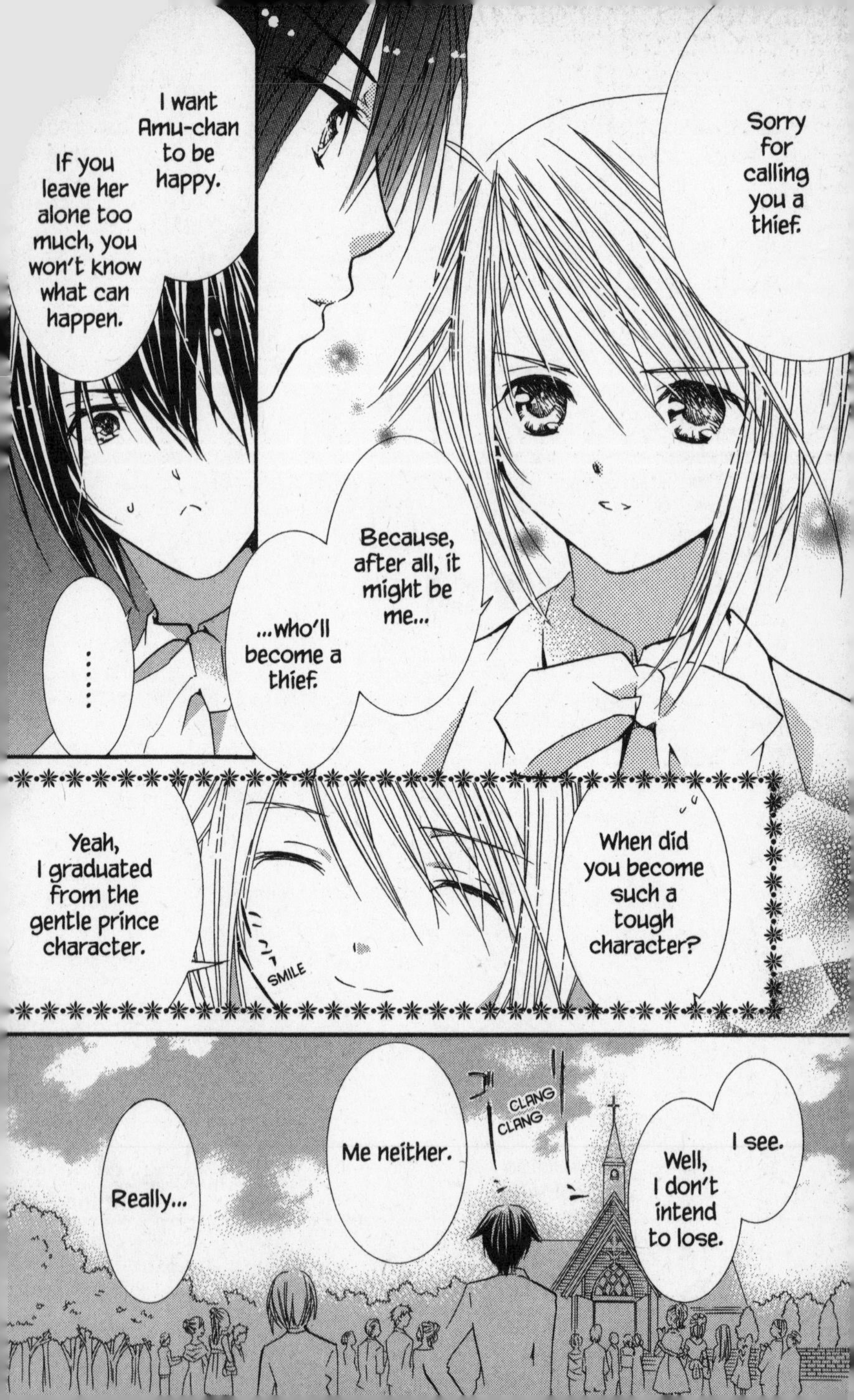

Sorry for calling you a thief.
Because, after all, it might be me...
...who'll become a thief.
I want Amu-chan to be happy.
If you leave her alone too much, you won't know what can happen.
......
When did you become such a tough character?
Yeah, I graduated from the gentle prince character.
SMILE
I see.
Well, I don't intend to lose.
CLANG CLANG
Me neither.
Really...

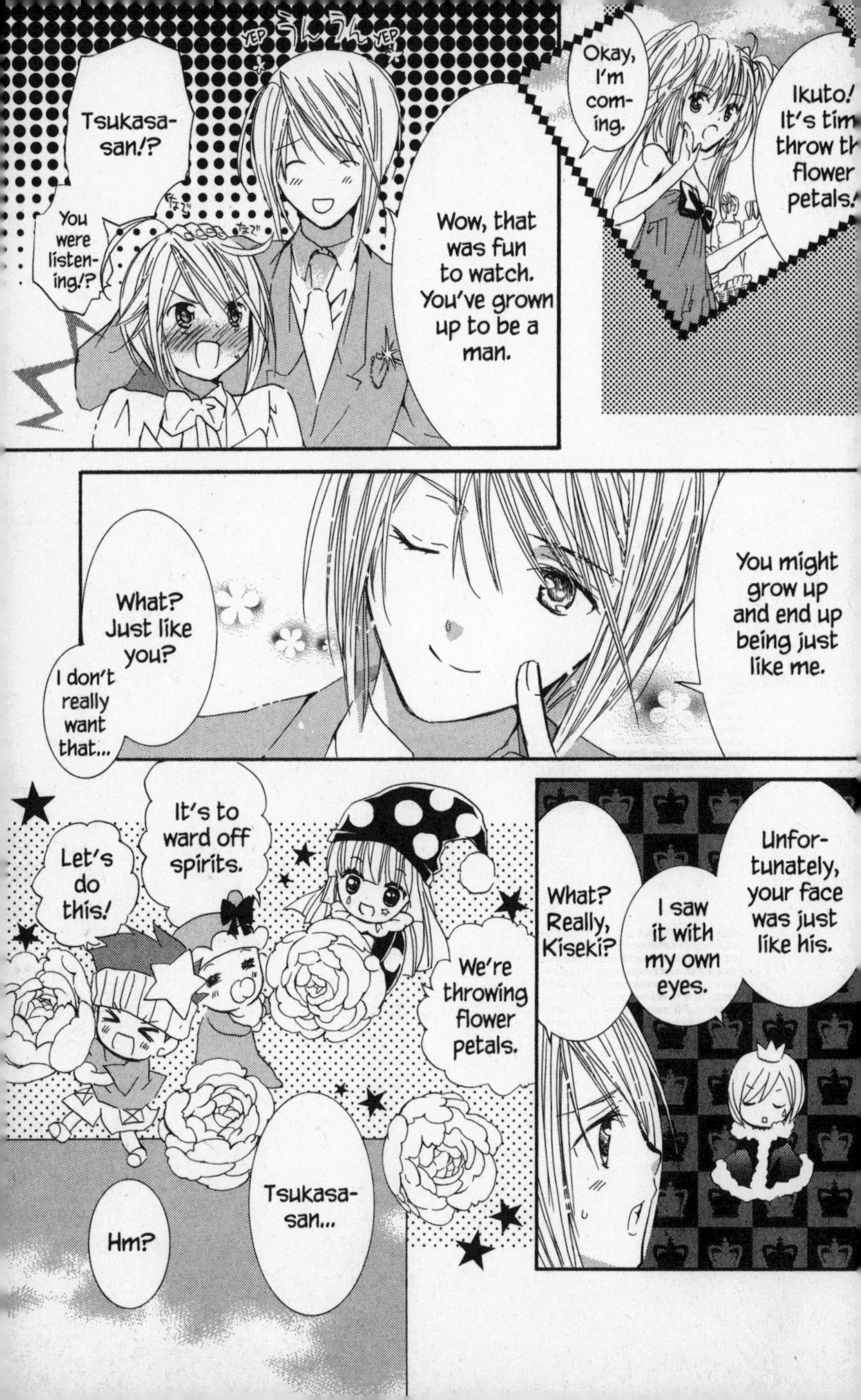
Ikuto! It's tim throw th flower petals!
Okay, I'm com- ing.
YEP うんうん YEP
Wow, that was fun to watch. You've grown up to be a man.
Tsukasa-san!?
You were listen- ing!?
You might grow up and end up being just like me.
What? Just like you?
I don't really want that...
Unfor- tunately, your face was just like his.
I saw it with my own eyes.
What? Really, Kiseki?
It's to ward off spirits.
Let's do this!
We're throwing flower petals.
Tsukasa- san...
Hm?

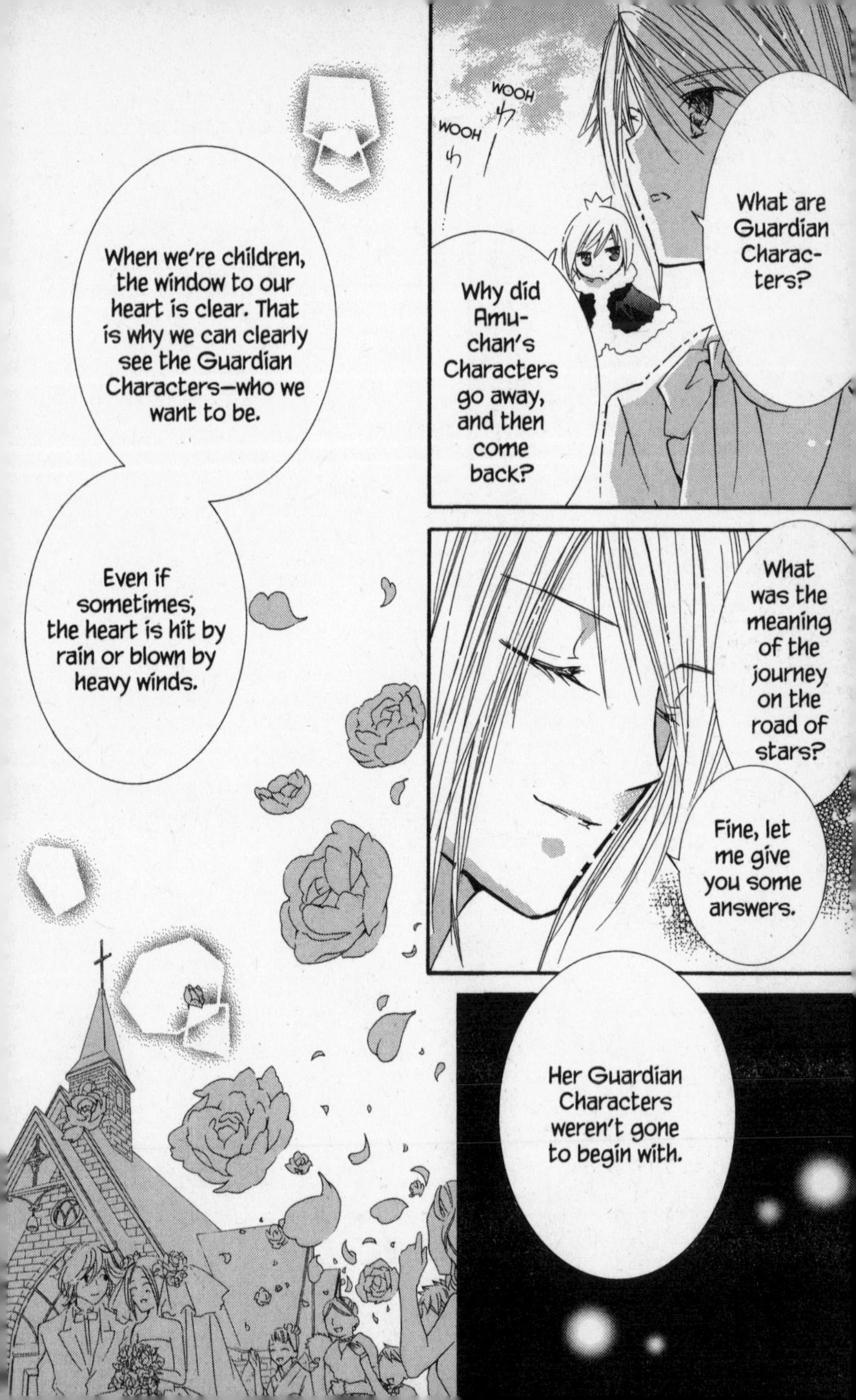

What are Guardian Characters?
WOOH
WOOH
Why did Amu-chan's Characters go away, and then come back?
What was the meaning of the journey on the road of stars?
Fine, let me give you some answers.
Her Guardian Characters weren't gone to begin with.
When we're children, the window to our heart is clear. That is why we can clearly see the Guardian Characters—who we want to be.
Even if sometimes, the heart is hit by rain or blown by heavy winds.

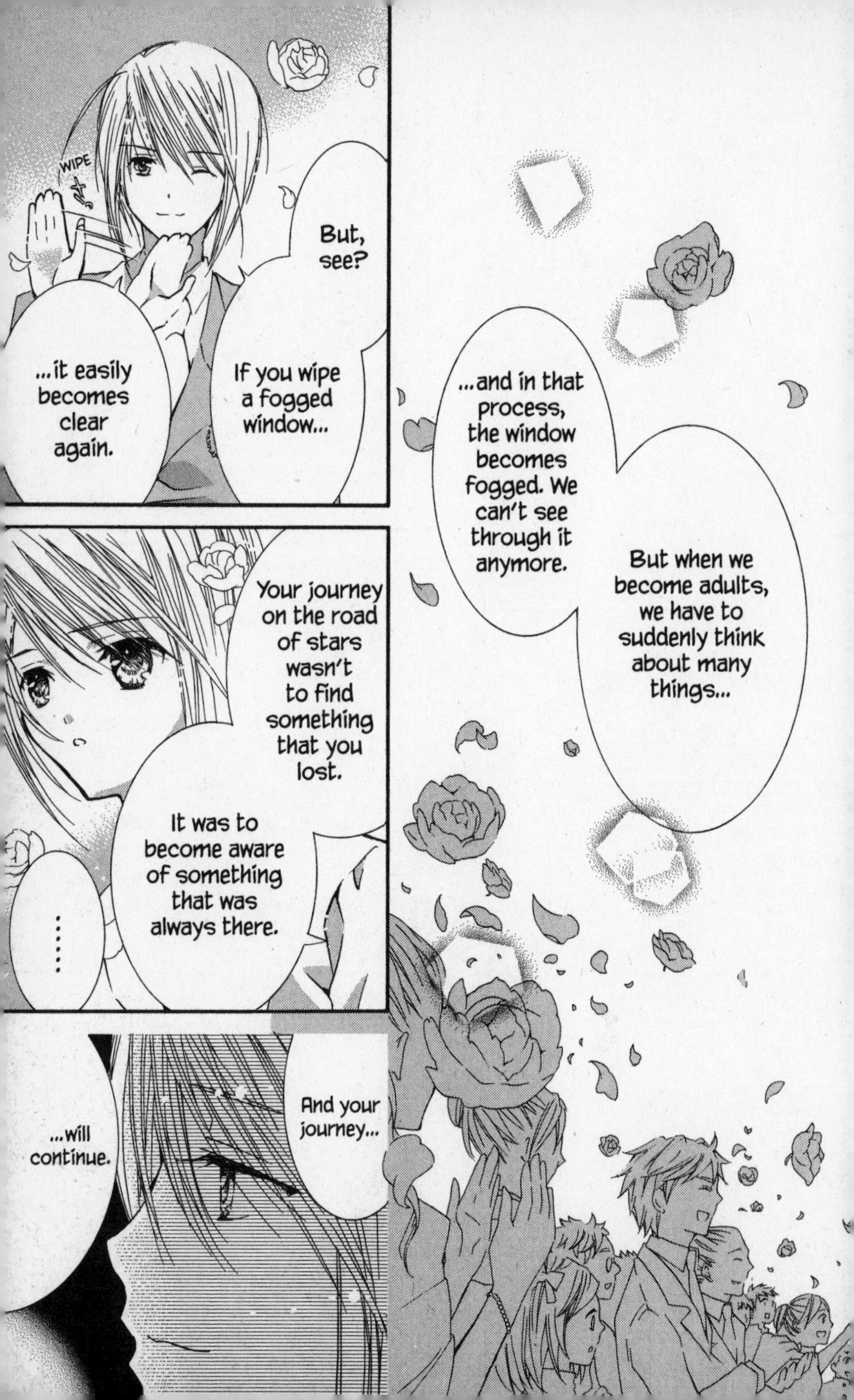
But when we become adults, we have to suddenly think about many things...
...and in that process, the window becomes fogged. We can't see through it anymore.
But, see?
If you wipe a fogged window...
WIPE
...it easily becomes clear again.
Your journey on the road of stars wasn't to find something that you lost.
It was to become aware of something that was always there.
......
And your journey...
...will continue.

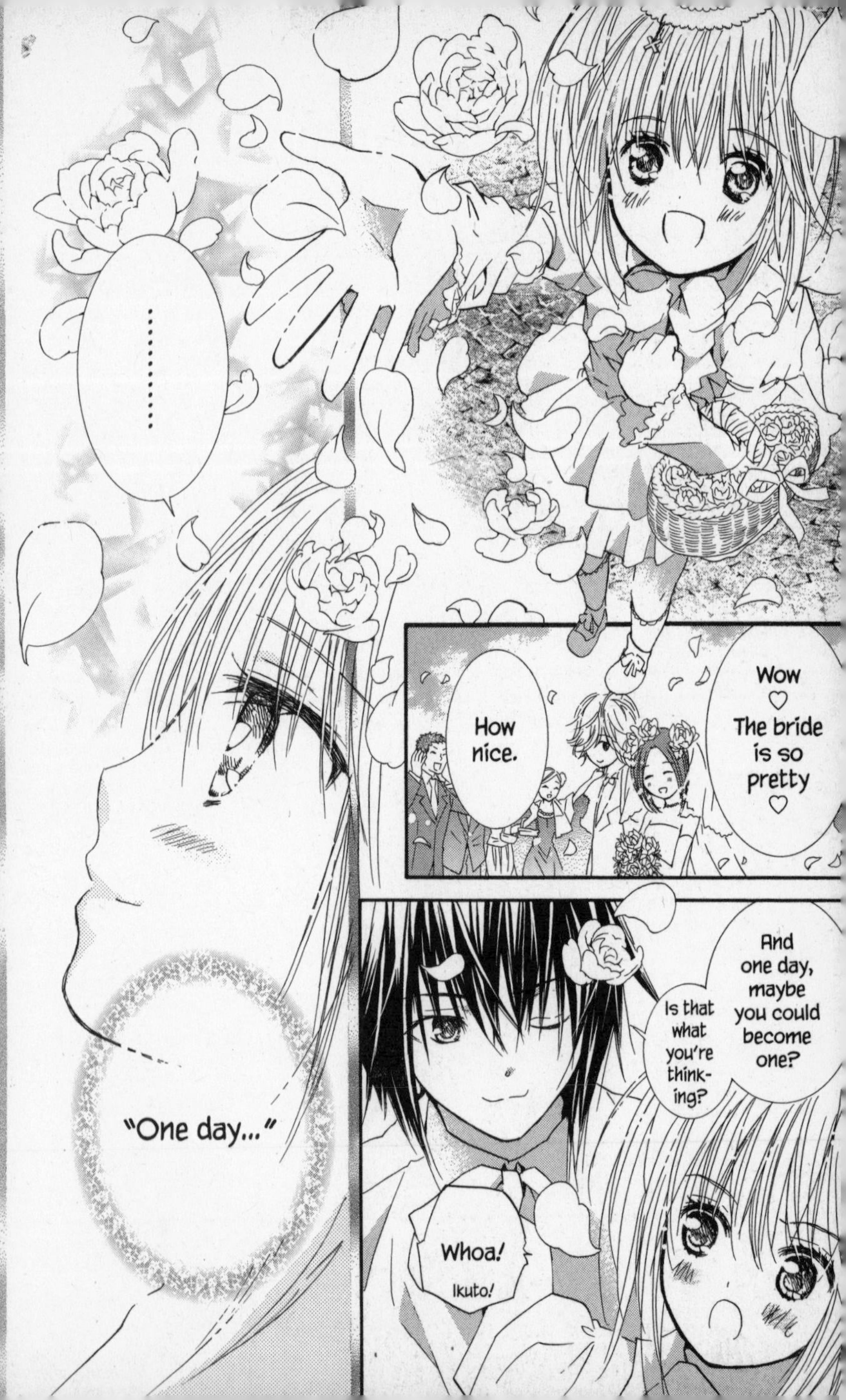
Wow ♡ The bride is so pretty ♡
How nice.
And one day, maybe you could become one?
Is that what you're think-ing?
Whoa!
Ikuto!
......
"One day..."

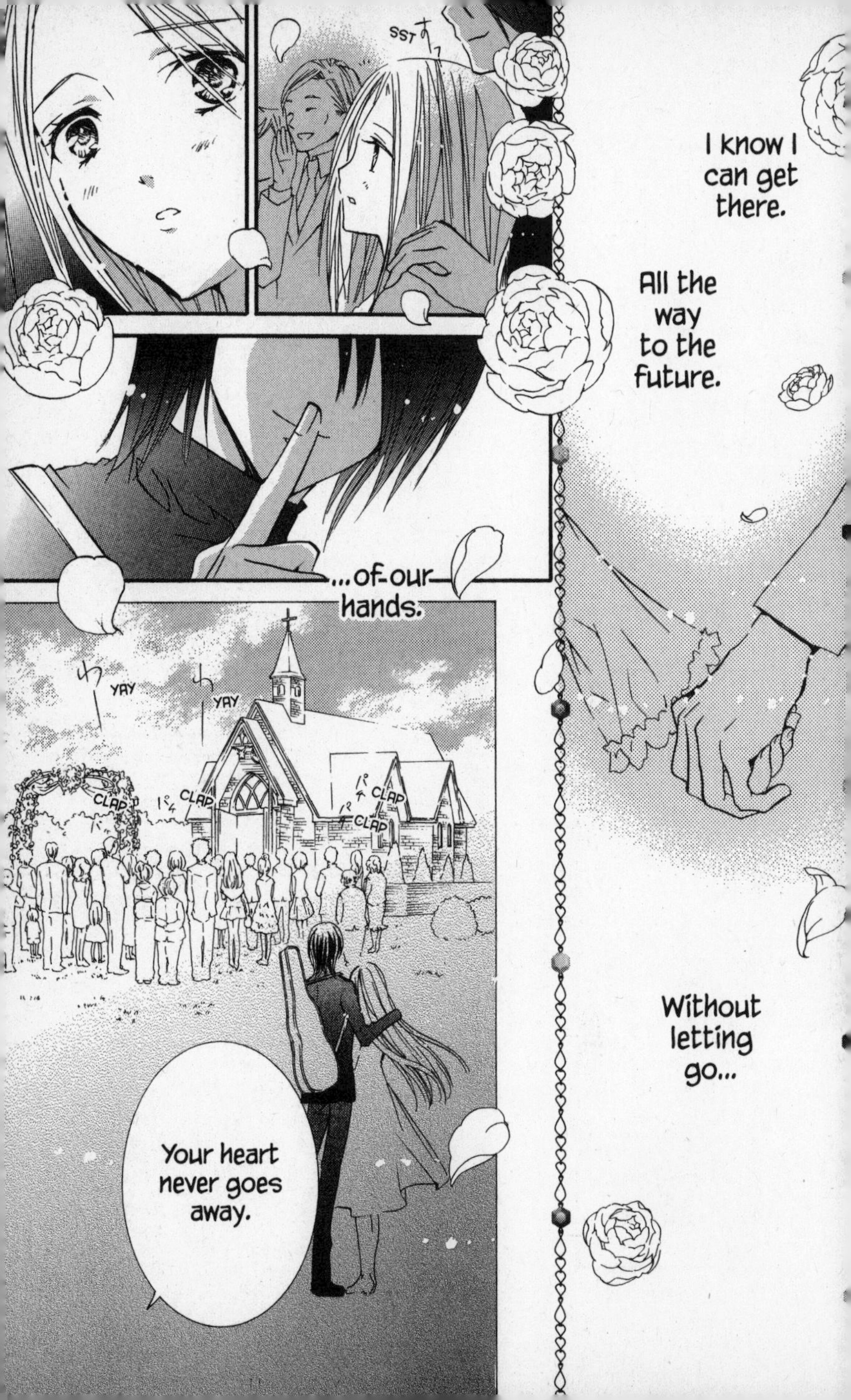
I know I can get there.
All the way to the future.
Without letting go...
SST
...of our hands.
YAY
YAY
CLAP
CLAP
CLAP
CLAP
Your heart never goes away.

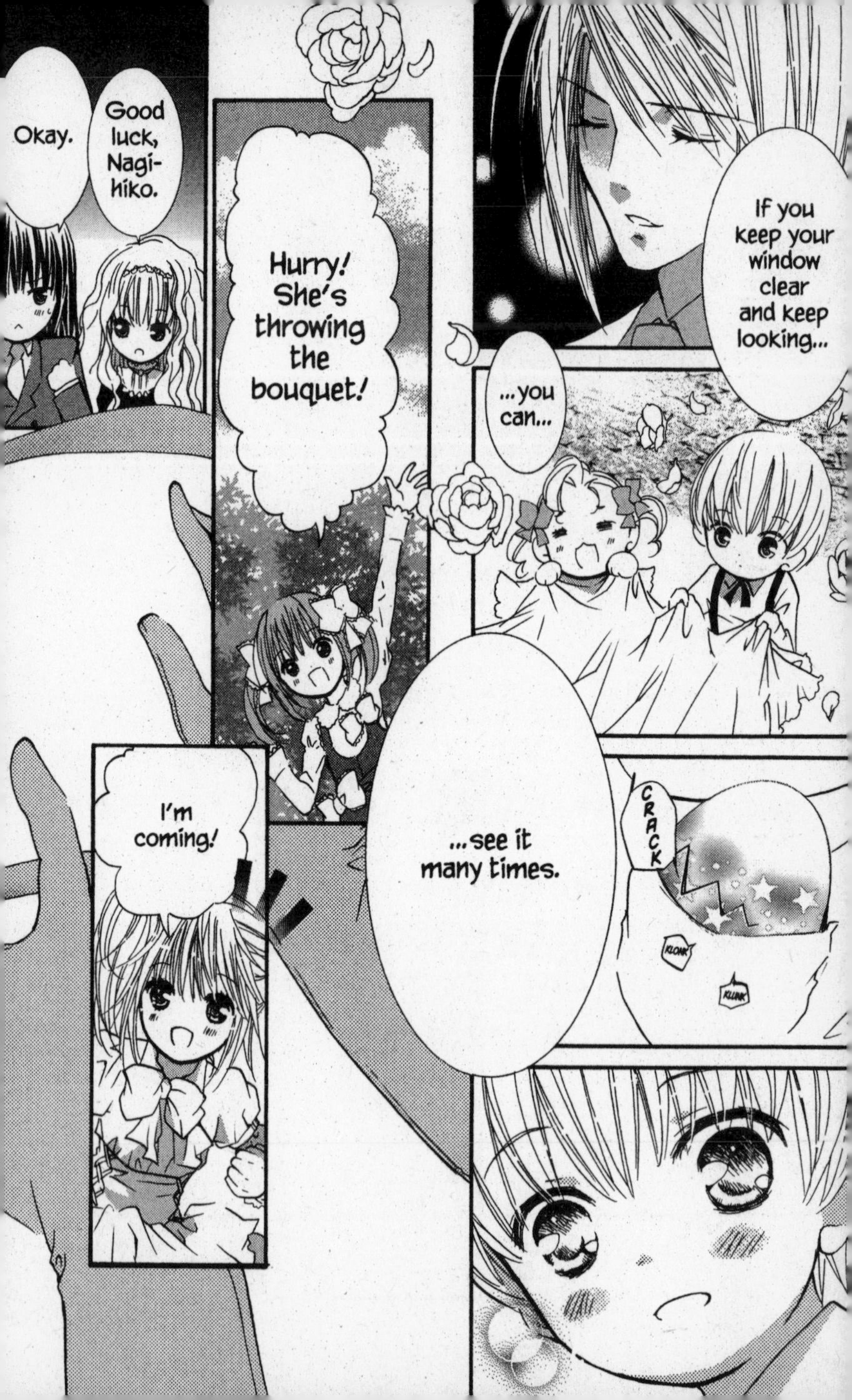
If you keep your window clear and keep looking...
...you can...
...see it many times.
CRACK
KLONK
KLUNK
Hurry! She's throwing the bouquet!
Good luck, Nagi-hiko.
Okay.
I'm coming!

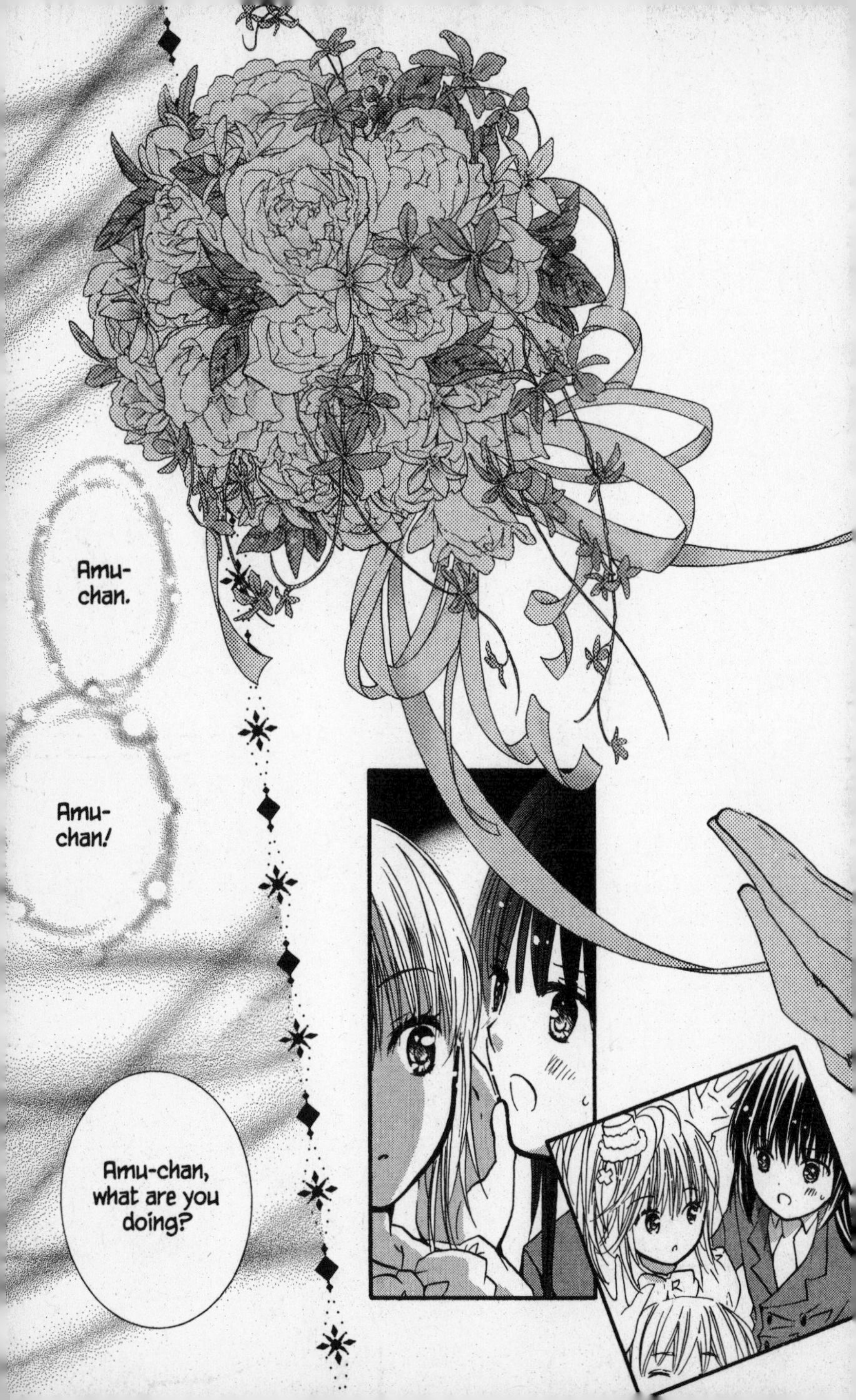
Amu-chan.
Amu-chan!
Amu-chan, what are you doing?

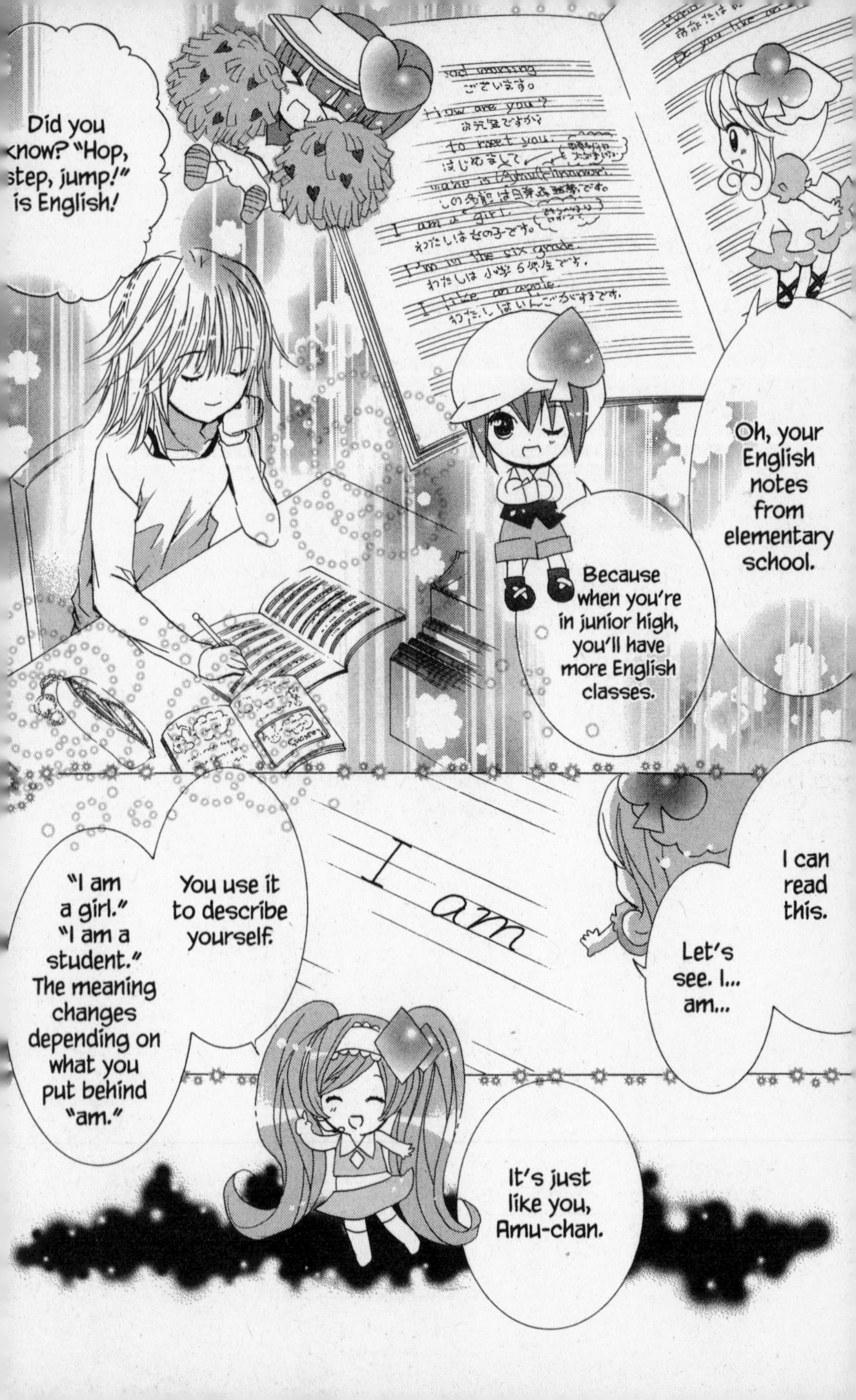

Oh, your English notes from elementary school.
Because when you're in junior high, you'll have more English classes.
Did you know? "Hop, step, jump!" is English!
I can read this.
Let's see. I... am...
I am
You use it to describe yourself.
"I am a girl." "I am a student." The meaning changes depending on what you put behind "am."
It's just like you, Amu-chan.

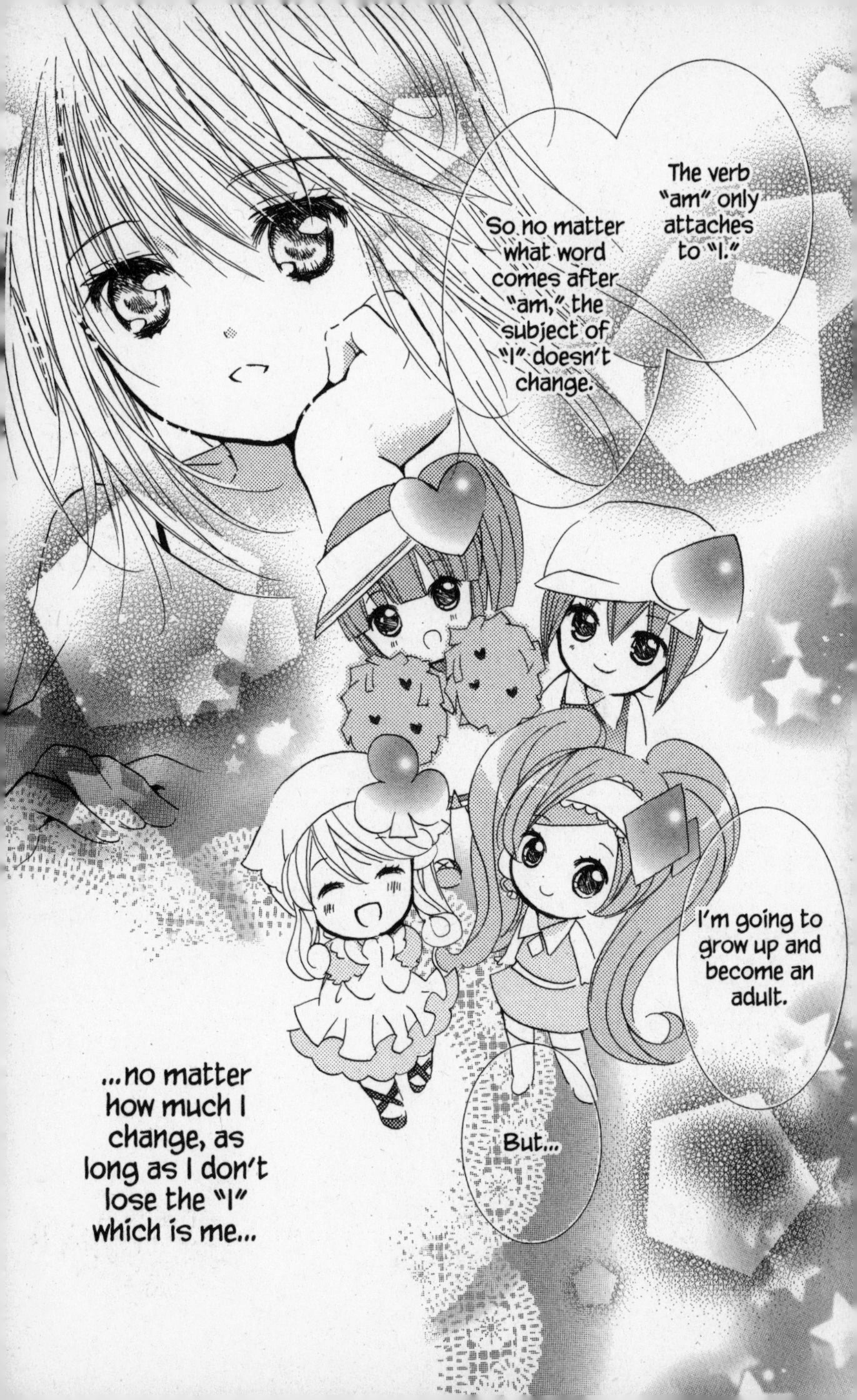
The verb "am" only attaches to "I."
So no matter what word comes after "am," the subject of "I" doesn't change.
I'm going to grow up and become an adult.
But...
...no matter how much I change, as long as I don't lose the "I" which is me...

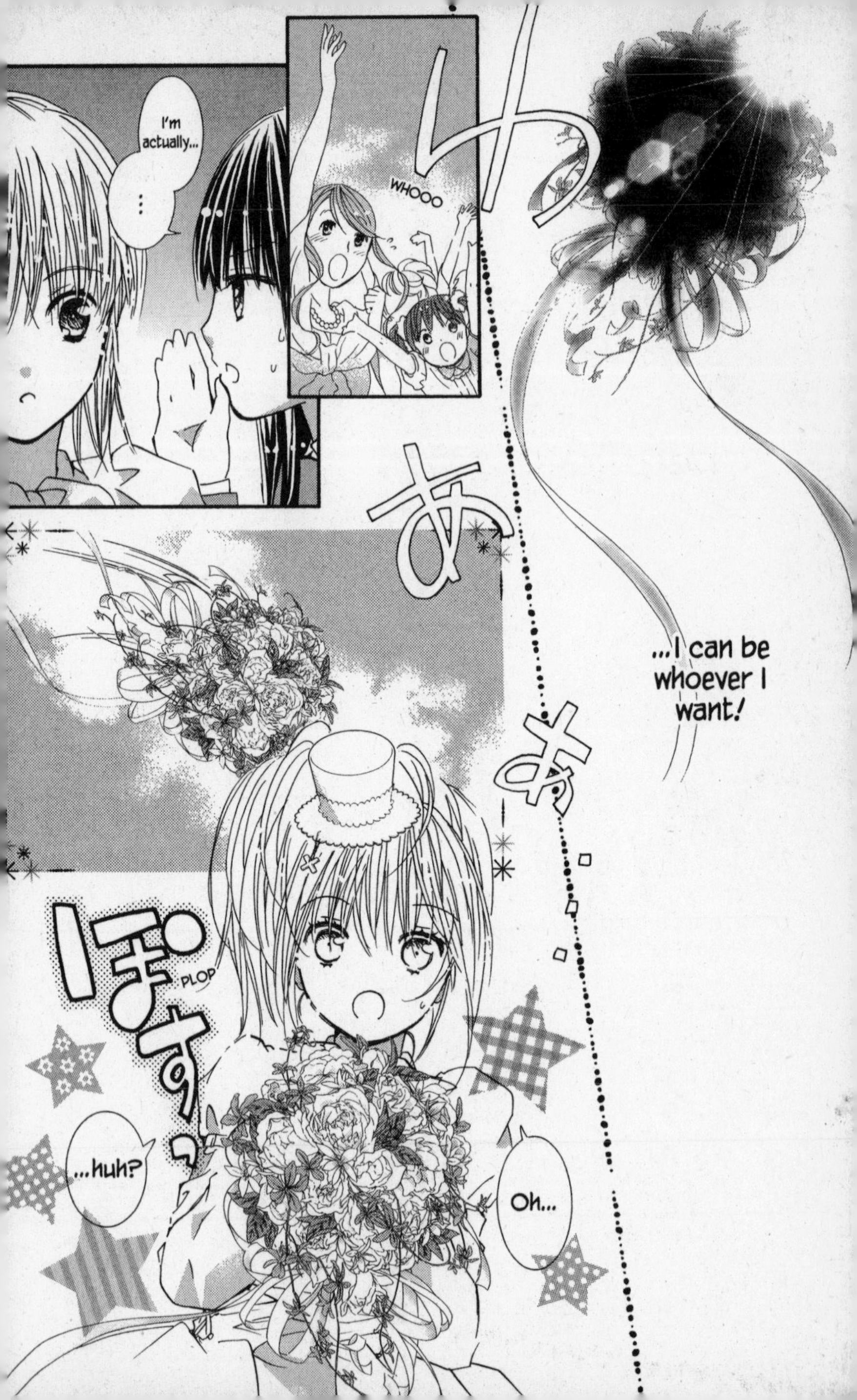
...I can be whoever I want!
わあああ
WHOOO
I'm actually...
...
Oh...
ぽすっ
PLOP
...huh?

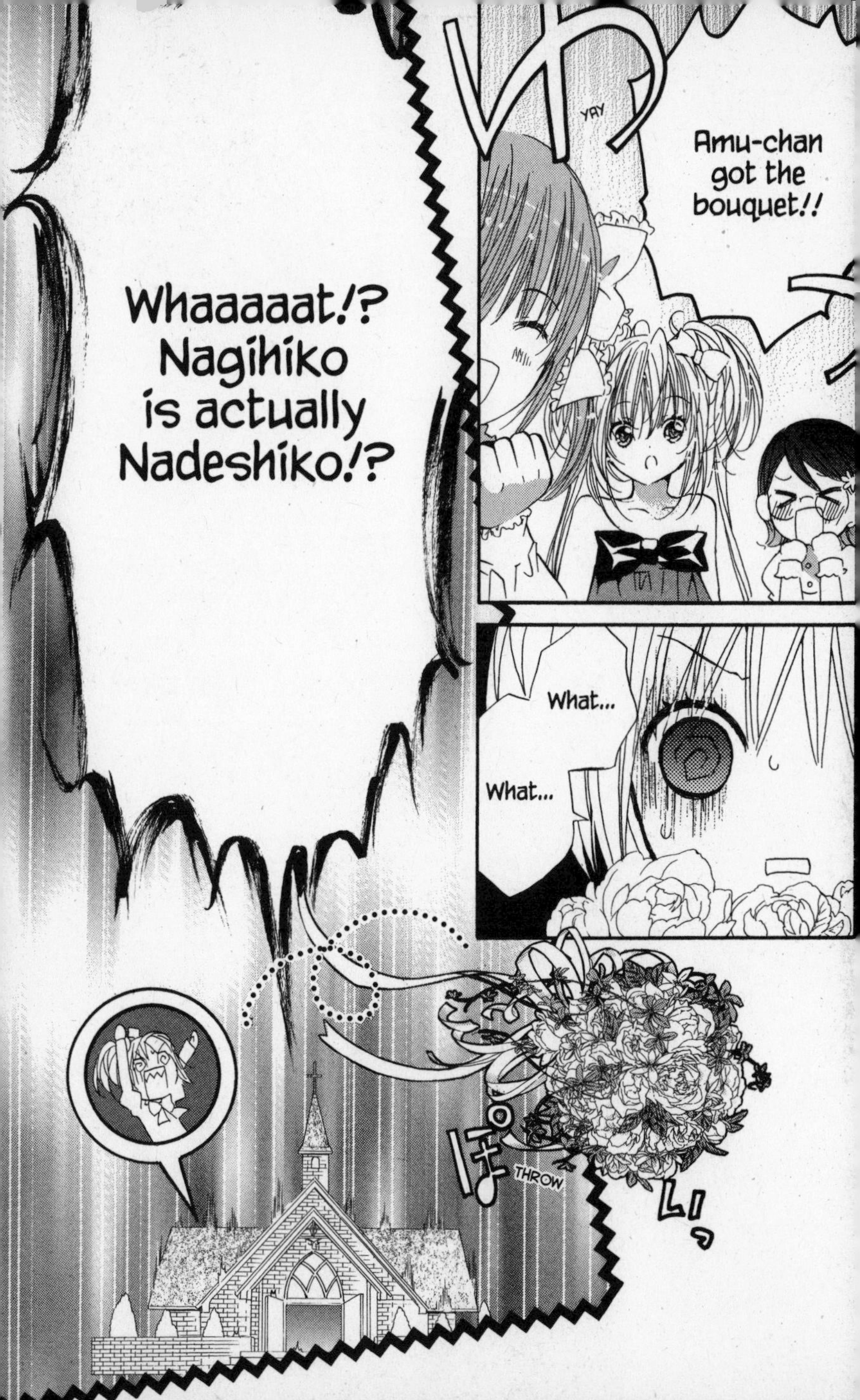
YAY
Amu-chan got the bouquet!!
What...
What...
Whaaaaat!? Nagihiko is actually Nadeshiko!?
THROW

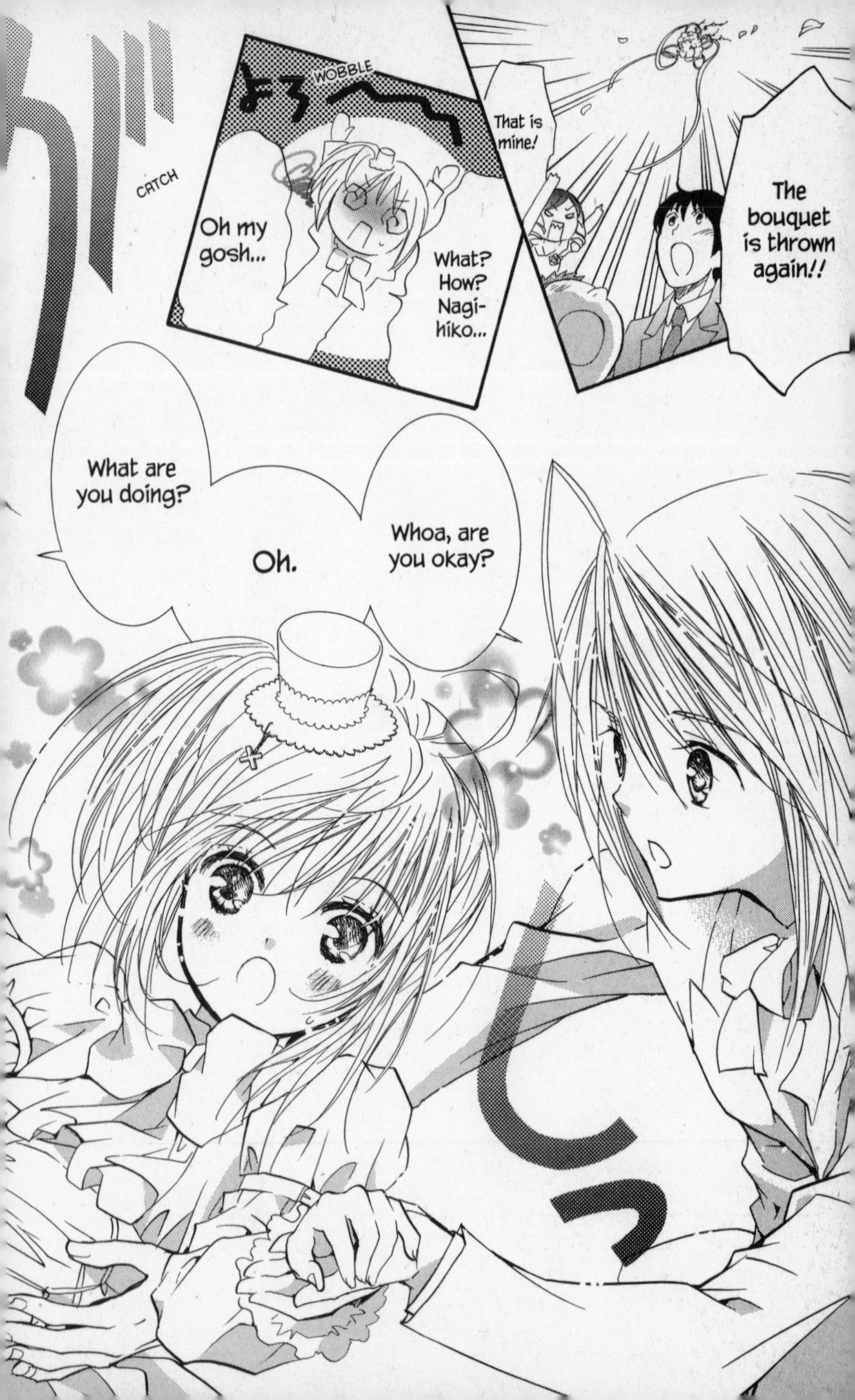
The bouquet is thrown again!!
That is mine!
WOBBLE
What? How? Nagi-hiko...
Oh my gosh...
CATCH
Whoa, are you okay?
Oh.
What are you doing?

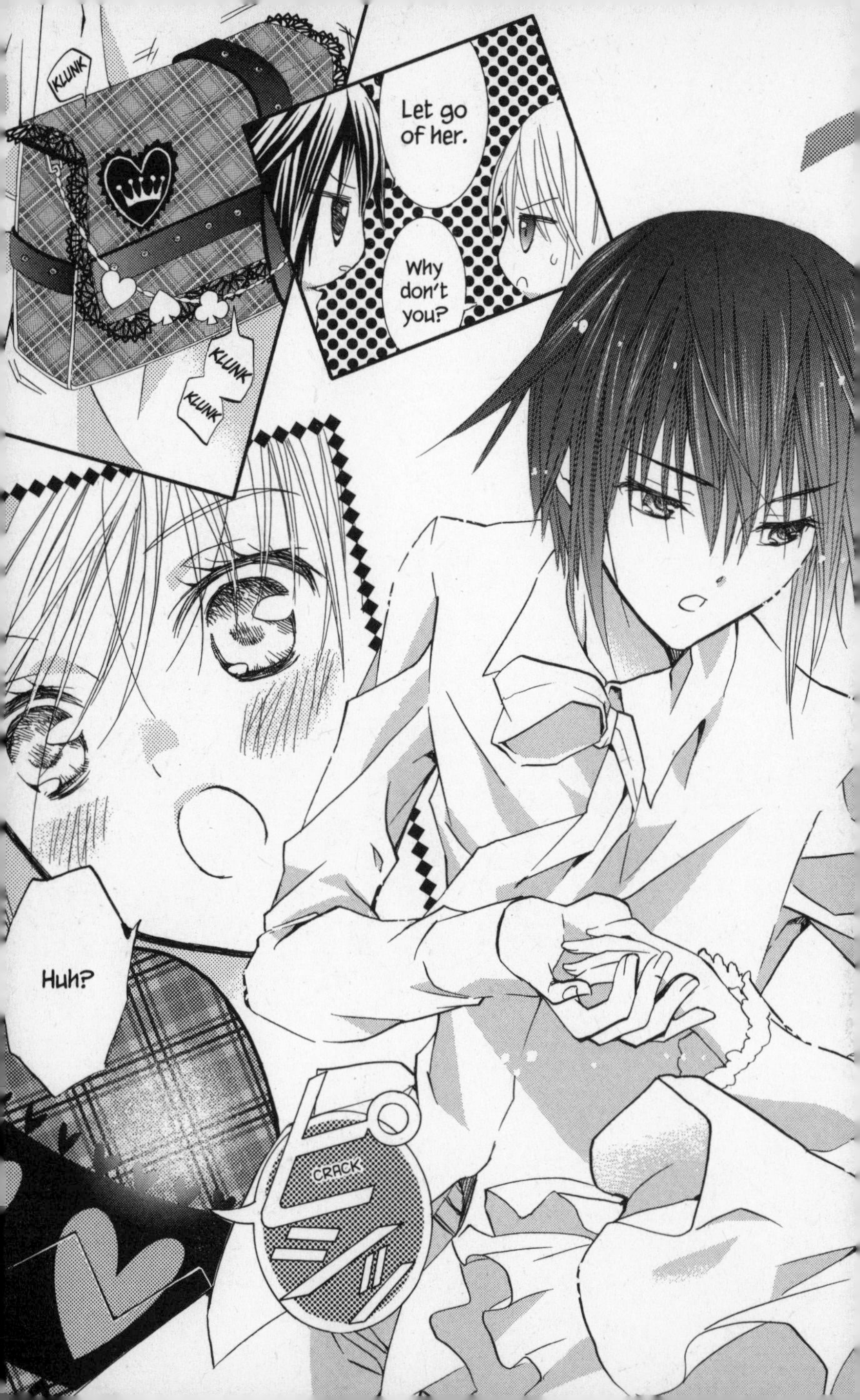

Let go of her.
Why don't you?
KLUNK
KLUNK
KLUNK
Huh?
CRACK

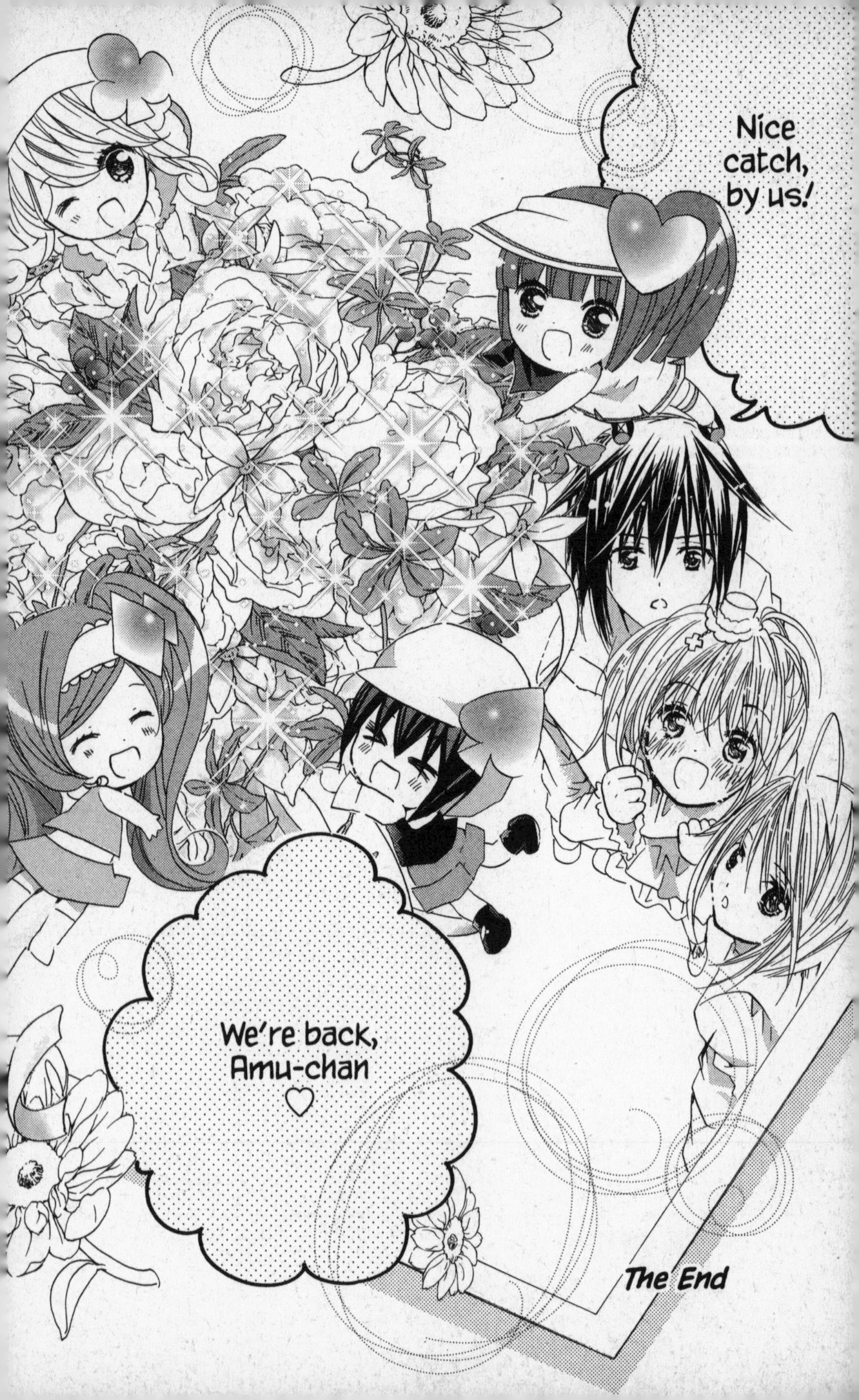
Nice catch, by us!
We're back, Amu-chan ♡
The End

# How we create

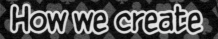Shugo
Chara!

## Presented by
PEACH-PIT

How does PEACH-PIT create Shugo Chara? We'll answer your question here!

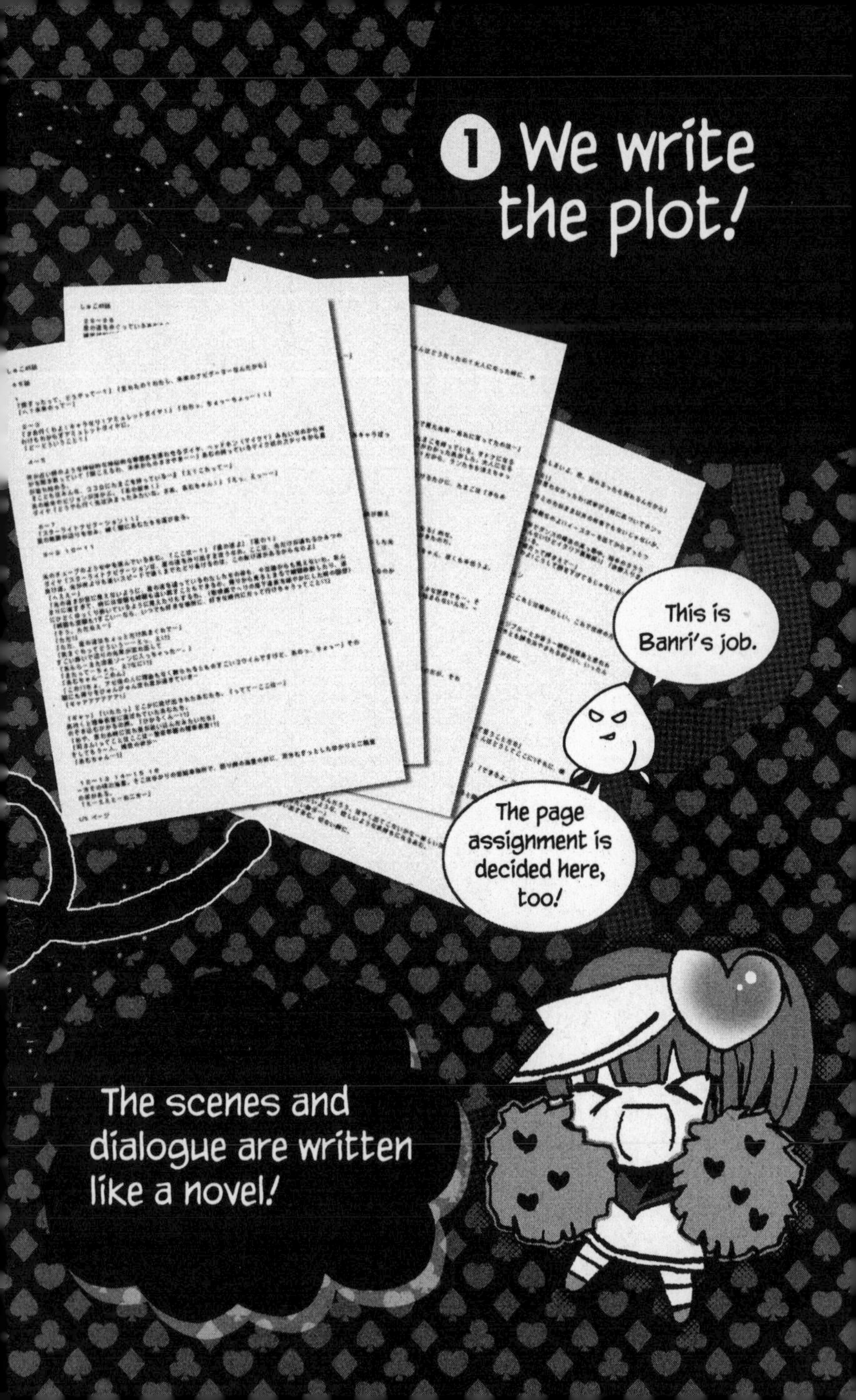
1 We write the plot!
This is Banri's job.
The page assignment is decided here, too!
The scenes and dialogue are written like a novel!

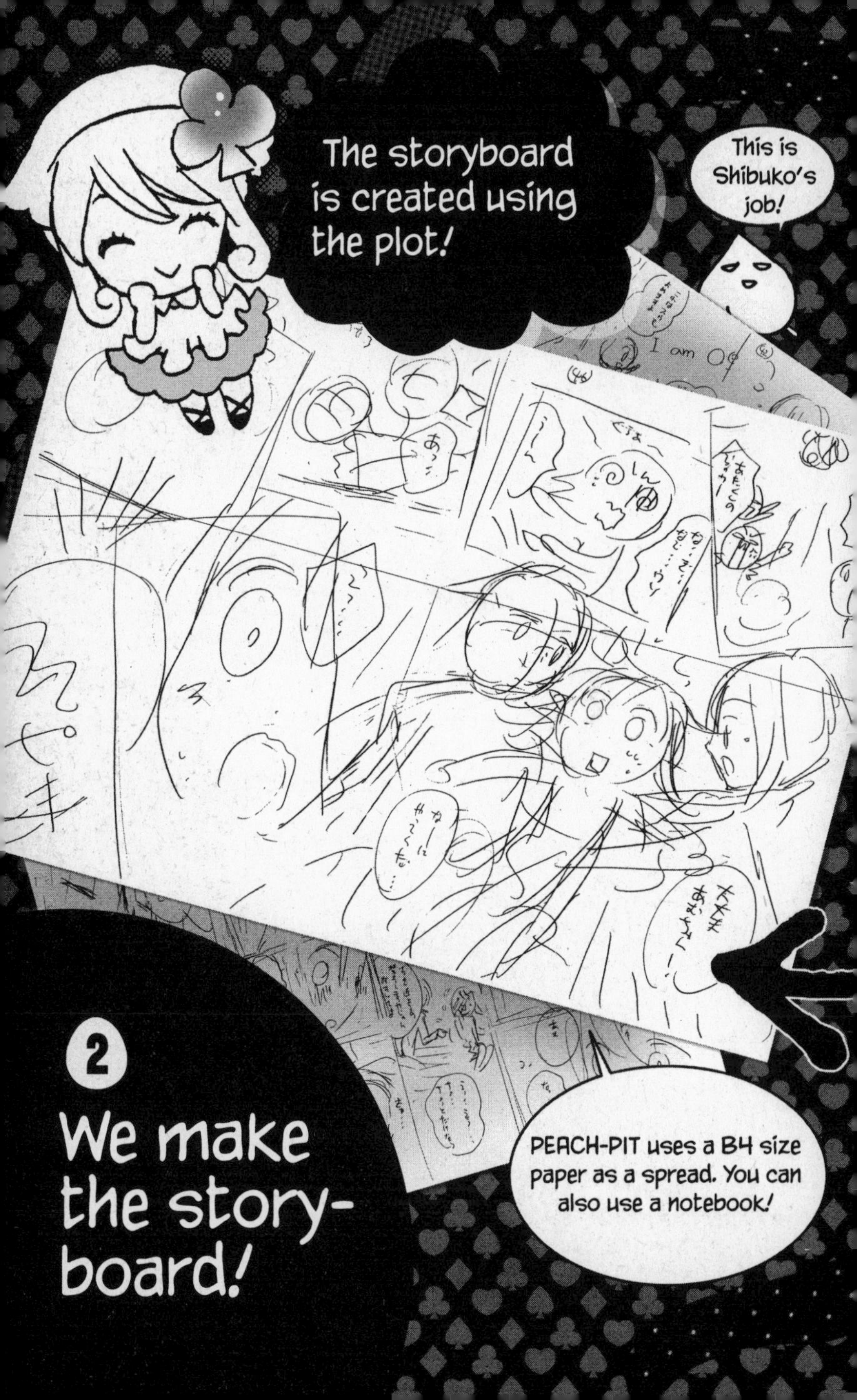
This is Shibuko's job!
The storyboard is created using the plot!
PEACH-PIT uses a B4 size paper as a spread. You can also use a notebook!
2
We make the story-board!

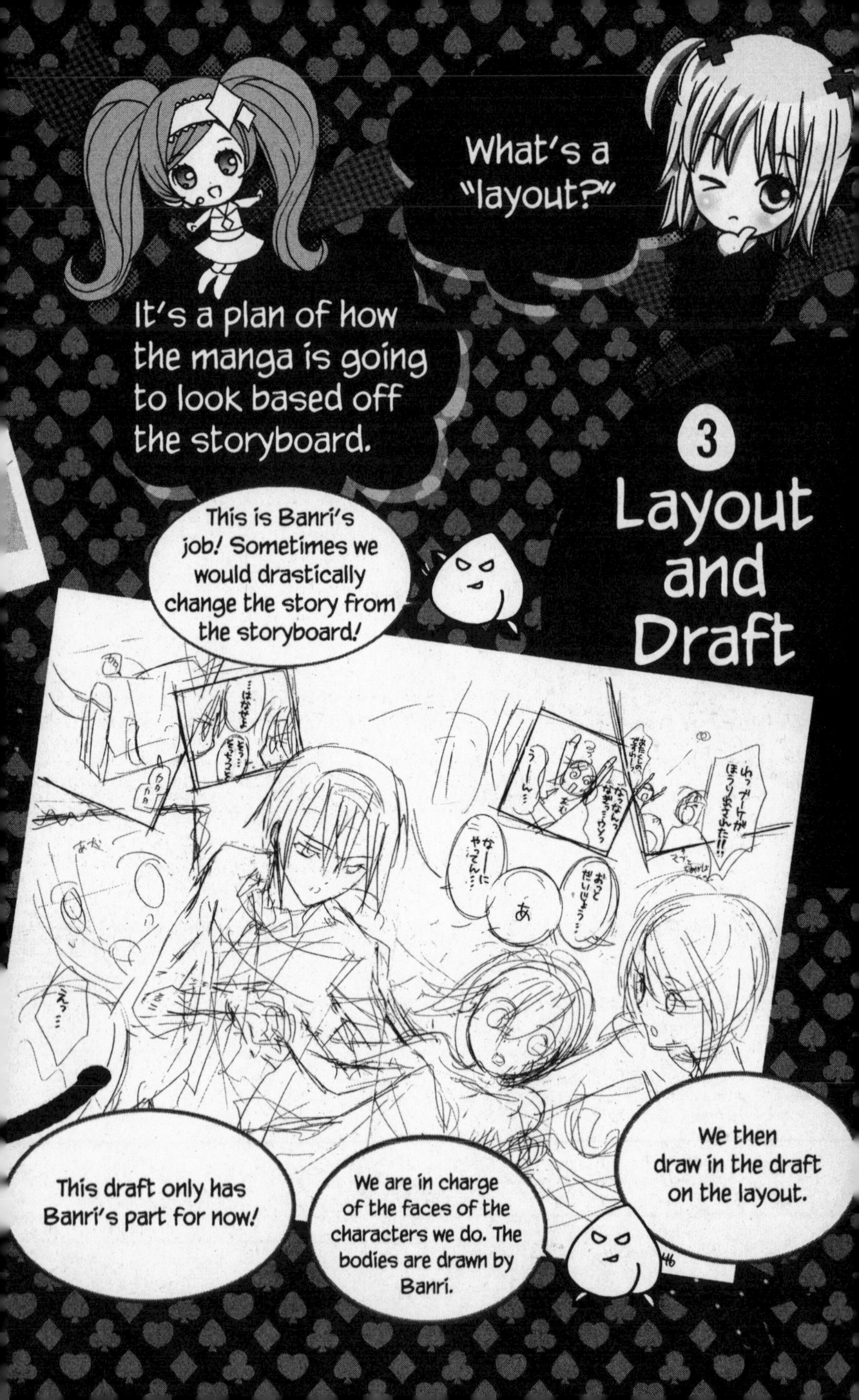
What's a "layout?"
It's a plan of how the manga is going to look based off the storyboard.
3 Layout and Draft
This is Banri's job! Sometimes we would drastically change the story from the storyboard!
We then draw in the draft on the layout.
We are in charge of the faces of the characters we do. The bodies are drawn by Banri.
This draft only has Banri's part for now!

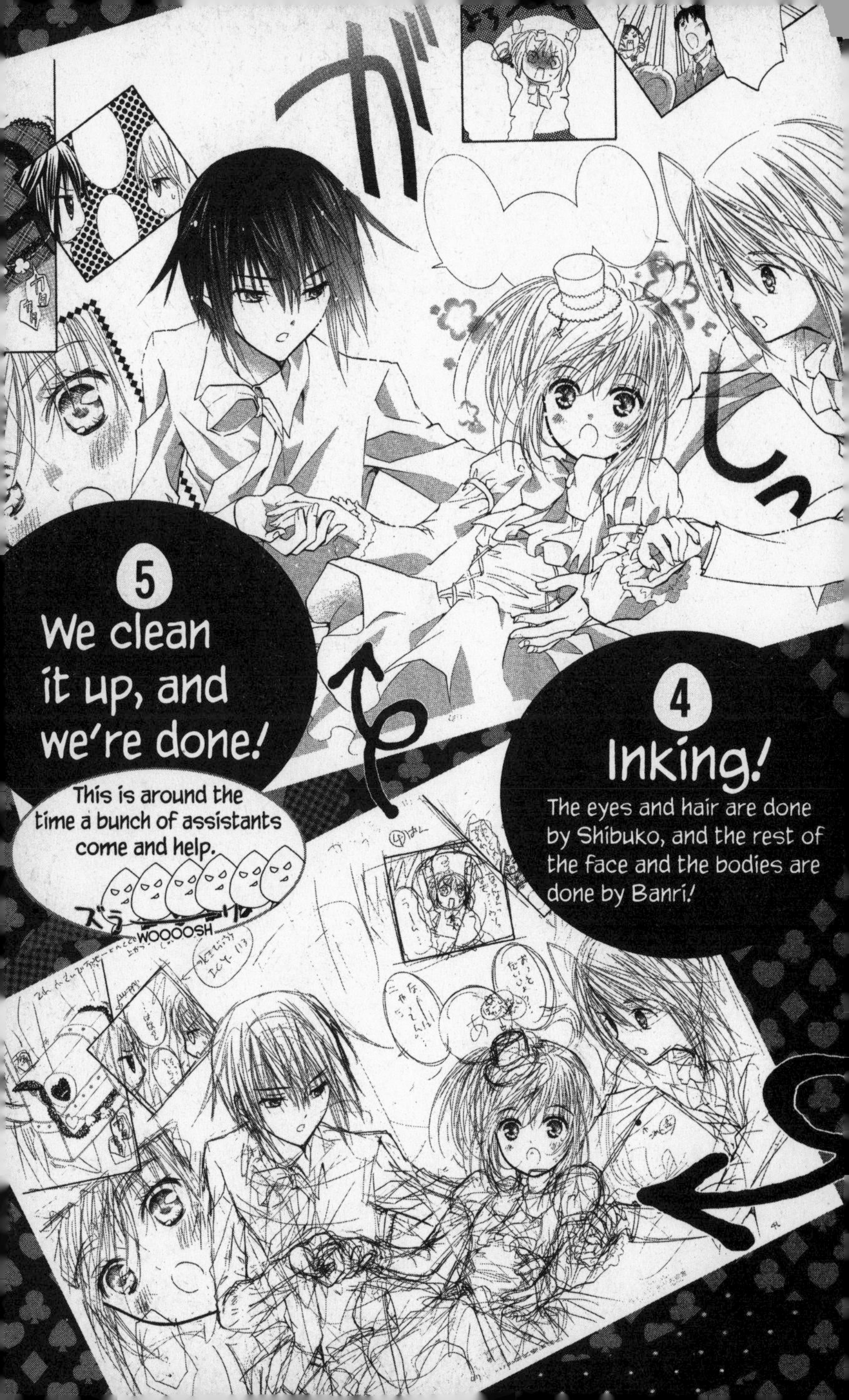
5
We clean it up, and we're done!
This is around the time a bunch of assistants come and help.
WOOOOSH
4
Inking!
The eyes and hair are done by Shibuko, and the rest of the face and the bodies are done by Banri!

# Thank you for reading until the end!

## Shibuko Ebara

I was really happy to be able to draw Amu-chan and the Guardian Characters for almost 5 years. We would receive letters that say, "I got courage from reading 'Shugo Chara!'" We got so much energy from these letters. We would feel great if, in the future, you have something that brings you down and you remember "Shugo Chara!" and pick it up again.
Thank you so much!

## Banri Sendo

Thank you, everyone, for reading until the end!
I had a lot of fun as a manga artist working on "Shugo Chara!" for almost 5 years.
We were able to draw everything we wanted to, and this is all thanks to everyone who kept reading.
All those who read "Shugo Chara!" and everyone who wrote us letters, thank you so much!
If you can have a special place in your Heart's Egg, even if it's in a corner, for Amu-chan and the gang, I would be happy.

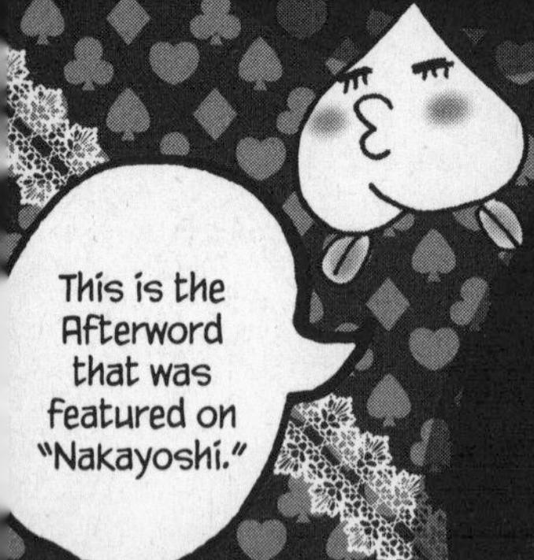
This is the Afterword that was featured on "Nakayoshi."

This is the end of "Shugo Chara!" Did you like it? I cannot express the gratitude I feel for all of you readers who read this long story until the end! "Shugo Chara!" was the first shojo series for us. PEACH-PIT, and every chapter was a trial and error, over and over again. We learned a lot and gained a lot. But the biggest treasure we gained was the encouragement we got from the readers. If we can give back to everyone with this series... if we were able to leave something in your heart, then there is nothing greater as manga artists. Thank you so much for reading until the end! I hope we can see you again soon!

**Banri Sendo**

This is the Afterword for the end of the manga.

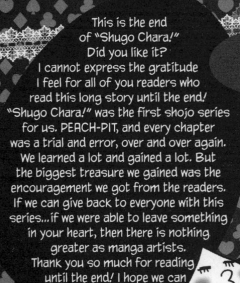

**Shibuko Ebara**

We had a grand finale on "Nakayoshi," and now with volume 12 being released as well as our second illustration book, this concludes "Shugo Chara!" officially. Thank you for staying with us until the end! As we drew Amu-chan's growth, we ran into walls and overcame them, being able to fulfill dreams on the way. Amu-chan and the Guardian Characters, thank you for working hard with us. And to the readers who cheered us on until the end, I give thanks from the bottom of my heart. If your Heart's Egg ever gets lost, please read "Shugo Chara!" and find it!

Let's meet again!

# PEACH-PIT

# About the Creators

PEACH-PIT:
**Banri Sendo** was born on June 7.
**Shibuko Ebara** was born on June 21st.
They are a pair of Gemini Manga artists
who work together. Sendo likes to eat
sweets, and Ebara likes to eat spicy stuff.

# Translation Notes

Japanese is a tricky language for most Westerners, and translation is often more art than science. For your edification and reading pleasure, here are notes on some of the places where we could have gone in a different direction in our translation of the work, or where a Japanese cultural reference is used.

## Momotaro, page 78

Momotaro is a folk hero from Japanese folklore. His name literally means, "Peach Boy," and he got his name because he was born from a large peach. There is also a version where an old couple eats some peaches, become younger, and gives birth to Momotaro. He eventually takes in a dog, monkey, and a pheasant to defeat some ogres that live on an island.

## Kusudama, page 80

A kusudama could mean various things, but here Yaya is referring to a decorative ball used in celebrations. The ball is hung up and cracks open and, along with a banner, different things fall out such as balloons or confetti.

## Taiyaki, page 87

A taiyaki is a Japanese snack made with batter and filled with red beans. It is shaped like a fish. There are variations in what you can fill it with, which include cream, custard, or chocolate.

## Matabee Zakura and Matabee Goto, page 92

The Matabee Zakura is a cherry tree located in Nara prefecture and is believed to be 300 years old. It is named after Matabee Goto (real name is Mototsugu Goto), a feudal warlord, because the tree is located on the site of where his residence used to be.

## Nade nade, page 117

Nade nade is a term derived from the verb "naderu," which is to stroke or pat. Nade nade is specifically to pat someone on the head.

# TOMARE!

## [STOP!]

You're going the wrong way!

Manga is a completely different type of reading experience.

To start at the *beginning,* go to the *end!*

That's right! Authentic manga is read the traditional Japanese way—from right to left. Exactly the *opposite* of how American books are read. It's easy to follow: Just go to the other end of the book, and read each page—and each panel—from right side to left side, starting at the top right. Now you're experiencing manga as it was meant to be!